THE CONQUEST OF WILL: INFORMATION PROCESSING IN HUMAN AFFAIRS

THE CONQUEST OF WILL: INFORMATION PROCESSING IN HUMAN AFFAIRS

ABBE MOWSHOWITZ

Department of Computer Science
University of British Columbia

ADDISON-WESLEY PUBLISHING COMPANY
Reading, Massachusetts · Menlo Park, California
London · Amsterdam · Don Mills, Ontario · Sydney

Reproduced by Addison-Wesley from camera-ready copy prepared by the author.

ISBN 0-201-04930-9
CDEFGHIJ-DO-79

To my mother and father.

Preface

Information is a basic ingredient of social organization. Its importance in the modern world is a consequence of the differentiation and diversification of human activities. Contemporary society exhibits a prodigal degree of complexity in its division of labor, interdependent functions, and large, mobile populations. Our economic, political, and cultural affairs are conducted as large-scale enterprises which require specialized structures for coordination and control. The management of such complexity depends on the use of sophisticated information-processing techniques. Partly in response to this need, a new technology of information whose central component is the general-purpose digital computer has come into existence in the twentieth century. This book is offered as a critical study of the effects of the new technology on contemporary society.

The organization of the work reflects the author's view of what constitute the overriding issues in the development of computer applications. Most computer-based information processing systems are seen to serve one of two general social functions: the coordination of diversity or the control of disorder. Coordination and control signify the extremes of a continuum of social choices. Aids to the delivery of social services exemplify the former; the latter is manifest in the use of databanks for surveillance purposes. Part I places the issues in perspective by sketching the social history of technology in the modern period, and examining the forces underlying the emergence of the computer. Part II focuses on the coordination of economic activities and social services. Following a survey of the distribution of computer applications, each of several major areas of computer use is considered in some detail. In Part III, the emphasis shifts to the implications of information technology for social control. Although computer utilities may come to play a prominent role in the delivery of social services, they are examined in this setting because of their potential impact on the political process. The principal issue is the effect of databanks and management science methods on political decision-making, and on the citizen's relationship to the apparatus of government. In the concluding part, the stress is on individual behavior. The social changes brought about by information technology are related to individual attitudes, values, and expectations.

Two fundamental themes permeate the entire discussion. One is the distribution of power in society; the other concerns individual responsibility. The growth of hierarchically structured bureaucratic organizations in industry and government reveals a firmly established trend in modern society. From the beginning of the industrial revolution to the present day, the twin goals of productivity and efficiency have achieved preeminence as determining factors in organizational change, and the principle of centrally directed hierarchical structure has facilitated the accomplishment of these objectives. Technological innovation is a salient feature of this development and its remarkable success in the economic sphere has recommended its elaboration in other areas of human activity. Although trying to disentangle causes and effects may be futile, there can be little doubt that advances in technology have accompanied the consolidation of economic and political power in the hands of elite groups. Information technology is no exception. Indeed, computer-based information systems furnish the means for centralizing power to an extent which could not have been imagined by absolute rulers of the past. Unfortunately, this presents a possibility too easily discounted. The threat does not stem primarily from malevolent groups seeking to usurp power in a democratic society; the pivotal issue is the alienation of individual responsibility which results from excessive bureaucratization of decision-making.

Perhaps the dominant model for social organization in the modern world is the factory system of production. The achievement of the factory system was made possible by resolving complex tasks into simple operations requiring relatively little skill. Bureaucracy exhibits an analogous division of labor and resolution of human task performance. In both cases, it would appear that productivity and efficiency are increased through large-scale operations; but at the same time, the specialization of function which this entails reduces the individual's responsibility for decisions affecting him. The introduction of computerized information systems in large organizations reinforces this tendency. It may not be an inevitable consequence of the technology, but there is little evidence to suggest that the use we make of our tools represents a free choice. Surely it is possible to use computers as well as other products of technology to achieve desirable social goals. However, so long as individuals acquiesce in the alienation of responsibility, power will continue to be concentrated in pyramidal corporate and state organizations.

There is no simple solution to this problem, and no prescription is given in this book. The remedy awaits a reappraisal of the functions of technology, and a strengthening of individual participation in community affairs.

Since the principal aim of this study is to explore the social consequences of information technology, technical details concerning specific computer applications have been largely suppressed. Some exposure to computers (such as might be obtained in an introductory course) is desirable but not indispensable for a determined reader. The discussion ranges over a broad spectrum of material so that coverage is necessarily compressed. Therefore, the reader is urged to do some browsing in the selected references cited for each of the chapter topics. The book is an outgrowth of lecture notes prepared for a one-semester course on computers and society offered by the Department of Computer Science at the University of British Columbia. A preliminary draft has been used as a text for this course.

I am indebted to my colleagues and students for many fruitful discussions concerning the social impact of technology. The comments and suggestions of W. Ash, E. Horowitz, J.M. Kennedy, M. Kuttner, A.K. Mackworth, Z.A. Melzak, H. Mowshowitz, R. Reiter, D.A.R. Seeley and others are gratefully acknowledged. O. Sutton has typed the manuscript and has helped with a variety of other tasks in preparing it for publication. W.B. Gruener of Addison-Wesley has followed the project with interest and has been helpful in seeing it through to completion. Research support through grants has been generously provided by the University of British Columbia and the National Research Council of Canada.

A. Mowshowitz
Vancouver, 1975

Contents

Part I.
Historical Perspectives

Motives for establishing continuity with the past are generally of two different types. One is associated with the process of achieving respectability and legitimacy; the other stems from a desire to understand the present so as to be able to plan intelligently for the future. The inclusion of historical material in studies of computer technology often reflects the former motive. Since the field is relatively new one may feel compelled to furnish it with a history replete with heroes and memorable exploits. The purpose of the present discussion is to lay a foundation for the analysis of the effects of computer applications on society; it is not our intention to develop a genealogy for the computer. Although the technology is of recent origin, it has intellectual antecedents which reach back at least to the beginning of the modern period; what is more important, it is linked to social movements which continue to influence its evolution. To appreciate the peculiar forms of computer applications and their effects on individuals and organizations, one must examine the role of technology in the formation of modern society as well as the growth of computational practices.

The rapid diffusion of computer applications in the post-war period is not a historical accident contingent upon the chance creation of a single instrument. Both the disposition to use the computer and the particular areas of its application have been conditioned by prior developments. Our inclination to use the computer is a natural extension of a pervasive commitment to technology in the solution of social problems. Western society has transformed opportunity into sacred duty. In practice, there is no real separation between the creation of an artifact and the obligation to use it. If this were an intrinsic feature of human society, there would be little point in searching for its origins in Western civilization. In fact, we have cultivated a peculiar attitude toward technology which is firmly embedded in our institutions and modes of behavior. Technological development has become a dominant factor in our economic, political, and cultural life. Thus it would appear that the growth of centralized bureaucracies in industry and government is a logical consequence of progress which, in turn, necessitates the elaboration of computer-based information-processing systems. We are conditioned to regard this trend as inevitable. Forebearance in the use of computer technology to assist in the solution of organizational problems is not consonant with our cultural disposition. Computer applications in the present are supported by traditional practices and beliefs; and if we are to deal rationally with our own compulsions, we must come to understand their etiology.

In addition to the influence of a special commitment to technology, computer utilization reflects historical trends in the application of computational methods and devices. The computer's association with scientific research, military systems, government bureaucracy, and commercial enterprises is rooted in the social history of computation. For example, the use of punched-card equipment for business and government data-processing prepared the ground for the subsequent introduction of computers. Indeed, the computer's commercial potential might not have been appreciated had it not been for this prior experience. Carrying the analysis back further, one discerns an evolutionary connection between the use of mechanical calculators and the emergence of electro-mechanical tabulating devices. The latter development was partly a response to the need for handling masses of data, but the need itself owes something to the expectations generated by the use of more primitive calculating machines. Each successive step on the road to the general-purpose digital computer created new opportunities and cemented old associations.

Perhaps the key to understanding the present disposition of computer applications lies in the fact that advances in computing technology accompanied the growth of large-scale industrial enterprise and centralized government administration. Even the early seventeenth century attempts to mechanize arithmetic operations must be viewed in light of the imperialist expansion of European civilization. Trade, exploration, and extensions of political power stimulated improvements in navigation and necessitated the creation of administrative controls. Mechanical aids to computation were needed in the preparation of tables of astronomical data, and for accounting purposes. Although scientific inquiry played a prominent part in stimulating experimentation with mechanical calculators, it seems doubtful that this would have been sufficient in the absence of a recognized social need. On the other hand, perception of need is partly a function of what is possible; and this is what leads us to focus on the interplay between technological innovation and social evolution.

The first two chapters are intended to provide historical perspective on the more specialized topics to follow. We will explore some of the major cultural and social factors in the emergence of the scientific-technological world-view, and discuss their relationship to contemporary problems. The more concrete issues underlying the development of contemporary computer applications will be examined as part of a survey of the evolution of computing devices.

Chapter 1.
Technology in Western Culture

The effects of computer applications on people and institutions cannot be understood apart from the larger issue of the role of science and technology in our society. The computer neither emerged in a vacuum nor is it used in a vacuum. Most, if not all, of the problems surrounding computer technology derive from well-established trends in the modern world. Industrial automation is a natural extension of the large-scale system of manufacturing elaborated during the industrial revolution with its standardization of parts and extensive division of labor. The cashless society toward which we appear to be moving has its roots in the financial developments which accompanied rapid industrial expansion. Computerized data-processing applications, from accounting and inventory control in large corporations to the myriad record-keeping activities of governments, have become necessary because of the increased size and complexity of organizations. But these complex organizations resulted from the application of other technologies in the creation of the modern industrialized, urbanized world. The birth of the electronic digital computer toward the end of World War II underscores its association with other technologies. The enormous computational requirements of research in atomic physics as well as other war-related efforts figured prominently in the creation of the modern computer. In short, the computer was developed in a historical context which made its emergence necessary, and in which its potentialities could be utilized.

The aim of this discussion of science and technology is to illuminate the origins of the dominant social problems associated with the use of computers. Both the disposition to exploit information technology and the changes brought about in doing so reveal the operation of historical forces. The widespread belief in the necessity of using computers to cope with social complexity may be traced to the modern conception of progress and our faith in its ultimate beneficence. Progress has come to mean the unending advance of civilization toward material perfection— a millennial future of abundance and ease made possible by the conquest of nature. This notion is based on an interpretation of history which began to take shape in the sixteenth century together with the emergence of the scientific outlook.[1] From a theory of human development concerned with intellectual events, the conception of progress gradually broadened during the seventeenth and eighteenth centuries to encompass the realm of social phenomena. The spectacular successes of science and technology provided the foundation for the modern view. As Bury points out, the idea of progress is an article of faith akin to the notions of providence and the immortality of the soul. One of its offspring is the doctrine of perpetual economic expansion which places a premium on productivity and efficiency. Like other products of technology, the computer is an instrument of the faith, so that it is not always clear whether the motive to use it reflects social necessity or sacred duty. Alternatives to the technological approach to social problems are rarely contemplated.[2]

The effects of computers on organizations must also be examined with reference to the evolution of modern society. In order to account for the observed consequences of computer-based information systems, it is necessary to look beyond the capabilities and limitations of the instruments themselves. It is not for purely technical nor accidental reasons that computers contribute to the centralization of decision-making in large organizations. Modern history shows a marked trend toward concentration of wealth and power, and technology is a major factor in this development. Other outcomes may be possible in principle, but it makes little sense to suppose that the choice lies in the way technology is applied. The commitment to use computers and other instruments is historically conditioned, and if we are not to be mastered by our tools, we must learn of their function in social evolution.

In this chapter, we will first discuss contemporary areas of concern with technology to gain some perspective on the relative importance of the social issues associated with computer technology. This will be followed by a brief survey of the social history of technology in the modern period. We will then examine the intellectual origins of the machine age and conclude with a closer look at the problematic nature of human-machine interaction.

1. Technology and the Contemporary Scene

Three areas of social concern related to technology are most noteworthy. First, one encounters the fear of nuclear war and the concern over the mounting economic and social costs of the arms race. A second area is the so-called ecological crisis brought about through imbalances in population growth, food production, consumption of non-renewable resources, industrial production, and pollution of the environment. Finally, there is considerable malaise associated with a condition many observers term a crisis of values. Seemingly a creature of industrialization and urbanization, it is manifest by the dissolution of the extended family and the imminent threat to the nuclear family, a general tendency toward institutionalization of impermanence in human relationships, and the erosion of human uniqueness in the face of expanding machine capabilities.

No one doubts that technology plays an important role in these problem areas. There would be no danger of nuclear war if there were no nuclear weapons; a less well-developed technology would pose a lesser threat to the environment; and a simpler, less mobile society would very likely be more stable than ours. The central question is the nature of technology's role in our society. Is it purely instrumental, as most observers believe; or has it become an autonomous, formative element in human affairs?

What has technology to do with an essentially political problem such as conflict among nations? It is instructive to study the motives for building and using the first atomic bombs. Robert Jungk(1960) paints a clear picture of the circumstances which led to the creation of the atomic bomb. The scientists who urged the United States government to embark on the nuclear enterprise and who later participated in the Manhattan Project were largely refugees from European fascism concerned that the Nazis would develop the bomb first. The bomb was completed after the surrender of Germany and at a time when preliminary feelers were being extended by the Japanese about ending the war. Although there was some opposition among the nuclear scientists to its use against Japan, the committee of experts established to advise President Truman concurred in the government's decision. The four atomic scientists on the advisory panel "felt themselves caught in a vast machinery and they certainly were inadequtely informed as to the true political and strategic situation." (Jungk, 1960, p. 190) Was the real motive to use the atomic bomb a genuine desire to shorten the war; or was it a foregone conclusion that the weapon would be used simply because it was available? The subsequent polarization of the world into mutually hostile armed camps, each devoting vast resources to the elaboration and refinement of nuclear weaponry suggests something more than passive instrumentality for the role of the new technology.

As the perceived immediacy of the threat of nuclear war has diminished, another problem has gained currency.[3] This problem is the degradation of the human environment. There is growing consternation over the consequences of unchecked population growth, depletion of resources, destruction of arable land, and pollution. All of these issues are linked to technology, directly or indirectly. The use of chemical fertilizers and pesticides to increase agricultural yields, for example, eventually has a deleterious effect on the soil and the ecology. The production of goods in an ever-expanding consumer economy leads to depletion of resources and pollution of the environment. The enormity of the problem is captured in the Report of the Club of Rome (Meadows, *et al.* , 1972, p. 29)

> If the present growth trends in world population, industrialization, pollution, food production, and resource depletion continue unchanged, the limits to growth on this planet will be reached sometime within the next one hundred years. The most probable result will be a rather sudden and uncontrollable decline in both population and industrial capacity.[4]

Although one may take issue with the specific projections of the Club of Rome, and question the assumptions of the world model which gave rise to them, it is impossible to deny that we are depleting our resources and degrading our environment and that a day of reckoning will surely come if we do not mend our ways. The important question is how we go about mending our ways. Can we rely on science and technology to provide solutions to the problems of over-population, resource depletion and pollution? Or is our faith in technology itself part of the problem?

Perhaps the strongest evidence (although less dramatic generally than the issues of nuclear war and ecological disaster) that technology may not be purely instrumental in our own society lies in the contemporary experience of alienation. Dostoyevsky's underground man provides a prototypical example of this phenomenon.

> Leave us alone without books and we shall be lost and in confusion at once. We shall not know what to join on to, what to cling to, what to love and what to hate, what to respect and what to despise. We are oppressed at being men— men with a real individual body and blood, we are ashamed of it, we think it a disgrace and try to contrive to be some sort of impossible generalized man. We are still-born, and for generations past have been begotten, not by living fathers, and that suits us better and better. We are developing a taste for it. Soon we shall contrive to be born somehow from an idea. (Dostoyevsky, 1864, p. 140)

Notes from Underground, published in 1864, reveals a powerful clash between the traditional Christian attitudes of Russian Orthodoxy and the rationalism of Western European science. In our own time the conflict is expressed in many different ways. The search for new (or perhaps older) forms of religious experience is often a consequence of the strict dichotomy between the spiritual and material aspects of modern life. Attempts to build new communities in the wilderness reveal a desire to integrate a seemingly meaningless, mechanical pattern of behavior into an organic whole.

The fundamental problem for Dostoyevsky's underground man, and the alienated individual of today lies in the collapse of traditional values, and the dissolution of communities capable of supporting genuine human commitment. The advanced form of this condition is what Emile Durkheim pointed to as an underlying cause of suicide. Michael Harrington(1966) sums up the profound sense of malaise experienced in the twentieth century.

> For more than fifty years, the Western world has haunted itself with rumors of its own death. Some said that the life of the instincts was being smothered, others that the spirit had become dry and brittle. There were those who recoiled before militant poverty and the revolt of the masses and those who feared the corruptions of affluence. Theologians announced a crisis of faith, secularists a crisis of reason. (Harrington, 1965, p. 13)[5]

The centrality of technology in the arms race and the current ecological crisis is apparent. That technology also plays a central role in the value crisis is neither well understood nor widely accepted. This state of affairs derives from the rather subtle character of technological influence on social institutions and value formation. The claim is that our dependence on science and technology has led us to adopt a world-view built on the rationalistic presupposition that all human and social problems can be resolved by the application of technique.[6] Scientific method is seen to be universally applicable to all well-defined problems. Although the scientific enterprise is justifiably proud of advancing human understanding, it has failed to generate an ethos capable of satisfying the psychic needs essential to the development of a moral basis for human conduct. Nevertheless, science and technology have furnished more than mere tools for use in dealing with the world; they have fostered a disposition to view the world in a certain way, and to act in accordance with that vision. The tools insist on being used in particular ways.

In a very important sense, developments in the computer field are closer to the problems of alienation than other technologies. Perhaps the key element in the mounting tension revealed in the uncertainty of contemporary life is the erosion of human identity. Both in the form of a tool aiding human performance, and as an autonomous entity, the computer is the embodiment of the ultimate conclusion of the mechanistic mentality. As a tool the computer usurps functions that were once thought to be uniquely human; as an autonomous entity, it forces direct comparison with human beings. If the comparison is accepted as legitimate (and many scientists do accept this), the human being may be regarded as nothing but a machine, and very often a rather unimpressive one. Retreat from rational thought as a response to this position is ominous, but not surprising.

2. Social History of Technology

We turn now to a brief examination of the ways in which technology has affected people and institutions. The study of the social history of technology is a relatively recent phenomenon, quite different in character from historical studies of particular technologies conducted from a technological point of view. Histories of industrial processes such as steel making and automobile manufacturing, or of instruments such as the lathe, focus on the internal development of some aspect of technology. Social histories of technology are concerned with the social organization surrounding the use of tools and processes, and the impact of their various applications, or, more generally, with the interaction between technology and social organization. Of course, without carefully documented studies of particular technologies, no social history is possible. However, the focus in social history is on the ways in which tools, materials, and energy are utilized in social contexts.

Two complementary problems are addressed. On the one hand, there is the question of how changes in technology affect social organization, for example, the consequences of improved agricultural techniques in the development of cities, or improvements in navigation, such as the invention of the rudder, in exploration and colonization. On the other hand, one is also concerned with the effects of social institutions and individual attitudes on the development of technology. The allocation of resources such as capital for industrial expansion is governed by social and economic factors which are thus seen to influence technological development. Samuel Lilley(1965) argued, for example, that the market economy of Western Europe and the United States acts as a brake on the introduction and elaboration of fully automatic production processes, as compared with the planned economy of the Soviet Union.

From the viewpoint of social history, technology involves the utilization of energy and materials in controlled situations to modify and organize man's physical and social environment. The character of the technology of a given historical period is determined by 1) its choice of materials, 2) its sources of power, 3) its varieties of tools, and 4) its modes of organization and control. The importance of the kinds of materials used in tools and implements is evident from the terms employed by archeologists to classify the periods of human prehistory. The shifts from stone to bronze to iron marked major turning points in human development. Moreover, the materials used in dwellings and shelters, utensils and furnishings leave their distinctive mark on the human environment.

The sources of energy harnessed for productive purposes also play a vital role in shaping social evolution. The domestication of animals for use in agriculture enormously amplified man's ability to procure a stable food supply and thus constituted a critical step on the road to civilization. In modern history the steam engine furnished a mobile and reliable source of power which contributed significantly to the creation of our industrialized society.

Two general categories of tools must be distinguished: those used in the production of commodities for consumption, and those employed in making other tools. Of course, a given tool might serve both purposes, but the distinction is important in connection with the division of labor in society. The latter category clearly requires a relatively high degree of social and cultural organization; or, at least, the willingness to defer immediate gratification for the sake of long-term objectives.

The fourth component of technology has come into sharp focus in the twentieth century. The nineteenth century witnessed the exploitation of important new sources of energy. Building on this technological achievement, we have revolutionized methods of organization and control. In the past seventy years, the innovations of the factory system of production have been carried to near perfection in the automated plants of the present day. Standardization and interchangeability of parts, in the context of large-scale manufacturing operations, provided the basis for the rationalization of the production process in the assembly line. This resolution of the assembly process into elementary operations, together with advances in control technology (and more recently the development of the computer), led to the automatic factory. Although the organizational aspect is a particularly salient feature of contemporary technology, it is a critical element in the technology of any period. The great pyramids of the third millennium B.C., for example, were made possible through a highly elaborate organization of thousands of human workers.

The accelerated pace of technological development beginning with the industrial revolution has led many observers (especially in the late nineteenth century) to belittle or ignore earlier achievements. This tendency to focus exclusively on the present inevitably produces distortions. Although the generation of power by means of windmills may not reveal much about electric power stations, there is a great deal to be learned about the social uses of electricity from examining its antecedents in the application of earlier sources of power. The experience of our predecessors may be extremely valuable in helping us to rationalize our own apparent needs for energy. It is largely for the purpose of countering the widespread ahistorical bias in contemporary discussions of technology that we undertake here a brief sketch of its development since the Medieval period.

The following discussion is based largely on Lewis Mumford's classic *Technics and Civilization* (1934). Three historical epochs (the eotechnic, paleotechnic, and neotechnic) spanning the past ten centuries (from 1000 AD to the present) are distinguished. Each one is characterized in terms of the four components of technology described above. The eotechnic period (1000-1750) stretches from the later middle ages to the beginning of the industrial revolution. Mumford calls this period the "dawn age of modern technics" in that it furnished the essential foundations for the industrialization of Western society which commenced in the middle of the eighteenth century. In terms of characteristic materials and sources of power, this was a water-and-wood complex. The principal material, both in commodities and in tools was wood; the key source of power was water.

The eotechnic period experienced an over-all increase in horsepower. This increase stemmed from several developments, the most important being the widespread use of water wheels. However, the introduction of the iron horseshoe, as early as the ninth century, and the adoption of the modern form of harness, which was in use by the tenth century, were not insignificant factors. The iron horseshoe increased the animal's range, and facilitated pulling by providing a better grip. The shoulder harness was a great improvement over the neck harness which dated back to Roman times; the former significantly increased the horse's ability to pull a load. It should be noted that the impact of these developments was not confined to agriculture. Animal power was used in mills for grinding corn, and in industrial operations such as mining for pumping water.

As noted above, the water wheel provided the most important contribution to the increase in horsepower, but the windmill also figured prominently. Both of these prime movers played a critical part in European history. Naturally, industrial development was favored in regions with abundant supplies of wind and water. The water wheel was used to provide power for pulping rags for paper in 1290; hammering and cutting machines in an ironworks were driven by waterpower in 1320; and a water wheel was used to saw wood in 1322. Other industrial uses of water power included the beating of hides in the tanning process, spinning silk, and operating grinding machines. For subsequent developments, one of the most important applications was the harnessing of water power in mining, mainly for drainage purposes.

The eotechnic economy relied on wood as a basic resource for its tools, instruments, products, and fuel. Wood was in evidence everywhere, from the machines of industry and the workman's tools to the implements and utensils of the farm and household. It was the principal material of ships as well as carts, buckets, and barrels, and was indispensable in building and mining. Although the use of metals was not insignificant, being essential in coinage and military equipment, wood dominated in virtually every phase of eotechnic activity. Viewed from the perspective of subsequent industrial development, wood provided a medium for experimentation with mechanical forms which served as prototypes for later inventions. This is especially important for understanding the dynamics of technological change. Past practices are discarded reluctantly, and human institutions have limited ability to accommodate innovations.

In its origins, modern technology is not an exclusively Western product. The eotechnic period exhibited a high degree of "technical syncretism," borrowing tools and methods from various cultures. Water wheels were used by the Egyptians to raise water; the windmill made its way into Europe from Persia in the eighth century. From China, the West learned the art of making paper and gunpowder as well as the use of the magnetic needle. Chemistry, physiology, and algebra came via the Arab world; and geometry and mechanics were the product of pre-Christian Greece.

The tools developed during this period are too numerous to catalogue here, but it should be noted that the foundations for subsequent technological achievements were rooted in the eotechnic economy. The compound crank and connecting rod for converting rotary into reciprocating motion, as well as other important inventions, came into use during the fifteenth century. Much of the later development of the industrial revolution can be seen in terms of refinement, consolidation, and the introduction of new materials and prime movers. Mumford goes so far as to assert that "the modern industrial revolution would have come into existence and gone on steadily had not a ton of coal been dug in England, and had not a new iron mine been opened" (p. 118). Perhaps the most critical innovation of the period was organizational: the separation of energy sources from the means of application and control. This step signals the beginning of the modern mode of mechanical production, which ultimately allowed for the emergence of the factory.

During the eighteenth century, forces which had been at work since the later Middle Ages erupted in a new technological order. The paleotechnic period (1750-1900) encompasses the first stage of the industrial revolution; the pace of technological expansion and change underwent a dramatic quickening, and new forms of production came into existence. This was a coal-and-iron complex. Coal fueled a new prime mover, the steam engine; and iron displaced wood as the characteristic material of the period. Every aspect of life was touched and irrevocably altered by the new order.

> A new movement appeared in industrial society which had been gathering headway almost unnoticed from the fifteenth century on: after 1750 industry passed into a new phase, with a different source of power, different materials, different social objectives. This second revolution multiplied, vulgarized, and spread the methods and goods produced by the first: above all it was directed toward the quantification of life, and its success could be gauged only in terms of the multiplication table. (Mumford, 1934, p. 151)

The interaction between technology and social institutions during this period has received much attention from social thinkers of widely varying persuasions. The separation between maker and artifact which had its roots in the eotechnic phase was carried to its penultimate conclusion in the factory system. We are still haunted by the legacy of developments in the paleotechnic period: degradation of the environment, concentration of capital and human resources in large-scale enterprises and the triumph of the materialistic conception of progress. Many questions have yet to be answered satisfactorily. Changing values make it difficult to compare conditions at different times; and many historical consequences of technology do not appear to be necessary ones. There is, for example, no inherent technological reason for the fruits of industry to be distributed in one way rather than another. The crucial problems that we face now derive from the factory system of production with its characteristic interchangeable manufacture. Even the digital computer was anticipated in the mechanical calculators and rudimentary forms of automatic control elaborated at the beginning of the nineteenth century. The Jacquard loom with its punched-card system for controlling the weaving of complicated patterns inspired Charles Babbage, and may have influenced the design of Herman Hollerith's punched-card tabulating system which was used in the 1890 United States census.[7]

The turn of the century is a convenient date to mark the transition to the neotechnic period. By this time technology had become a dominant force in social evolution. Earlier developments were undergoing refinement and consolidation as part of a systematic process of scientific and technological innovation. This current phase is an electricity-and-alloy complex. New materials, and new sources of power have been developed; and what is most critical for the future, new forms of organization and control have assumed a central position in twentieth century technology.

We are living in a time of ever-accelerating change. The paleotechnic factory has given way to the automated production line, with transfer machines and computer controlled devices. The crude transportation and communication systems of the industrial revolution are continually refined or replaced by more sophisticated ones. As many observers have remarked, the only certainty in contemporary life is change, a condition which derives from the nineteenth century addiction to the goal of perpetual economic growth. We are just beginning to experience some of the uncomfortable consequences of this doctrine of material progress. One of the great challenges of the future is the task of balancing production and consumption of both goods and services with resource allocation and waste.

3. Social and Cultural Origins of the Machine Age

The triumph of science and technology in Western civilization was long in the making. Although the ultimate sources for modern man's monumental obsession with the mastery of nature are rather obscure, we are not entirely ignorant of contributing elements. The habits, attitudes and values essential to the successful mechanization of life were rooted in the structure of Medieval society through the institutions it bequeathed to the modern world. Perhaps one of the greatest ironies of history lies in the consequences of the religious asceticism of the Reformation in that it spawned a completely secularized society.

Before examining some of the factors responsible for the emergence of the modern technological complex, let us make precise some of its attributes. Francis Bacon (1561-1626) was an articulate spokesman for the developing creed of science and technology; the *New Atlantis* reveals the goals and the empiricist underpinning of the scientific world-view. Bacon lived in the watershed period of intense scientific development; the sixteenth and seventeenth centuries witnessed the launching of the modern scientific juggernaut. Bacon was a contemporary of Johannes Kepler (1571-1630) and Galileo (1564-1642). He was preceded by Nicholas Copernicus (1473-1543) and followed by Isaac Newton (1642-1727).

In the *New Atlantis*, Bacon created a utopian vision which embodies the spirit of science and technology; he anticipated the philosophy of the Enlightenment in his view of a society ordered according to scientific principles. Bacon's chaplain and publisher, W. Rawley, remarked "this fable [*New Atlantis*] my Lord devised, to the end that he might exhibit therein a model or description of a college instituted for the interpreting of nature and the producing of great and marvellous works for the benefit of men, under the name of Salomon's House ..." In fact, the *New Atlantis* is an illustration of Bacon's famous dictum "knowledge is power." The aims of Salomon's House define the goals of science and technology. "The End of our Foundation is the knowledge of Causes and secret motions of things; and the enlarging of the bounds of Human Empire, to the effecting of all things possible." Here Bacon anticipates the modern conception of progress: that happiness consists in the satisfaction of ever-increasing material needs.

The prime importance of Bacon's work is not his description of the methods of empirical science, but his vision of a society governed by science and technology.

> In the *New Atlantis* the scientists form a caste endowed with a power superior to that of the king. The House of Salomon was not a society sponsored by the king and dependent on him; it was a State within a State, with seemingly limitless funds, secret agents, and the right to withhold secrets from the rest of the community. (Berneri, 1951, p. 128)

Although the modern world may not be strictly speaking a "scientocracy" or "technocracy," there is little question of the triumph of the world-view implicit in Bacon's utopia.

The view of science and technology which emerges from the textbooks we all used to learn about physics, chemistry, biology, etc. is a somewhat sanitized version of the reality. The bias of our own time (as evidenced by the dominance of logical positivism) is in favor of disembodied facts and theories. A distinction is drawn between discovery (an historical process) and verification (a logical process). The former reputedly has no validity in presentation of scientific theories. However, this position does in fact reflect on the historical process of discovery. The student is given the impression that progress in scientific development is from hypothesis to improved hypothesis in a strictly logical sequence. This is not only misleading, it is an arrant falsehood. This is important since we are accustomed to thinking that science has a monopoly on both method and truth. Without disputing this issue directly, let us examine the scientific enterprise as a sociological phenomenon.

What is central to scientific inquiry? According to philosophers of science, its single greatest strength is the objectivity of its methodology, the principle of intersubjective verifiability.[8] This principle asserts that any competent observer should be able to reproduce or verify the results of experiment. The scientist never appeals to any special faculty or province of knowledge, such as might be claimed by the metaphysician. There are no secrets (in principle) among scientists. In addition to the objectivity of its method, science claims to be universally applicable. Any problem which can be solved at all can be solved by the scientific method. Conversely, any problem not amenable to scientific analysis is a pseudo-problem, ill-formed, or meaningless.

What is the historical basis for these claims? The practice of science as articulated by Bacon in the *New Atlantis* developed gradually in a world dominated by the Medieval church. The appeal to experience as the ultimate arbiter of truth can be seen as a reaction against the arid scholastic speculation of the Medieval period. But science did not leave all of the Medieval heritage behind. The scientific construction of the material world requires an acceptance of the uniformity and regularity of natural laws. The medieval conception of a universe ordered by God played a central role in the emergence of scientific thought.

> [T]he greatest contribution of medievalism to the formation of the scientific movement [was] the inexpugnable belief that every detailed occurrence can be correlated with its antecedents in a perfectly definite manner, exemplifying general principles. Without this belief the incredible labours of scientists would be without hope. It is this instinctive conviction, vividly poised before the imagination, which is the motive power of research: that there is a secret, a secret which can be unveiled. How has this conviction been so vividly implanted on the European mind?
>
> When we compare this tone of thought in Europe with the attitude of other civilisations when left to themselves, there seems but one source for its origin. It must come from the medieval insistence on the rationality of God, conceived as with the personal energy of Jehovah and with the rationality of a Greek philosopher. Every detail was supervised and ordered: the search into nature could only result in the vindication of the faith in rationality. Remember that I am not talking of the explicit beliefs of a few individuals. What I mean is the impress on the European mind arising from the unquestioned faith of centuries. By this I mean the instinctive tone of thought and not a mere creed of words. (Whitehead, 1925, p. 19)

However, as Mumford(1934) observes, this belief was not in itself sufficient to account for the tremendous energy and success of the scientific enterprise. To appreciate this more fully, one must examine the institutions and practices in which the belief in a rational God were embedded, in particular, the iron discipline of the monastic life.

The spiritual foundation of the technological complex of the modern world rests on the peculiar rationalistic beliefs and practices of the Medieval period. Mumford points to the clock as the technical embodiment of the rationalistic principle of monastic life, which ultimately spread outside the monastery providing new regularity for workman and merchant. With the clock as an outgrowth of monastic rule, a transformation from organic to mechanical time is effected, and with this transformation comes a new preoccupation with the material here-and-now of secular activities rather than with the timeless life of the spirit. Thus practice is seen to buttress world-view. The dissociation of time from human events helped to create and sustain the belief in an independent world of measurable events which constitutes the foundation of the scientific edifice.

Yet it is not clear that the mechanistic mentality would have taken root had it not been for other influences. It is at least possible to imagine a world characterized by a belief in a rationally ordered universe with social institutions dedicated to a rational ordering of life, which rejects Bacon's admonition "knowledge is power." Indeed, preoccupation with the material world was not a virtue according to Medieval theology. It is certainly ironic that monasticism, an exemplary form of spiritual fulfillment, contributed to the development of this vice.

The peculiar institutions and thought of the High Middle Ages (1050-1270) and the succeeding two centuries prepared the ground for modern science and technology. Two critically important features of this foundation were the rationalization of daily life in the monastery, and the successful mechanization of time. But in spite of these powerful agents of change, theology dominated by eternity militated against the spread of the scientific outlook. One further ingredient was required. The construction of the edifice of modern society began in earnest with the Protestant Reformation of the sixteenth century.

Of course, this is not to suggest a particular cause and effect relationship between concomitant cultural and economic developments. To be complete, the analysis should incorporate the changes in both spheres. There can be little doubt that the revival of trade and commerce which occurred gradually from the eleventh to the sixteenth century contributed significantly to the changes which were wrought in Medieval society. The emergence of towns and a new class, the bourgeoisie, are key factors in the forging of the modern technological complex. Clearly, the future was in the hands of this new class; its values and institutions thus played a central role. In any case, without attempting to resolve the problem of cause and effect, we simply acknowledge the joint influence of the rise of capitalism and the new world-view which exploded in the Protestant Reformation.

Both science and capitalism share the belief in a rationally ordered universe. Time-keeping and orderly habits are as vital to the entrepreneurial spirit as to scientific progress. Herein lies one of the essential links between the Protestant Reformation and scientific world-view. Max Weber(1904-5) delineated the role of the Protestant ethic in the rise of capitalism. Weber raised the question of why the rationalistic temper applied to the pursuit of pecuniary profit triumphed over the conventional attitude which regarded unlimited lust for gain as antisocial and immoral. He answered, as suggested above, that this was a result of movements which had their source in the religious revolution of the sixteenth century. The key doctrine in Weber's analysis is the Calvinists' notion of a calling coupled with their peculiar view of salvation. The emphasis on predestination in matters of personal salvation led to the practical desirability of becoming immersed in and dedicated to a calling. The asceticism required for capital formation provided a natural expression for the acute moral anxiety generated by not knowing whether one would be saved or damned.

In tracing the social and cultural origins of the scientific-technological world-view, we have pointed to some of the prominent formative influences. Both science and capitalism, or perhaps more comprehensively, the modern mechanistic organization of human affairs were rooted in the institutions of the Medieval period and the innovations of the Protestant Reformation. The monastery exemplified the peculiar rationality of the Medieval world: its belief in an ordered universe. This belief together with the practice of the monastic orders in their adherence to iron-clad discipline provided the basis for the scientific belief in the regularity of natural phenomena and the empiricism of scientific practice. The Protestant Reformation of the sixteenth century with its focus on predestination and the necessity of a calling forged a link to worldly affairs. The new class of town-dwellers, the bourgeoisie, spawned by the revival of trade and commerce, were furnished by the Reformation with the rationalizations essential to the entrepreneurial spirit. It became possible to strive to accumulate capital and at the same time feel morally justified in the pursuit of one's calling. The calling of science and technology were part of the same spirit.

4. Some Consequences of the Mechanistic Mentality

By the time Adam Smith's treatise *The Wealth of Nations* appeared in 1776, the new world-view was firmly entrenched. The happiness of man was to be realized by the satisfaction of material needs. The division of labor in society was seen by Smith as a logical, necessary, and desirable step in the direction of improved task performance and ultimately in the direction of increased availability of goods. In our own time, this specialization has penetrated into every corner of human existence; virtually everyone is a specialist of some sort, and all the functions of living are handled by specialists. We are governed (or managed) increasingly by specialists; and we are even on the verge of abdicating the vestigial remains of our decision-making prerogatives in favor of specialists.

The triumph of the mechanistic mentality by the end of the eighteenth century is revealed in the literary record of the period. In a retrospective on the eighteenth century, Samuel Miller(1803) expressed the ardour of the recent convert to the faith. The emphasis is on the material aspects of life: the emergence of large-scale enterprise, the production of inexpensive goods, and the accomplishments of inventive genius. Comparisons with previous ages reflect a self-conscious materialistic bias.

> Perhaps it would not be extravagant to say that many of the higher orders of mechanics and day laborers now wear better clothes, and live, not more plentifully, but in some respects more conveniently, more neatly, and with more true taste, than many princes and kings were in the habit of doing two centuries ago ...

However, something is missing from the picture of productivity and apparent prosperity. This early hymn to progress is in sharp contrast to contemporaneous reports of the grim working conditions in the factories and the equally wretched living conditions among the new industrial poor.

> Children of very tender age were employed; many of them from the workhouses in London and Westminster, and transported in crowds as apprentices to masters resident many hundred miles distant where they serve unknown, unprotected and forgotten by those whose care nature or the laws had consigned them. These children are usually too long confined to work in closed rooms, often during the whole night; the air they breathe from the oil, etc., employed in the machinery, and other circumstances, is injurious; little regard is paid to their cleanliness; and frequent changes from a warm and dense to a cold and thin atmosphere are predisposing causes to sickness and disability, and particularly to the epidemic fever which is so generally to be met with in these factories.[9]

The work ethic, that legacy of Medieval rationalism and Protestant virtue, finds expression in a work attributed to James Reynolds(1802). This early nineteenth century piece created a utopian setting in which mechanical inventiveness is always rewarded and productive work is the highest virtue.

> Nothing excites ridicule so much as a man laboring with a bad instrument, or machine out of repair. On the other hand, nothing seems to give a Lithconian so much pleasure, as the sight of a dextrous workman, using an excellent machine.

One of the ironies of this utopian projection is that the reward of diligence is idleness, which as we have learned in the twentieth century presents serious problems.

The rapid transformation of society which took place at the beginning of the industrial revolution occasionally met with some violent resistance. The term Luddite, which is used to describe anyone who opposes technological innovation with violent action, derives from the name given to "an organized band of English mechanics and their friends, who (1811-16) set themselves to destroy manufacturing machinery in the midlands and north of England."[10] The advance of machinery, and consequent displacement of workers led to Luddite activity in the eighteenth and nineteenth centuries. Responding to the industrial revolution's callous disregard for human needs, Samuel Butler(1863) expressed the mounting anxiety over the direction of the doctrine of material progress. In a satire on Darwin's theory of natural selection, Butler raised some questions which are truly prophetic for our own time. He pointed to the possibility of machines evolving into higher forms of "mechanical existence" which could challenge the ascendancy of mankind— a theme which was developed further in his novel Erewhon.

That the twentieth century has ignored Butler's warnings is amply documented by our continued adherence to the doctrine of material progress. The theme of the early apostles of progress such as Adam Smith and Samuel Miller is echoed in the present day. Throughout the contemporary period, people have thrilled to the accomplishments of mechanized and automated production and the marvels of technology. The litany has not changed very much: greater productivity, improved living standards, cheaper goods and services, and more leisure time. Only very recently have we begun to question the relentless pursuit of these goals. Leisure is problematic in a culture attuned to the work ethic, and the institutionalization of change shows no signs of reaching an equilibrium.

5. Summary

The macroscopic effects of technological development are clearly evident to everyone. Moreover, that we are faced with challenging problems concerning the future role of technology is a matter of general agreement. We have already touched on the two opposing views of the social impact of technology. On the one hand, technology is seen as strictly instrumental in human affairs: it can equally well be used for constructive as for destructive ends.[11] On the other hand, some observers believe that technology acts as an autonomous force in modern civilization.[12] With these contrasting views in mind, we examined some of the major areas of contemporary concern: the arms race, the ecological crisis, and the collapse of traditional values. The mounting anxiety associated with these problems suggests a deeper human ambivalence; there seems to be a pervasive tension between man and his artifacts which grows in proportion as those artifacts more closely resemble man in their potentialities. The observation is especially significant for computer applications.

The evolution of civilization seems to entail the gradual alienation of man from the organic world. The first critical stage in this evolutionary process was the passage from hunter and food gatherer to pastoral herdsman and then to settled agriculturalist. This transition, which took place over a period of tens of thousands of years, carried man one step away from his natural environment; in gaining some measure of control over his habitat, man sacrificed the all-emcompassing certitude of the purely instinctual life. The other major landmarks in the development of civilization belong to the modern period. As intimated before, a subtle change took place in the relationship between producer and artifact during the eotechnic phase. This change resulted in the alienation of human labor during the period of rapid industrialization which followed. Labor was transformed into a commodity, and the intimate association of the artisan with his tools and the products of his craft was effectively destroyed. The factory system of production turned the human worker into an appendage of the machine. Further development and refinement of the factory system has heightened the sense of alienation. During the last half century, automated production techniques have been introduced, and with the advent of computers the means for automating the control of these processes is at hand.

Part of the problem we face in reaching an accommodation with technology stems from the way in which our tools have influenced our conception of the human being. By degrees, the realm of human uniqueness has eroded away. The seventeenth century image of man as an elaborate clockwork mechanism activated by a soul has been replaced by more sophisticated models. But in the process of refining the basic model, the soul was pushed from one corner to another until it finally vanished from the picture. The fusion of a mechanistic conception of man with the gradual displacement of human agency in securing the necessities of life has led to a crisis of identity which has been intensified by the creation of the computer. The computerized information-processing system poses a challenge to the continued dominance of human intelligence in the control of human destiny. This is the central issue to which this work is addressed.

[1] See Bury(1955)— a study of the evolution of the idea of progress.
[2] The proposal of Press(1974) for a moratorium on the development of community information utilities is a notable exception.
[3] This is not to suggest that nuclear war has become less probable, but that our perception has been dulled by fatigue.
[4] THE LIMITS TO GROWTH: *A Report for THE CLUB OF ROME's Project on the Predicament of Mankind*, by Donella H. Meadows, Dennis L. Meadows, Jorgen Randers, William H. Behrens III. A Potomic Associates book published by Universe Books, New York, 1972. Graphics by Potomic Associates.
[5] *The Accidental Century* by Michael Harrington (Copyright © Michael Harrington 1965), reprinted by permission of Macmillan Publishing Co., Inc., New York and George Weidenfeld and Nicolson Limited, London.
[6] Technique is used here in the sense defined by Ellul(1964). It characterizes the set of attitudes and dispositions underlying the use of technology in modern society.
[7] See Chapter 2, especially Section 3.
[8] See Reichenbach(1962), for example.
[9] From a book by John Aikin dealing with Manchester, published in 1795 (quoted in Inglis,1972).
[10] *Oxford English Dictionary*, 1971.
[11] Mesthene(1970), Forbes(1968), and Lilley(1965), for example.
[12] Ellul(1964) is perhaps the most prominent exponent of this view.

Chapter 2.
Computing in History

A definitive history of computation has yet to be written. Some aspects of the subject are treated in works on the history of mathematics and in surveys of calculating devices; in addition, some participants in the development of computers have produced monographs detailing more recent events. However, a comprehensive study tracing the evolution of the concepts, methods, and devices associated with computation may be a long time in the making. The extraordinary complexity of such a study is revealed in the following passage from Thomas M. Smith(1970).

> The appearance of computers late in the long history of counting and calculating provides a classic illustration of the phenomenon of convergence. Both historically and logically, computers owe their existence to many prior traditions. Among these are counting and reckoning, writing and the written record, the concept of quality, the engineering tradition, and many more. Before there were computers there were calculators, before calculators there were adders, and before adders there were counters. Before all of these there occurred to men whose names are lost to history notions of quantity. Probably before abstract ideas of quantity emerged there was already an ages-old tradition of enumerating. The origins of this presumed tradition, too, are shrouded in prehistory.

The absence of an authoritative guide to the intellectual origins of the computer age constitutes a severe impediment to any examination of the social matrix in which computing flourished and evolved. However, the issue is of sufficient interest to warrant the risk of possible errors and omissions in a premature effort. The principal aim of the present brief survey is to highlight certain salient features of the roles played by computation in Western history. It is offered with the hope of providing some perspective on the problems we face now, subverting Hegel's dictum that "peoples and governments never have learned anything from history."

In what follows, we will confine our attention to the modern period, beginning sometime in the fifteenth century. Of course, this choice is somewhat arbitrary in view of the intimate connection

24

between computation and the concepts of quantity and number and the long history of computational instruments such as the abacus. However, one discerns a striking continuity of development in computational methods from the fifteenth century to the present, which is clearly linked to the needs and expectations of modern society. The revival of trade and commerce, the reawakening of town life and emergence of a new social class, and efforts to extend the European hegemony across the oceans, which were well underway in the fifteenth century, created a strong need for improvements in computing. Merchants and tax collectors had to reckon accounts; navigators and cartographers needed accurate tables of astronomical measurements in order to determine positions on the earth's surface. The subsequent history of computation is almost invariably associated with expanding trade, growing governmental bureaucracies, and exploration and conquest either in the intellectual or the social domain. For the last four hundred years, the growth of computational skills has largely been in response to these social trends.

From our vantage point in the present, virtually all roads lead to the general-purpose, stored-program digital computer. In order to keep the discussion within manageable bounds, we will ignore the evolution of analog devices. Two landmark developments may be singled out on the tortuous path leading to the computer: the mechanization of arithmetic operations, and the automation of the control of computational procedures. We will examine each of these developments in turn, relating the technical accomplishments to social trends, and then focusing on the fusion of these ideas which first occurred in the nineteenth century. Most of the discernible trends in present-day computer applications have antecedents in the pre-computer world. This is especially true of information-processing systems in government. The discussion will conclude with a brief look at the role of computation in the early part of the twentieth century and some of the immediate factors responsible for the emergence of the computer.

1. Mechanization of Arithmetic: I. Exploration and Growth

Among the less-heralded changes brought about by the transformation of medieval society into modern European civilization was the increase in importance of computational skills. The principal source of this change was the expansion of trade and commerce which accompanied the growth of towns and the strengthening of national monarchies. Exploration and the search for overseas trade routes created a need for innovations in navigation. Taylor(1957, p. 544) observes "The methods of navigation developed first for the enclosed Mediterranean Sea and for the narrow seas on the continental shelf of northwestern Europe were inadequate for the new ocean navigation of the early fifteenth century sponsored by the Portuguese Prince Henry, the Navigator (1394-1460)."[1]

The medieval sailor made use of compass and chart and the technique of dead reckoning (the accounting of distance and direction travelled) to reach a desired destination. Prior to the fifteenth century the navigator used knowledge of astronomy largely as an aid in determining direction; he was unable to fix position out of sight of land. Prince Henry the Navigator introduced a new method of navigation which required observing the altitude of the pole star to obtain a fairly close approximation to the latitude. Since this observation could not be made near the equator, continued exploration southward along the west cost of Africa created an urgent need for a different method. Toward the end of the fifteenth century, astronomers and mathematicians in the service of Prince (later King) John of Portugal devised a technique for finding latitude by the noonday sun. This required computing a table of the daily declination of the sun.[2]

From the fifteenth century onwards navigation provided a powerful stimulus to the preparation and publication of tables of astronomical data. The Ephemerides of Regiomontanus (Johann Muller) published in 1471 was a milestone in this development. It contained tables prepared for navigation and other scientific purposes and eschewed astrological applications of astronomy. The information in these tables and others of a similar nature proved too inaccurate for use in determining longitude. Columbus and other explorers lost their way at sea as a result of attempting to use the data in such tables in conjunction with observations of the moon and the planets to find their longitude.[3]

The problem of accurate determination of longitude was particularly important in the development of mechanical aids to computation (see Goldstine(1972)). The solution of this problem awaited the fundamental advances in astronomy made in the sixteenth and seventeenth centuries by Copernicus, Kepler, Galileo, Newton, and others, as well as the design of an accurate chronometer. Several countries offered prizes in the eighteenth century for improved methods of determining position, and Great Britain established a Board of Longitude to examine such methods. During the eighteenth century a great many outstanding mathematicians attempted to improve Newton's theory of the moon's motions, in the hope of producing more accurate tables for use in navigation. The first *British Nautical Almanac and Astronomical Ephemeris for the Meridian of the Royal Observatory at Greenwich* was produced in 1767.

Apart from theoretical problems, the preparation of an ephemeris involves many laborious calculations. Since inaccuracies could result in costly navigational errors, precision is at a premium. Perhaps the earliest attempt to ease the burden of astronomical computations by mechanical means was that of Wilhelm Schickard (1592-1635), a professor of astronomy and mathematics at Tubingen.[4] Schickard designed and built a device in 1623 which was capable of performing addition and subtraction automatically and multiplication and division semi-automatically. The principal components of this machine were a train of gear wheels which functioned as an accumulator, a separate set of wheels for use in manually recording results, and a collection of six cylinders operating on the principle of Napier's numbering rods for multiplication.[5] Our knowledge of this device derives solely from sketches and descriptions contained in letters from Schickard to Kepler; the original machine was destroyed in a fire, and Schickard together with all his family subsequently fell victim to the plagues which ravished Europe during the Thirty Years War. It would appear that Schickard's ingenious device did not exert any influence on subsequent developments.

As suggested earlier, the growth of navigation was concomitant with the rapid expansion of trade and commerce. In addition to the exacting computational demands of navigation, commercial practice provided further incentives for mechanical aids. Lilley(1945) outlines three preconditions for the emergence of calculating machines: "a heavy demand for calculation, considerable mechanical experience, and a considerable development of physical science (the last, because the invention is not one that could be made from merely empirical approach)." By the early seventeenth century, all of these preconditions were satisfied. The time was ripe for the creation and application of mechanical computers. Since Schickard's work was obliterated and had no issue, the adding machine of Blaise Pascal (1623-1662) was effectively the first successful effort.

Pascal's machine, capable of addition and subtraction by means of a train of gear wheels acting as an accumulator, was completed in 1642. The precocious young mathematician apparently wanted to assist his father with his tax-collecting duties. Pascal's account of his invention reveals the motive to ease the burden of computational drudgery.

> Dear reader, this notice will serve to inform you that I submit to the public a small machine of my invention, by means of which you alone may, without any effort, perform all the operations of arithmetic, and may be relieved of the work which has often times fatigued your spirit, when you have worked with the counters or with the pen. (Reprinted in Smith, 1959, Vol. 1, p. 166)

Although a number of the machines were built and sold (one of which has been preserved in the Conservatoire des Arts et Metiers in Paris), the device proved too unreliable for commercial purposes, since the craftsmanship of the period was not sufficiently advanced to implement Pascal's design in a satisfactory practical form.

Another mechanical calculator designed for commercial applications was invented by Samuel Morland (1625-1695) in 1666. The principle of operation was similar to that of Pascal's device, but it was made specifically for adding and subtracting sums of money in British monetary units. Several other attempts were made in the course of the seventeenth century to construct practical calculating machines, the most noteworthy being that of Gottfried Wilhelm von Leibniz (1646-1716).

The mechanical calculator reached its penultimate form in Leibniz's invention which was conceived in 1671 and completed in 1694. Just as the mechanism contained the kernel of later refinements, Leibniz's account of the utility of his invention reveals a preeminently modern attitude.

> It is sufficiently clear how many applications will be found for this machine, as the elimination of all errors and of almost all work from the calculations with numbers is of great utility to the government and science.
>
> ...
>
> Also the astronomers surely will not have to continue to exercise the patience which is required for computation. It is this that deters them from computing or correcting tables, from the construction of Ephemerides, from working on hypotheses, and from discussion of observations with each other. For it is unworthy of excellent men to lose hours like slaves in the labor of calculation, which could be safely relegated to anyone else if the machine were used. (Reprinted in Smith, 1959, Vol. 1, pp. 18-0-181)

The Leibniz calculator constituted an advance over Pascal's machine in its ability to perform multiplication and division. Multiplication was implemented by means of repeated additions which could be performed simply by turning a handle and shifting the position of the carriage. Leibniz introduced a mechanism known as the "stepped reckoner" in his calculator, and also invented the "pinwheel." Both of these devices allow for the mechanical representation of the decimal digits, the former by means of a cylinder with fixed teeth of variable length arranged in parallel about its axis, and the latter by means of a wheel with movable teeth controlled by a cam-like ring. These two fundamental mechanisms figured prominently in many later machines. Thomas de Colmar employed the stepped reckoner in his "Arithmometer" of 1820, and made use of pinwheels in other machines. Pinwheels were also used in the nineteenth century by W.T. Odhner whose machine formed the prototype for the successful Brunsviga Calculator.

Although Leibniz's machine (which is preserved in the State Library in Hanover) formed the basis for subsequent mechanical calculators, it did not itself achieve success as a practical device. Technical problems affecting operational reliability had to be solved before the calculator was to become a practicable machine. The evolution of calculating machines from the end of the seventeenth century until the first commercially successful device was built in the middle of the nineteenth century was intimately associated with improvements in manufacturing techniques and the prodigious growth of computational requirements. Lilley(1945) sums up the situation.

> The Industrial Revolution gave a great impulse to the improvement of calculating machines, not only by providing the necessary technique, but also by increasing enormously the need for convenient methods of calculation, both for the accounting of the much larger businesses which arose and for the mathematical side of the scientific and technical problems which the Industrial Revolution produced.

2. Mechanization of Arithmetic: II. Government Record Keeping

The influence on computing of the record-keeping activities of large organizations is sufficiently important to warrant special treatment. Documentary records of human affairs are as old as civilization itself. In the modern period the growing division of labor and differentiation of function within society intensified the need for maintaining records. Government administration, in particular, has become ever more dependent on recorded information.

The term bureaucracy is used by sociologists to mean a formal organization established for the purpose of achieving some well-defined goal. Modern government bureaucracy as such resulted from the gradual separation of state administrative functions from the royal household. In England, the first step in this direction involved the formation of the treasury in the twelfth century. The increasing complexity of the affairs of state necessitated the further differentiation and elaboration of public administration. Perhaps the most significant influence in this trend was the centralization of power in the nation state. As the power of the state increased, new administrative functions were added, often at the expense of local self-government.[6] In any case, it is clear that the spectacular growth in the scope and complexity of government administration— military, police, fiscal, and judicial— during the seventeenth and eighteenth centuries necessitated vigorous record-keeping activity. The extent of this development in the seventeenth century may be judged by the growing concern for archives as evidenced by the appearance of numerous handbooks on archival administration. The French Revolution, however, marks the beginning of the all-powerful record-breathing leviathan that we are familiar with today. It was also during this period that the state began to take a systematic interest in science and technology, and to apply scientific methods to public affairs.

One particularly important area of record-keeping is associated with population census. Although census-taking was practiced to some extent in earlier times, the modern population census began to take shape in the seventeenth century. The pre-modern census was usually designed for highly selective purposes such as determining who should be taxed or conscripted into military or other forced service. The enumerations did not encompass the entire population— only those in particular categories were counted.

The major source of basic information on population in the eighteenth century was the civil register of vital events, which evolved from church records of christenings, marriages, and deaths. The information contained in these records was geared to the requirements of the simpler social order of the medieval world; it was not sufficient to satisfy the needs of government administration in the eighteenth century. Although censuses were taken, they were conducted sporadically, and the results were unreliable. A remark of Jean Jacques Rousseau written on the eve of the French Revolution reveals the concern of the Age of Enlightenment with these inadequacies.

> That government is infallibly the best, all other things being equal, under which, without the employment of any external means, without the naturalization of strangers, without receiving any new colonists, the citizens increase and multiply. That is the worst under which they lessen and decay. Calculators, it is now your affair; count, measure, and compare them. (Rousseau, 1762, p. 75)

In the past two hundred years the idea of a nation-wide enumeration for general administrative and scientific purposes has gained world-wide acceptance. This gradual evolution of modern census-taking reveals a shift in attitude toward the function of government which continues to exercise a powerful influence on the growth of computing. Since the eighteenth century, we have been relying more and more heavily on administrative solutions to social problems: this has generated a need for data documenting the condition of society. Although we may be more sophisticated than our eighteenth-century counterparts, who believed that appropriate presentation of facts would eliminate any possibility of disagreement over social questions, we share their enthusiasm for collecting facts. The modern state has acquired a taste for information, and its appetite is growing.

The periodic census came into existence at the end of the eighteenth century. The United States Constitution provided for a census to be taken every ten years beginning in 1790 to furnish a basis for the apportionment of representatives in Congress. France and England initiated periodic censuses in 1801. From 1790 to 1850, the number of items in the United States census inquiry expanded gradually from six to thirty-one, and the cost per capita in the same period underwent a sixfold increase.

The 1850 census is notable in that it "marked the beginning of scientific census inquiry in the United States." (Merriam, 1903). From this point on the need for automatic tabulating devices became more and more acute. The first three censuses required no clerks, all the work being handled by the enumerators. The number of clerks employed in 1850 jumped to 160, and by 1880 it had reached 1,495. Merriam comments on the need for mechanical assistance.

> By 1870 census inquiry had become so extended, and the increase in population and material development was so enormous, that tabulation by hand was necessarily inaccurate and extremely expensive. It was clear, moreover, that a point must be reached,

before many more decades had passed, where complete tabulation within the census period would be actually impossible. (Merriam, 1903, p. 839).

Some relief was forthcoming in the form of a machine invented by C.W. Seaton which was first used in 1872. This device served to display the tally sheets in a manner which facilitated the manual tabulation of results by the clerks. The Seaton machine was used extensively in the 1880 census, but it proved inadequate to deal with the relentlessly growing masses of data which had to be tabulated. It became evident that unless an effective method for fast and accurate tabulation were devised, the census inquiry would have to be reduced in scope. The latter was an unacceptable alternative, and Herman Hollerith's punched-card tabulating system made it unnecessary. With the aid of Hollerith's equipment, the state of the nation was duly tabulated in the 1890 census.

The mass society forged by the industrial revolution acquired in Hollerith's invention a tool well-suited to its needs. The representation of information as patterns of perforations in cards of uniform size afforded a flexible medium for recording enormous volumes of data; and the electric tabulating machines designed to read the cards provided the means for processing that data. Information is the life blood of large organizations, and this new class of computing devices constituted both adaptive response and powerful stimulus to the growth of large-scale enterprise.

3.   Automation of Control

Thus far we have examined some of the highlights in the reduction of arithmetic operations to elementary mechanical steps. A parallel development of equal importance in the evolution of computing devices involves the elaboration of automatic methods for controlling the order in which the elementary steps of a computation are performed. Devices incorporating a primitive form of sequence-control antedate the earliest known mechanical calculators. Elaborate clocks with mobile figures controlled by rotating pegged cylinders (a mechanism familiar from music boxes) were in evidence as early as the fourteenth century; and mechanical automata of every description were constructed in the ensuing period.

Man's fascination with robots and automata has a long and complex history with important consequences for the modern world.[7] The apparently barren imaginative genius of poets, philosophers and mystics who dreamed of mechanical men performing miraculous feats bore fruit in the Age of Reason. Valuable knowledge and skills were gradually accumulated by the makers of clocks, toys, and automata. During the sixteenth century the spirit of *homo ludens*[8] joined with *homo faber* to form a solid foundation for the practical inventiveness of the industrial revolution.

The early automata such as the figured clocks incorporated automatic control as an integral part of the mechanism. The differentiation of control from a sequence of actions occurred at the dawn of the industrial revolution. The pressure of increased demand for manufactured goods in the eighteenth century argued strongly for the replacement of human operators by machines in the performance of simple repetitive tasks. This led to experimentation with sequence-control mechanisms, first in the silk weaving industry of France. Intricate patterns could be produced with the draw-loom by drawing selected sets of warp-threads in a prescribed order and passing the shuttle between the drawn and stationary threads. The task of drawing the warp-threads required no particular skill and was usually performed by an assistant to the weaver working from a chart. "The inconvenience of employing an assistant, together with the errors it entailed, led to a search for a mechanism that would automatically perform the work of the draw-boy, and at the same time facilitate changes of pattern." (Patterson, 1957, pp. 166-167).[9]

The first notable development in the automation of the draw-boy's function was the mechanism designed by Basile Bouchon in 1725. Selection of the threads to be drawn was effected by means of a roll of paper perforated according to the pattern and wound onto a perforated cylinder. The warp-threads ran through a row of needles in a frame. When the cylinder was pushed toward the frame those needles passing through perforations left their attached threads stationary, while those which did not carried their threads along as they slid in the frame. Bouchon's design was improved three years later by Falcon who introduced several rows of needles, and substituted a string of perforated cards for the roll of paper.

These innovations were carried further by Jacques de Vaucanson (1709-1782) who was renowned as a maker of mechanical automata. Vaucanson constructed a loom in 1745 which embodied several improvements on the work of Bouchon and Falcon. The selecting apparatus was mounted above the loom, and so constructed as to eliminate completely the need for a draw-boy. This mechanism used perforated cards passing around a very complex cylinder, which made it too complicated for practical use.

Vaucanson's accomplishment in this area was to produce a device which served as the foundation for the Jacquard loom.

The automatic draw-loom was perfected by Joseph Marie Jacquard at the close of the eighteenth century. This loom used a perforated prism (in conjunction with cards) instead of a perforated cylinder, and incorporated a lifting mechanism which the weaver himself operated with a treadle. Jacquard succeeded in automating the selection of warp-threads in a practical device. Within eleven years of the invention's appearance at a Paris exhibition in 1801, there were 11,000 draw-looms using Jacquard's mechanism.

As indicated above the importance of these advances in the textile industry for computing technology lies in the elaboration of an automatic sequence-control mechanism which is differentiated from the process it controls. The system of cards used to encode a pattern in the Jacquard loom constituted an effectively unbounded medium for storing information, and lent itself quite naturally to the control of a sequence of computations, once the parallel was understood. That the parallel was understood may be a reflection of certain intrinsic features of modern society.

In the growth of cities, the expansion of trade and the creation of large-scale industrial enterprise, one discerns a trend toward highly interdependent and differentiated forms of social organization. Coordinating the diverse components of a manufacturing establishment or a trading company necessitated some degree of specialization of function. Manufacturing in particular came to depend less and less upon complex human skills. In order to achieve speed and reliability in production, the role of the craftsman was diminished by a systematic resolution of manufacturing processes into primitive operations. Scientific understanding advanced in proportion as the terms of ordinary human experience were isolated, refined and transformed into measurable quantities. The spirit of reductionism is an effective principle in the modern world. It is thus no accident that the automatic sequence-control mechanism of the Jacquard loom inspired the vision of Babbage.

4. Synthesis

The demand for computing power continued to grow in the nineteenth century. Business firms and governments required calculating devices for accounting and other purposes. We have already discussed the use of astronomical tables in navigation. The vital role played by trade and naval power in imperialist Europe added immeasurably to the importance of such tables. The preparation of mathematical tables for both general industrial and scientific applications as well as mortality tables for insurance purposes gained in importance. In addition to increasing society's computational needs, the industrial revolution stimulated improvements in machinery and provided further incentives for scientific investigation. Although European society in the early years of the nineteenth century was not quite ripe for the practical realization of the modern general-purpose digital computer, it did provide certain key conceptual ingredients.

The synthesis of ideas underlying the conception of the general-purpose digital computer was provided by Charles Babbage (1791-1871), a distinguished English mathematician who occupied the position of Lucasian Professor of Mathematics (once held by Isaac Newton) at Cambridge from 1827-1839. From his abiding interest in the construction of tables issued the fusion of the ideas of mechanical calculation with the notion of automatic sequence-control perfected in the textile industry. In 1822 he began work on a device known as the Difference Engine which was designed to tabulate polynomials by computing successive differences.[10] This work continued intermittently with support from the British government until 1833 when the project was abandoned. Around this time, Babbage conceived the plan for his most ambitious undertaking, the Analytical Engine.

The main features of this inspired conception took shape within three years of his preliminary investigations. By 1836, Babbage had rejected the rotary pegged cylinder as a control device and adopted the mechanism of the Jacquard loom instead. At this point, his plan for the Analytical Engine assumed the form of a general-purpose digital computer with a store, an arithmetic unit, and a punched-card input and output. As mentioned above, sequence-control was to be achieved by means of a Jacquard-like mechanism that provided iteration and conditional branching.

Babbage acknowledges his debt to the Jacquard loom in his discussion of the process of weaving with that device. "The analogy of the Analytical Engine with this well-known process is nearly perfect." (Babbage, 1864, p. 117). The comparison is carried further in a metaphor of Lady Lovelace. "We may say, most aptly, that the Analytical Engine *weaves algebraical* patterns just as the Jacquard loom weaves flowers and leaves. Here, it seems to us, resides much more of originality than the Difference Engine can be fairly entitled to claim." (Morrison, 1961, p. 252). The metaphor is not entirely fanciful despite the underlying invidious comparison. The warp and weft of the loom correspond to the store, the frame to the arithmetic unit (or the mill as Babbage termed it); and, of course, the perforated card control mechanism corresponds to the sequence-control apparatus of the Analytical Engine. One should recognize, however, that here the analogy ends. The Jacquard-loom did not embody a universal language for synthesizing patterns, replete with primitive operations and capabilities for logical expression. Babbage's remarkable insight placed it there.

It is clear from his own discussion of the Analytical Engine that Babbage appreciated the implications of his conception far beyond its application to table construction. " [I]t appears that the whole of the conditions which enable a *finite* machine to make calculations of unlimited extent are fulfilled in the Analytical Engine ... I have converted the infinity of space, which was required by the conditions of the problem, into the infinity of time." (Babbage, 1864, p. 128).

The capabilities and limitations of the Analytical Engine are discussed in an account [11] written by L.F. Menabrea and subsequently annotated by Augusta Ada, Countess of Lovelace (daughter of Lord Byron). Babbage presented a series of talks on his machine at a scientific meeting in Turin in 1840 which was attended by Menabrea, a young engineer who later became Prime Minister of Italy. Menabrea's account was based on these talks. Lady Lovelace translated the memoir into English and was encouraged by Babbage to add extensive notes of her own. The result is a valuable source of information on the Analytical Engine.

Babbage's dream of a general-purpose digital computer was not to be realized in his own time. The computational needs of the nineteenth century were not seen by his contemporaries to warrant the dedication of resources required for such a project. In addition the technology of the period was inadequate, perhaps even inappropriate, to the task. Babbage's continual modifications in the design also complicated matters. Too much a visionary, he could not compromise his grand design to translate possibility into feasibility. It is interesting to note that a Swedish contemporary, Pehr Georg Scheutz (1785-1873), inspired by Babbage's ideas, succeeded in building a difference engine which was displayed in London in 1854. Even in this less ambitious undertaking, Babbage failed to construct a machine.

Although Babbage's intellectual achievement was in advance of his time, he was very much a product of his time. The fundamental conceptual innovation embodied in the Analytical Engine derives from the resolution of computational processes into primitive operations. This resolution makes it possible to effect a computation by performing a sequence of operations and to introduce a mechanism to control the order of performance. Babbage's ideas were thus dependent on advances in mathematics, particularly those which led to the development of mathematical logic in the work of George Boole (1815-1864) and others.

Boole attempted to reduce the "laws of thought," codified principally by Aristotle, to an algebraic system. According to Goldstine(1972, p. 37)

> ... Babbage depended a great deal on Boole's ideas— as well as those of de Morgan, Herschel, and Peacock— for his understanding of what mathematical operations really are ... Babbage understood the notion of a mathematical operation and the quantities upon which it operated. This was made possible for the first time in this period by this group of English Algebraists.

Since Boole showed that logics can be reduced to very simple algebraic systems— known today as Boolean Algebras— it was possible for Babbage and his successors to design organs for a computer that could perform the necessary logical tasks. [12]

The reductionist spirit which laid the foundations of modern science and divorced the craftsman from his work conspired with the genius of the nineteenth century to give us the conception of the general purpose digital computer.

Babbage's plans for the Analytical Engine were carried further by his successors in the twentieth century.[13] Percy Ludgate designed an Analytical Machine in the early 1900's which introduced some important advances over Babbage's work. Leonardo Torres y Quevedo (1852-1936) explored the possibilities of using electromechanical technology in a digital calculating machine; and Louis Couffignal described a binary electromechanical program-controlled calculator in his Ph.D. Thesis of 1938. However, the computer awaited a propitious moment to be born. This moment was to be prepared by the practical success of punched-card tabulating systems, the refinement of developments in electrical engineering, and the computational needs of modern warfare.

5.   *Consolidation before Revolution*

As noted earlier (Section 2), the invention of Herman Hollerith marked a turning point in the history of data-processing. Hollerith's electric tabulating system is the ancestor of the punched-card equipment in use today. As used in the 1890 United States Census, it consisted of counting, sensing, punching, and sorting units. The information encoded on cards was sensed electrically rather than mechanically as in the Jacquard device. The sensing was accomplished by passing a card under a set of contact brushes which completed an electrical circuit. A completed circuit resulted in a one unit advance in a counter operated by an electromagnetic relay. Hollerith first employed rolls of paper in his machine, but the disadvantages of this medium became apparent in view of the requirements of processing data prepared in diverse locations or at different times. Punched-cards are clearly more suitable for sorting operations. Sorting was effected by means of an electromagnetic latch which opened when a hole was sensed. The dimensions of the Hollerith card were chosen to coincide with those of the United States dollar bill in order to secure the benefits of compatibility with existing equipment, a near poetic choice in view of the remarkable success of Hollerith machines in subsequent accounting applications.

Within a few years of the first major test of his system in the 1890 United States Census, Hollerith achieved international recognition, and his equipment was adopted for use in many countries. The experience gained in applications led to various improvements and added capabilities. In order to facilitate accounting operations, Hollerith devised a mechanism for addition employing an electromagnetic equivalent of the Leibniz stepped reckoner. In the course of the 1900 United States Census, automatic card-handling devices were added to the tabulators and sorters; and a manually operated decimal keypunch was developed.

Hollerith formed the Tabulating Machine Company in 1896 which enjoyed virtually undisputed preeminence in the field for several years. After 1900, Hollerith encountered difficulties with the Bureau of the Census, and the latter began manufacturing its own equipment for use in the 1910 census. James Powers was responsible for this operation which resulted in the development of a mechanical card-reading device. Part of the motivation for this innovation was the desire to circumvent the patents held by Hollerith. Powers left the Bureau and formed a company of his own which subsequently merged with Remington Rand in 1927. Hollerith sold his company in 1911, and it merged with two others to form the Computing-Tabulating-Recording Company. In 1914, Thomas J. Watson entered the picture and gave birth to the International Business Machines Corporation in 1924.

The first commercial use of Hollerith's system was an accounting application for the New York Central Railroad in 1895. In the ensuing years, tabulating machines found their way into banks, insurance companies, and retail stores, as well as government agencies. Competition between rival business-machine companies stimulated improvements in punched-card systems throughout the 1220's and 1930's. By the mid-1930's, business applications had become quite sophisticated. Several electro-mechanical accounting machines were designed and built. One for use in small banks was capable of storing the records of up to 10,000 accounts. Commercial applications also exploited the potentialities of systems of interconnected punched-card machines. One example, which anticipated contemporary computer applications in retail merchandising, involved an experimental system developed for a Pittsburgh Department Store. This system (Remote-Control Accounting) featured terminals connected to card-punch/tabulators and on-line typewriters which facilitated generation of sales records, customer billing, and also point-of-sale credit authorization.

Slowly the ground was being prepared for the emergence of the general-purpose digital computer. The commercial potential of accounting machines and data-processing equipment was explored. Designers gained invaluable experience in the application of advances in electrical engineering to punched-card machines. In addition, the sophisticated computational requirements of some areas of scientific research served to push the capabilities of punched-card equipment to the limit, thereby creating new opportunities. L.J. Comrie introduced Hollerith machines into the British National Almanac Office during his tenure as superintendent. Once again we encounter the influence of navigation on computing. In 1929, Comrie made calculations on the future positions of the moon, a task which required the punching of one-half million cards. Inspired by Comrie's success with punched-card equipment, Wallace J. Eckert with assistance from IBM established a scientific computing laboratory at Columbia University in 1934. Here Eckert assembled a system of punched-card machines for which he devised a centralized control mechanism, thus permitting automatic high-speed calculation in a chain of operations.

The pioneering work of Comrie, Eckert, and others led to the renaissance of Babbage's vision. Experiments with inter-connected punched-card machines under centralized control suggested the practical possibility of an electro-mechanical equivalent of the Analytical Engine. Vannevar Bush, inventor of the differential analyzer and wartime Director of the U.S. Office of Scientific Research was aware of this possibility in 1936. The lines of influence at this stage in the history of computing are too complex to sort out with much certainty, but it is clear that the demonstrable success of punched-card machines coupled with ever-growing computational needs overcame the resistance which had proved fatal to the Analytical Engine in the nineteenth century.

6. The Birth of the Computer

Efforts to design and build computing devices intensified under the wartime conditions of the late 1930's and have continued unabated ever since. Our proximity to the events of this era would argue against any claims to completeness or objectivity, but it is desirable to sketch the major developments and trace some of the interconnections among them. In what follows we will examine the growth of computer technology from the late 1930's to the early post-war period.

The earliest general-purpose program-controlled computer was built in Nazi-Germany. Konrad Zuse had conceived the basic design for a tape-controlled, floating-point, binary computer by 1936. The plan was put into practical form with some support from the government, the result being a floating-point binary machine with a 64-word store. This machine is known as the Z3 computer and was operational in 1941. It did not survive the war, and Zuse's work was virtually unknown outside of Germany until quite recently.

The mainstream of early computer developments centered in the United States and Great Britain. Howard Aiken of Harvard University, in cooperation with IBM, designed and built the Automatic Sequence Controlled Calculator, more commonly known as the Harvard Mark I. This largely mechanical device was operational in 1944, and first used on classified work for the United States Navy. Although the initial program-control of the Mark I did not allow for conditional branching, such facilities were later added in the form of a subsidiary sequence-control mechanism. Aiken designed several other machines at Harvard. The Mark II, completed in 1947 for the U.S. Naval Proving Ground in Dahlgren, Virginia, used electromagnetic relays and paper-tape sequence control. These were followed by Mark III in 1950 and Mark IV in 1952.

IBM's experience with the development of Aiken's Mark I launched the business-machine company in the computer field. The first effort after Mark I yielded the Pluggable Sequence Relay Calculator, a remote cousin of IBM's calculating punches. This was followed by the Selective Sequence Electronic Calculator (SSEC), a partly electronic machine with electromagnetic relays which appeared in 1948. An important feature of this machine was its ability to modify and then execute stored instructions. These early efforts provided invaluable experience for the scientists and engineers who were to design the commercially successful IBM 650 and later the IBM 701.

The Bell Telephone Laboratories's work on switching technology made it a natural environment in which to experiment with the use of electromagnetic relays for computing devices. George Stibitz and S.B. Williams designed a machine (Complex Number Computer) for performing arithmetic on complex numbers. This was completed in 1939 to become the first in a series of relay calculators built by Bell Labs. Stibitz's work on automatic sequencing and error detecting codes on the eve of United States involvement in World War II led to the design of the Relay Interpolater, a special purpose, tape-controlled device designed for use in fire-control problems. This was followed by three other models designed for military applications, the last of which was a general-purpose, program-controlled computer with conditional branching facilities.

Two further innovations on the way to the present day computer involved the exploitation of electronics technology, and the implementation of the stored program concept. John V. Atanasoff is credited with the first attempt to build an electronic digital calculating machine. Atanasoff's work at Iowa State College in the mid-1930's led him to the idea of a system using memory and logic circuits. During the 1930's and 1940's, several groups explored the possibilities of replacing mechanical or electromechanical devices by digital electronic circuits. The efforts of Zuse and Helmut Schreyer in Germany constituted perhaps the first attempts at utilizing electronics technology in the design of a general-purpose program-controlled computer.

The first major advance issued from the Moore School of Electrical Engineering at the University of Pennsylvania with the design and construction of the ENIAC (Electronic Numerical Integrator and Computer). The germ of the ENIAC concept was contained in a memorandum of John Mauchly in 1942 which discussed the use of vacuum tube devices for calculating. Like most other computing efforts of the period, this one was in response to military needs. The Moore School group, directed by J.G. Brainerd with Mauchly as principal consultant and J. Presper Eckert as chief engineer, completed the ENIAC in 1946.[14] This massive machine with its 18,000 vacuum tubes was the first electronic computer to become operational.

The final conceptual leap in the development of the computer was the idea of stored programs which appears to have originated with the ENIAC group. Although there are some unresolved questions concerning the parentage of the stored program concept, this critical idea was first documented in a 1945 draft report on the EDVAC (Electronic Discrete Variable Computer) written by John von Neumann of the Institute for Advanced Study at Princeton.[15] von Neumann became associated with the ENIAC effort in 1944, as a result of his work at the Los Alamos Scientific Laboratory (Manhattan Project). Details of the EDVAC project were presented in a series of lectures given at the Moore School in 1946, and thereby exerted a powerful influence on subsequent developments.

The earliest operational stored-program computer was a machine built at Manchester University (England) in 1948 primarily for the purpose of exploring the potentialities of the cathode ray-tube as a storage medium. Although this machine was not a practical computer, the Manchester project is historically significant in that it constitutes a line of development independent of the Moore School influence. Moreover, the experience led to the design of more powerful devices, in particular MADM (Manchester Automatic Digital Machine) which was built in cooperation with Ferranti, Ltd. The first practical stored program computer was the EDSAC (Electronic Delay Storage Automatic Computer) built at Cambridge University. The Cambridge group was lead by Maurice Wilkes who was a participant in the Moore School symposium. Although the EDSAC was based on the design of the EDVAC, the former was in operation by 1949; the EDVAC did not become operational until 1951.

Eckert and Mauchly left the Moore School to form the Eckert-Mauchly Computer Corporation, which designed and built the UNIVAC computer. UNIVAC was intended for both commercial and scientific applications, and the first one was delivered to the Bureau of the Census in 1951. The EDVAC group was further depleted by the departure of von Neumann. At the Institute for Advanced Study, von Neumann and colleagues designed the IAS computer which was completed in 1952. This random-access machine using electrostatic storage and parallel binary arithmetic provided a basis for several other computers. In particular, it influenced the development of the IBM 701, the first of IBM's 700 series. Also of considerable importance in the development of computer technology was the appearance in 1952 of the Massachusetts Institute of Technology's Whirlwind I computer. This machine marked a major advance in storage capacity, with its introduction of a coincident-current magnetic-core memory.

The evolution of computer technology since the emergence of the general-purpose, stored-program, electronic, digital computer is at least as complex as earlier developments.[16] Indeed, the details cover more than one college-level course of study. Since our principal aim in this brief survey is to indicate the interaction of computer technology with social forces, presenting further technical details would be inappropriate. One of the most disturbing features of the birth of the computer is its intimate association with military problems, an association whose legacy is still very much in evidence.[17] If this were simply an historical accident, a practical necessity born of a war for survival, it would be of relatively minor importance for society as a whole. But developments in the modern world suggest otherwise.

The marriage of science and government has its roots in the French Revolution, during which the improving spirit of the eighteenth century found practical expression. Government became a systematic patron of the sciences during this period. Napoleon was himself scientifically trained and had a shrewd appreciation for the practical utility of scientific investigation, especially for military purposes. What began as a partnership evolved into an intimate relationship. The demonstrable success in recent decades of society's ability to mobilize scientific resources testifies to this intimacy. The apparent freedom to use technology as we see fit diminishes in proportion as it becomes critical for the functioning of social institutions in a centralized state.

We have attempted to show in this chapter that the computer has a past which holds the key to its likely future in society. From the fifteenth century onward, the computational needs of society increased relentlessly. Under the tutelage of scientific and industrial expansion, modern man has cultivated a reductionist attitude toward experience. As industrial processes were resolved into simple component tasks, so computational processes were resolved into primitive operations, and control mechanisms elaborated in the one sphere were eventually translated into the other. Trade and the factory system of production aided by modern methods of transportation and communication institutionalized the conquest of space and time. The managerial revolution made possible by the emergence of computers with the ability to control complex chains of simple operations threatens to institutionalize the conquest of will.

[1] Reprinted by permission of the Oxford University Press, Oxford.
[2] For a brief discussion of the role of astronomy in navigation, see Parker and Scott(1953).
[3] The moon's position with respect to the fixed stars serves as a clock, and knowledge of the time enables one to determine longitude. However, the positions of the moon and stars must be known very exactly in order to obtain longitude accurately.
[4] Randell(1973) presents an extensive annotated bibliography on the history of computers, including early mechanical devices as well as excellent summaries of major developments from the first mechanical calculators to the birth of the modern electronic computer. See also Goldstine(1972), Smith(1958, Vol. II, Chapter III), Wolf(1935, Chapter XXIII, Part VIII), and Wolf(1939, Chapter XXVII, Part XI) for material on the history of computation.
[5] See Murray(1961) for descriptions of mathematical machines.
[6] The role of computers in the erosion of local autonomy is discussed at length in Chapter 12.
[7] See Cohen(1966), especially Chapter 6.
[8] Huizinga(1955) presents a convincing case for the importance of the play element in human culture.
[9] Reprited by permission of the Oxford University Press, Oxford.
[10] See Goldstine(1972, pp. 17-19) for a discussion of difference tables.
[11] Reprinted in Morrison(1961).
[12] *The Computer from Pascal to Von Neumann*, by Herman H. Goldstine (copyright © 1972 by Princeton University Press). Reprinted by permission of Princeton University Press.
[13] See Randell(1973), pp. 12-15.
[14] For an account by one of the participants, see Goldstine(1972).
[15] Randell(1972) conjectures that Alan Turing, whose pioneering work on the theory of computation can be seen to embody the idea in principle, may also have contributed to its practical development through his wartime contacts with von Neumann.
[16] Rosen(1969) presents a useful survey.
[17] See Chapter 14.

Part II.
Accomplishment and Promise: Coordination of Diversity

The need for distinctive mechanisms to coordinate activities increases with the number of parts involved and the diversity of their respective functions. In modern society, large concentrated populations and an extreme division of labor guarantee numerous interacting parts and great diversity. These conditions are the legacy of industrial development. The factory system of production consolidated capital and human resources in large-scale enterprises. Effective utilization of these resources necessitated a division of labor and specialization of function, and the innovations of the factory system have exercised a formative influence on the whole of society. An endless differentiation of occupations and functions is evident in every area of human endeavor, and each of them is linked to others in a vast chain of interdependencies. Our primary concern here is with the role of information technology in the coordination of these complex interactions. For purposes of discussion, it is convenient to distinguish between "extensive" and "intensive" forms of organization. Corporations and government bureaucracies exhibit the former type. The intensive variety is characteristic of the skilled performance of an individual such as a teacher or physician.

The coordination of activities in large organizations is normally the responsibility of a specialized group of individuals who form the upper levels in a hierarchical structure. Corporate and government operations provide the most prominent examples of this type of organization, but it is also to be found in educational institutions, hospitals, and other establishments which manipulate substantial social resources. Hierarchical structure facilitates specialization at all levels, and permits the functions of management to be differentiated from the operations of production. The advantages of this arrangement can be appreciated by analogy with the Jacquard loom in which control is exercised as a distinctive component of the weaving process (see Chapter 2). Management's peculiar specialized function is decision-making. This assumes a variety of forms at the different levels in the hierarchy, but what all types of decision-making have in common is their dependence on information.

In order to identify problems, form hypotheses and explore alternative courses of action, information must be gathered, processed, and structured appropriately. This holds whether the decision involves a routine matter of payroll deductions, a moderately complicated inventory control problem, or a strategic issue affecting the entire organization. The decision-maker in a large organization must contend with masses of data and complex interactions among many variables. As a fast and accurate processor of information, the computer is ideally suited to these tasks, and it is well on the way to becoming an indispensable instrument of management.

Socially significant problems of coordination are not confined to the management of large-scale enterprises. The performance of complex tasks by individuals or small groups is a basic component of medical practice, teaching, and scientific research. In these cases, too, information plays a vital role, and the activities of the physician, teacher, and scientist can be modeled as decision-making processes. For example, in the diagnosis and treatment of disease, information on the patient's condition must be gathered and processed so as to enable the physician to form hypotheses, draw inferences, and ultimately arrive at a decision and course of action. Although this kind of highly skilled behavior is often performed in the setting of complex institutions (schools, hospitals, etc.), the activities themselves are characterized by an "intensive organization" of knowledge. The information to be processed derives from a multitude of observations on a small number of events or transactions, rather than a few observations on a large number of transactions. Beyond routine data-processing applications, appropriate use of computers in this domain hinges on the development of techniques for mechanizing various facets of intelligent behavior.

Large organizations and skilled human performance pose problems which afford many opportunities for the effective utilization of computer technology. The potential benefits to society are mediated by gains in productivity and efficiency which result in more high-quality, inexpensive goods and services. However, computer applications have a pronounced tendency to contribute to organizational changes which may in the long run be inimical to democratic institutions. Coordination in hierarchical organizations is often a euphemism for command and control, and the computer may well serve as an instrument for the centralization of decision-making, leading to a dangerous concentration of power.

The main objective of Part II is to explore the social potentialities of computer technology. After surveying the distribution of computer applications in contemporary society and examining the computer industry, we will focus on some of the major areas in which information systems have been developed. The discussion of corporate decision-making is intended as a study of the macroscopic effects of computers on large organizations. This is followed by a look at automation from the point of view of the lower echelons in the organization. The subsequent treatment of education and health-care emphasizes the use of computers in augmenting skilled human performance, and the impact of these applications on the quality and availability of social services.

Chapter 3.
Computer Utilization

Since the end of World War II, the computer has emerged as a major force in contemporary society. An industry of mammoth proportions has come into existence, and virtually every major social activity from warfare to agriculture has felt its impact. One of the principal underlying causes of the rapid diffusion of computer applications is the diversity of contemporary society. The crowded urban centers in which most of us live embrace a staggering variety of activity. The force of numbers is of course an important component of this diversity, but equally important is the high degree of differentiation and interaction which characterizes the social structure. The self-sufficient individual and community are things of the past. The necessities of our daily existence are furnished by an exceedingly complex network of interdependent elements.

We are born in hospitals operated by a hierarchy of medical, technical and administrative specialists. Our food is grown and harvested on large farms employing sophisticated machines, and modern management techniques. The commodities we use are produced in factories which require a disciplined labor force and reliable supplies of energy and raw materials from all over the world. Their appearance in the market place depends on the coordination of processing, packaging, transportation, and communication facilities, as well as on an elaborate financial apparatus. We are educated by specially trained professionals in large institutions. Our jobs take us from place to place, and depend upon economic and political factors which transcend local and national boundaries. Even in death the interdependent character of our society manifests itself.

These observations are, of course, familiar to everyone. They bear repeating here because of the importance of social diversity as a force in spreading the use of computers. Neither the profit motive nor the will to innovate adequately account for this phenomenon. Increasing social complexity placed great strains on the technology available for processing information. The administration of public affairs and its dependence on population census is but one prominent example of this trend. As pointed out in Chapter 2, the ground was prepared in the twentieth century by the gradual penetration of punched-card equipment into government and industry. Many contemporary applications were anticipated in the uses of that equipment. The technical triumphs occasioned by World War II accelerated developments which were already well underway and, in addition, created new opportunities.

The objective of this chapter is to frame the range and scope of computer applications so as to place the various social issues associated with them in perspective. The critical task is the analysis of the role of information-processing technology in coordinating the interacting components of large organizations. To this end we will survey the areas in which computers are currently used, and assess their relative importance for society. No such discussion would be complete without an examination of the computer industry itself. We will consider the economic position of the industry and analyze its influence on public affairs. The dominant role of the United States in the diffusion of computer applications and in the computer industry tends to overshadow important developments elsewhere. Although most of the discussion will focus on the situation in North America, we will also deal with Western Europe and Japan, and to a lesser extent with the Soviet Bloc and Third World countries.

1. Computers and the Coordination of Diversity

Our primary concern is with the various social settings in which computers are used. Since computer applications in different contexts may be essentially the same from a computing point of view, it is useful to identify types of such applications. Most computer applications may be interpreted as belonging to one or more of five generic classes: clerical, information-processing, control, design, and decision-making.

Clerical applications encompass routine computing tasks such as payroll preparation, invoicing, and various accounting functions. Information-processing systems are designed to deal with the presentation and manipulation of data. Typical examples are stock-quotation, airline-reservation, and automated-library systems. The third class involves the control of operations such as occurs in certain industrial processes or in regulating traffic flow in a city. As the name suggests, the fourth class encompasses systems for facilitating the design process. Examples range from engineering problems to artistic efforts. The last class consists of systems developed principally to assist managers or decision-makers. These systems may utilize methods of operations research and other techniques to analyze the effects of alternative courses of action. Not all applications fit conveniently in these classes, but the scheme does provide a rough taxonomy.

The particular circumstances in which computers are used vary widely, but the underlying motives for virtually all such uses may be resolved into three different categories.[1] First, one observes a desire to achieve greater economy in an operation. This may take the form of reducing production or service costs, or it may involve an effort to secure more efficient utilization of resources. The declining cost per unit of computation which has accompanied advances in system design has made computers irresistable to many potential users.[2] Second, an operation may not be feasible at all without the use of a computer. Such is the case for large calculations in which the speed and accuracy of the computer is indispensable. In addition, there are problems which require solutions in "real-time" in order to be useful— weather forecasting is a notable example. Finally, the computer is often introduced for the purpose of achieving a deeper understanding of a complex process, or to rationalize an operation. This motive may enter in certain scientific investigations such as the simulation of social systems, or in the design of models for use in policy-planning.

Armed with a taxonomy of types and motives for computer applications, we turn now to the question of where these applications occur. In the present section we will survey the range of computer utilization in American society. There is virtually no loss of generality in restricting attention to the United States, since the entire spectrum of contemporary computer applications is represented. The issue of economic significance will be considered in Section 2. The form of available information on computer use places constraints on the types of questions we can readily answer. In keeping with characteristic statistical reporting practices, it is convenient to distinguish between government and the private sector on the highest level of abstraction. The sources consulted for this discussion present computer use data largely according to the economic divisions of the Standard Industrial Classification (SIC) system.[3] The classification scheme described here is not identical with, but does reflect, the SIC categories. Government is subdivided into federal, and state and local jurisdictions. Computer use in the former may then be analyzed according to locus of activity in the various departments and agencies. The latter, if differentiated at all, is usually resolved into its several operational responsibilities.

For present purposes, the private sector may be divided into five major categories: manufacturing, finance, wholesale and retail trade, services, and transportation and communication. In this framework, education (consisting mainly of primary- through university-level schools) is classified under services within the private sector. Electric and gas utilities are grouped with transportation and communication.

The most important area for computer applications is the federal government, and the military is by far the major user.[4] All of the five types of applications described above are represented. Clerical and information-processing uses are pandemic to all large organizations, the military being no exception. Weapons systems incorporate computers to provide control for guidance and targeting. Military strategists use decision-making systems in large-scale simulations, and sophisticated real-time applications occur in command-and-control systems. Although economy is not disregarded in military applications, the critical motive for introducing computers is feasibility. In response to the arms race, computer technology in conjunction with other technologies has been appropriated in order to facilitate operations that would otherwise be impossible.

Important non-military computer applications are supported by several federal government departments. The atomic energy program has historical ties with the computer (see Chapter 1) and continues to be a major area of computer use. Its principal nonmilitary rival is the space program, in which computerized flight-control operations have, through the popular media, assumed the epic proportions of the Old West.

Departments responsible for transportation, and national health, education, and social-security programs also make extensive use of computers. In addition to clerical uses, the Social Security Administration, for example, relies heavily on information-processing systems. Such systems have become indispensable in several functions of the federal bureaucracy: tax collecting and census-taking in particular. Data collected in the administration of these functions furnish information for use in policy-planning as well as in internal agency operations. Information-system applications also figure prominently in federal law-enforcement practices.

Computer use by state and local authorities parallels that of the federal government, but on a much smaller scale. Here, too, clerical and information-processing applications are widespread. Typical administrative jurisdictions where information-processing systems are used include motor-vehicle bureaus, law-enforcement agencies, and revenue departments. An additional area of increasing importance is urban planning, which calls for large-scale decision-making systems. The problems of coordinating day-to-day government functions, and of achieving orderly growth in congested urban centers have led administrators to experiment with computerized regional-simulation models.

The private sector supports a remarkable diversity of computer applications. As in government, clerical and information-processing systems are everywhere in evidence. In the manufacturing area, computers are used for process control and engineering design. The chemical, and oil refining industries in particular employ computers in the control of production processes. Complex machine and assembly operations such as occur in the automotive and electronics industries have also yielded to automation with the aid of computers.

Computing has long been an important element in financial operations. The insurance business added appreciably to the aggregate demand for fast and efficient calculating devices for use in statistical applications such as the preparation of mortality tables. Now, like other large organizations, insurance companies require computerized information-processing systems to handle their large volumes of client files. In addition to accounting-type clerical applications, banking practices have spurred the development of character recognition schemes to facilitate automatic check processing. Computer applications in financial transactions are likely to become increasingly more important in the future if the development of computer-communication networks permits implementation of automatic funds-transfer systems.[5] The widespread use of credit cards for retail purchases may mark the first step in the realization of computerized point-of-sale funds transfer.

The service area of the private sector is an extremely fertile source of computer applications. We will discuss the impact of computers on education and health-care in subsequent chapters. Companies which provide computer services of a clerical or information-processing nature to businesses account for a significant portion of computer applications. Other major users are the transportation and communications industries. The travelling public is familiar with airline-reservation systems, and computer-controlled ground transportation. A less visible (to the general public) use of computers is made by railroads for scheduling cars from origin to destination, and for handling the distribution of revenue to the carriers involved. Computers are also vitally important in communications, especially for message switching. The catalogue of computer applications is enormous and growing daily. Our aim in this brief survey is merely to indicate its range.

2. Social Investment in Computer Applications

The relative importance of the various computer applications is reflected in the level of resources committed to them. Unfortunately, there is no standardized method of accounting for this commitment. Statistics on computer usage, such as number and value of systems installed, vary from one source to another; and there is no universal agreement on the terms of reference. Nevertheless, the available evidence does allow us to estimate the relative extent of computerization in different countries and sectors of society.

The raw data on which most analyses of computer utilization are based fall into three classes: number of computing installations, value of installations, and number of persons employed in computing. The typical computer census distinguishes between general-purpose systems, mini and dedicated systems, and peripheral equipment. Figures for the total number of computer systems installed usually include only the first two items, whereas those for the value of installations (based on purchase price) often include all three.[6] Two main types of employment figures are compiled, one according to job classifications, the other by industry. In what follows, we will rely principally on number and value of installations, since these data are the most readily available for different countries.

By virtually any standard, the United States leads the world in computer utilization. At the end of 1969, the United States accounted for 57% of the total number of computer installations in the world;[7] Japan and West Germany each had 8%; Great Britain and France 6%; the Soviet Union 5%; with the bulk of the remaining 10% distributed among other industrialized nations such as Canada and Italy. There were an estimated 88,000 computing installations in the United States at the end of 1971. The value of these installations (including peripheral equipment) was in the neighborhood of $31 billion. The comparable aggregate figures for Western Europe (France, West Germany, Great Britain, and Italy) indicate 26,000 systems at a value of nearly $9 billion.[8] According to 1972 data,

Japan had moved into second place behind the United States with 15,000 systems valued at $4 billion.[9] As shown in Table 3.1, Great Britain and West Germany were roughly comparable, with France close behind.

Table 3.1   Computers, GNP, and Working Population — 1971.

Country	Number Install-ations	Value $ (x 10^9)	GNP $ (x 10^9)	Working Population (x 10^6)	Value: GNP (x 100)	Computers/ Million Working Population
U.S.	84,600	28.9	1068.8	79.12	2.71	1069
Japan	14,806[1]	4.1[1]	310.3[2]	32.01[2]	1.32	463
West Germany	7,800	2.9	217.4	26.67	1.33	292
U.K.	7,600	2.5	136.7	24.33	1.81	312
France	6,700	2.2	162.8	20.52	1.32	326
Italy	3,450	1.3	101.6	18.70	1.26	184
Canada	3,548[3]	1.1[4]	93.4[5]	8.63[5]	1.18	411

Source: Gassmann(1973); [1]Kurita(1973) giving 1972 figures; [2]*Japan Statistical Yearbook 1973/74;* [3]Canadian Information Processing Society (December 1971); [4]estimate based on rental figures; [5]*Canada Year Book 1973.*

These figures are useful to indicate the distribution of computing resources, but judging the relative intensities of computer development within different countries requires normalized measures. One such measure is given by the ratio of installed system value to GNP. For the United States this ratio is 2.7; it ranges between 1.3 and 1.8 for Western Europe and Japan. The number of computers per million of working population is another normalized measure which may be somewhat less sensitive to yearly fluctuations in economic activity.

The principal inference to be drawn from the figures on computer use is that a significant disparity exists between the United States and other industrialized countries. Although forecasts of growth are severely hampered by inadequate and ambiguous data, it is evident that the growth rate in the United States has slowed noticeably.[10] Moreover it is generally believed that the gap between the United States on the one hand, and Japan and Western Europe on the other, will narrow— especially as measured by the value of installations/GNP ratio.[11]

Thus far we have examined the distribution of computer resources across countries. We turn now to the question of which sectors of society make the most use of computers. As in Section 1, we will focus on the United States, with a look at Japan for comparative purposes. Of all the organizations in the United States, the federal government unquestionably makes the greatest use of computers.[12] As of June 30, 1971, there were 5,961 computing installations in the federal government. This figure represented about 7% of the total number of installations in the country. Within the federal government, the lion's share (approximately 57%) of installations belonged to the Department of Defense. The Atomic Energy Commission and the National Aeronautics and Space Administration accounted for an additional 30%, while the Departments of Transportation, and Health, Education, and Welfare contributed 4%, leaving 9% dispersed among the remaining federal agencies.

Of the major divisions defined in the Standard Industrial Classification (SIC) scheme, manufacturing showed the largest usage of computers, according to value of installations. The manufacturing group (including electrical and nonelectrical machinery, transportation equipment, metals, chemicals, food products, and printing and publishing) accounted for about 18% of the total value of computing installations in the United States. The services sector (consisting of education, medical and health, business, and miscellaneous services) and banking and insurance each accounted for about 14%. The transportation, communication, and electricity and gas division followed with 7%, while state and local government, and wholesale and retail trade each had 4%. The relative ordering of these industrial divisions in Japan was essentially the same, except for government.[13] Local and central government occupied the lowest ranks, each with 2% of the total value of computer installations.

A more revealing measure of the intensity of computerization within an industry group is afforded by the ratio of the value of computing installations to national income originating in the group. Applied to the United States, this measure shows the service area (particularly business services and education) to be most dependent on computers, while state and local government is least dependent. The relative positions of the other groups are the same as those produced in the ranking by value.

Employment associated with computer applications also gives some indication of the dependence of an industry group on computing. According to 1969 figures, the banking and life insurance groups employed 6.4% and 3.5% of their respective work forces in data-processing. This contrasts with 2.2% for utilities, 1.2% for chemicals, and 0.7% for railroads. Although not strictly comparable, these figures reinforce the ordering resulting from use of the ratio of value to industry income.

The importance of computer applications in the industrialized world is mirrored in the needs of developing countries. Computer technology is seen to be linked to the development of other technologies which are essential to the process of industrialization.[14] Economic and political conditions in countries of the Third World are too varied to permit many generalizations, but it is clear that one of the key areas for computer applications is management decision-making. Planning for economic development requires sophisticated models and considerable computing power. Although it may be premature to speculate, one is struck by the possibilities for abuse of power which the extensive use of computers by central governments could create or underwrite in developing nations.

3.   General Features of the Computer Industry

The computer industry plays an important role in determining the use of computer technology. As supplier of products and services, repository of expert knowledge, and economic force, the computer industry exerts a powerful influence on both the type and form of computer applications. An obvious kind of direct influence derives from the promotional efforts of individual companies, just as in other industries. Perhaps more consequential are the characteristic attitudes toward economic and social problems conveyed by the managerial and technical representatives of the computer industry. The widespread appeal of systems analysis as an approach to management problems must be due in no small measure to this influence. Although now a major economic unit, its comparative newness makes the computer industry difficult to analyze, insofar as much of the requisite data is unavailable. In this section we will discuss the principal components of the industry, mark its international character, and take a brief look at the dominant companies.

The report (OECD, 1969) on electronic computers sponsored by the Organization for Economic Cooperation and Development characterizes the computer industry in terms of the structure of computing systems. Three components are identified: computer proper (or central processing unit), peripherals, and software. Peripherals are taken to include input and output devices and auxiliary storage equipment. The software component is differentiated into basic software whose main element is the operating system, auxiliary software such as compilers and translators, and applications programs designed for specific tasks. This analysis reflects some of the divisions within the industry and also accords with the specialization which has occurred in certain countries. Some companies, for example, produce only peripheral equipment, and there are countries which do not have a computer manufacturing industry but are quite active in software design. In addition to this breakdown of the industry in terms of computing functions, it is also useful to consider a classification of computer companies based on market activity. Sharpe(1969) describes seven major categories of computer companies, four in the products area and three species of service firms. Computer manufacturers produce (or assemble from components made by other companies) general-purpose computers. The building blocks (such as logic modules, core memories, and peripheral devices) of computer systems are produced by components manufacturers. Users who prefer to lease equipment can turn to computer-leasing firms; and those in the market for used equipment can appeal to used computer brokers for assistance. Software firms are in the business of serving computer users and manufacturers by providing programs and programming skills. Computing services are furnished by conventional service bureaus and time-sharing vendors. Of course, these categories represent ideal types, since there is considerable overlap in the functions of existing companies and boundaries are not sharply drawn; but the range of activities delineated gives some indication of the diversification of the industry.[15]

The computer industry was launched in the United States in 1951 with the installation of Remington Rand's UNIVAC I. Prior to this time all the computers built were one-of-a-kind efforts destined for use primarily in government and university laboratories. OECD(1969, p. 37) presents a list of the main computer firms grouped by country giving the date of their first entry into the industry.[16] Commercial production of computers in Great Britain began in 1952, in Germany in 1954, and in France in 1956. Japan's computing industry was initiated, as was Italy's, in 1960. Although the United States assumed an early lead of some two to four years over other countries in the commercial development of computers, this factor is not regarded by OECD(1969) as significant in the continued American dominance of the industry.[17] Of greater importance was the magnitude of American enterprise in this area, and the stimulus provided by the federal government in absorbing a high proportion of the industry's output in the early 1950's.

The position of the United States in the computing field provides an instructive example of the ways in which technological development may be influenced by social organization. Although there are differences in the technological capabilities of firms in the United States, on the one hand, and Western Europe and Japan, on the other, the so-called "technological gap" is perhaps less important than differences in management organization and marketing techniques (Harman, 1971). This view is supported by the fact that most of the successful computer companies were not those with the initial advantage of greater sophistication in electronics technology. "The situation in the early and mid-fifties can be summarized thus: the business equipment manufacturers (IBM, Remington Rand, Burroughs, NCR, ICT, Bull) had the customers and the market, whereas the electronic firms had the technology. As it turned out, having the customers was more important than having the technology." (OECD, 1969, p. 98).

The international computer industry is dominated by a handful of American companies. The main computer firms from the industry's birth until 1969 included thirty-eight in the United States, eight in the United Kingdom, four in France, five in West Germany, and six in Japan. (OECD, 1969). By the time OECD compiled its list, the numbers had shrunk to twenty-six independent active companies in the United States, three in the United Kingdom, one in France, three in West Germany, and six in Japan. Of the firms active in 1969, eight dominated the industry. According to Sharpe(1969), these eight American companies (IBM, General Electric, Sperry Rand, Honeywell, RCA, Control Data, Burroughs, and NCR) accounted for approximately 98 per cent of the installed value of computing systems during the period 1962 to 1967.

The trend toward economic concentration in the computer industry does not appear to have abated. The "big eight" has been reduced to six, with the sale of General Electric's computer manufacturing operation to Honeywell in 1969, and RCA's abandonment of its computer division in 1971. The importance of the major American computer companies internationally is further evidenced by the various licensing agreements, joint ventures, and subsidiaries which make computing in Europe and Japan dependent on American technology.[18] But the single most remarkable fact about the international computer industry is the overwhelming share of the market controlled by one firm, IBM.

Ever since IBM overtook Remington Rand (later Sperry Rand) as the leading manufacturer in mid-1956, it has consistently held the lead. IBM's contribution to the installed value of computer systems from 1962 to 1967 was in the 70 to 80 per cent range (Sharpe, 1969). By 1972 IBM accounted for roughly 70 per cent of the domestic American market, and from 50 to 70 per cent of the West European market, with the exception of the United Kingdom where the British company ICL captured 43 per cent to IBM's 30 per cent (Kuo and Mills, 1972). Although IBM's share of the market is expected to drop, its position as the world's fifth largest corporation makes it a formidable economic force both in and out of computing.

4. Economic Position of the Computer Industry

Many observers believe that by the end of the century, the computer industry may be the world's largest.[19] Based on estimates of revenues from worldwide operations, the computer industry in the United States accounted for nearly 1.4 per cent of GNP in 1971. This compares with 3.9 per cent for the automobile industry. We have already examined the distribution and value of computer installations, and indicated some of the important characteristics of computer products and services. In this section, we will take a closer look at the size and growth of the computer industry.[20]

Table 3.2   World Shipments of U.S. Firms for 1971.

	Shipments in Millions of Dollars		
	U.S.	Overseas	World Total
General Purpose Computer Systems	4,200	3,300	7,500
Mini and Dedicated Application Computer Systems	250	60	310
Peripheral Equipment	630	*	*
TOTAL	5,080	*	*

Source: Gilchrist and Weber(1973); * no estimate available.

As mentioned before, the lack of certain types of data makes measurement difficult. Profit figures, for example, are not usable since it is generally not possible to separate profits associated with computer-related activities from other sectors within the industry. Available information includes the value of installations (considered earlier), revenues, and the value of shipments of new equipment. Taken together these indices of industry activity provide a reasonably accurate picture of size and growth rates.

In 1955 the value of world-wide shipments of new equipment by American computer companies was $65 million. By 1960 it had increased more than ten-fold to $720 million, and reached $2.4 billion in 1965. As shown in Table 3.2, the total for 1971 was in excess of $9.0 billion. The relative contributions of the domestic and overseas markets reveal the importance of international trade to the American computer industry. United States shipments by American-based firms amounted to $5.1 billion; overseas shipments came to more than $3.4 billion. In particular, 45 per cent of all shipments by manufacturers of general-purpose computers were overseas. By contrast, only about 20 per cent of the West European

Table 3.3   World Revenues ($ x 10⁶) of U.S. Firms in 1971.

	U.S.	Overseas	World Total
EQUIPMENT			
General Purpose Computer Systems	5,300	3,300	8,600
Mini & Dedicated application Computer Systems	250	60	310
Peripherals	695	380	1,075
Leasing	600	70	670
Used Comp. Sales	40	*	40
SERVICES			
Batch	950	110	1,060
On-Line	500	90	590
Software	750	40	790
Education	160	*	160
SUPPLIES	1,100	*	1,100
TOTAL	10,345	4,050	14,395

Source: Gilchrist and Weber (1973); * negligible.

market is supplied by European-owned manufacturers; and half of this part of the market comes from a single company, ICL (Gassmann, 1973). In France, Compagnie Internationale d'Informatique (CII) accounts for about 10 per cent of the domestic market, and Siemens has something less than 15 per cent of the German market. The multinational character of the United States companies is shown by the fact that 60 per cent ($2 billion) of shipments to overseas markets were produced overseas in 1971. Gilchrist and Weber(1973) report the AFIPS estimate of the growth in the annual value of domestic shipments to be in the 70 to 80 per cent range. No comparable estimate is given for the overseas market.

Total revenues of American firms reached $14.4 billion in 1971 (see Table 3.3). The overseas contribution to this figure was $4.1 billion, approximately 27 per cent. In the ten-year period 1961 to 1971, annual growth rates in revenues averaged 23 percent for general purpose computer systems. Mini and dedicated application systems revenues grew an average 27.5 per cent annually, while services and supplies increased by 23.8 and 8.0 per cent respectively. The growth of the services sector is notable in that it rose from practically nothing in 1956 to a 20 per cent share of 1971 revenues. From 1965 to 1971, the average annual growth in leasing revenues was 58.5 per cent. The total revenues of the United States firms are expected to be in the range $22.8 to $31.5 billion for 1976.

The economic significance of the computer industry is also revealed by its contribution to balance of trade figures. Net annual exports (exports minus imports) of the computer industry in the United States grew from $455 million in 1967 to $1,143 million in 1971. Exports in 1971 were $1,262 million while imports amounted to only $119 million. Moreover, even though a substantial percentage of overseas shipments are manufactured overseas, thus not contributing directly to a favorable balance of trade, the earnings on United States investments abroad generated by those shipments do contribute to a favorable balance of payments.

Employment figures furnish another index of the size of the computer industry. Gilchrist and Weber(1973) conjecture (of necessity in the absence of accurate data) that computer manufacturers employ at least 300,000 workers. An estimated one million people (roughly 1.3 per cent of the labor force) were employed in the United States in computer-related jobs during 1971, most of them by computer users. The largest category, which accounts for 44 per cent of the total, is that of keypunch operators. Programmers and computer operators account for 21 and 20 per cent, respectively, while systems analysts make up the remaining 15 per cent. The training requirements for this manpower are met by a variety of educational programs. Exclusive of private EDP schools, 91,650 graduates with computer-related training were produced in 1971 by educational programs ranging from the high-school to the Ph.D. level. In addition, an estimated 200,000 high-school graduates had received some computer training.

5. Politics of Computers

The facts and figures dealing with computer utilization make it abundantly clear that computer applications are firmly established, and the industry is vitally important to our economic life. This observation must be taken into account in assessing the impact of computer applications, and especially in formulating policy alternatives. The current position of computer technology is reminiscent of the automobile industry after World War I. At that time, the question of allocation of resources to transportation systems was still comparatively open. The railroads were in a healthy condition and various forms of public transportation operated in urban areas. The policy decisions which led to the adoption of the automobile as the major form of transportation have had profound consequences with which we are all too painfully familiar. Once resources have been committed to an enterprise on a large-scale, it is exceedingly difficult to shift course. Automobile "applications" gave rise to a network of highways and service facilities which absorbed substantial resources, and a vast economic empire was created. In this way we became dependent on the automobile not only as a form of transportation but as a basic element in our economic and social life.

The analogy with the computer may not be perfect, but it is revealing nonetheless. Both the automobile and the computer answer to real social needs. Although it would appear that the existence of viable alternatives to automobile transportation has no parallel in the case of computer applications, this is true only if one insists on certain forms of social organization. So long as banks, for example, must process billions of checks, or federal agencies are responsible for administering social welfare programs involving millions of people, computers will be essential. But it should not be heretical to raise the question of whether or not this is "the best of all possible worlds." Just as the automobile could be utilized as a partial answer to transportation needs, the computer too could be applied not simply wherever the opportunity arises, but only where it is deemed in the best interests of society. That this might entail dismantling or modifying existing social institutions should not in itself prevent us from considering the alternative.

The major impediment to rational analysis of social issues lies in the inability or unwillingness to act so as to optimize long-term utility. Automobile industry executives faced with declining revenues, and workers facing layoffs do not take kindly to suggestions that people buy fewer cars and support mass transit. Similarly, those with a vested interest in computer use are not likely to applaud scepticism toward computer applications. These are understandable human reactions which may be harmless in themselves, but when amplified by the apparatus of a multi-billion dollar industry, they may take socially destructive forms. Perhaps the only sure way to guarantee against such an eventuality is to prevent both excessive concentration of wealth and power and dependence on exclusive social choices.

As documented earlier, such concentration and dependence have already occurred in the case of computers. The handful of companies which dominate the industry and the apparent necessity of information-processing systems in large organizations constitute an effective deterrent against the raising of broad policy issues regarding computer applications. There may be no human necessity in developing computer-communication networks to facilitate the instantaneous transfer of funds from one account to another; but the pressure from the computer industry and allied forces is likely to prove irresistable. Quite apart from the merits of any one particular application, we all lose when policy choices are determined by the operation of economic opportunism.

Concern over concentration in the computer industry has focused on IBM's preeminent position. Several antitrust actions have been taken against the company in the past few years.[21] The suit filed by the United States Department of Justice in 1969 is likely to have the most far-reaching consequences for the industry. IBM has been charged with various monopolistic practices designed to manipulate the computer market. Since it has already captured a substantial share of that market, IBM can use its pricing policy as a weapon to undercut competitors. Moreover, the company is in a position to alter technical standards for its equipment in a way which reduces the ability of other firms to compete. Some observers even hold IBM responsible for inhibiting technological innovation through its determined efforts to maintain its favored position.[22]

Although there can be little doubt about the economic importance of the current actions against IBM, it is not likely that the outcome will lead to a decline in the power of the industry or to a significant broadening of social choices regarding computer use. The break-up of the great oil trusts did nothing to prevent an inordinate expansion of energy consumption; nor has the public-utility status of the telecommunications industry diluted its influence on our society. Splitting IBM into several smaller companies, or introducing government regulation might stimulate innovation through inter-firm competition, but such actions cannot alter the influence of the industry as a whole. Computers, like automobiles and telephones, will continue to absorb our energies and resources.

The issue of excessive dependence on computer technology for the solution of social problems is complicated by the strategic military importance of computers. This provides governments with an additional motive for cultivating computer applications, especially those which arise out of research and development programs sponsored by the military. The United States is not alone in this attitude, as evidenced by the action of European governments. Former President de Gaulle's *Plan Calcul* which created Compagnie Internationale de l'Informatique was partly in response to the need for national control of the computer industry to insure adequate computing power for France's nuclear program. The closer one looks, the less one sees computer technology as a passive instrument awaiting our choice for good or ill. Given the economic importance of the computer industry and the widespread diffusion of computer applications, the only feasible choice lies in exploring alternative forms of social organization which might lessen our dependence on computers.

---

[1] Gotlieb and Borodin(1973, Chapter 3) discuss the relative importance of these motives in some detail.

[2] See Gruenberger(1968, p.161) for a graph showing the trend in unit-computation cost from 1955 to 1968. This graph is reprinted in Gotlieb and Borodin(1973, p.14), and United Nations(1971, p.81).

[3] *Standard Industrial Classification Manual*. Washington, D.C.: United States Government Printing Office, 1972.

[4] The dominance of military computing is by no means universal, as evidenced by Japan and Canada as well as other countries.

[5] The implications of this development are discussed in Chapter 8.

[6] For example, see Gilchrist and Weber(1973).

[7] Gilchrist and Weber(1973) point out that since the size distribution of computing installations in the United States based on value and number corresponds closely with that of other countries, the worldwide distribution by number reflects the distribution by value.

[8] Gassmann(1973).

[9] Kurita(1973).

[10] Gilchrist and Weber(1973). See also Gotlieb and Borodin(1973) for a graph showing the growth in the number of computers from 1962 to 1971 for major Western nations.

[11] Kurita(1973) and Gassmann(1973).

[12] This discussion of computing in the United States is based on figures given in Gilchrist and Weber(1973).

[13] Kurita(1973).

[14] United Nations(1971).

[15] This diversification reflects the variety of users' needs, but it is also in response to shifts in the relative costs of hardware vs. software, and CPU's vs. peripherals. See OECD(1969) and Sharpe(1969).

[16] Based on date of first installation.

[17] In Section 4 we will examine the extent of American dominance.

[18] This is underscored by the recent decision of the French government to allow the merger of Compagnie Internationale pour l'Informatique (CII) with the Franco-American Honeywell-Bull Company.

[19] See, for example, Spangle(1972) and Beman(1973).

[20] This discussion is based largely on Gilchrist and Weber(1973).

[21] See Beman(1973).

[22] Guzy claims that IBM is the only company in the industry with the capital surplus essential for investment in new ideas and products.

Chapter 4.
Information Processing in Corporate Decision-Making

Information technology is playing an ever-increasing role in the conduct of corporate affairs. The effective utilization of information is vital to the proper functioning of large organizations. This makes the computer, with its prodigious capabilities for processing information, particularly attractive to management. Computer applications in business encompass a wide spectrum of activities ranging from routine clerical operations such as customer billing and payroll preparation to complex systems employing sophisticated analytical techniques. Virtually every facet of corporate activity from production and engineering to marketing and planning has been affected by the introduction of computers. But the greatest potential for altering the shape of corporate organization comes from the use of computers by management as aids in decision-making.

Although the initial euphoria associated with information systems for management has been tempered by actual experience with such systems, managerial decision-making has nonetheless been profoundly affected by computers. The introduction of information-processing systems has consequences beyond the functions for which they are intended. In the course of developing and using them, tasks and responsibilities come under scrutiny and organizational changes often result. The automation of activities within the corporation has been accompanied by changes in job content, patterns of communication, and the responsibilities of the different classes of managers. Our main concern in this discussion is with modifications in organizational structure brought about by these changes, and the attendant shifts in the locus of power.

The hierarchical structure of large organizations amplifies the effects of computer-aided decision-making. Increased dependence on information systems by top management tends to reduce the decision-making functions of the middle ranks. The evidence is by no means entirely unambiguous, but the question of the degree to which management decision-making is concentrated by computer applications warrants careful analysis. In the twentieth century, the operational responsibilities formerly exercised by the owners of capital have been assumed by professional managers. Galbraith(1967) compared this development with the shift in the locus of economic power from land to capital which began to occur some two centuries ago. Power in the modern industrial enterprise is wielded by management.

> With the rise of the modern corporation, the emergence of the organization required by modern technology and planning and the divorce of the owner of the capital from control of the enterprise, the entrepreneur no longer exists as an individual person in the mature industrial enterprise. Everyday discourse, except in the economics textbooks, recognizes this change. It replaces the entrepreneur, as the directing force of the enterprise, with management. (Galbraith, 1967, p. 71)

The overwhelming power of corporations leaves little doubt as to the significance of any trend toward the centralization of management decision-making.

In this chapter, we will examine the impact of computer applications on corporate decision-making. Of primary concern are the effects of information systems on corporate organization. These effects will be assessed in terms of power shifts within management, and between functional units in the corporation. We will conclude with a discussion of the extent to which centralized decision-making results from the introduction of computers.

1. Information Processing in Management

Information-processing plays a central role in all phases of management activity, from communication to problem-solving and decision-making.[1] The need to process large amounts of information in the modern organization derives from three sources: the organization's external environment, routine operating activities, and planning and control. The external environment includes dealings with customers and suppliers, as well as with the legal system which governs the organization's conduct. Routine operating activities usually refer to internal matters, whereas planning and control involve over-all corporate strategy. The early successes of computer applications in accounting and other areas, coupled with the development of operations research and allied methods, stimulated widespread interest in harnessing the computer as a management tool in the form of management information systems (familiarly known by the acronym MIS).

Discussion of management information systems reveals a common response to the emergence of a new technology. In the early 1960's, observers in the business world and academia speculated on the imminent possibility of replacing human managers by machines.[2] Chastened by experience, contemporary analysts are less sanguine in their expectations. The complexities of management in the dynamically changing corporate environment have proved more intractable to automation than anticipated. But here as elsewhere, the tackling of a difficult problem has led to deeper insight and better understanding as well as to a touch of scepticism. Despite the lack of agreement on a precise definition of management information systems, the designation is generally used to refer to information-processing activities in support of management. The most fundamental function of management is decision-making, and we turn now to an examination of its nature.

Decision-making may be resolved into several stages of activity. Occasions for making decisions must be identified, possible courses of action explored, and, finally, a particular choice made (Simon, 1965). One might extend this analysis to include the activities associated with implementation of the choice as well as the process of reviewing its consequences. However, as Simon points out, these activities add nothing essentially new to the basic paradigm. Implementation and review simply constitute further occasions for evaluating alternative actions and making policy choices.

The standard model of ideal executive behavior within this decision-making scheme is suggested by scientific method. The initial stage of identifying an occasion for decision involves making observations on the state of affairs. Exploring alternatives embraces two phases of scientific inquiry: hypothesis formation and testing. Tracing the consequences of different courses of action requires forming hypotheses or constructing models which allow for predicting the effects of policy choices. The process of evaluating or ranking different policies is dependent on goals, and may be effected by comparing the model's prediction with the desired outcome. The final stage of choosing among alternatives is analogous to adopting the "best" hypothesis or model for the phenomena under investigation.

Kriebel(1972) discerns four levels of sophistication in the development of information systems for management. These levels correspond roughly to stages in the decision process. The most primitive information system is a databank containing raw observations on some phase of corporate activity, such as profit and loss figures for various product divisions. This information may be stored in a computer file and so organized as to make it accessible to managers in a convenient form. However, systems of this type have no capacity to draw inferences or evaluate policy alternatives; they function solely as elaborate almanacs. The next level of sophistication involves some modeling capability. Management science methods (principally operations research) are used in conjunction with databanks to form systems which are able to provide answers to hypothetical questions. For example, an information system containing data on market trials of a new product might incorporate a linear programming model of market demand. A manager would then be able to obtain answers to questions concerning packaging, pricing, or product design in relation to expected market performance; but the evaluation of different courses of action on the basis of corporate goals would still have to be carried out by the manager.

The ability to evaluate alternative policy choices characterizes the third level in the development of information systems. In addition to being able to respond to hypothetical questions, such systems incorporate goals in a form which facilitates determining which course of action can best achieve the desired results. It remains for the manager to accept or reject the recommended policy. Kriebel(1972) points out that systems of this nature are most commonly realized in the activities of the advisory staff group or committee. "In this case line management delegates authority for a certain area of responsibility to a staff department, but retains final control for decision through review and certification." An example in which computers are used is in the area of industrial scheduling. Here optimal scheduling policies are formulated with the aid of linear programming or other algorithms. However, many applications of this type have proved unsuccessful.

In the most sophisticated information systems, all the functions of management decision-making are automated. Not only are policy alternatives evaluated but the final stage of choosing the "best" course of action is accomplished automatically. Thus far, only very well-defined management decisions have been fully automated. Computer systems for process control in oil refining and chemical production, and factory inventory control are notable examples. The development of computer-based systems outside of these areas has encountered difficulties which are not likely to be resolved in the very near future.

Of particular importance for the analysis of management information systems is the distinction drawn by Simon(1965) between programmed and non-programmed decisions. The distinction is meant to call attention to a continuum of decision types. On the programmed end of the continuum, decisions tend to be of a routine or highly structured character, involving definite procedures which can be applied in a large class of similar situations. Accounting procedures and inventory problems are typical areas in which repetitive decision-making of this type occurs. At the opposite end of the continuum, decisions are characterized by novel circumstances, lack of well-defined structure, and the absence of definite procedures. Most strategic decisions made by the higher echelons of management fall into this category.

The only automated information systems in management which have achieved some measure of success are those designed for programmed decision-making, such as the process control applications mentioned earlier. Attempts to design systems to assist human managers have foundered most often on inadequate or inappropriate models of user requirements. The nature of human problem-solving behavior is imperfectly understood, and it is exceedingly difficult to anticipate what kinds of information are likely to be most useful for making unstructured decisions. The accomplishments of management information systems have fallen short of expectations. Kriebel(1972) reports a remark attributed to Isaac Auerbach concerning the performance of automatic data-processing systems in business to the effect that "20 percent are successful, 40 percent are marginal, and 40 percent are failures." This may be a harsh judgment, but it does reflect the reaction to the naive optimism of the early 1960's.

2. Effects of Automation on Managers

The impact of information technology on corporate management can best be understood with reference to the different levels in the hierarchy. Figure 4.1 presents a simplified organizational chart of a typical (mythical) corporation.[3] Three levels of management are distinguished. At the apex of the pyramid, top management holds the responsibility for formulating strategic policy. Corporate goals are determined, and decisions affecting the entire organization are made at this level. Examples of questions decided by top management include the issuing of stock, establishing a foreign subsidiary, developing a new product, or buying out a competitor.

The heads of various corporate units and departments, and superintendents constitute the next level of management. The function of middle management is to carry out the policy objectives

Figure 4.1   Levels of Management in the Corporate Hierarchy

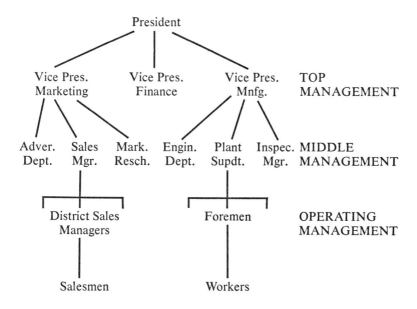

formulated at the highest level. This involves the elaboration of plans designed to translate broadly conceived policies into operational procedures. A top-level decision to manufacture a new product, for example, would leave middle management with the responsibility to determine what new equipment to purchase, how many salesmen to hire, and what advertising media to use for promotion. Operating management, which consists of foremen and supervisors, is situated at the base of the management pyramid. This level is responsible for implementing the procedures elaborated by middle management and directing the work of employees.

Since information-processing is a pervasive function in organizations, it is to be expected that the introduction of information systems will affect organizational structure. Although the evidence confirms this expectation, the precise form these effects will take is still difficult to ascertain. Part of the problem stems from having to distinguish between transitional and long-term effects. Moreover, much of the evidence is either anecdotal, or based on case studies which rely heavily on subjective reporting. The problems of interpretation are further compounded by organizational changes accompanying growth which make it difficult to isolate effects due specifically to the introduction of new technology. Nevertheless, it is possible to discern certain definite trends. In what follows we will examine the impact of information systems on managers, particularly shifts of position in the corporate hierarchy and changes in job content. Effects of a more global character will be discussed in Sections 4 and 5.

Middle management seems to have been affected more than other levels by the development of information systems. This is due in large measure to the types of systems introduced. As indicated in the preceding section, most applications involve the programmed type of decision-making, such as occur in some areas of accounting, scheduling, and inventory control. The role of middle management in these areas makes it particularly vulnerable. Huse(1967) describes a case study of the development of a computer-based management information system in a medium-sized manufacturing company. The system in question was designed to automate assembly and manufacturing scheduling, inventory control, supply management, and certain accounting operations. One of the effects observed was a contraction of the decision-making sphere of the middle manager. Operations formerly controlled by middle managers were incorporated into the information system.

Whisler(1967) reports on a similar case. The implementation of a computer system for production and inventory control in a major division of a very large corporation led to a substantial reduction in the number of middle management positions in these areas. Responsibility for all production, inventory, and accounting functions was shifted to the divisional vice president's staff.

In a comprehensive study of the organizational impact of computers in the life insurance industry, Whisler(1970) found that middle management's role in decision-making was reduced by the introduction of information systems. A minority of corporate respondents in the study indicated increased scope for middle management, but this apparent contradiction may be attributed to the transitional effects of system development, since middle management plays an important part in the development phase. Once the computer system is completed, however, the middle manager is reduced to handling exceptions and system changes. Supervisory personnel (operating management) are also affected by automated information systems. At this level, too, opportunities for making independent decisions are diminished. The focus on middle management may be due to the dramatic contrast revealed by their status and authority before and after the implementation of the automated information system. One general observation which we will return to later is the apparent shift of control to higher levels in the corporate hierarchy.

Although top management does in some cases make use of computer-based systems as aids in decision-making, this level in the hierarchy does not appear to have been significantly affected by the new technology. The non-programmed character of strategic policy formation is not about to yield to automation in the immediate future; and as Simon(1965) observes, even if this were feasible, human managers might continue to enjoy a relative advantage in terms of cost. Much of the discussion of top management's role centers about the extent to which high ranking company executives are involved in the development of computer-based management systems. The poor performance of such systems is often attributed to a lack of interest or understanding on the part of top management. This lack of involvement may be somewhat short-lived as organizational changes shift responsibilities for decision-making. In particular, it seems likely that the executive department in charge of computing facilities will gain in importance at the expense of others.

Many of the effects of information systems reported by corporate executives in Whisler's(1967,1970) investigations are related to the mere fact of change. Dissatisfaction and insecurity over changes in accustomed patterns of behavior, in addition to the threat of job loss in some middle and operating management positions, lead to confusion of transitional with long-term effects. No doubt the impact of management information systems is exaggerated as a result, but some long-term effects are beginning to manifest themselves. Individual autonomy, at all but the highest management levels, has been compromised by the introduction of computer-based systems. This is reflected in the emergence of a greater degree of corporate control over the timing of an individual's activities, and a trend toward the routinization of work.

The observed tendency of automated information systems to generate inflexibility in corporate operations has the effect of frustrating individual initiative. Whisler(1970) points to the paradoxical nature of this situation in that computer systems stimulate innovative ideas, but the high costs involved in making changes inhibit their implementation. The forced adaptation of human beings to machine systems is a characteristic feature of industrial and post-industrial society. DeCarlo(1967) speaks of the formalization of personnel relations occasioned by the development of computer systems and by concomitant organizational changes. The manager's autonomy in dealing with individuals within the corporation becomes more and more circumscribed. Moreover, the problem of evaluating individual performance under conditions of increasingly limited responsibility undermines the traditional incentive structure. This is but the latest stage in the process of alienating the human being from his work which began with the factory system of production. As in the automation of manufacturing methods, increased productivity and efficiency are the major objectives. There is little reason to believe that job satisfaction can be "arranged" for the corporate manager any more successfully than it has been for the assembly line worker by creating the illusion of participation in a socially useful activity.

3. The Corporate Computer Facility

Consolidation of information-processing activities within a new or modified corporate unit leads to important changes in organization and decision-making. The role and location of the computer facility vary from one company to another, depending largely on historical factors such as early applications and the expectations of management. Since computer use cuts across traditional departmental boundaries, the development of computing services acts as an agent of change. Having examined the impact of information systems on management, we turn now to the apparatus which supports those systems. After discussing the most common organizational locations for computer facilities, we will explore their influence on corporate structure and decision-making.

Withington(1966) identifies five different ways in which corporations have resolved the problem of integrating computer services into the organization: 1) locating the facility in an operating department such as manufacturing; 2) setting up a service bureau; 3) locating the facility in the accounting department; 4) placing it under the direction of central management; and 5) creating an independent department. Each location has its own peculiar advantages and disadvantages, but all reflect the corporate objective of providing computer services to the organization as a whole.

A large company with a department which can absorb a major share of computer services might locate the facility within that department. This solution suffers from a natural tendency on the part of the computing staff to discriminate in favor of their own department, thus promoting imbalance in service. The creation of a service bureau outside the departmental structure may eliminate this source of imbalance, but it too has shortcomings. The fact of operating independently of corporate departments may confer a separate identity on the service bureau. This could result in a charging policy designed to make the bureau financially solvent, thus inhibiting investment in anything but routine computer applications.

Since accounting applications figured prominently among the early uses of computers, the most common location for the computer facility is the accounting department. Despite the corporate wide role of the comptroller, this arrangement suffers from the same defects as locating the facility in an operating department. An alternative to the service bureau approach for remedying these defects involves assigning computer operations to a staff role under the direct control of top management. This is likely to prevent any one department from monopolizing the computer, but dependence on a high-ranking executive with little time to devote to the problems of running a computer center may leave it in a position similar to the service bureau. The creation of a separate operating department to accommodate computer operations is perhaps the most radical approach from an organizational standpoint. Decision-making is profoundly affected by the addition of a new department, especially one whose operating responsibilities take in the entire organization.

Whisler(1970) forecasts several significant changes in organizational structure linked to the role of computing within the corporation. The creation of a computer facility results in the aggregation of information-processing activities. The desire to make full use of the computer's capabilities argues strongly in favor of a centralized facility. Information-processing functions formerly handled in parallel by several departments shift to the new unit. This occurs partly as a consequence of the replacement of older data-processing methods and partly as a result of efforts to rationalize the functions of information-processing. The computer provides a means for reducing unit costs and streamlining operations by allowing for an increase in the scale of data-processing.

Transfer of information handling from operating departments to the computer center sometimes has the effect of reducing the size and relative importance of those departments. Naturally, activities which were based on the use of obsolete methods of data-handling disappear, and some consolidation occurs. In the process of restructuring the information function, opportunities are created for altering traditional departmental responsibilities. The introduction of new technology necessitates new forms of organization not clearly anticipated in the simple motive to reduce costs and increase efficiency. One major change observed by Whisler(1970) is the tendency to organize departments on a functional basis.

The aggregation of information functions in a central computer facility provides both motive and model for reducing redundancy in organization. Under conditions of relative autonomy, different operating departments develop activities in parallel with one another. This is especially so for activities of a universal character. In the past, departments responsible for particular product lines or specific geographical regions would each have their own arrangements for data-processing. Recognition of the advantages of centralizing data-processing has led to a reordering of these arrangements. But the effect of reordering goes beyond the mere transfer of functions to a separate facility or department for the purpose of securing the advantages of economy of scale. A general principle is established for reorganizing departments according to corporate-wide functions which has repercussions on patterns of control and decision-making.

The central computer facility signals the emergence of a new force in the corporation. Since so many elements depend on the computer, it is not surprising that the new facility has become a power to be reckoned with in the organization.

> As consolidation proceeds, riding on the back of computer systems, it seems inevitable that the group with computer responsibility will take on substantial authority in developing new decision systems. Thus, it is to be expected that there will be a lateral movement of decision-making in the organization. That is, certain decisions will move out of traditional departments into the computer and systems center, at least at the strategic planning stage. Day-to-day operations and maintenance of the new decision system may remain at the original location. (Whisler, 1970, p. 69)

Although the evidence accumulated to date does not warrant authoritative predictions, there can be little doubt concerning the increased influence of those responsible for information-processing. The anxiety expressed by corporate executives over computer personnel is indicative of this condition. Dorn(1972), for example, cites the problem of insuring the programmer's primary loyalty to corporate goals rather than the computing profession. This may be a relatively minor issue in the scheme of things, but it does signify the arrogance of newly acquired power.

One of the dangers in the centralization of any function lies in the tendency to promote rigidity and formalization. By eliminating much of the redundancy of parallel departmental organization, the centralized computer facility contributes to increased vulnerability. Measuring efficiency in terms of speed and unit-computation costs may be misleading. Gains in operational control may be offset by the inability to respond appropriately to changing conditions. Moreover, the effects of possible system failures must also be taken into account. The greater the dependence on computer systems, the greater the impact of errors and hidden biases. Systems designers have no special immunity to the imperfections shared by the rest of humanity, but the importance and prestige attached to the computer often lead management to overlook this detail.

As every businessman knows, the principal objective of the corporation is to maximize profits, so that the ultimate test of the efficacy of computer applications is their contribution to the balance sheet. However, this is an overly simplistic view, since the corporation has become a social institution wielding enormous influence in our society. Through involvement in educational and welfare programs, the contemporary corporation has accepted social responsibilities which transcend the profit motive. There is little justificatiion in viewing the elaboration of corporate policies as a strictly internal affair. The stock holders, and the managers and workers employed by the organization are not the only individuals affected by these policies. Thus, the manner in which decisions are reached, in particular the growing influence of the computer group within the corporate hierarchy, is a matter of general concern. As Blau(1956, p. 58) observes, "To administer a social organization according to purely technical criteria of rationality is irrational, because it ignores the nonrational aspects of social conduct."

4. Hierarchy as an Organizational Principle

Modern technology exerts a powerful influence on the models and metaphors used in the study of social organizations.[4] The executive structure of computer systems is a particularly fertile source of analogies. Large programs are typically divided into subprograms which are integrated by means of hierarchical control structures. This arrangement localizes the effects of disturbances. Errors can be handled without necessarily having to modify the entire program; and, generally speaking, changes can be made more easily in a modular design. Clearly, a greater economy of effort can be achieved through the "structured" approach to programming. By extension, this observation suggests that a hierarchy of specialized functional units under central control is an effective way to organize social activity.

In addition to programming practice, making optimal use of computer resources supports the hierarchical model. The computer's speed and accuracy can best be utilized by organizing computation on a flow basis with no outside intervention. In this way jobs can be completed with a minimum of errors and delays. Naturally, it would be inefficient to make some stage of a computerized process dependent on human participation if it were avoidable. Applied to multistage decision-making processes such as occur in corporate management, this points up the desirability of a hierarchy of compatible units performing specialized functions in a prescribed order.

In a widely cited paper, Simon(1965) analyzes the hierarchical principle in large organizations. The near universality of hierarchical structure in complex organizations suggests the operation of natural law. Biological organisms are differentiated into subsystems built of organs which are further subdivided into tissues composed of cell aggregates. Physical systems too are hierarchical in structure. Complex organic compounds contain molecular subassemblies which in turn consist of atoms made up of elementary particles. Even the cosmos with its galaxies differentiated into planetary systems and stars exhibits hierarchical organization. The pervasive character of hierarchy does not appear to be accidental.

By means of an instructive parable, Simon(1965) shows that systems of a certain size and complexity are likely to evolve hierarchical patterns of organization. A watchmaker who organizes his work into subassemblies can achieve more stable production than one who does not. The latter might have to reassemble the entire watch if his work is interrupted before completion, whereas the former would only have to reconstruct one subassembly. As in the development of large programs, disturbances are localized by arranging the work hierarchically. A further economy of effort is seen to derive from the reduced information transmission which obtains in hierarchical systems. Differentiation into subunits decreases the amount of information required by the individual parts, since the operation of a member of a subunit would require detailed information only for other elements in the same unit. Interactions between subunits could be accomplished with more limited knowledge based on information dealing with collective behavior.

This brief summary of Simon's analysis gives some indication of the basis for his conclusion that "The reasons for hierarchy go far beyond the need for unity of command or other considerations relating to authority." (Simon,1965,p. 101) Although this observation may be convincing when applied to physical and biological systems, it is misleading in the context of social organizations. The operation of an hierarchical system requires the subordination of the individual parts to the goals of the system. For a cell in the heart of an elephant or an amino acid molecule in a protein chain, this does not create any problems. Similarly, the individual parts of a watch are quite indifferent to the watchmaker's productive designs. The question of participation in goal setting obviously arises only for conscious beings, and individual humans functioning as parts of a social system are not indifferent to organizational aims.

The efficacy of hierarchical organization is intimately linked to goal structure. If the sole purpose of an organization is productive efficiency, then hierarchical structure may be warranted. But the subordination of individual aims required to secure this objective cannot be achieved without cost. Is there any reason to believe, for example, that reduced information transmission between individuals in different units of an organization is inherently desirable? In the short-run, one might anticipate certain savings in time and effort. However, the long-term consequences of diminished interaction are likely to show up as a kind of "genetic impoverishment" similar to that observed in populations with excessive inbreeding.

The role of hierarchy in promoting unity of command is more salient in social organizations than it is in physical or biological systems. Efficiency is only one particular motive among many, and beyond a certain level of productive capacity it may become destructive. Human associations answer to many needs. The satisfaction of a worker or manager in a corporation is not entirely defined in terms of his contribution to company profits or production statistics. The well-known Hawthorne effect reveals the sensitivity of workers to less tangible rewards. Work itself need not be an onerous duty performed strictly for the purpose of receiving a paycheck. Hierarchical structure in large organizations is not an intrinsic feature of social evolution. It is a response to a particular organizational goal, and is cultivated in order to achieve the disciplined effort of a large number of different individuals in the pursuit of that unitary goal.

The psychological need for stability and security may be more fundamental to hierarchy than economy of effort. This is especially evident under conditions of great uncertainty and disorder. Hobbes' defense of absolute monarchy, for example, was conceived during a turbulent period of civil strife in England. Since we no longer subscribe to the principle of political absolutism, other forms of authority must be sought. No historical period has a monopoly on rationalizations for its institutions. Whereas philosophers in the eighteenth century debated the divine right of kings, contemporary apologists for unity of command look to evolutionary principles. Lacking the convenient sanction of an ultimate moral authority, we are forced to appeal to the laws of nature. The "continuall feare, and danger of violent death" which characterized the natural condition of mankind for Hobbes is not entirely inappropriate for much of twentieth century civilization, and human imagination is capable of remarkable feats under duress.

The concept of hierarchical structure is congenial to contemporary thinkers because it appears to be rational in an evolutionary sense. While the inner personal need for security engenders a predisposition to accept, the doctrine of material progress furnishes the motive to justify. Modern man's faith in progress has promoted efficiency to the status of a sacred principle. Thus, it is possible to speak of hierarchy as a form of organization which transcends the needs of central control. It is a characteristic feature of religious faith that its fundamental tenets are never questioned. The commitment to progress establishes just such a privileged position for efficiency. If one does not question the desirability of efficiency as a goal, then it might indeed appear as though hierarchical structure were built into the ground plan of human history.

As noted earlier, the mark of technology is evident in modern conceptions of the organization. Since we cannot expect to examine the extensive literature of organization theory in a brief discussion, we have focused on one of the principal metaphors derived from technology. In an age less sophisticated than our own, a shrewd observer of social organizations might have seen the workings of an inscrutable logic. Our tendency to appeal to technological models serves much the same purpose. The impact of computers on organizational structure is inextricably bound up with our faith in the legitimacy of our models. In this sense, the computer is much more than an instrument of rational change. The use of computers in management decision-making is not likely to obliterate hierarchy. But not, as Simon(1965) argues, because of the action of an inexorable evolutionary process. The computer provides the means to achieve unity of command, and as the source of a particular model of organization, it reinforces the tendency to centralize control.

5. Centralization of Control

The effects of computer applications on the structure of control in the modern corporation is perhaps the most significant social issue associated with management information systems. Although the evidence is not completely unambiguous, there is substantial support for the conclusion that computers do contribute to centralized decision-making, at least in the short-run. Much of the disagreement over this issue stems from the difficulty of assessing the phenomenon in precise terms. The measures developed thus far tend to be crude, and do not adequately discriminate between the effects of computers and other characteristics of organizational change. This is especially problematic since the introduction of computer systems often affords an opportunity to reorganize departments or otherwise modify corporate structure in ways which are not always strictly essential to the operation of those systems. On the other hand, the changes accompanying computerized management systems may be regarded as part of the corporate response to a new way of thinking associated with computer utilization. We will adopt this broader view in the following discussion.

Before examining some of the evidence pertaining to centralization of control, let us consider the significance of the issue. It is difficult to overestimate the power of large corporations in contemporary society. " [T]he fact is that today the great American Corporations seem more like states within states than simply private businesses." (Mills, 1956, p. 124). Through the resources it controls, Big Business plays a dominant role in shaping public policy and in determining the character of everyday life. Corporate policies affect everything from the work people do to the products and services they believe are indispensable for the "good life." More generally, economic issues form the basis of political decisions, thus placing corporate interests in the position of power broker. In view of the influence exerted by corporations on society, it is clear, as asserted earlier, that the forms of decision-making are of vital social concern.

Concentration of decision-making in the upper echelons of management may possibly promote increased efficiency of production, but at the same time it poses a threat to democratic institutions. There is little difference between consolidation of power by a small group of political managers, and centralization of control in the large corporations which dominate our economic life. In either case, the average individual with limited resources has virtually no voice in shaping the course of events. One might argue, however, that the form of corporate decision-making does not materially affect the basis for corporate power. In some sense this is true, but the potential abuse of that power is inversely proportional to the number of individuals sharing it.

Centralization of control has the effect of isolating decision-makers from the lower levels of management and from the rank and file. As in the military, information flow is formalized, and responsibilities are rigidly defined. The will of authority is more easily exercised, but innovative thinking is discouraged. Distortions which inevitably occur in reporting are amplified, errors are more likely to have disastrous effects, and the organization is potentially more vulnerable as a result (DeCarlo, 1967). Examples of natural systems exhibiting hierarchical structure with central control are inappropriate models for social organizations. An individual in a corporation is not comparable to a liver cell. The latter is incapable of informing the brain of its views on the desirability of some action which does not have a direct effect on the liver. It is a mistake to suppose that specialization in social organizations extends to the point of requiring expert credentials for judging the desirability of organizational goals. Such judgments involve human values and call for wisdom in addition to expert testimony. The establishment of goals without the active participation of a large number of individuals works to the detriment of society as a whole.

The historical trend toward the centralization of power in society has been aided in no small measure by modern technology.[5] The question now is whether or not the computer is helping to accelerate the process. Whisler(1967) distinguishes between two forms of control in organizations.[6] System control refers to the direct influence of an individual on organizational achievement and is reflected in his share of compensation paid. Interpersonal control, on the other hand, involves the authority exercised by some individuals over others, and may be measured by the span of influence of superiors over subordinates. In a variety of examples of the development of computer systems, both types of control were found to increase for top management at the expense of the lower levels. The introduction of information systems results in fewer managers being paid more, and some levels in the decision hierarchy being eliminated, thus facilitating increased scope of control at the top. The expected concomitants of centralized control are also observed. There is tighter discipline in the utilization of time, and a noticeable routinization of activities at the lower levels in the hierarchy.

Whisler(1970) argues that computers can be expected to increase centralization of systems control for the following reasons.

> Computers tie together and integrate areas of decision-making and control that formerly were relatively independent of one another ... Given the typical pyramidal structure of business organizations, this integration results in shifting system control ... up higher in the organization than where it formerly was located. (Whisler, 1970, pp. 98-99)

The empirical evidence in the case of the insurance industry strongly corroborates this view. Respondents agreed almost unanimously that centralization of control accompanied computer use. The only difference of opinion on this issue was the degree of change brought about by computers.

The current trend is unmistakable, but it may not be an inevitable consequence of computer applications. Forrester(1967) views present organizational changes as characteristic of a transitional stage in the development of computer-based systems. The computer is seen as an instrument which can be used "to create either more confinement or more freedom." In principle, management information systems could be designed to inhibit excessive centralization of authority and promote individual autonomy. Whisler(1967) reasons that although the observed centralizing effects of computers will proceed for a time, there are limiting factors. Natural boundaries between independent corporate divisions act to limit extensions of central authority, and the high educational levels of professionalized managerial personnel militate against restrictive conditions.

Based on his analysis of hierarchical structure, Simon(1965) resolves the question of centralization of control into two distinct issues. The relative sizes of the building blocks in the organizational hierarchy determine the degree of centralization. Authority structure is seen as a separate matter governed by the relations between the building blocks. Exactly how an array of building blocks of various sizes can exhibit the property of centralization apart from the relations defining their interaction is not explained. This putative framework is interesting, however, as an example of an attempt to turn the issue of centralization into a purely technical problem, thereby rendering it socially innocuous. As noted in the previous section, hierarchical structure evolves in response to the needs of efficient production, and unity of command or centralized control is an inescapable feature of hierarchy.

The possibility that computer use in large organizations may ultimately lead to greater autonomy and personal satisfaction raises basic questions about hierarchical structure. One of the rallying cries of modern technology is the elimination of drudgery in work. The belief in the long-term contribution of management information systems to personal autonomy derives from a similar expectation, namely, that computers will free managers for creative tasks. However, just as the elaboration of machinery for factory production succeeded in alienating the craftsman from his work, there is no reason to believe that computers will not have a comparable effect on management in the context of hierarchically structured organizations.

The apparent limitations on centralization are not nearly so effective as the pressures for reductions in operating costs. Forrester(1967) may be justified in supposing that authoritarian direction of large organizations will prove to be inherently unstable in the long-run. But this supposition is rooted in a philosophical position which rejects social absolutism. It is just possible that the organizational changes taking place now in response to computer applications will alter this position before we have a chance to restructure the organizations.

[1] See Kriebel, *et al.*(1971) for a survey (Chapter 1) of the role of information-processing in management, and an extensive bibliography on the subject.

[2] Simon(1965) is a notable example. " [W]e will soon have the technological means ... to automate all management decisions ..." (p. 47).

[3] This description of the management hierarchy follows Mauser and Schwartz(1966).

[4] The influence of technology on models of man is discussed in Chapter 14.

[5] See Chapter 12.

[6] See also Whisler(1970, Chapter 5).

Chapter 5.
The Changing Character of Work

Changes in technology and modes of organization have profoundly altered the character of work in the modern world. The application of machinery to production has revolutionized our economic life and reshaped the role of work in human affairs. Although the central issue is the impact of computers, the effects of this new technology cannot be assessed apart from those of earlier innovations. Computer technology is but the latest development in a long chain of events stretching back to the rise of capitalism in Western civilization.

The consolidation of substantial capital resources in the factory led to the creation of labor as a distinct factor in production. Work was removed from the intimate surroundings of the home or small shop, and came to be dissociated from other aspects of daily life. Handicrafts could not long compete with factory production, as operations grew in size and articles were produced more cheaply. The factory system transformed human labor into a commodity to be bought and sold in the marketplace. This development has had far reaching consequences which continue to affect social institutions in the contemporary world.

The need for reliable sources of power to drive the machines of modern industry occasioned the perfection of the steam engine in the eighteenth century. The successful application of this new prime mover, first in the mine and later in the factory, contributed materially to the industrial revolution. But steam was not the only ingredient in the rapid growth of industry. The advantages of standardization and interchangeability of parts in large-scale manufacturing were recognized early in the nineteenth century.[1] The peculiar genius of nineteenth century technology is perhaps more to be found in its resolution of complex tasks into standardized repetitive operations than its elaboration of power. Many of the problems associated with automation in present-day industry are traceable to the accomplishments of the previous century, for it was during this period that the principle of treating human labor as an adjunct to machine-based processes was firmly established.

The rationalization of production methods was carried further in the development of the assembly line. Mass production of uniform, inexpensive goods became the central fact of modern life through the pioneering efforts of Henry Ford and others in the first decades of this century. Although mass production methods placed the products of industry within the ordinary worker's reach, they also condemned him to a work discipline characterized by endless monotony and the total absence of any intrinsic satisfaction. The alienation of labor was virtually complete at this stage. What remained for technology to accomplish was the complete elimination of the human element in production.

Automation became an issue of intense concern in the early 1950's, and innumerable books, articles, and reports have been written on the subject. A major fear shared by labor leaders and government officials alike was the possibility of widespread technological unemployment. Most observers recognized that the potential benefits of increased productivity, which were expected to result from the introduction of automated operations, could not be obtained without cost, social as well as capital.

In addition to unemployment, issues such as the consequences of increased leisure time, changing job requirements and other problems of worker satisfaction have been studied. The most striking feature of the literature dealing with automation is the absence of consensus. This state of affairs is largely a consequence of the extraordinary complexity of economic interaction. It is virtually impossible to disentangle the effects of automation from other factors governing employment and job requirements. Population growth, organizational changes, government fiscal and monetary policies, and changes in international trading patterns, to name a few factors, all influence employment directly or indirectly, thus making it hazardous to generalize about the particular effects of automation.

Despite the apparent difficulties, we are not entirely at a loss. When it is not possible to see general trends, qualified answers serve to inform speculation. In this chapter, we will examine some of the major problems posed by the use of automated methods, especially computer-based systems, for industrial and office workers. To set the stage for subsequent discussion, we will first survey the response to technological change recorded in the recent past. Then we will turn to contemporary issues associated with changes in job structure and the composition of the labor force. As indicated above, the social function of work has been drastically altered by technology. In the long-run, this may prove to be a decisive influence on the shape of the future. Be that as it may, the question is of sufficient interest to warrant careful study. The discussion concludes with an examination of the role of work in contemporary life, and an exploration of the so-called problem of alienation.

1. Responses to Technological Change

Progress through technological innovation has come to be accepted as a fact of life, inexorable as the proverbial death and taxes. Even those faced with loss of livelihood resulting from the introduction of new technology do not seriously contemplate destroying machines or attacking inventors. With rare exceptions the contemporary response to technological change ranges from polemical writing to contract bargaining and strikes by organized labor. The degree of concern is closely linked to the tide of prosperity. Conditions of low unemployment and strong economic growth breed complacency in workers and politicians alike. Concern mounts when material standards are threatened by declining economic activity. Apart from a residual wariness stemming from deeply rooted economic insecurity, our faith in the beneficence of technology is unshakable. Neither deadening monotony nor externally imposed work discipline poses a real challenge to the motive force of the pay envelope.

In the early days of the industrial revolution, displaced workers responded more vehemently. Starvation is obviously a greater threat than a mere reduction in living standards. But the recurrent outbreaks of violence during the eighteenth and nineteenth centuries also signify resistance to fundamental social change. Accustomed patterns of behavior were unceremoniously supplanted by the rigors of factory discipline. Although long hours and arduous toil were certainly commonplace in the pre-industrial period, the handicraft worker paced himself, and his work was a part of family life. The rural cottage was a rude place, but not nearly so oppressive as the wretched squalor of the early factory towns. Naturally, the new industrial worker needed some time to adjust.

Opposition to mechanization came from several sources. From the beginning of the modern period, capitalist expansion had to contend with the long-established power of the craft guilds. Examples of the resistance of guilds to technological change are well-known. In 1621, the weavers of Leyden, Holland succeeded in imposing a ban on the use of weaving machines which lasted for nearly a century and a half. Nevertheless, this type of opposition to machinery was successful to a very limited degree. The capitalist entrepreneur could easily escape the restrictions of the town guilds by locating in the country. Moreoever, many of the new industries were not subject to guild regulations at all. Despite the profound social changes brought about by the achievements of industrial technology, no powerful organized opposition ever materialized in the early stages of the industrial revolution.

The sporadic violence which preceded the trade union movement may have dramatized the plight of the worker, but it was clearly no match for the owners of capital backed up by the police power of the state. These acts were born of desperation and had no lasting effect on industrial progress. The adoption of some inventions was impeded temporarily by opposition from workers, as in the case of John Kay's loom which was perfected in 1733 but not in general use until thirty years later. Machinery was destroyed and inventors were occasionally harrassed.

> There were riots against the ribbon loom in 1676 and stocking frames in 1710. John Kay had his home wrecked in 1753 and was forced to leave the country. In 1768 the Blackburn spinners destroyed Hargreaves' jennies. In 1776 and subsequent years systematic attacks were made on Arkwright's machines. Crompton had to go into hiding. (Lilley, 1965)

One must be careful not to exaggerate the significance of these attempts to resist mechanization. As Lilley(1965) points out, even the well-known action of the Nottingham stocking-frame knitters, which gave rise to the term Luddism, was a response to oppressive working conditions and not an attack on machine-based technology. Moreoever, most instances of the introduction of machinery were not accompanied by violent resistance. This observation is, of course, subject to different interpretations, since factory owners were not powerless to take measures to preclude violent action. However, it is safe to conclude that changes in social organization were not the focal point of worker opposition. The immediacy of wage cuts and harsher working conditions provided more than adequate motive for action.

The shortness of human memory allows the passage of time to legitimize social upheaval. By the beginning of the nineteenth century, the factory system had become a respectable institution, with technological progress as a permanent fixture. Among those not directly affected by working conditions in the factories, the response to technology reflects the full range of human expectations. At one extreme, the apostles of progress viewed the unleashing of man's inventive spirit as the fulfillment of human destiny. The enormous increase in productivity achieved by the new manufacturing methods promised to create an abundance of inexpensive goods and ultimately to ease the burdens of work. Modern civilization was believed to have surpassed the culture of classical antiquity. Society was now ordered on rational principles, and everyone including the lowliest factory laborer could contribute through invention to the improvement of mechanized production. The machine was praised, and speculation on the future was an occasion for boundless optimism. Even socialist thinkers who pointed to the evils of capitalist production did not find fault with technology itself. The problem was seen to reside in the ownership of the means of production.

The negative response to technology often took the form of an escape into romantic fantasy. Nature and the simple pastoral life captured the imagination of those who rejected the mechanization of human existence. Rousseau's image of man's natural state exerted a powerful influence on succeeding generations. In sharp contrast to Hobbes (see Chapter 4), Rousseau held social institutions responsible for corrupting the pure innocence of natural man. Mumford(1934) points out that the impulse to "return to nature" was given ample opportunity for expression in the colonization of the new world. In effect this constituted a safety valve for the pressures created by a rapidly changing society. The return to nature was a strictly individualistic response, not a challenge to the new order, and its contemporary revival is not likely to have much greater social significance.

Between the two extremes of praise and censure, one finds the efforts of practical reformers who succeeded in curbing the most blatant abuses of industrial society. By accepting the basic premises of industrialization, and thus serving as its conscience, the reformist spirit helped to build a stable social order based on technological progress. The dominant contemporary attitudes toward technological change are part of the legacy of this spirit. Technology is seen to play a neutral role in social organization. The problems generated by automation and the use of computers, for example, simply require "appropriate" social adjustments.

With few exceptions present-day observers respond to continual technological change as an inevitable feature of human existence. Attitudes sometimes reveal ambivalence but rarely genuine opposition. Increased productivity is regarded as *a priori* desirable; the hardships caused by technological unemployment and related dislocations are recognized but not considered of major importance. The level of concern is superficial. The all-encompassing social context in which workers labor at well-regulated but meaningless jobs is entirely ignored. Suggestions that endless economic expansion may be irrelevant to the question of truly satisfying work are not taken seriously. So long as our machines produce large quantities of goods that we can afford, technology will be vindicated.

2.   Automation and the Work Environment

Worker productivity has risen steadily since the beginnings of the industrial revolution. Over the past one hundred years, the rate of growth in productivity, as measured by output per worker, has been in the neighborhood of 2 per cent per year (Jaffe and Froomkin, 1968). One of the principal reasons for introducing automated methods derives from the expectation of further productivity gains. Thus, it is natural to ask if there have been any appreciable gains since the end of World War II when automation began in earnest. Jaffe and Froomkin(1968) analyze productivity increases for several periods between 1870 and 1965. Their findings reveal that rates of increase in labor productivity during the 1950's were not above those of the 1920's. The same pattern is also evident in the first half of the 1960's. Judging from this recent over-all performance, there is little to suggest that automation will increase productivity any more than conventional mechanization has in the past, at least in the manufacturing sector. However, the continued spread of computer applications in nonmanufacturing areas such as banking, insurance, and business services may alter the picture.

The question of expected productivity gains is obviously of central importance to social issues associated with automation technology. This is of course not the only motive for developing computer applications (see Chapter 4), but as part of efforts to reduce costs, it is the one most often cited. In any event, these observations should help to keep the issues in perspective. Automation and computers in particular may exert their greatest effect on the kinds of work people do. In this section, we will examine the changes in production methods brought about by automation and the impact of those changes on the work environment, types of work, and skill requirements.

John Diebold is generally credited with having coined the term automation in the early 1950's, although it may have been used earlier. In his view, automation is something more than a new technology; it is a new way of analyzing and organizing work, which derives from developments in control theory and in information-processing systems (Diebold, 1962). The full implications of this innovation may take some time to unfold. More concretely, Froomkin(1968) distinguishes between two types of automation based on the essential character of the technology involved: 1) the feedback variety, and 2) the transfer type, or "Detroit Automation." The latter refers to methods for linking together a number of discrete production steps, so that the transfer of an item from one machine to another can be accomplished automatically. This type of automation was pioneered in the automotive industry.

Applications utilizing the feedback principle may be further subdivided into a) automatic information-handling systems using computers, b) process control systems (computer and integrated control systems for operation of an industrial process such as oil-refining or chemical production), and c) numerical control (the use of automatic control devices to direct the operation of complex special-purpose machines). In a more elaborate taxonomy, Bright(1958) describes seventeen levels of sophistication in automated systems, ranging from human labor assisted by hand tools to closed-loop feedback arrangements in which there is no human participation at all. For present purposes, Froomkin's classification provides an adequate basis for analyzing the effects of automation, since it accords well with the categories used in the literature on the subject.

Automation has resulted in reductions in the work force, and altered the nature of many industrial tasks together with the skills required to perform them. In the factory, there is a shift from operating jobs to maintenance type work, and a consequent change in job classifications. A hierarchy built on degree of skill replaces distinctions based on particular equipment operated, thus creating opportunities for advancement (Mann and Hoffman, 1960). The reorganization occasioned by automation usually involves the centralization of operating control systems, so that workers are somewhat freer to interact on the job than they were before. Perhaps the most significant observation concerns the apparent job enlargement resulting from automation. Although some workers are displaced, the types of work which remain to be done are more interesting and entail more responsibility.

The shift in emphasis to maintenance functions is especially prominent in the continuous-process industries (chemicals, oil refining, and steel), where skill levels are generally higher and more varied than in the typical assembly line operation (Walker, 1965).

Automation in the chemical industry has resulted in a greater variety of jobs and a more liberal time discipline as well as in more autonomy in the determination of work methods. The organizational emphasis on the process as a whole rather than particular jobs seems to make the enterprise less alien to the worker. An interesting feature of the process-control industries (which is being copied in some assembly situations) is the formation of task-oriented groups. The supervisory function is exercised here by the group itself, thus allowing greater autonomy with no loss of control.

The introduction of information-processing systems in the office (treated in Chapter 4 from the standpoint of management) produces major organizational changes (Rhee, 1968). Many clerical jobs are eliminated and workers must be retrained. Operations become standardized and more formally defined. The office worker has less autonomy, and many decision-making functions are either assumed by management, or built into the information system. Blum(1968) observes that the group most seriously affected by automation consists of experienced office personnel whose work requires considerable knowledge of company operations. Routine office workers engaged in filing or sorting activities can adjust relatively easily to comparable jobs associated with data-processing. The situation for more highly skilled and experienced personnel is quite different. There are no comparable jobs for them, and retraining is a serious problem. The status hierarchy within the office is significantly altered by the appearance of new classes of jobs connected with the computer system.

As this brief survey shows, the effects of automation on working conditions and job definition vary from one context to another. With the elimination of routine, repetitive assembly tasks, opportunities are created for more interesting work, at least for a few individuals. On the other hand, office automation exhibits some of the characteristics which attended the introduction of the assembly line in the factory. Computer-based information systems tend to reduce lower level office workers to machine tenders, with no opportunities for advancement. By contrast, automation in the factory represents a more advanced stage in technological development.

The effects of automation on skill requirements are difficult to determine. Comparing skill levels associated with different tasks is hampered by the lack of a normalized scheme of measurement and the inability to distinguish the effects of automation from those of other factors contributing to changes in job content. In spite of these problems, several studies of changing skill levels based on formal job requirements have been conducted. The findings do not reveal any over-all trend, since skill requirements increase in some cases and decrease in others. Froomkin(1968) reports there is some evidence to suggest that industries such as banking and insurance which have experienced high increases in worker productivity show a corresponding growth of skilled occupations. Conversely, skill requirements tend to decline in industries which do not undergo substantial productivity increases as a result of automation. This difference may be attributed to the degree of "technological saturation" characteristic of an industry. The absence of large productivity gains indicates a relatively stable situation in which automation is not likely to have a pronounced effect on jobs.

Borodin and Gotlieb(1972) present a summary of a study by Crossman and Laner(1969) indicating that direct skill requirements (those immediately essential to task performance) tend to increase, while indirect ones (such as occur in maintenance and support functions) tend to decrease. This helps to explain the contrasting effects of automation observed in different industries. For example, in banking and insurance, computer systems eliminate many jobs connected with support functions, while introducing new operating jobs with higher skill requirements. In some areas of manufacturing, on the other hand, automated methods shift the balance in favor of maintenance type jobs.

3. Effects of Automation on Employment

The relationship between technological change and levels of employment is not very well understood. Many theories have been advanced, but none of them adequately accounts for the complex empirical phenomena.[2] Availability of capital, consumer demand, income distribution, wage rates, and structural characteristics of the labor force are some of the factors which have been identified as determinants of employment levels. Jaffe and Froomkin(1968, p. 69) draw a qualified but optimistic conclusion: "It is only possible to generalize that the impact of technological change on unemployment is temporary and generally self-corrective." Nevertheless, even if one accepts this self-corrective notion, there can be little doubt that technological change creates very real social problems. Automation does in fact displace workers, and not all of them are able to find comparable jobs or acquire new skills. What is more, technology exerts a strong influence on the types of work society requires, which in turn affects educational and training needs. The following discussion will focus on some of the problems faced by individuals in their efforts to secure stable jobs under conditions of rapid technological change.

During the past few decades there has been a pronounced shift in the composition of the labor force. The number of people employed in service-related industries has increased dramatically in most industrialized countries. In the United States this number reached 49 million in 1971, compared with 22 million in the goods producing sector. Only 20 years earlier the numbers were roughly the same. The bulk of the service (as opposed to goods) producing occupations involve white-collar workers (professionals, managers or officials, salesmen and clerks); but the designation also includes service workers in the narrow sense (waiters, repairmen, etc.). Although the growth in the service sector, especially the white collar group, is striking, it does not signify the imminent disappearance of blue-collar workers (craftsmen, operatives, and nonfarm laborers). Jaffe and Froomkin(1968) note that changes in the composition of the labor force result from unequal growth rates for the different groups in particular time periods, rather than from replacement of one type of work by another.

As observed in Section 2, it is not possible to generalize about changes in skill levels linked to automation. Sometimes skill requirements are raised, and sometimes they are lowered. A related consequence of technological change, which received considerable attention in the early 1960's, is the apparently increasing need for educational and training programs designed to cope with worker displacement and skill obsolescence. This was not regarded simply as a matter of educating for increasing skill levels, but rather of providing the means for retraining workers for new jobs, and developing educational programs which teach general skills. Jaffe and Froomkin(1968) review several studies dealing with educational requirements for jobs, and conclude that high levels of education are not essential to task performance for the major part of the work in our technological society. A college education is often superfluous, and in a large number of cases so is a high school diploma. The concern expressed by politicians and labor leaders over educational opportunities for workers is certainly not misguided in its humanitarian objectives, but it has relatively little to do with the question of employability.[3] Even the retraining of workers displaced by automation poses less of a problem than was thought to be the case.

It is interesting to note that education plays no greater role in non-professional white-collar employment than it does in blue-collar jobs. The fact that during the 1950's and 1960's education was commonly cited as the key to employment reflects the preoccupations of status-conscious middle-class professionals. Educational attainment has increased generally during the twentieth century, but this is due largely to the productivity gains which have made protracted schooling economically feasible. Disproportionately high unemployment rates among unskilled and semiskilled groups are due more to employer bias than to the actual skill requirements of available jobs.

Changes in training requirements for computer personnel show clearly how technological change leads to greater simplicity in operations. In the early stages of computer development, programming required a very high degree of technical sophistication. In order to write a program, one had to have a detailed knowledge of the hardware capabilities of the machine. With the advent of assemblers, and compilers for problem-oriented languages such as FORTRAN, the computer became accessible to people with relatively modest technical backgrounds. The design of yet more powerful languages, coupled with the proliferation of software packages for scientific computation and commercial data-processing has further reduced the training required for routine programming. There is no need to speculate on how soon it will be possible to communicate with a computer using something resembling natural language to appreciate the trend.

The evolution of computer programming furnishes an instructive example of the role of organization in human task performance. Programming aids have an effect on the implementation of algorithms similar to that of the assembly line on manufacturing. In both cases a complex process has been broken down into simple operations requiring relatively little skill to perform. In principle, it should be possible to analyze service jobs in a similar way. It is not so much the intrinsic complexity of the final result that matters, but rather the process by which it is accomplished. Technology has not advanced by copying human methods. Thus it is hazardous to conjecture that automation will not affect the service activities including those which involve human interaction. Moreover, this observation does not presuppose the development of intelligent human-like machines, or any other major technological advance. Some indication of what is possible can be seen from innovations in equipment maintenance. By the use of a modular design which incorporates check procedures as an integral part of the equipment, the repair process is reduced to making a series of simple tests and replacing defective parts. Extending this kind of reduction to the activities of service workers or even professionals is not particularly far-fetched. The human content of such jobs is probably less of an impediment than cost.

The particular effects of automation on job content, skill levels, educational requirements, and other aspects of work may be less important than the general changes effected by technology in the organization of work. It is our love affair with technology itself that makes the issue so problematic. We are inclined to accept technological change in spite of our fears and misgivings. Automation is simply the latest phase of a continuing process, so that attempts to isolate its unique contribution constitute exercises in futility. Factory discipline and office routine were not created by transfer machines and computers.

The one observation that rises above the mass of trivia reported in the literature is that automation is accompanied by centralization of control. This holds for white-collar as well as blue-collar occupations. In Chapter 4 we examined the implications of increased centralization for management decision-making without reference to the ordinary worker. In fact there is little loss of generality in such an approach. For the average worker, the organizational changes introduced by automation are far from earth shaking. The substitution of work instructions produced by a computer for the orders of a foreman does not constitute a fundamental change. The foreman's role had already been mechanized. There is no less participation in decision-making or goal setting after automation than before. The current episode in the evolution of technology simply reinforces well-established trends.

Most work is performed in the context of large organizations, so that virtually everyone is affected by technology-induced organizational structure. Like muscles, will must be exercised to prevent it from atrophying. Centralization of control results in fewer opportunities for individual participation in decision-making and goal setting, and thus encourages action without responsibility. Nevertheless, there is every indication that the pursuit of productivity gains will contribute to the further expansion of large hierarchically structured organizations, and the continued concentration of wealth and power.

4. The Role of Work in Contemporary Society

The motive to improve productivity springs from different sources, but all of them reflect a shared social commitment to a peculiar conception of the "good life." Creating an abundance of commodities and easing the burdens of work are the central pillars of that conception, and technology is the vehicle for its realization. The world-view embodied in this definition of the "good life" has been shaped by many disparate historical forces. The Renaissance is credited with reawakening interest in man and his natural surroundings, and thus providing the cultural basis for a systematic accumulation of knowledge. Medieval institutions also played an important part. The rational discipline of monastic life furnished the concrete experience so vital to the spirit of scientific inquiry with its dependence on careful observation and measurement.[4] With the aid of scientific method, knowledge was transformed into an instrument of conquest. Success was rewarded with increasing confidence, and what started as an intellectual tool eventually became a powerful social influence.

The extension of the scientific outlook to the social realm was a very gradual process. After the fact, one sees the result as a belief in the perfectability of man to be accomplished through the elaboration of appropriate human institutions. The scientific enterprise gave rise to certain habits of thought centered on the manipulation of the material world. These habits were ideally suited to the task of establishing a rational basis for social production. The only additional requirement was a moral sanction capable of supporting a total dedication to that task. As suggested by Weber(1958), the missing ingredient was supplied by the Reformation.

The success of the industrial revolution hinged on the ability of the entrepreneur to accumulate capital and on society's readiness to provide the necessary labor. That both conditions were met with great regularity cannot be attributed to chance. De Grazia(1962, p. 41) remarks

> [O]ut of the reformation came a new atmosphere. Labor commanded a new tone. Once, man worked for a livelihood, to be able to live. Now he worked for something beyond his daily bread. He worked because somehow it was the right or moral thing to do.[5]

The aggressive materialistic attitude of science found expression in a new social undertaking with the aid of this moral imperative.

Work in the modern world embodies a curious paradox. As the industrial revolution advanced and technological change gained social approval, the new order came to be justified on the basis of its long-run promise to reduce the need for human labor. The utopian visions of the eighteenth and nineteenth centuries all paid tribute to this expectation.[6] Society was to be ordered on rational principles, production accomplished by human workers making effective use of machines, and the fruits of industry distributed equitably. It was left to the imagination of the twentieth century to eliminate the human element in production. The paradox arises from the fact that work is not simply a means to the end of securing commodities. Industrial expansion was facilitated by the moral basis for work; the tendency to eliminate the need for work undermines that basis.

It may be objected that technology does not eliminate work but merely alters the kind of work performed. The shift from production of goods to services might be cited as a case in point. Moreover, the number of people working has grown steadily since the beginning of the industrial revolution. To resolve this issue one must look more closely at the role of technology. The question of whether or not technological change results in unemployment is misleading. Work can be redistributed in many ways. Productivity increases can be absorbed by decreasing the number of hours people work. The critical observation is that new machines and methods are introduced for the purpose of increasing worker productivity and thus reducing labor requirements. The proximate result is easily obscured, but the significance of the intention is not thereby diminished.

Leaving aside for the moment the question of the actual content of jobs, it would appear that contemporary society has inherited the best of two worlds. Living standards in industrialized countries are higher than ever before, and most people continue to work. Technology has been used to increase worker productivity without creating massive unemployment. In addition, the so-called work ethic, the moral component of work, is still very much alive. The appearance is deceptive insofar as one might attribute this state of affairs to the beneficent influence of technology. The fact is that the effects of technological change are mitigated by other social forces. Perhaps the most potent countervailing influence is cost. Human labor persists in many jobs simply because of its relative cost advantage. The long-run expectation is clear, and this is not without effect on the worker.

Having a job serves many purposes in contemporary life, in addition to providing money. It creates a stable routine and secures one a place in the community. For some people it may furnish an essential source of personal identity, and for most it confers a definite social status.

> Today the American without a job is a misfit. To hold a job means
> to have status, to belong in the way of life. Between the ages of
> twenty-five and fifty-five, that is, after school and before

retirement age, nearly 95 per cent of all males work, and about 35 per cent of all females. Being without a job in prosperous times is bad enough, but being without one in a depression is worse yet. Then the American without work— or the German or Englishman— is a damned soul. Various studies have portrayed the unemployed man as confused, panicky, prone to suicide, mayhem, and revolt. Totalitarian regimes seem to know what unemployment can mean: They never permit it. (De Grazia, 1962, p. 41)

Although De Grazia's description is for the most part as appropriate today as it was in the early 1960's, there are some indications of a weakening of the force of the work ethic.[7]

The generations born after the Great Depression of the 1930's have grown up under the protective umbrella of state social welfare programs. Although welfare benefits provide only basic subsistence, they are often comparable to the wages of unskilled workers. Since many of the jobs open to the unskilled and semiskilled offer little in the way of personal satisfaction, the motivation to work is undermined. What technology could not accomplish in a frontal attack may yet be effected by a rearguard action. The economic feasibility of welfare schemes derives from the increased productivity of workers which in turn is a consequence of technological development.

5. Technology and Alienation

Alienation is a common theme in contemporary society. At one time or another it has been fashionable to speak of the alienation of just about everyone: poor people, minority groups, intellectuals, artists, workers, and people under thirty. The phenomenon did not originate in the twentieth century. Karl Marx pointed to the alienation of labor resulting from its transformation into a saleable commodity. Dostoyevsky portrayed the condition of alienated men in his *Notes from Underground* as well as in other writings. The pervasive character of the condition suggests the operation of powerful historical forces. Industrialization has transformed social institutions and altered the foundations of our world-view. The traditional norms supported by cohesive family life have all but disappeared with the decay of that basic social unit. Alienation is not confined to work, but changes in the nature of work are central to its etiology.

In the period preceding the industrial revolution, work functioned as an integral part of family life. Work meant participation in an organic enterprise, whose goal was not the accumulation of money or goods but the perpetuation of the family unit. The concrete experience of contributing to a common goal served to cement bonds of loyalty and mutual trust. An individual was defined by his role in the family, and was secure in that position. The discipline of family life was rigid but not alien. Conditions were far from idyllic— extreme hardship was the rule and life expectancy about half of what it is today. But the comparison with current conditions is an invidious one.

Industrialization altered the very foundations of social organization. The removal of work from the home completely changed the structure of the family. Equating labor with money transformed work into an alien activity. The worker became alienated from the tools and products of his labor, from the activity itself, from other human beings, and worst of all from his own human nature. Contemporary studies focus on the problem of alienation from work activity. One assumes that nothing can be done about ownership of the instruments of production; and we have grown indifferent to what we produce.

> Alienation exists when workers are unable to control their immediate work processes, to develop a sense of purpose and function which connects their job to the over-all organization of production, to belong to integrated industrial communities, and when they fail to become involved in the activity of work as a mode of personal self-expression. In modern industrial employment, control, purpose, social integration, and self-involvement are all problematic. (Blauner, 1964, p. 15)[8]

Powerlessness, meaninglessness, social alienation, and self-estrangement are the terms used to describe the worker's sense of alienation. The symptoms are not hard to identify; causes and solutions are rather more obscure. Causes are attributed to those aspects of work which can readily be modified. It is possible, for example, to contemplate changes in factory or office routine which give the worker more control over his own immediate work activity, or at least the illusion of control. Altering the basic form of production is another matter entirely; and beyond the prospect of manipulating the worker's perception of his work there is little to be done within the given framework.

The idea of fabricating meaning in jobs devoid of human content is a vain hope. Industrialization changed the character of work in two fundamental ways. As observed earlier, work was removed from the home and divorced from family life; in addition, the factory method of production incorporated technology which reduced human skill requirements to the performance of simple repetitive operations. Perhaps the industrial psychologist can neutralize the effects of monotonous work by making certain changes in the work environment. However, no superficial change in working conditions can be expected to supply meaning and social connection to a purely mechanical activity. Both office and factory workers participate in an abstract ritual having no essential connection to the rest of their lives. Indeed, this is probably true of most people who work in large organizations. The erosion of personal accountability which results from this ritual performance sometimes leads to monstrous acts, as evidenced by Nazi bureaucrats like Adolf Eichmann.

Folk wisdom holds that idleness leads to vice. But this does not imply that one should keep busy for the sake of occupying time. The belief derives from the preindustrial era, and points to the function of work in establishing balance and definition in a person's life. Modern jobs are capable of doing this to a very limited extent, so that in many cases the job itself may become a source of evil. The growth of humanistic values is stunted in the office and factory. For the shared experience which supported each member's sense of loyalty to the family, the modern organization has substituted the pep talk. A job could in principle provide the discipline and regulation that all human beings require, but only through the exercise of moral force.

> [D]iscipline can be useful only if considered just by the peoples subject to it. When it is maintained only by custom and force, peace and harmony are illusory; the spirit of unrest and discontent are latent; appetites superficially restrained are ready to revolt. (Durkheim, 1897, p. 251)[9]

The natural tendency of automation is to centralize the functions of control and decision-making, to concentrate these functions in the upper levels of the management hierarchy. From the very beginning, factory life was patterned on army discipline. Just as modern armies consist of highly mobile task forces characterized by a high degree of horizontal integration, the modern automated factory or office also has its task forces. And again, just as an army task force has a goal imposed upon it by anonymous policy makers, so does the industrial task force. Ever since the famous study of Western Electric's Hawthorne Works in the late 1920's and early 1930's (Roethlesberger and Dickson, 1939), industrial psychologists have been at work studying ways of improving worker productivity and morale. The latest trend is to give people the illusion of autonomous decision-making, in order to disguise their real powerlessness. The tyranny of group pressure replaces the close supervision of a foreman.

> Now the ever-more-complete mechanization of labor in advanced capitalism, while sustaining exploitation, modifies the attitude and the status of the exploited. (Marcuse, 1964, p. 25)

However, Marcuse does not see the problem as intrinsic to the technology itself, but rather as a feature of the capitalist system. Perhaps Butler was closer to the mark in the view expressed by his Erewhonian philosopher:

> [T]he servant glides by imperceptible approaches into the master; and we have come to such a pass that, even now, man must suffer terribly on ceasing to benefit the machines. (Butler, 1872, p. 180)

[1] See Lilley(1957, Chapter II) for a brief but incisive discussion of the pre-history of automation.

[2] Jaffe and Froomkin(1968, Chapter 5) present a concise summary of various theoretical positions.

[3] Friedrichs(1972), who points with pride to the progressive educational policy of the German metal workers' union, illustrates this gratuitous concern.

[4] See Chapter 1.

[5] Sebastian De Grazia, OF TIME, WORK AND LEISURE. © 1962 by the Twentieth Century Fund, New York. First published in 1962. First Anchor Book Paperback Edition, 1964.

[6] See Chapter 15.

[7] See Berg(1974) for a discussion of contemporary attitudes toward work.

[8] © 1964 by The University of Chicago Press, reprinted by permission.

[9] Copyright 1951 by The Free Press. Reprinted by permission of Macmillan Publishing Co., Inc.

Chapter 6.
Education and the Growth of Knowledge

The rapid increase in the number of school-age children resulting from the so-called post-war "baby boom" placed great strains on the educational establishment in the late 1950's and early 1960's. Added to the pressure of numbers, was the generally accepted belief that education is the royal road to job and career success. Thus not only was it necessary to process large numbers of people, but to do so without any decline in the "quality of instruction." Naturally, the experts turned to technology for the needed miracle. The educator's interest in computers has much in common with that of the corporate manager or government bureaucrat. Schools are complex organizations whose information-processing requirements furnish many opportunities for computer applications. Classroom scheduling, maintenance of student records, and various accounting operations are typical of such requirements. Computers were first employed in administrative tasks of this kind, but the potentialities of using them as instructional aids were recognized quite early.

Education for the masses in a pluralistic society calls for an extraordinary balancing act. Homogeneity and diversity are antagonistic principles under conditions of high student-teacher ratios and scarce resources. Sensitivity to individual differences is a luxury in the traditional American classroom. If there is to be any technological revolution in education, it is most likely to come from computer applications in the learning environment which allow for individualized programs. Administrative applications may have important consequences for the organization of educational institutions; but computer-assisted instruction holds out the promise of fundamental changes in the process of education.

The development of automated instructional programs is somewhat analogous to that of management-information systems. Modest success with routine problems raised great expectations which later proved to be overly optimistic. In essence, it was discovered that technology cannot substitute for a genuine understanding of how people learn and what constitutes good teaching.

The most interesting current research efforts in computer-assisted instruction are characterized by their attempts to make appropriate use of the computer, rather than merely copying the methods of mediocre teachers. Clearly, making appropriate use of the tool presupposes some knowledge of what is possible, and even more important, what is desirable. As in other areas of potential computer use, the allure of an enormous, virgin market was too strong to prevent premature efforts by various enterprising companies. Turning a profit rarely calls for deep understanding of basic issues; there is only one criterion for the success of a product, and that is how well it sells.

The educational enterprise encompasses the pursuit of knowledge as well as its communication and preservation. Thus we are led to consider the role of computers in research and scholarship. Computers have been associated with scientific research since they were first created. The computational needs of investigations in nuclear physics played an important role in the early development of computers. In fact, Goldstine(1972) remarks that the first problem run on the ENIAC involved "a very large-scale calculation as a test of the feasibility of a process that was then felt to be of great importance to Los Alamos."[1] This close association with research has continued and spread to virtually all areas of inquiry, from the sciences to the humanities. It is probably fair to say that we have only just begun to appreciate how to use the computer in the pursuit of knowledge.

Most of the chapter will be devoted to computer applications in formal education. We will first look at the accomplishments to date and characterize the different types of systems. After a brief examination of two avant-garde projects, we will survey the controversy surrounding computer-assisted instruction in general. The discussion will conclude with a glance at the role of computers in scholarship, and implications of computer technology for the "information explosion."

1.   Computers and the Aims of Education

To assess the current impact and potential contributions of computers in education, we must first consider the goals of the enterprise. According to Alfred North Whitehead(1929, p. 16) "Education is the acquisition of the art of the utilization of knowledge." Clearly, this process is a complex affair. It involves acquiring specialized skills, developing an awareness of one's own society, and discovering the continuity of human development. Put in other terms, it is the task of education to socialize the individual or to provide each succeeding generation with the knowledge and skills essential for it to carry on from its predecessor. From this point of view, the vital importance of education can be seen in terms of the cumulative nature of human experience. The founder of general semantics, Alfred Korzybski(1921), coined the term "time-binding" to describe what he believed to be a distinguishing feature of the human being, namely, the capacity to accumulate knowledge from one generation to the next, and to continue adding to the general store. Clearly, the way and the form in which our accumulated knowledge is passed on to the next generation will have a decisive effect on what happens next.

Proceeding from a broad statement of goals to prescriptions for their implementation is difficult at best. Whitehead's remarks at the beginning of this century on the prevailing curricula of his time are no less valid today.

> The solution which I am urging, is to eradicate the fatal disconnection of subjects which kills the vitality of our modern curriculum. There is only one subject-matter for education, and that is Life in all its manifestations. Instead of this single unity, we offer children— Algebra, from which nothing follows; Geometry, from which nothing follows; a couple of languages, never mastered; and lastly, most dreary of all, Literature, represented by plays of Shakespeare, with philological notes and short analysis of plot and character to be in substance committed to memory. Can such a list be said to represent Life, as it is known in the midst of the living of it? The best that can be said of it is, that it is a rapid table of contents which a deity might run over in his mind while he was thinking of creating a world, and had not yet determined how to put it together. (Whitehead, 1929, pp. 18-19)

Various experiments have been tried, since Whitehead made these comments, in the expectation of providing a unified and dynamic approach to the presentation of knowledge. This is not the place to discuss them, but one general observation is warranted. At least part of the difficulty in achieving Whitehead's ideal curriculum is the simple fact of having too many students for the number of teachers. Coupled with an emphasis on skill acquisition, this imbalance works to create uniformity in the learning environment.

Our society is committed to the principle of education for everyone. This means that large numbers of individuals from diverse social backgrounds must be "educated" simultaneously.

The traditional response to this problem has been to design curricula for the greatest common denominator. Given the fact of one teacher and a large group of pupils, this response, although certainly not the only one conceivable, is a predictable one. The existence of the computer makes possible the design of programs tailored to individual needs, without sacrificing the democratic principle of universal education. Computer applications in both administration and instruction can be expected to contribute to this end. Administrative applications which increase operating efficiency and decrease costs may have the effect of making more resources available for teaching and curriculum development. Instructional uses of computers are aimed at having a more direct impact on the learning process.

Before discussing these applications at greater length, let us consider the extent of computer use in the schools. In a survey of the 23,033 secondary schools in the United States conducted in 1970, Darby, *et al.*(1972) found that approximately 35 per cent make some use of computers. Administrative applications are reported in 25 to 30 per cent of all secondary schools, while 10 to 15 per cent use computers for instructional purposes. This latter figure compares with less than 2 per cent found by Bangs and Hillestad(1970) in a 1966 survey. Schools which use computers for both administration and instruction account for 5 to 10 per cent of the total.

Although the majority of schools make no use of computers, the number that do is increasing rapidly, as evidenced by the eight-fold increase in the case of instructional applications from 1966 to 1970. An interesting feature of computer use is that it seems to follow an all or nothing pattern: schools which use computers are prone to be heavy users. Applications have a tendency to cluster about administrative and guidance functions, or the teaching of problem-solving and data-processing skills. Thus far, the main use of the computer in secondary school instructional programs has been as a tool for solving problems.

Since computer applications in school administration are quite similar to those in the corporate environment, we will focus here on the peculiar characteristics of automated instructional systems. Several classroom uses of computers have been described. As indicated above, computers are widely used as computational aids in problem-solving courses such as mathematics and accounting. Instruction in electronic data-processing has also become fairly common in secondary schools. Computers function as control devices for presentation of multimedia material in the classroom (computer-mediated instruction), and as diagnostic instruments for assessing student performance and prescribing individual instruction (management of instruction). Between administration and instruction are the guidance and counseling programs which make use of computer-based retrieval systems for student records, together with automatic scoring and analysis of tests of performance and ability.

The most significant application of computer technology in education is computer-assisted instruction (CAI). This is a development with the potential to restructure the learning environment itself. CAI promises to create special programs for each individual student which recognize his peculiar needs and allow him to learn at his own pace. Suppes(1968) paints an interesting picture of the future: students at interactive terminals, communicating with a computer via written and spoken language as well as graphical images. The possibility is suggested of eliminating the lock-step, self-contained classroom of the present by using the computer to tailor courses and programs to individual needs. Individualized instruction will facilitate continuous monitoring of a student's progress: diagnosis of problems, suggestions for improvement, and evaluation of performance. Such arrangements are expected to improve efficiency in the learning of basic skills. Conveniently located remote terminals or teaching stations will place at the student's disposal sophisticated learning-resource centers consisting of automated libraries of multimedia material. The need for regularly scheduled courses will disappear as the computer assumes the function of coordinating the allocation of resources to groups and individuals.

Three levels of development in CAI are distinguished: drill and practice, tutorial, and dialogue systems.[2] The simplest and most common variety of CAI is the drill and practice system designed to supplement the regular curriculum. In this type of system, the student sits at a terminal and practices procedures illustrating concepts introduced by the teacher or memorizes facts presented by the computer program. Typical areas in which drill and practice systems are used include the teaching of elementary mathematics and science and beginning language instruction. One of the main advantages of such systems is the fact that they allow the student to progress at his own speed, free of the sometimes oppressive scrutiny of teacher and peers.

Tutorial systems offer reasonably sophisticated interaction capabilities between student and program. Concepts are presented and skills in using them developed. When the student exhibits the requisite mastery, a new concept is presented. A common approach to this type of system involves the automation of programmed instruction. We will look at an example of a more interesting approach in Section 2.

The dialogue system is seen as the next stage in the evolution of CAI. Whereas tutorial systems allow for interaction, the dialogue system will permit communication between student and computer program. As the name implies, genuine dialogue is the goal. Many obstacles must be overcome. Suppes(1968) points to the basic problems of recognizing spoken speech and performing semantic analysis on natural language text. However, he is quite optimistic about early solutions.

> I would predict that within the next decade many children will use individualized drill-and-practice systems in elementary school; and by the time they reach high school, tutorial systems will be available on a broad basis. Their children may use dialogue systems throughout their school experience (Suppes, 1968, p. 422).

2. Some Innovative Systems

Discrepancies between promise and reality are often embarrassing and sometimes even painful. It is not difficult, for example, to detect inadequacies in computer-based educational systems. The application of new technology characteristically follows well-established patterns until its potentialities for innovation are adequately explored. Like the internal combustion engine, the computer has been harnessed to a vehicle whose design was constrained by an earlier technology. In most cases, only rather routine teaching practices have been automated. Drill and practice and primitive tutorial techniques do not reflect the most sophisticated pedagogical skills. So long as no outrageous claims are made for the replacement of human teachers by machines, one is inclined to admit that comparisons between the two are strictly invidious.

The possibility of using the computer in nontrivial learning environments is being actively pursued in several experimental programs. We will discuss two such efforts: PLATO and LOGO. These systems are radically different from one another. PLATO is an extension of conventional tutorial systems; the LOGO project embodies a novel conception of the acquisition of problem-solving skills. The reason for including both of them here is that each in its own way promises to be exceedingly influential in the development of computer-assisted instruction.

PLATO is a product of the Computer-Based Education Research Laboratory of the University of Illinois.[3] Since the early 1960's, the system has grown from a single, computer-controlled student-station to several hundred interactive terminals linked to a large, remote computer. The typical learning environment of PLATO III consists mainly of a terminal device through which the student interacts with the computer program. This terminal combines a keyset (containing the usual alphanumeric characters and variable sets of special purpose symbols) with a video display. Information displayed on the student's television screen derives from two main sources: an "electronic book" and an "electronic blackboard." The former consists of a bank of slides stored in a computer-controlled random-access slide selector. The electronic blackboard is a short-term storage medium associated with the terminal. In addition to slides and blackboard material, the system also controls a movie projector and lights.

PLATO III can accommodate different approaches to teaching. The development of a course involves the design of a computer program embodying the "teaching logic" written in the language of the system, a modified and augmented version of FORTRAN. Two teaching logics, tutorial and inquiry, have been extensively explored using PLATO. In the tutorial approach, the student is guided through a fixed sequence of topics. Facts and examples are presented and questions asked. Presentation of successive items in the main sequence is contingent upon the questions being answered correctly. The student has some control over the process in that he can branch to a "help" sequence if a question is found to be too difficult. However, the student's communication with the program is restricted to answering questions or requesting help in a predetermined form.

The opportunities for interaction between student and program are greatly increased in the inquiry teaching logic, which constitutes a small step in the direction of the dialogue system. In this learning environment, the student must specify the information required to solve a problem presented by the system. In effect, the teaching logic provides a syntax for the student to use in communicating with the computer. This ability to ask questions makes for greater flexibility and student control of the learning process.

An example of the types of questions allowed is given by the following sequence from a maternity nursing lesson (Bitzer, *et al.*,

1969). The student is asked to list two cardiovascular compensations which result from increased blood volume during pregnancy. At this stage the student's request for information is a fixed response which prompts the system to list possible areas of investigation. After an area (anatomical and physiological changes of pregnancy) is chosen, the student is asked to specify a sub-area. Following the specification (circulatory system), the student is presented with computer-generated information dealing with the given request. As this example shows, questions in the inquiry logic must be translated into a sequence of discriminations. Although this may appear to be somewhat artificial, "it resembles the way one locates merchandise in a department store, and even elementary school children adapt to it easily" (Bitzer and Easley, 1965).

Comparisons between post-test scores of students using the PLATO system and those taking conventional courses do not indicate significant differences in performance. But the time required for preparing lessons appears to be lower in the computer-based learning environment, and what is more there is greater retention of material. The apparent economic feasibility of extending PLATO to a computer-controlled teaching system capable of handling 4000 stations lends practical significance to these observations.

Both the tutorial and inquiry teaching logics of the PLATO system are designed to facilitate the acquisition of facts, concepts and skills. This process is accomplished by means of a computer program which controls the sequence of events in a teaching session. Learning in this environment is largely a passive experience for the student. The LOGO project constitutes a radical departure from this approach to education (Feurzeig, *et al.*, 1971). The basic idea involves the use of the computer as an experimental problem-solving environment. Programming the computer and solving a problem are not viewed as separate activities. The programming language LOGO was created for the purpose of providing a medium for the exploration of mathematical concepts.

According to Papert(1971a, p. 25), "Our image of teaching mathematics concentrates on teaching concepts and terminology to enable children to be articulate about the process of developing a mathematical analysis." In addition to a teletypewriter connected to a computer, the LOGO laboratory contains an apparatus known as a "turtle" which operates under the computer's control and may be equipped with various kinds of sense, voice, and writing organs. One variant of the turtle is a vehicle which is capable of backward and forward movements relative to its own orientation, and rotations about its central axis. Attached to this device is a pen which may be up or down. Thus, the turtle can be used to draw figures. In this context, it is possible for a child to experiment with geometric ideas by writing LOGO procedures to direct the movements of the turtle.

The educational philosophy underlying this approach is based on the observation that "children learn by doing and by thinking about what they do" (Papert, 1971b, p. 11). This suggests the formation of a learning environment which encourages experimentation and a critical attitude. Earlier investigations by Moore(1964) of the effects of "responsive environments" on the learning process anticipated this approach. Perhaps the central feature of Moore's "demonstration experiments" is the emphasis on intrinsic reward as a motive for learning. Although his "talking typewriter" is a rather primitive device compared to LOGO's cybernetic toys, the principle underlying their use is much the same: encourage a child to explore the world by providing a means for him to act on it concretely. If the environment is sufficiently rich and cleverly arranged, the child's experiments are likely to lead to greater mastery. Moore's talking typewriter proved quite effective in teaching children basic symbolic skills. The immensely more versatile turtles show great promise as agents of the experimental method in education. As experience with LOGO learning environments accumulates, the potentialities for making intelligent use of computers in education will be more fully explored.

3. Prospects for Computer-Assisted Instruction

The long-range aims of CAI are universally applauded. Few educators would quarrel with the desire to improve instruction and curricula through the design of individualized programs, just as few politicians would publicly denigrate patriotism. However, as Oettinger(1968) points out these objectives are ambiguous. First, there is the rather serious inadequacy of a lack of an empirically validated theory of teaching, to say nothing of a universally accepted philosophy of education. The nature and objectives of individualized instruction, and the expected role of the human teacher are problematic issues which tend to become submerged in a swirl of technical exuberance.

Suppes(1968), for example, speaks confidently of the importance of various elements such as learning by ear in terms of incorporating audio messages into the computer's repertoire, but he neglects to consider the role of human interaction in the learning process. The technological bias here is evident. Only those elements which can be incorporated into a computer-based system are regarded as important. There is no particular reason to suppose that receiving messages by ear is more important than receiving messages from another person. Secondly, there is the question of allocation of resources. This is particularly important, since any widespread commitment to computer technology in the schools would be very expensive; and once installed, it would be difficult to justify any further expense connected with major modifications.

Although declining school enrolments and a general disenchantment with education may dampen enthusiasm for expensive technological innovations, school officials are not likely to ignore the promotional campaigns of companies manufacturing CAI systems. The prospects for computer displacement of substantial numbers of teachers is of course rather remote, especially in view of the growing power of teachers' organizations. However, computer-based systems may still exert a formative influence on the educational environment. Clearly, the types of systems chosen, and the way in which they are implemented will affect the character of the teaching process.

Computer-assisted instruction concentrates on the acquisition of intellectual skills to the exclusion of other aspects of education. The limited capabilities of existing systems coupled with inappropriate use of the technology in the schools encourages this narrowness. Teaching human values cannot be accomplished by means of abstract exercises, nor is an appreciation of cultural traditions likely to emerge out of a protracted association with a computer terminal. Even the creative learning environment of LOGO is no guarantee against a one-sided development of cognitive skills. Becoming socialized involves learning to respect the needs of other people. One may become proficient in many areas of knowledge without acquiring any sensitivity to other human beings. There is little comfort in the thought that these problems are not intrinsic to computer systems. The fact is that educational technology like other applications, promotes those functions which are most readily implemented. When the Russians launched the first Sputnik in the late 1950's, the training of scientists and engineers became a number-one priority of American educational policy. The legacy of the Cold War is still very much in evidence in the schools, and the attempts to design efficient learning systems reflect the desire to transform education into skills training. This is not meant to suggest that the acquisition of skills is unnecessary, but the pursuit of knowledge as a form of "nutcracking" leads to underdimensioned human beings. Norbert Wiener captured the essence of current trends in an incisive metaphor.

> The goose that lays the golden egg has become a Strasbourg goose with his feet nailed securely to the floor of his coop, to be crammed with information, not cracked corn, to the end that from the degeneration of his brain, not his liver, a profitable commodity may ultimately be drawn.[4]

Surely there is a legitimate role for computer-assisted instruction. None of the social functions of education can be achieved without teaching facts and skills. The activities of drill and practice in some form are necessary to the mastery of concepts, and the memorization of basic facts. If computer systems can be designed to facilitate these tasks, and perhaps do them better than human teachers, why should they not be used? The problem is that technology is not applied in a vacuum. Schools are social institutions with well-defined operating procedures and goals. The real danger of CAI lies in pandering to certain institutional rigidities. If computer technology were adopted in the spirit of the LOGO project, it could serve as part of a creative learning environment. There is no *a priori* reason to suggest the impossibility of using computers intelligently in the schools. A system capable of encouraging self-motivated development of cognitive skills would certainly be a desirable part of the curriculum. Unfortunately, only very few logical possibilities ever become practical realities.

The potential benefits of a sophisticated system like PLATO could very well become a bureaucratic nightmare. In principle, scholastic records are kept to monitor a student's progress, to identify weaknesses and strengths, and to assist in counseling. The reality is somewhat different, however. Records are used primarily for administrative convenience. Students are classified and labelled, and haunted by the official record of their performance. Designers of computer-based systems claim that individualized instruction would obviate the need for labeling. Given the structure of school administration this is a dubious proposition. It is more likely that the extensive information gathered in the course of computer-controlled teaching sessions would be used to refine student classification schemes. Unless the technology forms part of a teaching environment which can accommodate a large number of students pursuing individualized programs, it will serve to reinforce existing administrative practices.

The motives cited for the development of CAI indicate the restricted aims of the technology.

> A shortage of qualified teachers and a rapidly increasing number of students have resulted in a critical overload in our educational system. In addition, the technological advances of our society within the last 25 years have increased tremendously the amount of knowledge that must be mastered in all areas of learning. (Bitzer and Easley, 1965, p. 89).

With some exceptions (notably LOGO), computer-based teaching systems are designed to process large numbers of students, where processing means cramming with specialized information. The imminent decline in the general student population tends to undercut the need for CAI. A recent New York Times report contrasts sharply with the earlier observations of Bitzer and Easley.

> The number of elementary school pupils has been falling since 1970, mainly because the children of the post-World War II "baby boom" are beginning to pass through the school system and the national birth rate has fallen to an all-time low of 1.9 children per woman. Empty classrooms and even surplus schools are commonplace. ... Secondary school population is expected to peak this year, and colleges, many of which have been slow to read the demographic figures, will move from declining growth to a levelling off— or even an absolute decline— in the nineteen-eighties.(Fiske, 1975)[5]

In addition to the drop in enrolments, there is growing dissatisfaction over formal education. Schools as well as other institutions in the United States are suffering from erosion of public confidence. This is especially noticeable in secondary schools where the percentage of high school graduates going to college has been declining since 1970. Education is no longer a guarantee against unemployment.

The strategic problem of altering attitudes within the educational establishment may prove to be a lethal deterrent to the intelligent use of computers in the schools. Oettinger(1969) documents the powerful resistance to change within the public school system. Although sympathetic to the ends of CAI, he takes issue with the exaggerated claims of current capabilities, and the naive expectation that teachers and administrators will embrace the new technology with open arms. In addition, he points to the lack of understanding of appropriate uses of technology in education and the impracticality of introducing innovations given the enormous costs and public resistance to increased tax burdens. As noted above, the schools are going through a painful period of contraction.

Basic survival is the issue for many institutions. The public is not in a mood to examine the merits of anything that does not reduce expenses. If this is any indication of future attitudes toward education, the prospects for innovative CAI programs are not particularly good.

> [A]lthough computers may revolutionize possibilities, they alter the facts of life not at all. When we go to schools where computers are actually in use we find them serving as expensive page turners, mimicking programmed instruction texts. Yes, computers have practically infinite branching capabilities, but this matters little when we are unable to foresee more than a very few of the most commom possible learner responses. Restricted to narrow ranges of preordained alternatives, the learner is constrained to answer in the program's terms... . If we want real technological change— not just the appearance of it— we must, as in all enterprises, invest money in better ideas and better people. The scale of investment is found to be large. With 46.5 million pupils expected in public elementary and secondary schools by 1975, each additional dollar to be spent on one child translates in $46.5 million on a national scale. (Oettinger, 1969, pp. 50-51)

Oettinger does not take issue with the beneficent view of computer applications in education; his comments underscore the need to distinguish between ultimate promise and immediate possibility. He is particularly sensitive to the political problems of conducting research in the field of CAI. It may be expedient to focus on immediate returns, but in the long-run, this is a poor policy. Not only is knowledge sacrificed, but opinion is likely to be prejudiced against the ultimate value of the research.

4. Computers in Research

It would not be an exaggeration to say that the entire scholarly world has discovered the computer in earnest. From the approximate solutions of systems of partial differential equations to the preparation of concordances as an aid to stylistic analysis of literary texts, the computer has been drafted in the service of knowledge. Let us consider the more important uses of the computer, and the effects these uses are having on scholarship.

We have already had occasion to note the historical connections of the computer with atomic physics. In a discussion of the uses of computers in science, Oettinger(1971) distinguishes between two aspects of the computer's role: as instrument and as actor. The distinction is sometimes blurred in practice, but it is a useful one nonetheless. As a research instrument, the computer is helping to bridge the gap between what the scientist observes in his experiments and what he understands of the phenomena under investigation. The computer can perform the long and complicated chain of calculations necessary to utilize observations at a speed which allows the scientist to test his ideas in "real time," so to speak. Examples in which this capability is important include X-ray crystallography, analysis of particle-track photographs in high-energy physics and the study of brain tumors by radioactive-isotope techniques. In addition to providing computational power for hypothesis testing, the computer is being used in the laboratory to control experiments.

Computers also play an instrumental role in the formation of hypotheses. Conjectures often result from an examination of special cases. As an example, consider the problem of determining the sum of the integers from 1 to n, for a given value of n. One way to approach this problem is to study the sums for the first few values of n, and to try to infer the general result. With a computer it is possible to examine a large number of cases for much more complicated problems, and this type of exploration is becoming more common in such fields as number theory and combinatorial mathematics.

Perhaps the more important role of the computer is as actor in scientific investigation. In this capacity, the computer program itself embodies a dynamic expression of theory, analogous to the use of mathematics as a language in science. This dynamic expression is achieved through the simulation of models. Here the computer is not simply a computational instrument but rather serves as a vehicle for the theory itself. This use is most dramatically evident in simulations of complex economic or social phenomena. In these cases, there is no alternative mathematical formulation, so that the computer program is the only expression of the theory. Examples abound: war games, command and control simulations, stock market models, voting behavior, demographic and related studies, and computer-based models of problem-solving behavior.

In the context of simulations of social systems, the political questions of research strategy mentioned earlier become exceedingly important. Consider a simulation of an urban area, designed for the purpose of providing policy-makers with a tool for answering questions about the effects of specific policy measures on the future development of the region. City planners might be interested, for example, in the effects of residential development in a certain area of the city on population densities, traffic patterns, property values, etc. The practical importance of the specific projections revealed by the simulations is obvious. Moreover, only a little reflection is required to appreciate the danger of a research strategy aimed at achieving immediate results. We know even less about the dynamics of urban development than we do about the learning process, and clearly run the risk of contributing to the making of bad decisions and discrediting the ultimate value of this type of research. We will examine this problem in greater depth, later, in connection with decision-making in government.

Before leaving the subject, however, let us examine an assertion of De Sola Pool(1968) to the effect that a definite statement produced by a simulation is better than a vague one based on an informal model of a social system. Insofar as no action proceeds from a vague statement, it is preferable to a bad decision based on a definite statement. Our inclination is to use the tools we have created whether their use is warranted or not. The computer is certainly no exception. Unfortunately, both the vague and the definite statements have something in common: they often proceed from the same basic desire on the part of scientists to obtain more research funds.

Although the computer is unquestionably an asset in many areas of scholarship and research, there is some concern over the possibility of cultivating excessive dependence on its use. As computers become more and more accessible, the likelihood of inappropriate applications increases. The computer's data-processing capabilities can easily be misused in ill-conceived and poorly designed research projects. This applies to all disciplines, the humanities as well as the sciences. The collection and processing of data can become an end in itself, or worse yet an excuse for publishing results which serve no other purpose than to enhance the author's status. The temptation to perform experiments or to determine word frequencies in a literary corpus, simply because a computer is available to process the data, is often irresistible, especially when career advancement hinges on scholarly production. But, of course, this type of intellectual masturbation antedates the computer.

Creativity is an elusive human quality, and the influence of computer technology on scholarly creativity is a matter of pure speculation. According to one often repeated conjecture, if a computer had been available to Copernicus, he would have been content to patch up the Ptolemaic system rather than propose a new model of the cosmos. It is not always clear that declining computation costs are in the best interests of intellectual progress. Computers can be used as substitutes for thought: when in doubt, collect data and compute. Instead of trying to find an analytical solution to a problem, one may be inclined to write a computer program to explore different possibilities. This procedure is perfectly reasonable in some cases, but in others it may disguise incompetence.

The principal impact of the computer on scientific research and scholarship derives from the modes of inquiry which are possible only with its use. We have acquired a new methodology having capabilities we are ill-equipped to appreciate at this early stage in its development. Just as mathematical concepts and symbolism helped to sharpen our understanding of natural phenomena, the language of computer programs promises to pave the way for deeper insights into complex systems. But the promise may be compromised by our continued adherence to the Baconian dictum "knowledge is power." True understanding is not necessarily achieved by successive approximations, nor is it likely to be obtained in the pursuit of intellectual fashions. Creativity involves the taking of risks, both intellectual and personal. It remains to be seen whether or not contemporary scholars will rise to the occasion.

> they are good clockworks; but take care to wind them correctly!
> Then they indicate the hour without fail and make a modest noise.
> They work like mills and like stamps: throw down your seed-corn
> to them and they will know how to grind it small and reduce it to
> white dust. (Nietzsche, 1892, p. 237)[6]

5. *Computers and the Growth of Knowledge*

We turn now to the general issue of the role of information and knowledge in contemporary society. The emergence of the expert is one indication of the growing importance of information. In our complex society, vast amounts of information must be processed both in everyday operation of our organizations and institutions, and in policy making. This observation has become so commonplace as to find its way into the mass media. According to the now orthodox view, we are experiencing an information explosion. The main evidence for this view hinges on a measure of knowledge by the foot, i.e., if all the books and articles produced in a year were to be placed in a stack it would stretch from here to there. The situation for scientific research was characterized by Vannevar Bush(1945, p. 102).

There is a growing mountain of research. But there is increased evidence that we are being bogged down today as specialization extends. The investigator is staggered by the findings and conclusions of thousands of other workers— conclusions which he cannot find time to grasp, much less to remember as they appear. Yet specialization becomes increasingly necessary for progress, and the effort to bridge between disciplines is correspondingly superficial. ... The difficulty seems to be, not so much that we publish unduly in view of the extent and variety of present day interests, but rather that publication has been extended far beyond our present ability to make real use of the record. The summation of human experience is being extended at a prodigious rate, and the means we use for threading through the consequent maze to the momentarily important item is the same as was used in the days of square-rigged ships.[7]

One of the principal causes of the so-called information explosion is seen to be the extreme specialization of function in our society. This is just as true of government operations as it is of scientific research; and few observers see any need to question the trend. The most common response is to propose technological methods for processing information so as to make available to the specialist precisely what he needs. This is what Isaac Asimov(1973) advocates in connection with direct mail advertising. In his view everyone is a specialist of some sort.

Asimov heralds the rise of a new individualism in which the supermarket of the intellect is extended to the whole of our social existence. Personal definition is to be achieved through the information we receive. The use of a personality profile which reflects our particular needs, tastes, expectations, and values will eliminate superfluous material, so that we need no longer bear the onerous burden of deciding who we are. For the Socratic doctrine of personal knowledge, Asimov would substitute personalized consumption. To cope with the information explosion, man must become a sponge, a passive element in an information network, absorbing messages as they filter through to his particular corner of the universe.

This fantastic view of the future is reflected in the technological response to the information explosion. Licklider(1965) presents a futuristic scenario which he uses to characterize a powerful, interactive, information storage and retrieval system containing the whole of human knowledge for its data base. Needless to say, we are very far from developing any such system. Although one might very well argue about feasibility and what constitutes human knowledge, it is nonetheless true that we will eventually be able to design a system which approximates, albeit crudely, the one described by Licklider. However, if it is to subsitute for conventional sources of information such as libraries, and other people, the design itself becomes extremely important. The information one selects for use in decision-making, research or, what have you, plays a determinative role in the decisions and hypotheses which are ultimately generated. Thus organization of information is not innocent; it reflects the biases of the organizer and will influence the ideas of the user. The possible influence becomes enormously amplified when concentrated for use by a specialist. The inherent dangers in Licklider's so-called "procognitive" system both for political decision-making and human development may be greater than the potential benefits.

The development of large-scale information storage and retrieval systems as a response to the information explosion, will inevitably reinforce the tendency toward specialization. In particular, it makes it easier for a scientist to obtain references relevant to a very narrow problem area. Services of this nature have been around for some time now: the researcher furnishes a profile of interests and obtains lists of references periodically. These aids are quite useful to the individual researcher, but they form part of a positive feedback cycle. Specialization leads to yet greater pressures for selectivity in information dissemination, which in turn facilitate more specialization. The dangers of fragmentation of knowledge are often cited in efforts to establish interdisciplinary programs and institutes. But these efforts may be, strictly speaking, rearguard actions, having little effect on the general trend. After all, the members of interdisciplinary institutes are specialists, and so are the people they train. This follows naturally from our attitudes toward research. The value of scholarly production is inversely proportional to the dimension of the underlying intellectual interest.

The ideal of the Renaissance man has been pronounced dead in the twentieth century. One is no longer entitled to an opinion unless duly certified as an expert on the particular subject. This doctrine has become unwritten law in academic circles. The proliferation of material in countless books and articles makes it impossible for a single individual to master more than a small segment of human knowledge. Learned societies ponder the problem of accommodating the ever-increasing flow of scholarly production. One wonders if the world would not come to an end were the journals to stop accepting articles.

The computer is a timely invention. We now have a tool ideally suited to our retentive compulsions. It is much easier to record everything than to face the problem of making discriminations. The real danger of the trend toward specialization lies in the erosion of personal responsibility. Habits paralyze the will. The practice of relying on expert judgments fosters an attitude of acquiescence in matters outside one's "special competence." Unfortunately, this is not limited to intellectual disciplines. Matters of great social importance are deemed beyond the scope of the ordinary individual. The democratic ideal of an informed citizenry participating in decisions affecting the common welfare seems destined to share the fate of the Renaissance man.

[1] Los Alamos was the location of the principal United States Government laboratory of the Manhattan Project.

[2] For a more detailed treatment of these systems, see Ellis(1974).

[3] Bitzer and Easley(1965); Bitzer, et al.(1967); Bitzer and Easley(1969); Bitzer and Skaperdas(1970).

[4] Quoted in Piel(1962,p.224).

[5] © 1975 by The New York Times Company. Reprinted by permission.

[6] From *The Portable Nietzsche* edited and translated by Walter Kaufmann. Copyright 1954 by the Viking Press, Inc. Reprinted by permission of The Viking Press, Inc.

[7] Copyright © 1945 R 1973, by The Atlantic Monthly Company. Boston, Mass. Reprinted with permission.

Chapter 7.
Computers in Health-Care

Increased demand for medical services has placed severe strains on existing resources, and there is widespread concern over mounting costs and inadequate health-care for large segments of American society. A number of factors have contributed to this state of affairs. Health-care, like other social services, has come to be regarded as a right rather than a privilege, so that demand for services has increased beyond what might be expected on the basis of population growth alone. Structural changes in the medical profession have also affected the availability of health-care. The trend toward professional specialization and centralized facilities in the form of clinics, group practices, and large hospitals tends naturally to concentrate resources in urban areas, leaving sparsely populated regions with inadequate services. In addition, advances in medical technology lead to increased costs as a result of the large capital investment required for sophisticated devices and associated expenses for supporting personnel. Although the over-all deficiencies are relatively easy to specify, remedies are far from obvious. The problem is to provide more services for more people without sacrificing quality and without increasing unit costs. Graduating more physicians and building additional facilities is a partial solution, but it fails to come to grips with the cost factor. What seems to be required is increased productivity, and here is where the computer enters the picture.

As in industry and education, computer applications in medicine are largely a response to information-processing needs. For example, hospitals present administrative problems analogous to those of other complex organizations, and, predictably enough, one of the major uses of computers is in routine accounting functions such as payroll, billing, and receipting. More generally, the computer is being employed to assist in the management of patients, coordination of services, and the diagnosis and treatment of health problems. The ultimate objective is, of course, better medical care, which in practical terms translates into increased productivity of medical personnel and more efficient utilization of resources. Improvements in information-processing are seen to be critical to the realization of these goals, especially as they relate to the physician's activities. Every phase of diagnosis and treatment involves the gathering and analysis of data. Recording the patient's history, analyzing clinical observations and test results, diagnosing probable causes of the patient's condition, and monitoring treatment are all areas where information-processing plays a major role, and computer applications seem warranted. Automation of these functions, at least in part, promises to increase the physician's effectiveness by providing reliable information when and where it is needed, and by reducing time spent in clerical chores. We have already encountered this expectation in corporate management, education and research. Computer applications in these contexts serve to refine the division of labor so as to optimize system performance. Ideally, tasks are allocated to human professionals and machines according to their respective capabilities.

The development of computer applications in medicine reveals a familiar pattern.[1] Efforts to implement computer-based systems have met with success in some areas (notably administration and the clinical laboratory), but the optimistic predictions of the early 1960's have given way to a realistic assessment of the difficulties involved.[2] According to Taylor(1970), experience with large on-line information systems has contributed to this change. "Our ignorance about the precise function and value of medical data in hospital records becomes more obvious than ever when we try to automate data-handling in hospitals." As in other fields, the initial focus of computer applications in medicine was on administrative tasks and record processing. In addition, laboratory uses were developed. More recently, medical history taking has been automated at several centers, and computer-assisted diagnosis has received considerable attention. Although a substantial investment in computer technology has been made, medical practice has yet to be revolutionized by automation. The promise for the future is enormous, but much depends on rationalizing the organization of health-care services.

Our aim here is to examine some of the principal medical uses of computers in light of the objectives and the over-all social organization of health-care. To this end, we will first characterize computer applications in medicine, and then turn to questions concerning their effectiveness. The success of technological innovations must be measured in terms of their effects on the quality, availability, and cost of medical services. We will discuss these issues and conclude with a look at the broader problems of providing adequate health-care.

1. Information Systems in Health-Care

Record-keeping is an essential component of medical practice. The administration of health-care facilities (hospitals, clinics, physician's offices, etc.) and the activities more directly concerned with the patient's welfare both require the maintenance and processing of records. In the former case, records are used for purposes analogous to those served in corporations and other organizations with a large volume of transactions: payroll accounting, inventory control, resource allocation, billing, etc. What is peculiar to health-care is the information generated in the course of transactions between patients and medical professionals— physicians, technicians and nurses who are directly involved with diagnosis and treatment. In the following discussion, we will focus principally on computer-based systems for processing the records of these transactions.

Since one of the more important medical applications of computers is addressed to hospital activities, we will first examine hospital information systems. According to Dunn(1973, p. 6), "[a] hospital information system is a method or system to acquire, store, manage, and recall information about the operation of processes that interact within the hospital environment."[3] Five major subsystems are identified: medical records, quality control, manpower management, resource allocation, and general administration. The medical record is the heart of the information system. It contains data from the patient's history, clinical tests and observations, and provides an account of the treatment administered. Information may be added to the record by different personnel at various locations, such as nursing and laboratory stations in the hospital, and retrieved for use by medical personnel and administrators. All the other components of the system depend on effective processing and utilization of medical records. Quality control, for example, concerns the monitoring of activities associated with patient care: tests, clinical procedures, drug administration, etc. This subsystem is designed partly to serve a watchdog function to guard against inappropriate actions such as a prescription for a lethal dosage of a drug. The remaining components of the information system are sufficiently familiar from the corporate setting as to require no further comment here.

A number of computer-based hospital information systems are now commercially available. Singer(1969) characterizes four basic categories of systems. Large-scale, multi-hospital systems are designed for use by a group of hospitals, and encompass patient-care applications as well as administrative functions. Single-hospital systems serve the same purposes within a given hospital. Service bureaus offer systems typically limited to accounting applications, and dedicated computer systems are available for other uses. The first two categories embrace the "total system" concept and reveal a wide range of medical computer applications, not all of which have been successfully implemented. Generally speaking, the large-scale design features a time-sharing system consisting of remote communication terminals linked to a central computer in the hospital or elsewhere.[4] These systems usually have message switching capabilities so that information entered from an input device at one location in the hospital can be routed to output devices at other locations. This facilitates the storage and retrieval of information in medical records. Although elements of design vary from one case to another, most systems are predicated on the idea of creating an integrated database for use in all phases of hospital activity. Apart from cost, which we will discuss later, the greatest technical impediment to the development of effective hospital information systems is the lack of uniform and systematic procedures for recording medical observations.

Physicians have made use of some sort of medical record in the diagnosis and treatment of disease since classical Greek civilization (Anderson, 1970a). Attention has focused recently on the purposes of medical records since their essentially unstructured character makes for difficulties in incorporating them into computer-based information systems. John Jacquez (Bemer, 1971, p. 372) characterizes the problem in terms of differing interpretations of the functions served by medical records as seen by practicing physicians and the "reformers" who would like to systematize the process of recording.

> There are real differences between the physicians, who use the medical record, and the reformers who want to change the system. One reason for what should be called a succession of failures in the automation of medical record systems is misperception by the reformers of what the physician sees as the function of the record. The reformers view medical records as an accumulating data base to be used for research. For the practicing physician, the medical record ... is just a scratchpad to aid his memory in managing a particular episode in the life of one patient. When that episode is over, he couldn't care less about that record.[5]

Physicians' reluctance to adopt a new approach to medical records is due in part to the fact that they do not see any clear advantage in doing so. As Jacquez points out, in order to effect a change it will be necessary to devise a system which, at the very least, serves the functions of the "scratchpad" with less effort on the physician's part. But this is not the only problem. The amount of information which may be included in a record is virtually limitless, and experienced judgment is required to distinguish relevant material from irrelevant. Moreover, the design of a universal scheme demands uniformity in the terms used to describe observations. (Anderson, 1970b).

Information used in medical decision-making derives from several sources: interviews, physical examinations and laboratory tests. One area in which the terms of reference are relatively unambiguous and systematic procedures are used is the analysis and reporting of clinical test data. Some types of laboratory testing have been completely automated, and computers are being used to analyze, store and extract data from test results for review by physicians. Computerized analysis has been developed largely for applications in clinical chemistry, but some success has also been achieved in other areas such as automating the analysis of electrocardiograms.[6] Data from tests performed in automated laboratories may be transmitted directly to a computer from the instruments involved, or entered manually from a terminal. Systems designed for use in clinical chemistry range from single instruments coupled to a small computer to complex arrangements of multiple instruments and remote data entry devices linked to medium-size computers. Data-processing in the automated laboratory consists mainly of raw-data acquisition, simple computation and storage. In the simplest case, computations are performed on data collected on-line from a single test. More complex systems process data collected from ten or twelve tests, store results, and produce formatted reports printed by patient name. "However, no current system includes all the chemical tests, the urinalyses, the hematological tests, the microbiological tests, and the blood banking data reduction in a comprehensive manner." (Berkeley Scientific Laboratories, 1971, p. 187). Sophisticated retrieval systems for complex laboratory information also await development.

Computer-assisted laboratory techniques are being used in automated multiphasic health-testing (AMHT).[7] This application involves the screening of patients before they are interviewed or examined by a physician. Various test results, such as laboratory analysis, electrocardiogram interpretation, chest X-ray, blood pressure and other measurements, are recorded together with information from the patient's history. In a typical automated multiphasic examination, the patient's history is obtained through questionnaires presented at a terminal. The patient then proceeds to other stations in the AMHT unit for clinical tests. Data from test results may be collected automatically or entered manually, as in the computerized clinical chemistry laboratory. After testing is completed, a structured report of findings is generated by the computer for the physician's use.

The common element in the applications we have discussed so far is their dependence on a primitive form of computer-based information storage and retrieval. Somewhat more sophisticated information-retrieval systems have been developed to handle medical literature. A pioneering effort, which has been in operation since 1964, is the Medical Literature and Retrieval System (MEDLARS) of the U.S. National Library of Medicine. Although primarily an aid to medical researchers, document retrieval systems of this type are also used by practicing physicians to obtain bibliographic material.[8]

2. Computers in Diagnosis and Treatment

As suggested before, computer applications in medicine are conceptually indebted to management information systems. Computerized medical data acquisition, storage, and retrieval correspond to the first stage in the development of such systems (see Chapter 4). The next level of sophistication involves the automation of decision processes. Like his counterpart in corporate management, the physician must draw inferences, make decisions and initiate actions on the basis of incomplete information under conditions of uncertainty. The greatest challenge for computer applications in medicine lies in automating the decision processes in diagnosis and treatment. Some progress has been made in the design of experimental systems, and computer-assisted diagnosis has been used successfully in medical education; but practical programs capable of simulating the problem-solving skills of the physician are not within our grasp.[9] In this section, we will examine some computer applications in medical diagnosis and patient monitoring whose main objective is the automation of decision processes.

Boyle(1969) differentiates diagnostic situations into three categories. The simplest one involves the interpretation of clinical test results such as obtained from electrocardiograms and electroencephalograms. As noted in the previous section, considerable progress has been made in harnessing the computer as a diagnostic aid in the clinical laboratory. These applications are by no means trivial, but the problems encountered are relatively well-defined. At the other extreme, one finds the highly non-programmed decision-making associated with diagnosing the condition of a new patient. The range of possibilities is virtually unlimited, and the physician must draw on his accumulated fund of medical knowledge and experience to devise a strategy for arriving at a diagnosis. For these reasons, complete automation in this case remains a distant possibility. Nevertheless, some interesting results have been obtained. Boyle reports on a study in which the performance of a computer program is compared with that of a clinician in making diagnoses based on analysis of the results of the Cornell Medical Index Questionnaire (CMI). In a sample consisting of 350 patients, 48 per cent of the computer's choices were correct, as opposed to 43 per cent for the clinician. Despite the marginally superior performance of the computer, this comparison probably says more about the limitations of the CMI than it does about the respective abilities of diagnostic programs and physicians.

Diagnostic situations holding the most promise for the development of significant computer applications are those characterized by a relatively small number of alternatives. Here the physician has a rough idea of what to expect; for example, certain key symptoms may limit the possible diagnoses to disorders in a particular organ. One approach to automatic diagnosis is based on what might be termed a "static decision model." The term "static" implies that a decision is reached only after all the information from the patient's history, both from physical examinations and clinical tests, is available. Differential diagnosis is accomplished in this model by means of a matrix of conditional probabilities which signify the relative frequencies of occurrence of clinical symptoms in various disorders.[10] This matrix is constructed from statistical samples of patients with established diagnoses. A typical entry may be interpreted as the probability that a certain symptom will occur in the presence of a given disease. For example, in the case of suspected thyroid disease, the probability that a precipitin test will be negative given the presence of a simple goiter is shown in Boyle's illustration to be .999. Using these conditional probabilities, together with the relative frequencies of occurrence of the diseases in question, it is possible to compute the likelihood that a particular disease is indicated by the clinical symptoms.[11] The essential step in arriving at a diagnosis requires computing likelihoods for the various possible diseases based on the medical observations and tests performed on the patient. This approach has been carried out experimentally in the diagnosis of congenital heart disease and thyroid disorders with creditable results.

Taylor(1970) argues that the static decision model does not accurately reflect diagnostic methods in clinical practice. "[C]linicians, in practice, do not normally collect all the data on any one patient but select the tests in a sequence, being guided in the selection of the next test by the outcome of the current one." This leads him to propose a sequential or multi-stage decision model of diagnosis. In addition to the Bayesian machinery of the static model, a measure is defined which allows for choosing successive tests so as to maximize the information obtained. Taylor describes a computer program embodying this approach. Initially, the program selects the "best" or "most informative" of a given set of tests, and waits for the physician to enter the results. The likelihoods of each disease are then computed on the basis of the test results, and the next most informative test is determined. This process continues until the physician is satisfied with the discrimination achieved, or until the tests are exhausted. Taylor claims an accuracy for his system of 93 per cent in the diagnosis of non-toxic goiter.

Although the results achieved in special cases are encouraging, the practical utility of computer-assisted diagnosis in real-life situations has yet to be demonstrated. Current developments are limited by lack of knowledge about the incidence of diseases in the population and their accompanying signs and symptoms. In addition, the precision and accuracy of clinical observations leaves much to be desired. The automation of decision processes depends on the availability of reliable and consistent information for use in drawing inferences. As yet, the non-standardized medical record does not afford such information. But these considerations pale into insignificance when one considers the formidable complexity of the problem-solving behavior of the experienced clinician. Although programs exhibiting problem-solving skills have been constructed (see Chapter 14), general-purpose diagnostic systems are not likely to emerge in the very near future. One area in which computer-assisted diagnosis can be expected to play an increasingly important role is medical education. In this context, diagnostic systems serve as instructional aids similar to the tutorial systems described in Chapter 6.

To conclude our brief survey of computer applications in

medicine, we turn now to automation in the context of treatment. Although the decision processes encountered in these applications are of a rudimentary nature, the opportunities for extending the computer's role are considerable. A number of instruments have been developed for recording physiological activity, and computers are being used in conjunction with such instruments to monitor patients. One of the main purposes of computer-assisted monitoring in medical treatment is the detection of potentially dangerous conditions which require prompt action. Typical applications are found in the care of critically ill patients where continuous surveillance is required. The most advanced systems currently in use are those designed for monitoring cardiovascular activity in coronary cases. These systems are capable of measuring intravascular pressures, calculating cardiac output and peripheral resistance, and recording, analyzing and displaying electrocardiograms. (Rawles, 1972)

The effectiveness of computer-assisted monitoring relative to more conventional methods is difficult to assess. Comparisons of mortality rates in fully automated and partially automated monitoring situations are inconclusive. There is, however, a decided difference between general wards and coronary care units. Rawles expresses a skeptical attitude toward current techniques for automated patient monitoring: "In my opinion ... the best monitor of them all is a nurse, if you can get one." Technical difficulties with existing systems provide some justification for this view. "Noisy" sensor instruments often introduce errors in the analysis of data which may result in a false alarm triggered by detection of a non-existent condition. This of course does not reflect on the computer's function, but again reliable information is indispensable to the over-all system design. Advances in instrumentation for physiological monitoring have been stimulated in recent years by the space program, and continued efforts to adapt new devices and techniques to medical practice are likely to exert an influence on both treatment and diagnosis.[12]

3. The Changing Character of Medical Practice

Contemporary computer applications in health-care have not revolutionized medical practice. Recognition of the computer's potential for innovative change generated a great deal of excitement beginning in the late 1950's, but actual accomplishments have fallen short of expectations. As Hall(1972) observes, "most of the computer applications are administrative and only a few are medical or clinical or even oriented towards patient care." Although the interest and enthusiasm do not appear to have diminished, opinions expressed by workers in the field of medical computing reflect judgments sobered by vicissitude. The slow pace of progress in developing practical medical uses of computers have been attributed to a number of factors, most of which are familiar from other domains. Imperfect communication between medical and computer professionals, inappropriate or premature undertakings, lack of innovative approaches, failure to appreciate the complexity of the problems addressed, and physicians' resistance to change are some of the commonly cited reasons for the current state of affairs. It is not our intention to assess the relative importance of these factors. They are noted simply to help counterbalance any tendency to exaggerate the impact of computers on present day medical practice. In this section and the next, we will explore the likely effects of computers on the form and quality of medical services and on their cost and availability in the population as a whole.

The benefits expected from computer applications in health-care may be divided into two categories. One includes improvements related to medical-information-processing; the other encompasses the results of a more efficient utilization of resources. In principle, comprehensive, reliable, and timely information makes for greater diagnostic capabilities and, ultimately, better medical care. The introduction of automated interviewing techniques for compiling the medical history, the automation of testing in the clinical laboratory and in multiphasic screening programs, and the use of computer-based retrieval systems for patient records constitute important contributions to the management of medical information. These applications free the physician and ancillary medical personnel from time-consuming, routine tasks and provide ready access to information required in diagnosis and treatment.[13] In addition to reducing the time spent by the physician with a patient, medical resources can be allocated more effectively. Automated testing, in particular, is seen to improve the capacity for rapid diagnosis thus yielding shorter periods of hospitalization. This in turn increases the number of hospital beds available for the acutely ill, and relieves the heavy burden placed on in-patient facilities. From the patient's point of view, it would appear that automation expedites treatment and reduces inconvenience. If all the necessary clinical tests are conducted in an automated laboratory or as part of a multiphasic examination, one avoids having to make multiple appointments at a variety of offices and laboratories. Moreover, efficient processing of medical information saves the patient time by reducing delays and insuring prompt attention.

The patient's welfare is naturally the prime consideration in any medical procedure. To the extent that computer applications can be said to contribute to the maintenance or restoration of the patient's health, they must be deemed beneficial. However, this criterion is deceptively simple. A solution to one problem may give rise to another. For example, medication which is effective in the treatment of a given ailment may have undesirable side effects. This poses a delicate question which cannot be resolved on technical grounds alone. It is necessary to weigh the respective risks of the treatment and the disease in light of human values and social norms. Just what constitutes a tolerable risk is determined by the community, and prevailing attitudes are reflected in the decisions made by physicians and public health officials. These decisions become exceedingly difficult, however, when reliable information about risk is unavailable. One would not dream of launching a mass immunization program without first conducting pilot studies to determine failure rates and potentially dangerous side effects. Although it is not always a routine matter to obtain such data, the problem is trivial in comparison with investigating the consequences of wholesale technological change.[14] Apart from ritualistic platitudes concerning the humanization of computer-based health-care systems, precious little has been said by those involved with the technology about the effects of such computer applications on individuals and communities. The concepts and methods of management science are useful for considering questions of efficiency and productivity, but they are of little help in understanding the long-term influence of technological innovation on human welfare. We simply do not know what the side effects might be, nor do we have any assurance that we are even asking the right questions.

There is one area in which it is possible to investigate the direct impact of computers on patients. Contrary to most applications, the automated interview presents a situation in which the patient interacts with a computer program. Here the computer is manifest in the form of a communication terminal. From the standpoint of the designer, the importance of the patient's acceptance of the system is second only to its usefulness to the physician. Data on attitudes toward automated medical histories has been collected in several applications. In one study (Haessler, 1969) patients were asked at the end of the interview to indicate whether they would prefer to relate their history to a machine, a physician, or a nurse; or whether they have no preference. Of the 200 patient-reactions tabulated, more than half indicated no preference. The rest showed a preference for the machine over a physician by a margin of almost three to one; and the machine was preferred to a nurse by a six to one margin. Comparable results have been obtained in several other studies. The significance of these favorable reactions to the computer is not clear. Perhaps the patient feels more at ease communicating intimate personal details to a completely neutral respondent. On the other hand, it may be that medical personnel in their professional roles have become so remote from the individual's problems that the patient prefers to deal with a real machine rather than a simulated one.

Medical specialization and a mobile population have altered the traditional physician-patient relationship. The specialist who sees a patient once or twice cannot assume the role of the family doctor who is familiar with the individual's life history from an extended association. On the patient's side, there is little justification for regarding the specialized physician as a repository of human wisdom and thus treating him as a professional confidant. Here as elsewhere, discontinuity makes for impersonal relationships. Whether or not this change is desirable, it is a fact of contemporary life, and the course of modern medicine suggests that we must learn to live with it. Denenberg(1975) argues that the dramatic increase in malpractice suits in recent years is symptomatic of the trend.

> With each medical advance, with each addition to the maze of medical specialization, the doctor-patient relationship becomes colder and more remote. We would hardly think of suing a friendly family physician, almost one of the family, but we hardly think twice about suing the remote specialists who manipulate technology and lose touch with people.[15]

Computer applications are likely to encourage further specialization. One of the main reasons for introducing computer-based medical systems is to increase the productivity of medical personnel. This objective is pursued after the fashion of industry by refining the division of labor. Efficiency demands that complex tasks be resolved into simple ones which can be performed by relatively unskilled personnel.[16] More patients can be processed in less time by fewer personnel if the medical activities associated with diagnosis and treatment are hierarchically organized.

Automation of routine information-processing tasks constitutes one step in the direction of hierarchically structured medical services. In particular, it becomes possible to assign some of the tasks formerly executed by physicians to paramedical personnel. Computerized interviews, clinical testing, screening procedures, and patient monitoring contribute to a growing division of labor in the medical profession. The physician begins to take on the characteristics of the corporate manager whose principle function is to make strategic decisions. In a study of ambulatory care, Sherman, et al.(1973) describe medical practice of the future.

> Rather than relating directly to every patient himself, [the physician] would become a manager of a team of paramedics who relate to patients on his behalf, paramedics who would be following his standing orders in routine situations. Only non-routine cases would be referred to him for disposition.

Physicians who have been instrumental in developing automated multiphasic health-testing do not believe that computers will depersonalize medicine. Collen(1973), for example, asserts the contrary. Individualized medical reports, like individualized instruction and individualized junk mail, are seen to define personalized service.

4. Delivery of Health-Care Services

The most immediate and critical problems facing health-care delivery are cost and availability of service. Costs have mounted steadily and the supply of services is inadequate to meet demand. Annual expenditures on medical care in the United States amount to approximately eight per cent of the gross national product. The development of computer applications in medicine appears to some observers as a necessity. By increasing productivity, the computer can help to compensate for manpower shortages and spiralling wage bills. This point of view has much to recommend it, but there is no guarantee that over-all costs will be reduced in the short-run. For example, automated clinical testing permits unit cost reductions through high volume operations; but the availability of these facilities encourages the physician to order more tests thus neutralizing the potential savings to the patient.

In the long-run, such innovations as automated screening procedures may lead to lower costs by facilitating preventive medical practices. This, however, is difficult to demonstrate, and one might ask whether the demand for services could be partially satisfied by other means. The return on investment for computer technology must be weighed against alternative strategies for allocating social resources. Perhaps the demand for medical services would be reduced by eliminating the environmental factors in various ailments. Industrial pollution, inadequate nutrition, sedentary physical habits, overcrowding, and generalized stress are all believed to contribute to ill health. If corrective measures were taken at this stage in the etiology of disease, even the need for preventive screening procedures might become less acute. Considerations of this sort are no less realistic than proposals to automate medical practice on a grand scale or to increase the number of physicians graduated from medical schools. These all involve long-term programs whose chances for success are largely a matter of speculation.

Our aim in this discussion is to raise pertinent questions about the technological response to the problems of health-care delivery. We begin by taking a closer look at the cost and the benefits of computer applications in medicine. Singer's(1969) survey of computer-based hospital information systems shows development costs to be high. The range for a typical on-site system with terminals was found to be $350,000 to $700,000, although in some cases the figures were much higher. A substantial part of these development costs resulted from the need to modify or augment inadequate software supplied by manufacturers. Operating costs associated with on-line, real-time systems are expected to approach $3 to $5 per patient-day. Nevertheless, information systems designed for administrative uses can reduce hospital expenses. Schmitz(1973) reports on a system which effected a 2 per cent decrease in a hospital's total expenses per patient-day during a period when expenses were climbing generally by 14 per cent and more. The improved performance in this case is attributed largely to better inventory control and resource allocation. The available evidence suggests that medium-size systems for administrative applications can be cost-effective.

Automation has been successful in holding down costs in the clinical laboratory. Berkeley Scientific Laboratories'(1971) study of five large hospital facilities indicates that unit costs have been reduced by increasing productivity. Compared with the growth in over-all hospital costs, increases in laboratory direct costs appear to be well controlled. Analogous results are anticipated for the use of computerized patient history taking. Ryan and Monroe(1971) refer to a pilot project in a practitioner's office. The automated patient history saved "20-30 minutes of the one hour of personal physician time allocated for the new-patient work-up." This translates into a monetary savings of $17 to $25 (at internist's rates of $50 per hour) purchased at a cost of $12 per automated history. Here again, unit costs can be expected to decline in proportion to the volume of patients processed. Evaluating the cost-effectiveness of other computer applications in medicine is more complicated. Automated multiphasic health-testing, for example, involves a new approach to medical care which stresses screening for preventive as well as diagnostic purposes. Thus, as Collen(1973) points out, it is not enough to examine the costs of individual tests; one must also take into account the consequences of improved detection of health problems in the population served. Generally, the introduction of automated information systems is seen to be accompanied by structural changes in the organization of health-care services, which makes it difficult to design appropriate measures of cost-effectiveness.[17] (Vallbona, 1970)

No one expects that the mere presence of computers in health-care will miraculously solve the problems of cost and availability. A more rational form of health-care delivery is required to make effective use of the new technology. Garfield(1973) argues that the failure of the price mechanism of the market system to allocate services satisfactorily can be traced to the evolution of costly medical technology and procedures. Medical care, in effect, priced itself beyond the means of most people. This occasioned the development of various insurance schemes which contributed to inflationary costs and created overwhelming demand for services. The net result is a vicious circle defined "by increasing demand, increasing costs, and increasing unavailability of services." To appreciate the nature of this vicious circle, one must analyze the dynamics of demand for medical services. The different states of health present a continuum ranging from well to definitely sick with intermediate points which Garfield calls "worried well" and "early sick." A potential demand for service is generated by uncertainty as to one's exact position in the continuum. Uncertainty is seen to create a highly elastic demand among the well, worried well, and early sick, as opposed to the inelastic demand of the definitely sick. The fee mechanism inhibits elastic demand but not the inelastic variety, so that its elimination by means of insurance schemes serves to increase demand and overload the health-care system.

Since health-care services are essentially inelastic, they cannot expand quickly enough to accommodate drastically increased demand. This results in competition for services and increased costs. Garfield proposes changes in the structure of health-care delivery designed to provide greater flexibility of response. The basic idea involves making use of automated techniques and paramedical personnel to handle patients in the well, worried well, and early sick categories, leaving the physician to deal with the more complex medical problems of the definitely sick.[18] Four categories of service are distinguished: health-testing, health-care, preventive maintenance, and sick care. Coordination is to be accomplished by a computer-based information system. Patients would first be screened by paramedical personnel in the health-testing division using the automated history and automated clinical laboratory to identify problems and to make appropriate referrals. The health-care component is conceived as a new branch of medicine whose purpose is to "improve health and keep people well." This too would be staffed with paramedical personnel and presumably would accommodate the well and worried well. Preventive maintenance would be designed to meet the needs of the early sick and some classes of chronically ill patients. Paramedical personnel in this division would process patients and report findings to the appropriate physicians. Finally, sick care is envisioned as the proper sphere of the physician, acting as a "manager of patient care" aided by the other three divisions. This scheme is predicated on the belief that the costs of patient care are substantially lowered by the extensive use of automated procedures supervised by paramedical personnel; and as we saw earlier, it is not without some justification. We will discuss the implications of making structural changes in medical care in the next section.

Another factor which affects the availability of medical services is the mobility of the population. Each time an individual seeks care as a patient in a new location, a history must be recorded and other pertinent medical data obtained. Since much of the information is often on file elsewhere, this constitutes an unnecessary duplication of effort and adds to the overload on the health-care system. Conventional means of transferring records between medical centers may save the patient some effort, but it is a relatively costly procedure because of the administrative and clerical work involved. Computerized record systems could alleviate the problem if records were maintained on a regional or national basis. This might be achieved by some form of medical information utility with remote terminals located in hospitals and physician's offices.[19] Apart from providing a permanent medical file for the patient, such a system would be a great boon to medical research and public health planning. However, controlling access to the information on file is not a simple matter, and the potential for invasion of privacy constitutes a serious threat to individual autonomy.[20]

5. Computers, Health, and the Public Interest

There are many potential benefits to be derived from the use of computers in medicine, all of which may be expected to contribute to improvements in health-care. Specialized applications in medical research, education, administration, health-testing, diagnosis, and patient monitoring are conceived largely for the purpose of increasing the productivity of medical and paramedical personnel or promoting the optimal use of resources. The object of greater productivity and efficiency is, of course, reduced costs, and more and better services. In a word, the crisis in health-care is to be met through the use of technology to rationalize the delivery of services. The question we must address at this point is whether or not the potential of computer technology in medicine can be transformed into actuality under existing conditions.

Thus far, we have discussed computer applications within the framework of the health-care establishment. Although some modifications in medical practice are required by the introduction of computer-based systems, the fundamental mechanisms of control and decision-making remain intact. The power and interests of bureaucrats and medical professionals and the institutional arrangements on which they are based are unchallenged by these systems. Under the new technological dispensation, the more refined division of labor may transform the physician into a medical manager and the administrator into a modern corporate executive, but the locus of authority remains unchanged. If the dramatic rise in costs and the inadequacies in delivery of services were of recent origin, skepticism over the technological response could be dismissed as idle speculation. Unfortunately, this is not the case. As Alford(1972) points out "[i]f health-care is in 'crisis' now, then it was in crisis ten, twenty, and forty years ago as well." What is more, the proposed remedies are basically variations on an old theme. In this concluding section, we will examine the prospects for success of the most recent proposals.

The shortage of physicians and medical facilities is evident throughout the population, but as in any situation of scarcity, low-income groups suffer the most. For the affluent individual, inadequate health-care delivery means inconvenience and higher medical or insurance bills; for those who are less fortunate, medical care is simply unavailable or of inferior quality. The urban poor constitute the most deprived group. Lacking accessible treatment facilities in the community and the means for obtaining care elsewhere, low-income residents in large metropolitan areas seek medical attention only when the need is acute. Of the four states of health analyzed by Garfield as affecting demand for services, only the definitely sick category is relevant. In their present form, the primary medical-care facilities— city-county hospitals, health departments, and neighborhood clinics, cannot accommodate more comprehensive programs of health-care. This has promoted the establishment of neighborhood health centers as part of a program to provide access to comprehensive care. In an effort to furnish such care at an "acceptable cost," computer-based patient-management systems are being explored. This involves the implementation of a health-care scheme along the lines proposed by Garfield. The objective is to make use of paramedical personnel to "carry out many of the preventive services ... provide care for some common acute self-limiting diseases, and follow up patients who are in a stable phase of a chronic disease." (Vallbona, et al., 1973). Neighborhood health centers using computer-based systems are still largely experimental projects, but the experience of related attempts to provide health-care in neighborhood clinics suggests that success does not hinge on technological factors.

Alford(1972) characterizes the establishment of neighborhood health centers in the United States as an exercise in futility. The reasons for inevitable failure are seen to be social and political in nature. Such efforts are doomed by the consequences of excessive demand for services, the formation of a two-class health system, and the likelihood of short-term funding. Neighborhood health centers are typically located in poor areas with relatively few physicians. The introduction of inexpensive, high-quality, medical care initially unleashes an overwhelming demand for services which formerly had no means for actualization. This may lead eventually to a degradation of service and disillusionment on the part of both staff and the community, which in turn affects the prospects for establishing new centers. The absence of any real improvement generates cycnicism in the community so that new ventures are likely to be ignored or rejected. Ironically, the problem then becomes one of underutilization which provides justification for dismantling the program. The attempt to restrict services to low-income residents also contributes to the failure of the neighborhood-health-center concept. This policy effects a two-class system of health-care, with all the inequities attendant upon separate services for the rich and poor. The indignity of means tests erodes respect for patients, and the institutionalization of two classes of services inevitably results in lower status for the staff serving the poor. Such conditions are not conducive to attracting and holding highly qualified personnel, and the turnover of staff prevents the formation of continuing relationships with the community. Added to these instabilities is the insecurity of financing. As part of a piecemeal approach to health-care reform, the neighborhood center is always in danger of being replaced by a new program which affords greater political leverage.

The reliance on technology to solve what is essentially a complex social issue is not peculiar to medicine. Failure to recognize the interplay of social forces underlying a problem makes for inappropriate and wasteful uses of scarce resources. Perhaps the most notable recent example is American policy in Southeast Asia. The technological capability for transforming the region into a parking lot contributed rather little to an intelligent assessment of the evolving political situation. Despite the obvious differences in objectives, there are instructive parallels between the respective technological approaches to foreign policy and health-care. Productivity and efficiency figure prominently in both cases. After all, American foreign policy was based in large measure on a belief in the irresistable power of productive military personnel coupled with efficient command-control systems. The demand for health-care services is no more likely to be met by the simple expedient of increased productivity and efficiency than was the corresponding demand for "social services" in Vietnam. To see why this is so, one must probe more deeply into the structure of health-care delivery.

Medical practice is dominated by powerful vested interests which are highly resistant to changes that might threaten their authority and priviledge. Alford identifies two groups: the "professional monopolists" and the "bureaucratic rationalizers." The first consists mainly of physicians, specialists, and medical researchers whose professional position supports a nearly complete monopoly over the conditions of their work. This monopoly is sustained by the traditions of the medical profession and the absence of any independent means of evaluating the effectiveness of medical services. The second group is made up of the chief executives of the health establishment: hospital administrators, medical-school directors, heads of quasi-public insurance, and government officials responsible for public health. For this group, authority and prestige are linked to organizational control. The health administrator's power is proportional to the extent of the apparatus at his disposal, and rationalizing the organizational structure is a means for increasing that power. Although the two groups occasionally form alliances within a given institution for the purpose of obtaining public funds, their basic interests are opposed. The existence of these competing interests acts as a deterrent to comprehensive reform in the delivery of health-care services.

While the professional monopolists stress reforms which increase the physician's productivity by putting him in charge of systems staffed by paramedical personnel, the bureaucratic rationalizers seek to integrate fragmented health services within the hospital or other centralized facility so as to create efficient organizations subject to their control. Inevitably, technology serves to enhance the power and influence of one or the other group. In the competition for scarce resources, the public interest is the chief victim. "The integration of all aspects of the health-care system ... would require the defeat or consolidation of the social power that has been appropriated by various discrete interest groups and that preserves existing allocations of social values and resources." (Alford, 1972). The ability of the computer to facilitate increases in productivity and efficiency does not guarantee an equitable distribution of health-care services.

[1] Recall the discussion of management information systems in Chapter 4 and related observations concerning computer applications in education (Chapter 6).

[2] Michael G. Saunders (in Bemer, 1971, p. 366) comments: "Although some 5 to 10 million persons visit the physicians of North America daily, only a few thousand will have had any part of their medical care affected in any way by the computer."

[3] This definition has much in common with the notion of management information systems (see Chapter 4).

[4] See Ball(1973) for a description of several commercially designed hospital information systems.

[5] Copyright 1971, Association for Computing Machinery Inc., reprinted by permission.

[6] See Berkeley Scientific Laboratories(1971) for details on automated laboratory equipment and systems.

[7] AMHT was pioneered in the Kaiser Permanente plan of prepaid group practice in the United States. According to Ryan and Monroe(1971) there are "122 active or planned multiphasic programs in the country, many of which are automated."

[8]   We have already discussed the role of computerized document retrieval systems in scientific research (see Chapter 6).

[9]   In Chapter 14, problem-solving behavior is considered in the general setting of research in artificial intelligence.

[10] See Boyle(1969) for an example of such a matrix.

[11] This computation is based on Bayes' Theorem. For a discussion of decision models in medicine see Lusted(1968).

[12] See Sandler, *et al.*(1973).

[13] Assuming, of course, that information is presented to the physician in a usable form. See Collen(1970) for a discussion of this issue.

[14] In Section 5, we discuss some of the political implications of medical computer technology.

[15] Reprinted by permission from *The Progressive*, 408 West Gorham Street, Madison, Wisconsin 53703. Copyright © 1975[4]. The Progressive, Inc.

[16] Recall the discussion in Chapters 4 and 5.

[17] This phenomenon is evident in corporations as well; see Chapter 4.

[18] This is essentially an extension of the use of automated multiphasic health-testing and entails the kind of hierarchical organization discussed in Section 3.

[19] Computer utilities are discussed in Chapter 8.

[20] These issues are treated in Chapter 9.

Part III.
Challenge: Control
of Disorder

The distinction between coordination of diversity and control of disorder is often very subtle. It is largely a function of attitudes and intentions rather than properties of the instruments used. Modern communications technology makes it possible for us to sustain a great variety of activities routinely; but it also provides the opportunity for virtually continuous surveillance of an individual's behavior. Centralized administration of social services may afford a more equitable distribution of those services; but such administration requires the collection and maintenance of information files on the recipients. Although there is always an element of control in coordination, the distinction, even though largely a matter of emphasis, is vitally important because of the social commitment associated with large-scale technological development.

The important question is the impact of the social commitment on particular policy choices. In theory an individual is free to use a tool such as a computer as he sees fit. An employee of a bank, for example, may attempt to improve customer services, or he may try to modify an existing program so as to divert funds into his own account. But the operation of society cannot be understood purely in terms of the aggregation of individual choices. The interaction of technology with social institutions leaves neither one unchanged. Society is not free to utilize the technology it supports in any manner whatsoever. Quite apart from inherent technical limitations, commitments to develop technology are constrained and guided by the disposition of society at large. The post-war development of nuclear weapons, for example, was neither anticipated nor effectively controlled by those responsible for the decision to build an atomic bomb. Initially, social resources were committed for what was regarded as a highly specific objective: to develop an atomic bomb ahead of the Germans; but the consequences of this choice extended far beyond the concrete military situation in which it was conceived. Who would have predicted then that a mere fifteen years after the first atomic explosion, it would become respectable to speak of megadeaths in connection with the role of nuclear exchanges in diplo-military strategy.[1]

The shift from coordination to control is imperceptible. Viewed simply as technological development, the fusion of computers with communication systems, can be regarded as a turning point in our ability to cope with diversity. However, it is extremely naive and historically unjustified to view the development in this way; computer-communication networks will not be used in a social vacuum. This new technology provides a powerful vehicle for centralized control of societal functions. Coordination usually involves the orderly interaction of relatively autonomous units, such as might be expected in a loose federation of independent states; control, on the other hand, is characteristic of centrally directed components of an organism. Social commitment to the development of a computer utility may ultimately serve to accelerate the emergence of an absolutist state, in which, as a Nazi theorist once said "not only is the individual inferior to the state, he has no right to exist."

In the next five chapters we will explore the impact of computer technology on the distribution of power in society. The discussion begins with the emerging computer utility. Time-sharing services have become viable commercial enterprises, and computer networks are beginning to pass beyond the experimental stage. The technical feasibility of regional or national computer-communication networks is no longer in doubt, and this fact must be taken into account in assessing the desirability of computer applications, especially those which affect the political process. One of the fundamental problems of a democratic society is to preserve a balance between the rights of citizens and the authority of the state. Individual and organizational privacy play a critical role in guaranteeing democratic freedoms. Our treatment of the consequences of computer-based data surveillance will focus on the nature of privacy and the efficacy of projected safeguards.

The political process is particularly sensitive to the introduction of computer technology in government decision-making. There are two closely related aspects of this issue which we will examine separately. One concerns the collection, storage, and processing of information in government operations; the other involves the use of systems methods in exploring policy alternatives. The main concerns here are the quality of decisions and the extent to which members of the community have a voice in matters affecting their welfare. Part III concludes with a discussion of the relationship between power and social information. Computer applications are a response to growing social complexity, but the latter is partly a consequence of the centralization of power and information technology appears to facilitate this trend. We will argue that the conditions which seem to necessitate the elaboration of computer applications are not an inexorable result of social evolution; they are the product of a particular historical development and can be modified by community action.

---

[1] Herman Kahn's first major effort to think about the unthinkable appeared in 1960.

Chapter 8.
Computer Utilities

The growth of the computer industry and the widespread diffusion of computer applications bear witness to society's dependence on the new technology. Such is the importance of this development that the computer has come to be regarded as a vital social resource. Numerous independent applications have demonstrated its capabilities and established a predisposition to extend its use. As an isolated tool employed in unrelated activities, the computer has already exerted a considerable influence on contemporary affairs. The possibility of consolidating computing power in the form of utilities signals a new stage in the evolution of computer technology, pregnant with consequences for the future of society.

The next step is not without precedent. Railroads began as "stand-alone" transportation systems linking a handful of different locations. With the spread of independent lines, it became evident that more efficient use of existing capital resources could be made through the sharing of facilities. Similarly, the automobile would be of limited value in the absence of a generally accessible network of highways. The concept of sharing is crucial for the effective utilization of social resources. If each user of electric power required a separate generating station, many people would still be using candles. The integration of transportation, communication, and power facilities into large networks has made service more economical, reliable, and universally available.

The technological basis for computer utilities is not a matter of speculation. Service bureaus operating time-sharing systems have proved to be commercially viable, and experimental computer networks have already been constructed. It is too early to predict the form computer utilities are likely to assume, but the main components are readily identifiable. The purpose of a computer utility is to provide a full range of information processing services: computer time, programs, and data. This requires three basic elements: computers, data communications facilities, and terminals. Data communications facilities serve as the common message carrier for computers and users; terminals are the means by which human users interact with the network. The advantage of a computer utility over stand-alone systems is not primarily one of cost, although this is an important factor. Of greater significance is the ability to make use of resources, programs, and data, located at different centers within the network.

The potential impact of computer utilities on society is difficult to exaggerate. Even for a world grown accustomed to global transportation and communication, the possibilities of universally accessible computer networks are truly revolutionary. Thus far the computer has impinged on everyday life in a somewhat abstract and indirect fashion. The computer utility proposes to bring the computer into the home, to eliminate cash as a medium of exchange, and to transform government into an omniscient and ubiquitous force. Social control is the keynote of this eventuality. Home terminals may allow for a wider choice of entertainment, make possible an electronic form of catalogue shopping, and even provide the means for continual education; but the principal social effect lies in the concentration of information in the hands of bureaucrats and officials.

The establishment of computerized databanks in private organizations and government agencies has already generated concern over the invasion of privacy and possible abuses of power. Although these issues are real enough today, they are likely to become several orders of magnitude more significant with the advent of computer utilities. A national databank may be created by default. Unfortunately, the technical problems of system security (insuring against unauthorized access to data) tend to obscure the overriding danger of excessive centralization of power. As dramatically evidenced by totalitarian regimes, information is critical to the apparatus of state control. Since political legitimacy is often indistinguishable from political fact, the mere existence of democratic institutions is no guarantee against extensions of state power.

In the following discussion, we will explore the emerging forms of computer-communication systems. After examining the basic concept in some detail, and reviewing current developments, we will turn to the issue of social need and the expected contributions of computer utilities. Since financial applications figure prominently in current plans, we will take a closer look at developments in this area, and then analyze the potential effects of computer networks on the structure of social control.

1. The Computer Utility Concept

The idea of a computer or information utility reflects a particular attitude toward computer-communication systems. This attitude is expressed in the belief that mass communication facilities which permit access to computers and associated information files from remote terminals should be viewed as a utility and developed in the public interest. Sackman and Nie(1970) remark in their preface to the proceedings of a conference on the information utility that the participants "agreed that government and concerned groups should attempt to exercise as much influence as possible to see to it that these systems provide more than simple commercial services."[1] In its general form, the underlying system for an information utility is a computer network— a configuration of interconnected computers, remote terminals, and support facilities. Although computer utilities in this broad sense have yet to emerge, the development of remote-access time-sharing systems and experimental networks give some indication of future possibilities. In what follows, we will explore the notion of a utility and examine some of the general features of computer networks and time-sharing services.

Baran(1967) characterizes a utility as "a 'natural monopoly' in which the government issues an exclusive franchise to provide service to the public on a noncompetitive basis." Existing computer-communication systems (notably time-sharing services) differ from this conception in two important respects. Service is provided on a competitive basis, and not all users are treated equally. The present stage of development of computer-communications is reminiscent of the early history of the telegraph and telephone. In each of these cases, competing systems established by private companies evolved into interconnected units providing regional and national service. It remains to be seen whether or not computer networks will evolve along similar lines.

The criteria for public utility status derive from two basic considerations: relationship to the public interest, and tendency to form a natural monopoly.[2] An industry whose activities are of public consequence may be the target of government regulation. If, in addition, the most efficient mode of operation demands centralized planning and control which can only be realized in a monopolistic enterprise, the state may grant a legal monopoly. In return for this privilege, the utility is expected to provide reasonably adequate service to anyone who wants it, and to treat all customers equitably. As Parkhill(1966) points out, the kinds of industries regarded as public utilities vary over time according to changes in technical, economic, and political conditions. Just how the public interest is defined depends in large measure on prevailing social attitudes.

The case for treating computer networks as public utilities is based on projections of their likely social role in the future, and the presumed necessity of monopolistic practices. Parkhill(1966) observes that public utilities share in certain common features which argue strongly for monopoly status: high fixed capital, a centralized supply service, variable service demands, and a capacity which far exceeds average service loads. Moreover, the obligation to honor all demands for service necessitates the maintenance of substantial reserve capacities. These factors, coupled with the economies made possible by large-scale operation, serve to justify the granting of special privileges in order to serve the public interest. Although experience is limited, it appears likely that computer networks will exhibit the characteristics of existing public utilities.

Farber(1972, p. 36) characterizes a computer network as "an interconnected set of dependent or independent computer systems which communicate with each other in order to share certain resources such as programs or data, and/or for load sharing and reliability reasons."[3] Licklider(1970, p. 7) stresses the general-purpose multiple-access character of the computer systems. "In such networks, the computers will talk with one another, and people will talk with the computers— and through the computers with one another— and will be able to use procedures and data stored at any node in the country or, eventually, in the world." Many technical problems remain to be solved before large-scale computer networks become commercially practicable, but there is no doubt that solutions will be forthcoming in the near future. Thus the questions of control and regulation associated with the public utility concept are real and immediate.

The ability to share resources is perhaps the most powerful feature of computer networks. This ability amplifies the social importance of remote access to computing facilities. Time-sharing services may be seen to impinge on the public interest, but computer networks will be of incomparably greater significance. The existence of databanks, for example, poses serious problems for insuring data confidentiality, and protecting individual privacy. These problems will be compounded by the advent of networks in which many databanks may become accessible to a user. In a civilization predicated on continual technological change, it is hazardous to predict the future. Nevertheless, one risks little in projecting a central role for computer utilities in determining the shape of social institutions during the next few decades.

Computer utilities have been made possible by advances in data communications, message-switching technology, and the elaboration of remote-access time-sharing systems.[4] Digital communications equipment for transmission of computer-usable data came into existence in the mid 1950's. Since that time, systems have been designed which permit computer to computer communication; and facilities for handling data communications terminals have been developed. Digital communication has become especially important in connection with time-sharing systems. The successful realization of remote access to a central computing facility is perhaps the most significant development on the road to computer utilities. Remote access to computing power and other resources by a large population of users is essential to the applications envisioned for computer networks.

In response to the growing need for digital communications services, data transmission facilities have been improved and new common carriers have come into being. Dunlop(1970) suggests that the establishment of special-service common carriers providing microwave links between cities may signal the birth of a major inter-urban communications network. In conjunction with the resources of Community Antenna Television (CATV), this "could provide a powerful alternative to Bell system facilities, especially for high-speed data transmission." A computer utility may be as near as one's television set.

The successful operation of time-sharing services is paving the way for commercial computer networks. These services are based on technological developments which began in the early 1950's. "[S]pecial purpose computer utilities of a rudimentary type, but capable of providing simultaneous service of a limited sort to multiple remotely located users, have long been in use." (Parkhill, 1966, p.53). Notable early achievements include a primitive airline reservation system in use in 1952, and the highly influential Semi Automatic Ground Environment (SAGE) system developed during the late 1950's for the U.S. Air Force.

Time-sharing services are of two main types. One provides computer time to users at remote locations. The user typically designs and maintains his own programs, which are supplemented by a system library of general-purpose routines. Programs are run through terminals usually on the user's premises. The second type provides specialized functional or industry oriented services. Examples include hotel and airline reservation systems, stock-quotation systems, services for real estate property management, doctor's and dentist's billing services, order entry and invoicing systems, text editing, and message-transfer and information-retrieval systems. In all of these cases, the user has only a limited capability to modify the programs used and the services provided.

Specialized time-sharing operations usually have more customers than those providing remote computational services. Both of these applications are helping to create a favorable climate for the growth of computer networks.

2. Computer Network Development

Several computer networks are currently in operation, and many more are under construction or being planned. The technology is no longer experimental, and most industrialized countries are participating in the development. International concern over the establishment of standards for data transmission gives some indication of the advanced state of network implementation. In order to place the discussion of social issues in perspective, we will examine the general features of computer networks, and describe selected systems. Details will be kept to a minimum, but some technical considerations are unavoidable, since our main purpose here is to assess the prospects for the creation of universally accessible computer utilities.

Networks can be differentiated in terms of the computational services they provide and their communications facilities.[5] The computers attached to a network in a computational capacity are known as "hosts" to distinguish them from machines whose exclusive function is in support of communications. If the host computers are all of similar type, the network composition is said to be homogeneous; otherwise, it is heterogeneous. This is an important distinction since the latter case entails a number of technical problems such as data conversion between computers and software compatibility. The sites on a network are called nodes, and the structure formed by their interconnections may be centralized or distributed. In the centralized arrangement all the computers are linked together through one central site, whereas interconnections in a distributed network may be direct or through intermediate sites.

The communications part of a network consists of data transmission facilities, such as telephone lines, coaxial cables, microwave or satellite links, and computers for interface processing. Transmission may be analog or digital. In the analog case, a modulator-demodulator (modem) is required at each end. The critical parameters of communications channels are maximum transmission rate, error and delay characteristics, and possible directional limitations. Transmission rate requirements are governed by the type of equipment involved in the communication.

Slow-speed teletypewriter terminals can be supported by a channel rate of 60 to 100 bits per second, whereas high-speed transmission between computers may involve rates in the tens of thousands of bits per second.

One of the major innovations introduced in network communications is the concept of packet switching. In this mode of transmission, messages are broken up into small bundles called packets. Each packet carries information specifying its identity and destination address. This procedure allows for independent transmission of the packets through the system as communication lines become available, thus providing a means for optimizing the utilization of resources. The scheduling and routing algorithms required to handle this type of transmission bear some resemblance to the operations of postal services.

Farber(1972) reviews the characteristics of several computer networks developed in the United States. The most important example, both from a technical point of view and in terms of large-scale commercial possibilities, is the ARPA Network designed under the auspices of the Advanced Research Projects Agency of the Department of Defense. This network, which pioneered in the development of packet switching, links (as of 1972) computing installations at 23 sites. The host computers vary from a Digital Equipment Corporation PDP-11 to the University of Illinois' Illiac IV. The geographical range of this heterogeneous, distributed network is continental in scope, and the principal transmission medium consists of leased telephone lines. The communication system is message oriented and operates on a store-and-forward basis, i.e., messages, which may be decomposed into packets, are stored at intermediate points as they progress through the system toward their destination. Mounting pressure for wider participation from universities, government agencies, and other organizations interested in joining the ARPA network testifies to its success.

Control Data Corporation's Cybernet is an example of a commercially operated network offering general computation services to its users. This is a heterogeneous, distributed network linking 36 of CDC's data centers throughout the United States. The TSS network developed by IBM in cooperation with some of its model 360/67 customers also has a wide geographical range, although it is an experimental system. The homogeneous character of this network allows for program and data interchange among the host computers. More notable is the fact that standard hardware is used so that as Farber(1972) notes a copy of this network could in principle be purchased from any IBM salesman.

Several regional and local networks have also been developed. The MERIT Network (Michigan Educational Research Information Triad) is a heterogeneous, distributed system linking the computing centers at three major universities in the state of Michigan for the purpose of sharing resources in an educational computing environment. A similar educational computing alliance was formed among three universities in North Carolina in 1966. The TUCC Network (Triangle Universities Computation Center) is a relatively simple centralized arrangement consisting of homogeneous computers. Lawrence Berkeley Laboratory's Octopus system is an elaborate network connecting several different computers on the Laboratory's premises. Another local network, of an experimental nature (DCS, the Distributed Computer System) is being developed at the University of California at Irvine.

Computer networks in various stages of design and implementation are to be found in Europe and Japan as well as in North America.[6] The National Physical Laboratory (NPL) in Great Britain, which implemented a local packet-switched network, was an early contributor to the technology. In France, the government-sponsored CYCLADES network with its packet-switched communications subnet CIGALE, will link five major installations and is expected to provide information resources for central government administration. Data-transmissions facilities capable of supporting computer networks are being installed in most European countries, and an international network (EIN, the European Information Network) is currently being planned. A system similar to the ARPA Network, linking university computing centers across Canada (CANUNET, the Canadian University Network) is also on the drawing boards. In Japan a large-scale computer network capable of furnishing computer services on a nationwide basis is under consideration.

As suggested earlier, networks have several important advantages over isolated computer services. Work loads can be distributed among the computers of the network so as to achieve more efficient utilization of available resources and greater service reliability. Although this capability is not currently operational in all networks, it can in principle be added. A feature which is universal is program sharing. Data can be transmitted to a host computer which contains a particular program. The converse, data sharing, is also possible. This facility is useful in cases where it is more economical to ship the program to the location of the data. Some networks allow for dynamic file access, which enables a user to access data sets at different locations as if they were local. This feature may prove especially important for the integration of regional databanks.

The networks constructed to date reveal a multiplicity of service objectives.[7] Homogeneous systems are particularly well suited for resource sharing since data conversion problems do not arise. Some networks may limit access to a restricted class of users for economic, technical, or organizational reasons. This situation could arise where data security is a paramount issue such as in military or law enforcement applications. A different service criterion operates in cases where high-speed data transmission facilities are required for handling massive volumes of data. Applications involving production programs for payroll or other accounting operations have such a requirement. It is possible to imagine a national computer network which encompasses various subnets designed to meet these special objectives. Although the interconnection of different networks poses serious problems for resource management, the basic technology of network design is a reality, and we are not likely to escape its influence.

3. The Computer as Social Resource

The technological feasibility of computer utilities has served to transform the computer from an instrument for specific commercial and governmental applications into a global social resource. What we have seen so far is merely a preview of dramatic events to come. Technology was not invented in the modern world; it is a component of every social order and therefore impinges on the individual no matter what form it takes. A society's peculiar commitment to technology defines its distinctive character in a particular culture. Transportation and communication, for example, are basic social functions which play a role among primitive groups as well as advanced industrial societies. Before the railroad and the telegraph, these functions were largely local in character, in the sense that disruptions or failures had limited consequences for society as a whole. Now that the integrity of our society is dependent upon transportation and communication, they are no longer transparent. Herein lies the essential meaning of social resource.

We are in the process of cultivating a new dependence on technology. In spite of the many uses of the computer and the importance of the associated industry, one is inclined to agree with Weizenbaum's(1972) assessment of the computer's social effects. The most far-reaching consequences are of an indirect character; the main impact inheres in the potentiality for future exploitation of the computer as a social resource. This is a critical juncture because we are still free to choose. We can rush headlong into the development of computer utilities, or we can restrict that development.[8] The first step in a rational analysis of the issue is a careful examination of putative need and expected benefits.

The principal reason given to justify the development of computer utilities is the growing complexity of society. This complexity manifests itself in many forms. Increasing population and social diversity result in prodigious growth of social transactions. Early computer applications in banking reflect this pressure of numbers. Fano(1972) observes that check handling by computer was pioneered in the 1950's by the Bank of America because it was believed that eventually "manual handling of checks would have required the entire adult population of California." The computer's penetration of business and government was in response to the same need to process a mounting volume of transactions. But the need for computers is seen to transcend their function as mere electronic bookkeepers.

Complexity, as evidenced by diversity, specialization and interdependency, creates problems of management and control. As the individual becomes less self sufficient, society assumes the obligation of providing for more and more of his basic needs. Social services proliferate and become formalized functions of government. In most industrialized countries education, health-care and social security are public concerns. The gargantuan administrative tasks associated with these activities necessitate the use of computers. In addition to the provision of social services, there is the parallel need for the formal exercise of social authority. Law enforcement too requires computers. Information is the life blood of bureaucracy, and increasing dependence on formal organizations renders bureaucracy socially indispensable.

The mere fact that information is a vital element in the operations of industry, social services and other areas of government administration does not adequately account for the trend towards the development of computer utilities. Conceivably, independent computer applications might be sufficient to satisfy administrative requirements for information-processing. The pervasive need for information and computer services suggests the desirability of sharing resources— programs as well as data. One of the reasons for this is cost. Several different organizations may require the same data. Most government agencies, for example, have some need for demographic and economic material such as statistics dealing with population and income distribution. The cost of collecting and processing this information is considerable, and unnecessary duplications of programs could also be reduced by making computing services available on a shared basis.

Although cost reductions may be the force behind commercial exploitation of computer-communications, some observers see the survival of society as the real issue. Fano(1972) expresses this belief by asserting that "society may well crack under the weight of its own complexity" unless we are successful in extending the capabilities of the human mind through the development of a large-scale computer-communication network. Human resources are believed to be inadequate to the task of managing complexity. Computer utilities are essential for mass production of services, just as power utilities and transportation systems are required to support mass production of goods. Individuals as well as organizations must have access to information-processing facilities in order to function effectively.

The underlying rationale for this position stems from the belief that information utilities are the only means to facilitate informed decision-making under the demanding conditions of contemporary life. This applies to all sectors and strata of society. Large organizations must deal with a bewildering complexity of interacting variables. Day-to-day operations no less than long-range planning require sophisticated analytical techniques for processing mountains of data. The intuition of experienced managers no longer suffices for the problems faced by industry and government. Rapidly changing circumstances present comparable difficulties in every day life. Individuals must cope with technological change at work, and increasingly more complicated political issues. Conventional modes of education and information dissemination are believed to be inadequate for these tasks and responsibilities. The survival of democratic institutions may be at stake.

Nothing short of Licklider's "procognitive systems" will do, and for such an intellectual tool to be effective we must have information utilities.[9] Through the medium of universally accessible computer networks, managers, officials and ordinary citizens will be able to obtain the information and services essential to their work and for effective participation in the political process. Presumably the vast resources made available to the community at large will contribute to more informed decision-making, and thus lead to the perfection of our institutions, and the realization of a more satisfying form of existence.

The bridge to the future may be completed before most people are aware that it has been started. As indicated in the previous section, computer networks have reached the stage of commercial feasibility. Data communication facilities are extensive and becoming more so. Cable TV could provide the means for introducing two-way communication terminals in the home. Parker(1970) points out that the first step in this direction might involve marketing a device to convert ordinary television sets into cathode-ray-tube display terminals. The success of time-sharing services is enough to suggest that people could be induced to buy such adapters. Services could expand gradually, beginning with computer-based games and household computation, and later extending to computer-assisted instruction packages and library services. It is likely that in the initial stages, only the upper middle classes would be affected. No doubt there are potential customers for stock market and financial information services. But eventually, reduced costs, a broader range of offerings, and aggressive marketing might make the home terminal as commonplace as the ubiquitous television set itself.

The home terminal is the chief symbol of the coming information utility. It signifies anticipated acceptance of the technology's inevitability. The question of desirability of the underlying commitment is too diffuse to enter into here, so we confine the discussion to consideration of projected benefits.[10] The contributions to be expected from computer utilities encompass all real and imagined computer applications. The Canadian Computer/Communication Task Force summarizes the state of affairs.

> Computer/Communication services of the future may be universally accessible from terminals in offices, factories or even homes. Consolidation of computer and communications facilities, and of data stored in public databanks, and the ready availability of common application programs in an integrated system would provide ... universal accessibility at a fraction of today's costs through the shared use of common resources. Conceptually, this could make universal access economically feasible and could promote the multiplicity of services required. (Communications Canada, 1972a, p. 8)[3]

Armer(1966) and others enumerate this multiplicity of services in visions of an electronic future. Straightforward extensions of existing time-sharing services are likely to be first on the agenda. Financial transactions will be conducted by means of an electronic cash and credit system with terminals in retail outlets and communication links to the banks, making possible an instantaneous transfer of funds from one account to another. Industries with extensive client transactions will offer greatly improved services. Insurance companies, for example, will have terminals in branch offices which are connected by a communications network to computer systems in the home office, thus providing immediate access to customer files.

Computer utilities may revolutionize the nature of publishing. At first the network capability might be used for periodic updating of printed texts and documents. In the long-run, electronic publishing via home terminals might replace the printed word as the principal source of information. Health-care will be improved by the dissemination of current knowledge, and the maintenance of files containing medical histories. The goal of continual education could be realized through computer-based instruction programs developed for home use.

Perhaps the most significant contribution lies in the area of government operations. Administration will become more effective through the increased availability of accurate information and the pooled resources of many different agencies. Moreover, the possibility of public participation through electronic opinion polling or other means could make government more responsive to the ordinary citizen. Law enforcement will also be improved by the ability to utilize information located at different points in computer networks. As in some time-sharing systems currently used by police forces, real-time access to databanks containing files on suspected or convicted criminals would facilitate the apprehension of law-breakers. This unsystematic catalogue of possibilities is offered simply to give some idea of current thinking. It requires only a little imagination to continue the list *ad nauseum*.

4. The Coming Financial Computer Utility

The special case of the financial computer utility furnishes an instructive example of the issues associated with computer utilities in general. Electronic funds transfer would constitute a natural extension of existing financial services; the requisite technology is currently available, and economic feasibility is just around the corner. The need for such a system is evidenced by the phenomenal growth of financial transactions. Demand deposit accounts in the

United States have grown from 60 million in 1960 to about 78 million in 1970; the number of checks processed yearly has increased from 12 billion to approximately 24 billion in the same period (Novick and Levin, 1971). The manpower and capital resources committed to processing all that paper are enormous. Although the main attraction of electronic funds transfer lies in expected cost reductions, the convenience afforded by a universal credit card scheme is also a strong incentive for development.

Charles Block gives a realistic appraisal of what to expect in this decade.

> [T]he 70's may see emergence of 2 interbank systems: a payment mechanism to more fully support credit and debit flows, and a security mechanism system for handling investment data flows between banks, brokers, and stock exchanges. ... We may see some payment subsystems; some may be paperless, a few may be instantaneous, but none will be universal to the extent of supplanting cash or checks (Bemer, 1971, p. 157).[12]

Evidently, the transition to the cashless society will not occur overnight. Current practices are likely to be extended gradually. Preauthorized loan-payment plans will beget automatic payment arrangements in selected businesses. The payroll check may disappear as industry adopts automatic transfer schemes, and bill paying services for individuals may become widespread.

Although the basic technology needed to support computer-based funds transfer and credit verification exists in principle, certain refinements are still required.[13] In addition to low-cost, reliable, terminal devices, centralized financial-information files, and a large-scale data-communications network, a secure mechanism for customer identification must be developed. In order to avoid delays in transactions, an identification scheme would have to be fully automatic. Machine readable cards similar to those currently in use might be considered, but the possibilities of fraud pose thorny problems. Voice prints may provide a more acceptable alternative in the long-run. For those of us with "nothing to hide" this might be viewed as a small sacrifice of personal autonomy for the convenience of an efficient payment system.

As in all commercial ventures, the incentive for development is profit. Despite their reputedly conservative character, financial institutions have been pioneers in the introduction of computer technology. The impulse to exploit potentially lucrative markets is clearly more powerful than the inhibiting influences of traditional business practices. Electronic funds-transfer systems in conjunction with credit-card operations offer many opportunities for profitable ventures. Payment and credit services, securities transactions and other extensions of familiar services are the obvious examples. The existence of centralized financial files might also encourage the growth of investment management programs for individuals, as well as applications not yet imagined.

The attractive commercial possibilities of expanded services will no doubt lead to keen competition over the introduction of financial computer utilities. Anderson, *et al.* (1966) identify several groups with a natural stake in this development. First, of course, are the commercial banks whose activities and experience place them in a central position. Other financial institutions may also figure prominently. Credit bureaus have an interest in protecting their information files and retaining their clients. The national operations of finance companies coupled with their considerable experience in the consumer credit field argue strongly for their participation in a credit scheme. Retailers too have a strong interest in credit financing, and national associations could bargain effectively with financial institutions. Possible development arrangements are further complicated by the essential participation of communications companies and manufacturers of computers and data-processing equipment. The latter, in particular, might be tempted to bid for part of the service market as an extension of equipment sales.

The importance of the question of participation in the development of a financial computer utility goes beyond the prospects for sharing in a profitable market. Control of funds transfer and credit operations is of vital concern to society at large. A monopoly or dominant interest would confer considerable power on the holder, and would almost certainly require strict government regulation. In fact one might argue that it would be desirable for the federal government to assume control from the start. Through the federal reserve system and treasury operations, the federal government is already deeply involved in banking and funds transfer. Moreover, many other agencies of government would naturally play an important part in any financial utility. The public interest might best be served by a government-operated system which would eliminate the problem of a private monopoly, and encourage improvements in economic planning.

The latter issue presents interesting possiblities. Centralized financial-information files in government hands could provide the means for fine tuning the economy. More precise data on monetary and fiscal conditions would allow for more responsive government action. Tax collection might eventually be accomplished automatically, and revenue forecasting could be greatly improved. A universal identification scheme would make tax evasion more difficult, and would provide government authorities with valuable information on individual and business activities. In principle , it would be possible to detect changes in consumer spending, and to monitor the vital signs of economic activity on a day-to-day basis.

Electronic funds transfer will of course create some problems. The elimination of processing delays would change the character of financial operations. Individuals as well as large organizations often rely on floating assets, funds committed but not yet transfered, to cover payments. Also, the use of checks currently allows for second thoughts in financial transactions, since it is possible. to stop payment once a check has been issued. On the other hand, some sort of delay mechanism could be incorporated into an automatic transfer system. Another class of problems might arise from the elaboration of the credit-card mode of payment. Financial irresponsibility in the form of a credit spree might accompany the generalized use of credit cards. But these are minor issues in comparison with the possible impact on individual privacy and the opportunities for political control.

No matter what arrangements are made for development, ownership, and regulation, the existence of a financial computer utility will result in the consolidation of private information about individuals. A computer-based funds transfer system would provide the means for recording a person's movements, the organizations he belongs to or supports, the material he reads, his amusements and patterns of consumption. The amount of information available would depend on the extent to which automatic funds transfer replaces cash or other non-accountable forms of exchange. Since for most law-abiding citizens, convenience is next to godliness, cash would probably become extinct in short order. Privacy safeguards will almost certainly be incorporated in any system with such capabilities for collecting personal data. The question is whether or not safeguards can be effective against society's occasional determination to ignore them.

5. Computer Utilities and the Public Interest

The example of electronic funds-transfer systems reveals many of the problematic issues associated with computer utilities. As often happens, public debate rages after the fact. Primitive specimens of the information utility have already materialized in the form of time-sharing services and data communications networks. Just what sort of creature will survive to maturity remains to be seen, but the broad outlines of its development are now coming into focus. Although computer networks may ultimately provide the technological substratum, the evolution of information utilities depends on many factors and is proceeding in parallel with the growth of these sophisticated systems. In this concluding section, we will examine the regulatory context of the emerging information utility, and consider its relation to the public interest.

The impetus for introducing computer-communication systems stems mainly from economic opportunity. Social need is a precondition, but it is not sufficient to stimulate investment. As noted before, the commercial success of computer applications, particularly time-sharing services, has proven the opportunities for profitable exploitation of the apparent social need for computer-communications. The leading actors in this drama of technological innovation are the computer-equipment manufacturers, service bureaus and software houses, computer-based information services such as credit inquiry and stock market quotations, and common carrier communications services (Kestenbaum, 1970). The diversity of experience and interest of the participants is reflected in the many facets of the development of computer utilities, which ranges from the construction of microwave links between cities and the design of communications terminals to the crystallization of new markets for computer-based services.

The social importance of computer utilities leads one to expect some form of government regulation. Since the evolution of the technology is a piecemeal affair, the elaboration of regulatory mechanisms follows no master plan. Kestenbaum(1970) describes a regulatory spectrum which encompasses the different circumstances of the participants in the emerging information utilities. Comprehensive regulatory structures define one end of the spectrum. Such structures apply to common carrier services. Typically, a government agency is created to monitor the activities of the industry, and has the power to control the entry of new firms, to set rates and profit levels, and to supervise practices and conditions of service. The middle of the spectrum is occupied by partial systems of regulation. An example of this type of government supervision is the broadcasting industry. In this case, entry and mergers are regulated, but there is no control over rates. Moreover, most service conditions are determined by the industry.

The absence of explicit government regulation defines the other end of the spectrum. This arrangement is characteristic of the computer-manufacturing industry, data-processing services and other non-communications areas of information utilities. Although there may be no explicit controls, this does not mean that government exercises no influence. Government expenditures and antitrust activity act as implicit regulatory mechanisms. Apart from government controls, there are private constraints which limit and shape development. Economic conditions are quite effective in this way. High entry costs, such as obtain in the newspaper industry, inhibit the growth of new companies. On the other hand, the lure of economic gain acts as a powerful incentive to offer particular services. Regulation interacts with these private constraints and serves to modify the effects of economic conditions.

Kestenbaum(1970) observes that a comprehensive regulatory system for computer utilities is unlikely. However, limited controls are being considered to deal with specific problems. It may be desirable, for example, to regard certain information utilities as common carriers, depending on the nature of their communications operations. Monopolistic practices constitute another area for regulation, but this can probably be handled under existing laws. Questions of security and confidentiality may also lead to regulatory action. The need to protect sensitive information such as trade secrets is a particularly important area.

The regulatory context for information utilities is dominated by economic considerations. Political problems are either too remote or ill-understood. This is especially evident in recent changes in policies regarding the communications industry. Impediments to the growth of information utilities are being removed. Kestenbaum(1970) observes that regulatory policy governing "attachments, interconnection, line sharing, specialized data carriers, and other issues" is giving way to the emerging information utilities. This encouragement of growth is further evidenced by a favorable attitude toward CATV and its potential applications in computer utility services.

The most widely cited non-economic issue is the possible effects of databanks on individual privacy. Since this problem will be treated at length in Chapter 9, we will focus here on some of the broader questions raised by the existence of computer utilities. The history of the modern period reveals a pronounced trend toward the centralization of state power.[14] Like transportation and communication systems, computer utilities place at the disposal of government an instrument capable of sustaining and accelerating that trend. The new technology is claimed to be the child of growing social complexity, which means that the tool is needed by governments to ward off chaos. But it is also believed that centralization of power is not a necessary consequence of computer technology. The possibility exists for using computer information utilities to revitalize the political process.

Fano(1968) argues that effective utilization of information is the only means of safeguarding democratic institutions.

> Perhaps the primary reason why we have to resort to hierarchical control in human organizations is that spontaneous coordination of activities would require more effective information flow than can be achieved today. (Fano, 1968, p. 46)

According to this view, a society with better means for handling and disseminating information would be able to tolerate more freedom and diversity. Of course, there is no *a priori* reason to suppose otherwise, but history is filled with discarded logical possibilities. The record of how technology has actually been used in the modern world does not support Fano's supposition. In principle, transportation and communication might have been expected to contribute to a broadening of human experience, and greater tolerance for different customs and beliefs. Instead, these technologies have served to promote the consolidation of power in the nation state, and a concomitant homogenization of culture. The ability to travel with ease on a global scale and communicate across great distances has not led to increased understanding or greater compassion. There is no evidence to suggest that international tensions have been lowered as a consequence of increased information flow. The dominant impulses articulated in our information rich society are those of the Ugly American or the Ugly National of whatever country. Differences in human circumstances are to be leveled, or observed with morbid curiosity.

The problems of human interaction cannot be reduced to information flow, nor can the shortcomings of existing social arrangements be attributed to imperfections in our instruments of communication. Is there any reason to believe that a two-way terminal in the home would materially alter an individual's response to television broadcasts showing scenes of violence or human misery? The mere fact of having access to information does not create the disposition to act appropriately. Information is not a substitute for human experience. The potentialities of information utilities for promoting free exchange of ideas so as to effect "spontaneous coordination of activities" must be viewed in the same historical context which shaped the role of transportation and communication in the present. It is purely wishful thinking to suppose that improved information flow will result in spontaneous efforts to resolve conflict and create more responsive social environments. The historical evidence points to further concentration of power.

Information is necessary for rational decision-making and conflict resolution, but it is certainly not sufficient. It seems doubtful that the kinds of experience and knowledge people require for achieving harmonious social interaction can be provided by an information utility, no matter how sophisticated. The various forms of human experience are not intertranslatable, and knowledge is selective: facts are not given *a priori*, "the map is not the territory." There are many alternative models of the "real world," each reflecting a particular set of biases. A conflict of interest may stem from different values, rather than ignorance of so-called facts.

Inasmuch as the facts chosen to represent a situation reflect the observer's model of reality, the control of information dissemination may serve as a powerful propogandistic tool. This problem is ignored in Fano's analysis. Sackman(1968, 1970), too, appeals to the constructive possiblities of real-time information systems, without taking into account the political context in which the technology is introduced. The pragmatist traditions of American philosophy, especially the work of John Dewey, provide the basis for Sackman's discussion.

> We take then our point of departure from the objective fact that human acts have consequences upon others, that some of these consequences are perceived, and that their perception leads to subsequent effort to control action so as to secure some consequences and avoid others.(Dewey, 1927, p. 12)

Information utilities could provide the means for realizing the free social inquiry and communication which is central to Dewey's political philosophy. But Dewey(1927, p.182) also observed that "the smoothest road to control of political conduct is by control of opinion." In the absence of the will to define itself, the public is bound to remain a creature of political power, comforted and cajoled by its mechanical intelligence.

---

[1] A contrary position is stated by Wilkes(1968, p. 74).
[2] See Parkhill(1966, Chapter 7) for a more detailed discussion of these issues.

[3] Reprinted with the permission of DATAMATION (R) Copyright 1972 by Technical Publishing Company, Greenwich, Connecticut 06830.

[4] We will discuss some examples of computer networks in Section 8.3.

[5] See Parkhill(1966, Chapters 3 and 4), Bauer(1968), and Dunlop(1970) for detailed treatment of these technological advances.

[6] This discussion of general features is based largely on Farber(1972) and Pyke and Blanc(1973).

[7] See Davies(1974), Allery(1974), Pouzin(1974) and Martel, *et al.*(1974).

[8] See Hootman(1972) for a discussion of the marketing aspects of networks.

[9] Press(1974) argues for a moratorium on the development of computer utilities.

[10] See Chapter 6.

[11] The question of desirability is the focal point of the subsequent chapters of Part III.

[12] Reproduced by permission of Information Canada.

[13] Copyright 1971, Association for Computing Machinery, Inc., reprinted by permission.

[14] Much of the following discussion is based on Anderson, *et al.*(1966).

[15] See Chapter 12.

Chapter 9.
Privacy and Surveillance

The invasion of privacy is perhaps the most controversial issue associated with computer technology. Much of the notoriety derives from the popular theme of computer as sleuth. The use of computer-based information-retrieval systems by law-enforcement agencies is a dramatic illustration of the technology's potential for surveillance. Another area of intense public concern is the record-keeping activities of government and private organizations. Census data, educational records, and credit-agency files, for example, contribute to the exteriorization of our private selves. Some of the more direct consequences of the growth of record-keeping have been widely publicized. People have been denied credit, refused employment, and disqualified for insurance because of errors or misleading information filed in inaccessible databanks. These problems are symptomatic of impending change: the computer is forcing us to reformulate the very distinction between public and private acts.

Privacy has long been recognized as an important component of life in a democratic society. It is essential to the physical, psychological, and spiritual integrity of the individual. At the same time, the general welfare of society requires the imposition of limits on individual behavior. The evolution of social institutions reveals a series of compromises between autonomy and coercion. Naturally, the particular balance achieved depends in part on the instruments available for exercising coercion. Throughout most of human history, these instruments were severely limited in scope. Time and distance thwarted the designs of the most ambitious rulers. The development of technology in the modern period has required the elaboration of institutional safeguards to restrict the growing power of social authority.

The apparent opposition between individual autonomy and social authority is a multifaceted issue. We will concentrate on one aspect of that opposition: the balance between the individual's need for privacy and society's requirements for information. The growing complexity of social administration is accompanied by ever increasing demands for data. Corporations, government agencies, police forces, and schools must gather and store information on individuals in order to support routine operations and policy-planning functions. Computers facilitate these tasks, but their use has consequences beyond improving efficiency.

As noted earlier (see Chapter 2), the gathering of information for administrative purposes became organized on a systematic basis during the eighteenth century. Since the birth of periodic census-taking at the beginning of the nineteenth century, the demand for information has grown relentlessly. Although the problem of insuring some measure of privacy is not entirely new, computer technology poses a new challenge. The moral and legal safeguards which served to provide a precarious balance between individual privacy and social inquiry in the nineteenth century are no longer adequate. By comparison with modern methods of surveillance, the techniques used in the past seem crude and ineffectual. It would appear that technology has swept away the natural barriers against the abuse of power.

The following discussion will focus on the computer's role in redrawing the boundaries between the public and private spheres. After delineating the different types of surveillance, we will examine the philosophical basis for the dichotomy between individual and society. This examination will serve as point of departure for a consideration of the functions of privacy in a democratic society. The main problem we face is the development of effective mechanisms for safeguarding privacy. We will explore some proposals and conclude with a critical analysis of their potentialities.

1. Forms of Surveillance

The urbanized mass society has replaced the neighborly solicitousness of a simpler era with the impersonal concern of large organizations. When conduct is scrutinized in the course of social interaction among the members of a stable community, formal surveillance is largely superfluous. For some people, the anonymity and loneliness of urban living may be mitigated by the existence of records which bear their names. In any case, there is little choice in the matter. The normal functions of society can no longer be discharged without extensive records of people and transactions. These records betoken a form of surveillance of growing importance in contemporary life.

Westin(1967a) distinguishes three types of surveillance: physical, psychological, and information (or data), all three of which have been dramatically altered by modern technology. The physical variety of surveillance has probably received the most attention in recent times. In addition to spies and paid informants, our advanced civilization requires sophisticated gadgets. The widespread use of electronic eavesdropping devices by law enforcement agencies and private interests has led to the enactment of restrictive legislation. In the psychological realm, the twentieth century has produced a whole complement of new surveillance methods. Polygraph devices, one variant of which is the lie detector apparatus, are used routinely in police and personnel work. Testing procedures designed to reveal various attributes of behavior have become standard tools of employers and educators. But technology has much more in store for the future, as the wild imaginings of science fiction take shape in the form of drugs capable of inducing specific states of consciousness, and behavioral monitoring devices which can be implanted in the human body.

The primary concern here is with data surveillance. Like the other types, this one does not involve an entirely new concept; only the methods at our disposal are new. The lack of a real-time storage and retrieval medium forced governments in the past to be highly selective in their efforts to monitor individual activity. Nevertheless, the dossier system elaborated for purposes of controlling political dissidents was far from harmless. The Gestapo used it quite effectively, as did other secret police organizations. Now that the computer has replaced the filing cabinet, the need for selectivity is no longer so acute. Modern governments can avail themselves of vast stores of information documenting the activities of virtually everyone.

The three forms of surveillance are not entirely independent. Improved methods of data surveillance allow for more extensive applications of the other types. The value of information often lies in its potential for future use, so that efficient storage and retrieval systems are at least as important as the means for obtaining the information. A file of individuals who are believed to be potential assassins, for example, might contain material gleaned from bugged conversations and psychological test results. For such information to be effective, it must be possible to process requests in real-time.

Two historical developments contributed to the present state of data surveillance: the growth of record-keeping and improvements in information-processing technology. The need for accurate demographic material for purposes of taxation and general government administration became apparent in the eighteenth century, and since then record keeping has become a permanent feature of governmental activity. The scope of record keeping in our society is staggering. Information on individuals derives from medical records, school reports, IQ test results, psychological profiles, social security and employment histories, files on military service or classified jobs, social records detailing marital status and family make-up, assorted material associated with the use of credit cards (e.g., travel and purchases), and police records. Technological improvements have made this proliferation of record keeping possible, and also have encouraged the trend.

> As information-recording processes have become cheaper and more efficient, the government's appetite for data has intensified and been accompanied by a predilection toward centralization and collation of file material. As if responding to something akin to Parkinson's Law, technological improvements in information-handling capability have been followed by a tendency to engage in more extensive manipulation and analysis of recorded data. This in turn has motivated the collection of data pertaining to a larger number of variables, which results in more personal information being extracted from individuals. The availability of electronic data storage and retrieval has accelerated this pattern in a number of contexts .... (Miller, 1971, p. 21)

The appetite for information is by no means restricted to government. Corporations and other organizations also gather information about individuals. Perhaps the largest demand outside of government comes from social scientists conducting research on individual and group behavior. But the distinction between government and private organizations is less important than the power controlled by the organization itself. Record keeping is primarily an administrative function, and may not constitute surveillance in the strict sense of monitoring individuals' activities. The administrative use of information is transformed into surveillance by the exercise of power, the use of information to influence decisions affecting particular individuals.

The existence of computer-based databanks opens up many possibilities for extensions and refinements of data surveillance methods. Different agencies may pool information resources, or establish centralized files. This means that previously scattered material becomes integrated into comprehensive record-keeping systems. It is not essential to imagine the merging of files, since integration can be accomplished in an appropriately managed network arrangement with resource sharing capabilities. In addition to data consolidation, automated information systems allow for more intensive use of available records. Information may be extracted and processed in many different ways to serve a variety of ends.

It is instructive to differentiate between indirect and direct data surveillance. The former refers to the record-keeping associated with the administration of government services such as health and welfare. The direct variety is linked to police activities. This distinction is more commonly embedded in the division of databanks into statistical and intelligence types. The critical point to observe is that the difference is becoming exceedingly difficult to specify. Statistical information must be labeled with its source, ultimately an individual by name or number, in order for it to be usable in policy studies. Moreover, inter-agency cooperation in "urgent" investigations often compromises the character of information originally collected for use in research or administration.[1]

The most immediate problems created by surveillance concern abuse of power and betrayal of trust. These problems pose a serious challenge to democratic institutions. However, even if it is possible to develop mechanisms to deal with the outward manifestations of these threats, there remain subtle issues which cannot be resolved by fiat or regulation. Extensive record-keeping and surveillance support a homogeneous and uniform vision of reality, with neither boundaries nor frontiers. Global settlement has effectively destroyed the phsyical frontier. Now we are witnessing the disappearance of its psychological counterpart. Our ability to observe, test, and record behavior seems destined to constrain our capacity to dream. Perhaps this is unnecessary, but computers, like domestic animals, too often resemble their masters, and the latter may be encouraged to emulate the Bourbons, forgetting nothing and learning nothing.

2.   Public and Private

The concept of privacy has no fixed universal meaning, and cannot be understood apart from a particular socio-cultural context. An act may be interpreted as having social significance even if it is performed by a solitary individual and has no direct consequences for anyone else. In contemporary society, it is customary to invoke the general welfare to distinguish between public and private behavior. Reading a particular book, riding in an automobile without wearing a seat belt, and obtaining an abortion are examples of acts which many people regard as private matters. But books may influence opinion, treatment of personal injuries requires social resources, and the practice of abortion may be seen to diminish the value of human life. In each case, the community may perceive indirect consequences bearing on its collective interests, and seek to regulate individual behavior.

The increased scope of institutional functions and their associated record-keeping requirements places severe strains on traditional notions of privacy. Public safety, education, health-care, and other basic services have become formal social responsibilities, whose performance necessitates information surveillance. Since computers are instrumental in these tasks, the technology itself is a powerful agent of change. The major problem we face is a redefinition of the respective spheres of public and private behavior which takes into account the central role of computer-based information systems. In order to create appropriate regulatory mechanisms, we must have a clear idea of what constitutes infringements of privacy. The principles which guided the relevant social arrangements in the past may no longer be servicable; our concept of the public welfare has changed, and earlier notions of self-sufficiency and individualism no longer apply. Thus we turn to an examination of the respective limitations of individual action and social authority as a prelude to further discussion of the principles underlying the protection of privacy.

The origins and legitimacy of authority are fundamental problems in social and political philosophy. At the risk of oversimplifying the issues, we will briefly consider some of the more important ideas which have influenced modern conceptions of political justice. Western democratic governments are based on the principle of consent of the governed. This principle is rooted in a philosophical tradition known as the social-contract school which flourished in the seventeenth and eighteenth centuries. A social contract or covenant, entered into by a collection of individuals, was regarded as the primal act in the formation of civil society. Before the social contract, men existed in a state of nature, variously characterized on a scale from intolerable to idyllic. In the process of creating civil society, the parties to the contract renounced certain rights and gave their consent to the establishment of a sovereign authority.

The character of the state of nature and the social contract itself were seen to determine the basic constitution of political power. For Hobbes(1651), the transition to civil society is an inevitable consequence of the intolerable conditions of life in the state of nature. In his view, the social contract confirmed a total alienation of rights. This contrasts with Locke's(1690) version, in which rationality substitutes for inevitability. The state of nature is governed by natural law, and the social contract is a consequence of human reason: individuals acting to secure the benefits of organized society. For Locke, the renunciation of rights is partial, inasmuch as life, liberty, and estate are regarded as inalienable. Moreover, the principle of consent functions on two levels. The legitimacy of government is based on the consent of individuals in the social contract, and the consent of the majority provides the foundation of just laws.

Current attitudes toward privacy owe much to Locke's analysis of political justice. The purpose of government is two-fold: to preserve property (life, liberty, and estate) and to secure the public good. This distinction is basic to the private-public dichotomy which differentiates between individual rights on the one hand, and collective interests on the other. The balance between the two is maintained by a government based on the consent of the governed. "The supreme power cannot take from any man any part of his property without his own consent." (Locke,1690,p. 93). The social contract does not confer arbitrary powers on government, since moral values are antecedent to the creation of political authority. This is at variance with Hobbes' belief that moral values (or justice) derive from government.

Modern conceptions of the state have also been strongly influenced by Rousseau's(1762) attempt to justify social authority. Like Hobbes and Locke, Rousseau hypothesizes a social contract among consenting individuals to account for the existence of government. The renunciation of rights is total, but the supreme authority so endowed is not a sovereign, as for Hobbes, but the whole community whose ideal interests are expressed in the "general will." This latter differs from the "will of all" which is the totality of particular wills, or private interests. Perhaps the most important consequence of Rousseau's notion of the general will is that all rights derive from the community. Insofar as the will of all may be confused with the general will, this observation lends itself to justification for "totalitarian democracy." A government may declare itself the oracle of the general will and thereby become the sole arbiter of social justice.

The notion of social contract as the source of political legitimacy was largely abandoned by nineteenth century philosophers. Our own ideas have been powerfully conditioned by a school of thought known as utilitarianism. Instead of focusing on the origins of government, the utilitarians sought to build a normative and descriptive theory based on the "principle of utility." According to Bentham(1823), "Nature has placed mankind under the governance of two sovereign masters, *pain* and *pleasure*. It is in them alone to point out what we ought to do, as well as to determine what we shall do." (p. 1). Bentham rejected the appeals to the law of nature as sheer caprice, because they were used to justify the powers and prerogatives of conservative and reactionary elements in his own time.

The principle of utility was intended as the foundation of a science of morals and legislation, a logic of the will. As such, it provides a fundamental criterion for judging the legitimacy of actions, and a tool for analyzing human behavior. The utilitarians believe that human conduct is guided by the pursuit of pleasure, but it is not necessarily known what will lead to the greatest pleasure. Thus the development of rules for conduct and decision-making requires knowledge of the consequences of actions. Dewey(1927) incorporates this idea into his doctrine of social inquiry, and in this form it is central to some recent proposals for making effective use of computer utilities.[2]

One of the leading utilitarian thinkers of the nineteenth century was John Stuart Mill, whose analysis (Mill,1859,1879) of the necessary restrictions on individual freedom and social authority serves as the framework for much of contemporary discussion of the privacy question. Mill enunciates a principle, on the basis of which the sphere of individual liberties may be ascertained. The sole end for man, individually or collectively, is self-protection, so that the only purpose for which power can be exercised over individuals is the protection of others. An individual has the right to do anything he likes, so long as it does not harm anyone else. Mill was concerned about the tyranny of society at large, as well as that of government, and identified three main areas of individual liberties: the inward domain of consciousness, liberty of expression, and the freedom to unite. Society's permanent interests require the preservation of individual liberties. Private acts are those in which the individual is sovereign, and in this realm there is no justification for the exercise of social coercion.

Whereas Mill posits a moral principle from which individual freedom flows as a consequence, Dewey(1927) builds a theory of social freedom based on an observation concerning acts and their perceived consequences. Dewey rejects the dichotomy between individual and society. This position suggests the existence of a fluid boundary between private and public. In Mill's view, if the consequences of an action affect only the individual who performs it, the action is private; if others are affected, the action becomes public and thus subject to social control. Dewey's distinction between private and public is based on a refinement of this division.

> Many private acts are social; their consequences contribute to the welfare of the community or affect its status and prospects. In the broad sense any transaction deliberately carried on between two or more persons is social in quality. It is a form of associated behavior and its consequences may influence further associations. (Dewey, 1927, p. 13)

The consequences of acts impinge directly on those engaged in a transaction, and indirectly on others. "The public consists of all those who are affected by the indirect consequences of transactions to such an extent that it is deemed necessary to have those consequences systematically cared for." (Dewey, 1927, p. 15) From Dewey's point of view, the group replaces the individual as the fundamental unit of social analysis.

The concept of social inquiry or experimentation plays a key role in Dewey's theory of the state. Social groups must have the freedom to explore the consequences of actions so as to make decisions in the public interest. But, in addition to avoiding the imposition of restraints on social inquiry, this essential function must be encouraged and reinforced by positive action: the public must provide for the dissemination of the results of social inquiry. A universally accessible computer network would appear to be ideally suited to this purpose. However, the main object of social inquiry is to provide the empirical evidence needed to guide the formation and change of social and political institutions. This requires a certain plasticity in those institutions. Where social differentiation is based on special interest and privilege, the instruments of free information flow may be used to perpetuate the power of a few. In principle, the invasion of privacy is a non-issue in Dewey's conception of society. But just as the will of all may be a perversion of the general will, unrestricted information flow does not necessarily guarantee unrestricted experimentation.

3. Privacy in a Pluralistic Society

Privacy is a property of human social interaction which is most often characterized by some notion of distance between the self and others. In some cases this distance is fixed by custom or tradition, and in others by formal rules. Since privacy assumes so many different cultural forms, it is difficult to devise a satisfactory taxonomy. In Western tradition, three general types are commonly distinguished in relation to property, the person, and information.[3] Privacy in the form of spatial distance or individual territory is linked to property. The home, for example, defines a private realm as well as a shelter. Privacy of the person involves physical and psychic distance. Moral sanctions and legal doctrine support the integrity of the individual by protecting him from physical harrassment and by guaranteeing freedom of movement and expression. The use of information may alter the social or psychic distance between the individual and society. A persons's reputation may be damaged through the revelation of private information, or he may be subject to manipulation by other people. This area of privacy is the one most directly affected by data surveillance.

Whether or not there is a universal human need for privacy is less important than the fact that it plays a vital role in our own culture.[4] As suggested in the previous section, the concept of individual privacy is a central component in theories of political legitimacy. The critical issue here revolves around the functions of privacy in a democratic society. Invasion of privacy through information surveillance raises questions of social control. Information may be used to coerce, intimidate or otherwise manipulate individuals and groups. The problem we face is ultimately political in nature. Studies of different cultures show that man is capable of thriving under conditions which exhibit varying degrees of personal privacy, and it may well be that information technology will spearhead a significant change in our own arrangements. But the real issue is the continued maintenance of the balance between freedom and authority which has shaped our political system. In what follows, we will examine the functions of privacy in individual and group behavior and discuss the question of society's need for information. The focus of our inquiry reflects Mill's concern for placing limits on social authority.

In a widely cited study, Westin(1967b) analyzes the functions served by privacy in a democracy. Four major categories are identified: personal autonomy, emotional release, self-evaluation, and limited and protected communication. Each one reveals an aspect of individual behavior for which the lack of privacy might facilitate social control. Westin says of personal autonomy:

> In democratic societies there is a fundamental belief in the
> uniqueness of the individual, in his basic dignity and worth as a

creature of God and a human being, and in the need to maintain social processes that safeguard his sacred individuality. Psychologists and sociologists have linked the development and maintenance of this sense of individuality to the human need for autonomy— the desire to avoid being manipulated or dominated wholly by others. (Westin, 1967b, p. 33)[5]

Beyond its psychological role, personal autonomy is indispensable to effective participation in the political life of a free society.

The necessity of emotional release is seen to derive from the tensions of life in society and is universally accepted as an important element of physical and mental health. Privacy provides the individual an opportunity to shed the various masks of his social roles and thus to realize emotional release from the tensions and stimulation of daily life. Westin speaks of this aspect of privacy as a "safety-valve" function.

Privacy is also essential to self-evaluation, the integration of experience into a meaningful pattern which articulates the individual personality. Some measure of solitude or withdrawal is necessary for making use of the information which confronts us at every turn, so that plans can be formulated and decisions made. Moreover, reflection on the moral consequences of actions also involves a form of self evaluation for which privacy is generally considered desirable.

Of the fourth function of privacy, limited and protected communication, Westin comments:

The greatest threat to civilized social life would be a situation in which each individual was utterly candid in his communications with others, saying exactly what he knew or felt at all times. The havoc done to interpersonal relations by children, saints, mental patients, and adult "innocents" is legendary. (Westin, 1967b, p. 37)

There are two aspects to limited and protected communication. First, it allows an individual to share confidences with those he trusts— intimate friends and relations on the one hand and professionals such as doctors, lawyers and priests on the other. The second general aspect serves to delimit the contours of mental distance in all types of interpersonal situations. This is especially important in the crowded urban settings in which most people live. It is essential for the individual to restrict communication about himself in order to preserve some measure of psychic integrity.

These four functions of privacy also operate on the level of organizations. Organizational autonomy is just as threatened by violations of privacy as is individual autonomy. Examples range from government security operations to civic organizations advocating controversial ideas. Lack of organizational autonomy would seriously jeopardize the system of checks on governmental power which exists in our society.

Release from public roles corresponds to the emotional release for individuals. Everyone knows that public statements reflect idealized versions of organizational positions. The real bargaining between labor and management, for example, takes place behind closed doors. Similarly, sensitive diplomatic negotiations involve practical compromises which could not be openly admitted.

Organizations also need privacy to plan their actions, i.e., evaluative periods for decision-making. Political parties plan strategy and make policy decisions in closed caucus rooms. Moreover, public officials require privacy in order to consult freely with their staffs. Closely related to privacy for evaluation, is privacy involving protected communications.

> The organization's need to communicate in confidence with its outside advisors and sources of information and to negotiate privately with other organizations corresponds to the individual's need for protected communication. (Westin, 1967b, p. 49)

Bargaining positions are particularly sensitive to premature divulgence of information. The use of carefully planted public releases designed to sabotage negotiations testifies to the importance of this function.

As much as we value individual privacy, we also recognize the social necessity of some forms of information surveillance. The main problem we face is preserving an equilibrium between the two. Westin(1967b) surveys the ways in which Western democracies have resolved this problem. The balance achieved in British society exhibits a bias in favor of privacy. This may be attributed to the relatively high degree of public confidence in social institutions which acts to reduce the necessity for surveillance. The West German situation, on the other hand, reflects an authoritarian bias towards surveillance. The United States falls somewhere in between these poles. American society reveals a fundamental tension between social egalitarianism and individualism. Infringements on privacy are resented, but at the same time the leveling influences in American life promote acceptance of information surveillance.

Society's right to discovery has been reinforced during the past century and a half with the expansion of governmental activities in the sphere of social welfare. The abuses of the industrial revolution led to central government regulation of private business and to its entry into an area formerly occupied largely by charitable groups and local governments. The introduction of social-security schemes and various programs designed to provide for the disabled and the handicapped under centralized administration carried its own rather convincing rationale for collecting and processing information about individuals.

The rapid expansion of government's role in social welfare during the last fifty years has strained our ability to deal with the requisite information. The proposal for a national data center in the United States was aimed at improving the situation. Kaysen(1967) points to the inadequacies of an overly decentralized statistical system. Before the introduction of computers, the characteristic method of presenting information was to publish summaries of data. Kaysen contends that summaries substitute worse for better information, and less for more refined information. These shortcomings are seen to limit the precision of the policy making process, since the less informed we are, the worse will be our decisions. Thus, the principal advantage of a national data center would be the gain in our ability to handle the requirements of informed decision-making. Decentralized organization also entails unnecessary duplication of effort in that information on related subjects is collected by different agencies. It goes without saying that greater efficiency of information-handling would also be expected.

The balance between privacy and social inquiry may be upset in favor of the latter merely by default. Michael(1964) argues that the wide acceptance of ability as the basis of success leads to acquiescence in testing procedures and the interpretation of private information. Moreover, there are enormous pressures from personnel workers, managers, and educators for information about the private person as well as efforts to gain access to existing stores of data. Convenience and creature comforts seem to exercise great sway over us. We appear willing to sacrifice our privacy for credit cards and mobility. The most disturbing aspect of the problem of achieving balance is the apparent remoteness of the consequences of each small incursion into our private selves. The ultimate problem of the distribution of power in society seems ever so remote from the question of filling out a credit card application. Miller(1971, p. 207) indicates one of the greatest dangers we now face.

> Beyond the dangers to particular individuals, the unregulated computerization of personal information may have a numbing effect on the value of privacy as a societal norm. As is true of

electronic surveillance, the climate or atmosphere of suspicion created by an accumulation of invasion of privacy is of far greater concern than the direct harm caused by the incidents themselves.

4.   Formal Mechanisms for Protecting Privacy

The most widely held view on the question of balancing society's need for information against the requirements of individual privacy is a compromise position. The dangers of expanding use of information in society are recognized, but it is felt that through a combination of legislative, regulatory, and technical security measures, these dangers can be minimized and kept in check. In the following discussion we will focus on legislative and regulatory safeguards against the invasion of privacy. The question of system security, providing protection for personal information and insuring against fraudulent use of data-processing facilities, is largely a technical problem and peripheral to our main concern.[6]

Westin(1967a) explores the legal framework for dealing with the problems of information surveillance. Four current weaknesses in American law are identified. First, there is no workable definition of personal information as a precious commodity. The classes of information which are recognized by law all relate to property rights. Proprietary information, corporate records and other business data are well-established notions in legal practice, but information whose significance is not primarily economic has been sadly neglected. A second shortcoming concerns the flow of information in government operations. No comprehensive system for regulating access to, or use of, information in government controlled databanks has been developed. The legal restrictions which apply to income tax records and census data do not protect other material.

The absence of procedures to protect against improper practices in the collection and handling of information constitutes a third area for remedial action. In order to guarantee accuracy and reliability, it is essential to establish guidelines for the collection of information, and its verification. The kinds of information which may be collected, the manner of collection, who has access to it, and how it can be verified or corrected must be specified. The damaging effects of secret files on individuals was amply demonstrated in the early post-war years in connection with loyalty-security investigations. Apart from the need to protect individuals, the public interest requires that information used in administration and policy-planning be as accurate as possible. Finally, the fact that data employed for statistical purposes must be identified with a name or number raises questions about the possible use of databanks for intelligence operations. In order to use data derived from different sources, there must be some means of matching items pertaining to a given individual. The proliferation of databanks in government and large organizations thus poses a serious potential threat to individual privacy.

To cope with these problems, Westin proposes general corrective guidelines for the future. First, it is necessary to establish as a legal principle an individual's right to limit the circulation of personal information about himself.[7] This principle must be accepted as part of a fundamental right to privacy which can only be waived for good cause. A second policy proposal deals with procedures for classifying information in order to facilitate implementation of the first guideline. Information must be distinguished according to the use for which it is intended. Such a scheme which might, for example, differentiate between matters of public record, confidential, or strictly secret information would provide a means for controlling the circulation of data about individuals.

The implications of a right to privacy guaranteeing individual control of personal information have been detailed in several major studies. Westin and Baker(1972) discuss the question of individual access to records, rules for confidentiality and data sharing, and limiting unnecessary data collection. The right to see records about oneself is particularly important for insuring due process. One of the basic problems is learning of the existence of files. Although it may be impractical to require government agencies to notify individuals that information concerning them is on file, some systematic means for discovering what records are being kept is necessary.[8] Westin and Baker(1972) propose that government issue a "Citizen's Guide to Files."

> This Guide to Files would contain a listing for every government agency, specifying the nature and content of each of its files containing information about individuals; the statutory authority for its maintenance; the class and number of persons covered; the type of information contained in it; the uses to which the file is put; whether identified information from the file is shared and, if so, with whom, and under what authority; whether the individual has access to all or part of his record in the file; and similar information. (Westin and Baker, 1972, pp. 362-363).

Knowledge of the existence of records is the first step in the process of gaining access, but such knowledge is useless without the right to inspect those records. Westin and Baker(1972, p. 364) urge "that any record about an individual which is consulted by government officials in the determination of the individual's rights, opportunities, and benefits under a government program should be open to inspection." Records used for intelligence or other purposes would be excluded. Beyond the need to inspect records, the protection of privacy demands a mechanism for challenging the information contained in personal records. "[A]n individual should be given by law a proper succession of remedies for contesting the accuracy, completeness, or propriety of information he finds there." (Westin and Baker, 1972, p. 370)

The elaboration of rules for confidentiality and data sharing is another major area for legal action. In order to protect the private interests of individuals, access to files by third parties must be controlled, and the conditions under which data may be shared strictly regulated. Westin and Baker examine these needs in connection with national welfare-reform proposals. The detailed personal information to be maintained by such a system would provide an attractive source of material for various federal, state, and local officials. Policies governing access would have to be worked out. In addition to records kept by government agencies, there is the problem of policing access to private databanks. Current laws are not sufficient to cope with the pressure on privately held information from investigative agencies such as tax authorities, law enforcement bodies, and legislative committees.

The most problematic aspect of the regulatory approach to privacy concerns the development of policies designed to limit unnecessary data collection. Denying government agencies or large private organizations the right to gather whatever information they please would be like trying to snatch away a bone from a hungry dog. Nevertheless, a few cautious steps have been taken.

> American society has seen the necessity to impose restrictions on organizations which collect information in order to make discriminatory judgments on the basis of religion, race, nationality, and most recently as to sex. When we move beyond these, however, and the civil-liberties claim is made that certain other personal information is not truly relevant to a given decision, the policymaker must decide how he can judge what is a relevant piece of information for a national security investigation, or hearing on credit, parole, scholarships, employment suitability, etc. (Westin and Baker, 1972, p. 374).

The "Code of Fair Information Practice" recommended in a report of the U.S. Department of Health, Education and Welfare (Ware, 1973) echoes the Baker and Westin proposals. Five basic principles serve as points of departure for the Code.

- There must be no personal data record-keeping systems whose very existence is secret.
- There must be a way for an individual to find out what information about him is in a record and how it is used.
- There must be a way for an individual to prevent information about him that was obtained for one purpose from being used or made available for other purposes without his consent.
- There must be a way for an individual to correct or amend a record of identifiable information about him.
- Any organization creating, maintaining, using or disseminating records of identifiable personal data must assure the reliability of the data for their intended use and must take precautions to prevent misuse of the data. (Ware, 1973, pp. xx-xxi)

Regulatory mechanisms proposed by Communications Canada(1972b) combine statutes containing rules governing databank practices with administrative machinery for implementing the rules. The implications of establishing "an independent regulatory tribunal, a surveillance agency, and a complaint mechanism or Ombudsman" are considered.

Some progress in the regulatory area has already been made. Various laws pertaining to the accuracy of credit information have been enacted as well as laws guaranteeing the right of access to credit files. Educational and medical records have also come under the protective umbrella of government regulation. In addition to private databanks, the files of certain government agencies are now subject to statutory controls.[9] Perhaps the most comprehensive regulatory program enacted so far is the Swedish Data Act which became law in 1973.[10] The Act sets up a Data Inspection Board (DIB) which is empowered to issue permits for the establishment and maintenance of personal-information files. Many of the recommendations discussed earlier for protecting privacy are incorporated in the statutory authority of DIB. The purposes for which a databank is intended must be specified in the permit issued by the Data Inspectorate, and directives governing conditions of use, access, disclosure and maintenance must be given. Duties of the keepers of personal records files are also defined in the Act, as well as penalties for improper action. The Swedish experience with this model piece of legislation warrants careful study.

5.   On the Efficacy of Formal Safeguards

The legal-regulatory-security approach to the protection of privacy is based on two beliefs. First, there is the tacit acceptance of the legitimacy of databanks and some forms of data surveillance. This is rooted in the notion that contemporary society is too complex to function without extensive record keeping. The second belief is that our social and political institutions are sufficiently robust to handle the alleged threat to individual privacy. While not minimizing the dangers of information surveillance, Westin and Baker(1972), for example, conclude that computer technology has not yet created the conditions most feared by critics.

> [C]omputer usage has not created the revolutionary new powers of data surveillance predicted by some commentators. Specifically, the great majority of organizations we studied are not, as a result of computerizing their records, collecting or exchanging more information about individuals than they did in the precomputer era. They are not sharing identified information more widely among organizations that did not carry out such exchanges in the precomputer era. And individuals are not receiving less due process in computerized data systems than law and practice mandated in each field of record-keeping when decisions were made using manual files. (Westin and Baker, 1972, p. 341.)

This assessment of the current situation is not particularly surprising. Attitudes and habits which have been sustained by institutional practice for many generations are not likely to change overnight. After all, computer applications began in earnest only twenty-five years ago. Extrapolation from present trends must be guided by historical perspective. Projection of future behavior depends on making appropriate regularity assumptions. Two conflicting tendencies are in evidence. One is the evolution of democratic institutions which have proved capable of preserving a balance between individual freedom and social authority under changing circumstances. The other is the trend toward the centralization of power. Effective safeguards for privacy, and political freedom generally, depend on the acceptance of the rule of law by all segments of society. The greatest uncertainty in forecasting the probable effects of computerized databanks lies in their potential for misuse by centralized bureaucracies.

Of course, there is no solid evidence for supposing that the rule of law will weaken in the future; one must be careful not to exaggerate the role of computer technology as a formative influence in social policy. Nevertheless, it cannot be denied that information-processing systems provide a powerful tool for the exercise of political control. The fact is that the opportunities for abuse of power are magnified by the presence of the tool. This is not to say that anti-democratic practices would disappear in its absence, but that the impact of such practices might be less devastating. That a legitimate government may use its information gathering authority for purposes of political or social control is by no means idle conjecture. The preservation of apartheid in South Africa is a case in point.

> Under a Population Registration Act passed by the South African Parliament in 1970, the government will computerize the record system to maintain apartheid...
>
> Under the registration program, every black African is required to carry a 50-page blue identification document, with information on age, sex, race, citizenship, district in which he normally resides, ethnic group or tribe to which he belongs, permits to leave the country, education, etc. (Lundell, 1971)[11]

The crucial problem we now face is how to protect ourselves from the dangers of arbitrary police action by the state. The United States government did not act under law when it uprooted one-hundred thousand Japanese Americans in 1942 and held them in "relocation centers" until the war was over. In retrospect, it is easy to declare such action illegal, but that is small consolation for the loss of property and personal hardship suffered by the individuals affected. The massive logistical problems occasioned by the relocation program were solved without computers. In this case, information surveillance was not especially important, since the community in question was readily identifiable. The existence of computerized databanks would facilitate similar moves against less homogeneous groups. Legal restraints are not always sufficient to prevent determined governments from violating individual rights. It is not so far-fetched to imagine that a politically troubled democratic regime would exploit a so-called crisis situation to justify promulgating emergency measures, and then use confidential information to round up "undesirable" elements.

According to Lasswell(1965), databanks and information-processing systems appear to have a built-in bias for centralization, concentration, monopoly and regimentation. He cites the tendency to capitalize on economies of scale as one of the underlying reasons. The net effect of our focus on social inquiry is an exaggeration of the attitude of inquiry at the expense of commitment, conviction and argumentation. Thus, preference becomes translated into the need for further information. People get out of the habit of exercising value choices. There is a tendency for society to be run for the benefit of special interest groups. It is questionable whether in fact this tendency can be neutralized or reversed following the formal legalistic approach to safeguarding individual rights. "Such preventive legislation might do some good; but if the great impersonal forces now menacing freedom continue to gather momentum, they cannot do much good for very long."(Huxley, 1958, p. 110) Lasswell's socio-political recommendations suggest needed policy alternatives to bolster the rule of law. Explicit training in commitment is required to promote the willingness to act responsibly, and this cannot be achieved without genuine participation in power sharing. Under such conditions, it might be possible to create a realistic awareness of the threat to privacy posed by data surveillance, and to generate meaningful debate.

[1] We will explore this problem more fully in Chapter 10.
[2] See Chapter 8.
[3] Communications Canada(1972b)
[4] See Westin(1967b) for a discussion of the human need for privacy and its origins in Western culture.
[5] Copyright © 1967 by The Association of the Bar of the City of New York. This and the following passages are reprinted by permission of Atheneum Publications, New York, and The Bodley Head, London.
[6] For a treatment of the problems of system security, see, for example, Hamilton(1972), Parker, Nycum and Oura(1973), Van Tassel(1972), and Weiss (1974).
[7] The question of whether or not certain data should be collected at all will be considered at length in Chapter 10.
[8] U.S. Federal Government files alone account for several billion person-records.
[9] Poage(1975) discusses federal legislation in the United States restricting personal information-gathering, particularly the Fair Credit Reporting Act of 1970, and the recently enacted Privacy Act of 1974. For further material on federal and state laws concerned with data surveillance, see the *Privacy Journal*, Washington, D.C.

[10] See Iverath(1973).
[11] Copyright by Computerworld, Newton, Mass. 02160.

Chapter 10.
Information and the Political Process

Our discussion of surveillance has led us to consider some of the motives for introducing computerized information systems into government. Generally speaking, the basic reason cited by most observers is the growing complexity of society. Modern government administration is responsible for coordinating and controlling economic and social activities, preserving public order, and providing a variety of services for highly mobile populations. On all levels of government, these tasks require the processing of vast quantities of information, for which computers have become an indispensable tool. Beyond their role in data-handling, computer-based information systems are seen as important adjuncts to the decision-making process. In this chapter and the next, we will focus on two complementary aspects of such systems: databanks and systems analysis methods.

The problems of information flow in government are common to all large organizations. Like private corporations, government bureaucracies are hierarchically structured and exhibit a spectrum of problem-solving and decision-making functions ranging from routine administrative tasks to strategic policy formation. Payrolls must be met, resources accounted for, jobs scheduled, policies elaborated, and plans devised for their implementation. But there is one obvious and critical difference between governments and private organizations. Ideally, the former aim to secure the public good, rather than the particular interests of any special group. This distinction is especially important for planning and policy formation. Since the public interest is at stake, the needs and desires of ordinary citizens must somehow be incorporated into the decision-making environment. It is in this area that computer-based information systems may make their most distinctive contribution to government administration.

The development of information systems in government exhibits a pattern familiar from the private sector. Just as management information systems (see Chapter 4) have fallen short of initial expectations, databanks and the systems approach to problem-solving have thus far failed to revolutionize government decision-making. Most computer applications are of the routine data-processing type involving accounting transactions or record-keeping operations within a single agency. The opportunities for resource sharing afforded by databanks have not yet been realized to any appreciable extent. This is partly due to the difficulties inherent in the design of flexible information-storage and retrieval systems, but perhaps more important is the institutional resistance to change. A databank is more than a collection of facts or records; it contains structured information organized to serve the needs of particular classes of users. Effective utilization of databanks calls for reorganization of operations along functional lines. Anticipated cost reductions, resulting from removal of duplication and improvements in the information available to decision-makers, are hindered by the perpetuation of an outmoded division of labor.

These retarding influences on the rational use of information technology in government may also be viewed in a positive light. Resource sharing is not necessarily an unmitigated blessing. The availability of databanks containing personal information on individuals allows for consolidation of files for use by government officials. This capability intensifies the problems caused by data surveillance, and could very well contribute to the centralization of political power. It does not, of course, follow that imperfect information systems and traditional forms of organization should be cultivated as a hedge against the designs of power hungry bureaucrats. What we must aim for is a broader concept of rationality which reflects the long range interests of the public as a whole. We cannot afford to allow the technical requirements of information systems to dictate the form of government organization.

Inasmuch as the information requirements of government decision-makers parallel those of corporate managers, we will focus here on problems which are linked to the political character of public administration. The key issue is the distribution of political power. Information technology may create opportunities for wider participation in decision-making, or it may serve as an instrument of manipulation and coercion. As background to this issue, we will explore the development of databanks in different levels of government, and take a close look at their role in planning and policy formation. Various ways of encouraging citizen participation in government have been suggested. We will discuss some of these possiblities and then examine their potentialities in relation to the structure of government and the needs of public administration.

1. Databanks: Distribution and Variety

Concern over the proliferation of databanks is evidenced by the mounting volume of government reports dealing with the effects of record-keeping on democratic institutions.[1] Databanks are maintained by all levels of government, but are most prominent at the highest level.[2] In the United States, computerized files containing personal information have been created within at least a dozen of the major federal agencies. (Westin and Baker, 1972). Databanks in the Defense Department include non-classified files on several million persons in various programs. The FBI's National Crime Information Center contains files on 95,000 persons on an average day. Forty million names are listed in the master index of the Immigration and Naturalization Service, and 2.6 million persons are on file in the National Driver Register Service of the National Highway Safety Bureau. The centralized computer files of the Social Security Administration contain records on more than 150 million citizens.

In addition to the records on individuals held by government agencies for internal bookkeeping and administration of social services, there are databanks containing statistical information. Wallis'(1971, pp. 61-63) catalogue of the "sources of primary statistical data used by the Federal Government" gives some idea of the scope of statistical reporting in the United States. Material collected by federal agencies derives from observations of respondents, direct measurements (excluding surveillance data), and internal records. Observations of respondents include information on persons and activities drawn from the population-at-large and data on participants in federal programs as well as those subject to government regulation. The population census is a critical source of statistical information on all members of the population; various sample surveys, such as the National Health Survey and Current Population Survey, supplement and complement this material. Eligibility information supplied by recipients of social security benefits and other services furnishes additional data; and, of course, the income tax records of individuals and businesses constitute an extensive store of information. Direct measurements include counts, surveys and experiments generated, for example, by weather reports, customs information, surveys of resources, and results of medical experiments and treatments. The internal records of agencies contribute reports on operations, accounts and audits.

Joint federal-state programs serve as another major source of statistics used by the federal government. Reports on employment, hours worked, earnings, educational statistics, and material derived from vital records are examples of respondent observations. Direct measurements supply data on crop yields, traffic counts, highway statistics, and enumerations of births and deaths. State and loca. summaries provide further information on crime and other social conditions. A third source of material comes from state and local governments: regulatory, law-enforcement and criminal-justice programs, as well as government operations. Examples include statistics on unemployment compensation, registration and licensing of medical personnel and health-care facilities, and state prisons. Private organizations, such as professional and trade associations, unions, and non-profit establishments, also contribute to the supply of federal government statistics.

The databank concept suffers from much the same confusion that attaches to management information systems. There is no general agreement on what constitutes a databank, nor is there a universally accepted classification scheme.[3] A broad distinction is generally drawn between statistical and intelligence (or inquiry) databanks. Roughly speaking, the former refers to information systems designed to provide data for research or policy-planning studies. Intelligence databanks provide dossier type information on individuals for use in administration, regulatory operations, or law enforcement activities. The adminstrative function of intelligence systems is sometimes used to distinguish a separate category of databanks. Ware(1973), for example, classifies records into three categories (administrative, statistical, and intelligence) on the basis of their respective functions in government operations. Administrative data are generated and used in the everyday management of individual transactions. Planning and program evaluation require statistical data; and intelligence records must be kept for purposes of assessing people's character and qualifications.

According to Lenk(1973), databanks are most often characterized as organizationally distinct information repositories, in which data is structured independently of any specific applications so as to serve the needs of a wide variety of users. This conception is seen to be inappropriate on several grounds. First, it implies an artificial separation of data-processing from other aspects of public administration, which obscures the complex organizational structure of information handling systems. Furthermore it is not generally true that databanks are available to a wide variety of users.

As suggested earlier, the changing view of databanks reflects a similar shift in management information systems from the "total systems concept" to database development.

As part of a survey of databanks in government, Westin(1971) presents a typology based on purpose, and organizational location of a databank. Five different kinds are identified. First there is the statistical databank for policy studies which forms an agency with no operating responsibilities to administer, regulate, or prosecute. Its principal function is to provide data for research and policy-planning. Detroit's physical and social databank (Black and Shaw, 1967) and the District of Columbia Real Property Databank are examples of this type.

The second type Westin calls the independent agency (or coordinating) databank. This one is set up to provide data for use by various line agencies. Again it forms an independent organization which has no administrative, regulatory or prosecutive functions. The New York State Identification and Intelligence System (Gallati, 1971) is a notable example. Other criminal information systems of this type, such as the California Criminal Justice Information System, are in operation in various parts of the United States. Another example is the SPEDE databank (System for Processing Educational Data Electronically) introduced by Florida's state Department of Education. A third type of databank is one for general administration. This one is attached to the political executive and is thus far in evidence only in city and county governments. The purpose of such a databank is to serve as the nucleus of a total management information system.

Implicit in Westin's classification scheme is a distinction between the administrative and the policy-planning functions of government. The statistical databank is designed exclusively for policy-planning. The coordinating databank serves both functions. The databank for general administration is designed for the administrative function. The fourth type, single agency or intra-agency databank, is similar to the coordinating databank in that it serves both the administrative and policy-planning functions. However, the intra-agency databank is attached to an executive agency, whereas the coordinating databank forms an independent agency by itself. Examples of the intra-agency type of databank include the U.S. Secret Service's file on dangerous persons who might attempt to assassinate the president, the FBI's National Crime Information Center, and the California Department of Motor Vehicles information system.

The last category of Westin's scheme is the mixed, public-private statistical databank exemplified by the Social Data Bank of the United Planning Organization, a private corporation financed by federal government funds. Although this classification is useful for descriptive purposes for prevailing conditions in the United States, it is not sufficiently refined as an analytical tool. It would be useful to further differentiate the purposes served by databanks and to take into account the way information is shared among different agencies as well as the over-all organization of its use.

It is difficult to overestimate the importance of computerized databanks in government operations. Some indication of the range of databanks in use by the United States government was given above. A report of the Senate's constitutional rights subcommittee(1974) reveals that more than 1.25 billion "pieces of information" about United States citizens have been incorporated into information databanks by 54 federal agencies.

> [A]s Americans entered the post-World War II era, it seemed as though the role of the Three Fates [of Greek mythology] might be reappearing in modern dress. The life thread of each man was now spun in the formal records that gatekeeper organizations began to keep about him at birth. He was measured at each step of his growth according to information woven into these proliferating files. ... The Three Sisters with shuttle and shears had been replaced by the record weaving looms of large organizations. (Westin and Baker, 1972, p. 3)

2. Databanks: Expected Contributions

Databanks by any other name would serve the same essential functions of providing information for government operations. Their ultimate form may not yet be visible, but it is possible nonetheless to analyze the conditions of their evolution as elements of administrative practice. The first question to consider is the putative need for computer-based information systems in public administration. Armer(1966) observes that information has traditionally been organized according to its use. That is to say, information is recorded in a form suitable for use by separate agencies such as law enforcement, welfare, accounting, education, employment, etc. This practice has resulted in an enormous amount of duplication of data files, since several different agencies collect and store the same information for different purposes.

The opportunities for duplication are truly staggering in view of the multiplicity of government agencies and levels of jurisdiction. Armer gives the figure 91,236 for the number of separate political regions within the United States. The need for some mechanism to alleviate the waste of unnecessary duplication is apparent: databanks offer some hope of accomplishing this. Computer-based information systems could reduce the costs of duplication by rationalizing data collection and storage. The development of databanks which store information by person and property, for example, rather than by agency use, would allow for data sharing among many different agencies.

In addition to reducing costs, the interagency sharing which might result from the use of databanks, would give rise to more comprehensive information, thus in principle improving the decision-making process. Presumably, the more comprehensive information would arise from two sources: an agency's ability to spend more to get information— the extra money coming from savings in data-processing; and also, what is more important, a shared databank would make information available that an agency might not previously have known existed at all. In the long-run, these improvements might be expected to yield better and expanded public services.

The existence and spread of databanks became a controversial issue in the mid 1960's with the emergence of proposals for a national data center in the United States.[4] These proposals were embodied in a series of government sponsored reports dealing with the problems of federal statistical services and with the potential contributions of information technology to their solution. The first report (issued by a committee of the Social Science Research Council chaired by Richard Ruggles) pointed to the need for extracting information from existing records in different forms and preserving administrative data for subsequent use. Computers were seen as the key to meeting these needs. The report recommended the establishment of a federal data center to preserve records, provide storage and retrieval facilities, and promote the integration of data from different sources.

This early report was examined by the Office of Statistical Standards of the Bureau of the Budget (with Edgar S. Dunn acting as consultant) from the point of view of implementing its recommendations. Dunn focused on the inter-relationship of records. The federal statistical system was criticized for its failure to furnish adequate mechanisms for integrating elements of data sets.

Such facility is essential for assessing the relationships among independent activities. This inadequacy led Dunn to recommend the formation of a National Data Service Center for the expressed purpose of serving both government and private users of federal statistical data.

The idea of a national data center provoked strong reactions in the press and in Congress, where concern was voiced over potential threats to individual privacy. A highly influential report was issued in this period by the Special Subcommittee on Invasion of Privacy of the Committee on Government Operations, under the chairmanship of Congressman Cornelius E. Gallagher. At the same time, another comprehensive proposal for a national data center was drafted by a committee reporting to the Bureau of the Budget on the question of storage and accessibility of government statistics. This committee, headed by Carl Kaysen, pointed to the need to counter the tendency toward decentralization of statistical files in order to achieve the integration of data required for an effective statistical service.[5] The recommendations of the Kaysen committee built on those of the earlier reports.

The Federal Statistical System has three basic functions; namely, (1) collection, (2) integration and storage in accessible form, and (3) analysis, tabulation, and publication. It is reorganizing the second that offers the most promise. This function is now the least well-performed of the three, and it is the one which is most easily separated out from the present organizational structure. However, it must be done on a substantial scale, and in such a way as to recognize the interaction of this function with the other two. Further, the new organization must not be confined to a merely archival function. If it is defined along the lines suggested below, it offers the best promise, in the judgment of the Committee, for starting the development of the Federal Statistical System toward a more integrated and efficient form.

Accordingly, the committee proposes the creation of a National Data Center.—This Center would be given the responsibility for: (1) assembling in a single facility all large-scale systematic bodies cf demographic, economic, and social data generated by the present data-collection or administrative processes of the Federal Government, (2) integrating the data to the maximum feasible extent, and in such a way as to preserve as much as possible of the original information content of the whole body of records, and (3) providing ready access to the information, within the laws governing disclosure, to all users in the Government and, where appropriate, to qualified users outside the Government on suitable compensatory terms. The Center would be further charged with cooperation with state and local government agencies to assist in providing uniformity in their data bases, and to receive from them, integrated into the federally generated data stock, store, and make accessible, the further information these agencies generate. (Kaysen, 1966, p. 31)

Quite apart from its implications for invasion of privacy, the creation of a national data center would entail many problems and might not provide the quality of service expected. The costs of a comprehensive system for integrating and linking micro records appear much greater than anticipated by proponents of a centralized databank. Hansen(1971) argues that many of the services expected to flow from such a scheme can be provided more effectively and at a lower cost on a sample basis by making use of *ad hoc* record-matching for particular applications. One of the difficulties in operating a large-scale integrated databank arises from the problem of linking records in different files. Even if the records have unique identifiers, such as name and address, they may be given incorrectly. As a result, many comparisons may have to be made in order to insure optimal linking of matching records. As the size of the file increases, so does the cost of linking and the potential for error.

> The additional statistical results that can be achieved by comprehensive linking of federal records would be far less than seems to be anticipated by many who advocate this major development. While the records available to be matched do contain many important items of information, they frequently lack information that is essential to a particular study. Moreover, the desired integration of information can often be more readily accomplished by a sample survey or from the Census, or by record linking as needed for a small sample, or by a combination of these.(Hansen,1971,p. 6)

3.   Urban Information Systems

The outward signs of society's growing complexity are clearly evident in the urban environment. Indeed, cities often seem entirely unmanageable. The chaos produced by the occasional failure to deliver basic services in such areas as public safety and sanitation lends credence to this view. Unfortunately, the difficulties of urban management do not disappear when services are restored to normal. Administration requires the coordination of a large number of interdependent activities, from accounting and budgeting to the operation of traffic lights and garbage collection. Planning for orderly growth involves the development of models based on current conditions and projected needs. The one element common to these diverse activities is information, which must be collected, stored, and made available in appropriate forms to administrators and planners.

Sturman(1972) analyzes computer applications in urban management from the point of view of information flow in decision-making. Five categories of activities, forming a "process loop," are identified: data acquisition and monitoring, data management, analysis, decisions, and action.[6]

> The urban system process begins with data acquisition for the purposes of problem identification. Because the volume of data is great and must be manipulated in many ways by many agencies, the information must be structured, stored, sorted, updated, edited, and retrieved, that is, managed. The information is then analyzed, and decisions are made and acted on. The results are then monitored to provide further data with which the decisions and activated policies can be checked. (Sturman,1972,p. 652)[7]

The critical issue in this discussion is the acquisition and mǎnagement of information intended to serve decision-makers and planners. Despite technical and economic difficulties, urban databanks containing information on people (e.g., vital statistics, demographic material, income and employment data, and crime rates) and facilities (e.g., housing, streets, transportation, parks, museums, etc.) are likely to become increasingly more important in the future. The development of geographic data bases, in particular, which present information according to geographical location, may lead to substantial improvements in the quality of information available to urban managers. Information systems have already proved valuable in providing the data necesary to rationalize allocation of police and fire services. However, the problems of designing and managing a databank are considerable. Budgetary and technical constraints limit file size as well as the use of data. Hardware and software incompatibilities between different files make effective integration difficult and costly. Moreover, as indicated in the previous section, record linkage between files is not a trivial problem. In general, the experience of a number of cities indicates that substantial programming, maintenance and operation costs make large databanks "marginally cost-effective." (Sturman, 1972).

Dial(1968) emphasizes the political structure of decision-making in differentiating urban management processes into five partially overlapping subsystems: administration, support of operations, support of planning, management, and research. The administrative subsystem incorporates such functions as personnel accounting, property inventory and control, finance management, billing and receipting, etc. As in private organizations, this is the most well-developed part of existing information systems. Support of operations encompasses the service functions. This subsystem constitutes a resource for dispatching police, fire and other emergency vehicles and also for controlling traffic lights, etc. A subsystem for support of planning might maintain a computerized geographic database with some built-in analytic and modeling capability. The management subsystem is the least developed of all the components.[8] This subsystem is meant to automate a large part of urban government decision-making, or at the very least, to provide managers with reliable information concerning the consequences of various policy alternatives. Finally, a research facility would support planning with comprehensive studies of historical data.

One of the obstacles to the development of urban information systems is the lack of appropriate organizational structures. As Dial points out, the use of a computer does not assure such organization. Very often duplication of records is inherited from the conventional organization; useless information is not expunged, and conventionally reported information is uncritically incorporated into the computerized information system. But this may be attributed to the novelty of modern information technology. New technologies have a tendency to borrow forms from older technologies, whether appropriate or not. In any case, it seems safe to assume that after a period of transition, new forms will evolve which will be more suited to computer-based information technology.

The final or ultimate payoffs of urban information systems are seen by Downs(1967) as actual improvements in government or private action, as opposed to improvements in the information on which action is based. Such payoffs always involve improvements in the effectiveness of decision-making and can be divided into two classes: technical payoffs and power payoffs. The former are potentially beneficial to all participants in decision-making, whereas the latter (power payoffs) are characterized by redistribution of the benefits of decision-making, i.e., gains in one person's decision-making effectiveness over another's.

The technical payoffs expected from information systems in urban government are essentially the same as those which lead to computer applications in other large organizations. Reducing data-processing costs and achieving greater operational efficiency are as important here as they are in corporate management. Computer-based information systems can provide faster access to information, promote wider distribution, and free administrators from routine record-keeping activities. In addition to improving efficiency, such systems are expected to provide better information, and to generate data never before observed or recorded. Greater consistency in reporting data and less distortion in the information destined for policy makers are also possible in principle. What is more, there is the added attraction of developing enormous data inventories for general use.

These payoffs are of course not to be achieved without sacrifice. On the debit side of the ledger, one finds substantial outlays for new capital equipment, and demands for much more highly skilled personnel. The character of decision-making may also be adversely affected. Automated information systems encourage an exaggerated dependence on quantifiable variables, and contribute to increased organizational rigidity by formalizing functions. The ability to comprehend incipient changes in the environment may be impaired as a result of formalized information flow. There also appears to be a tendency to reduce the participation of intermediate level officials in the decision-making process just as observed in the corporate setting.

In general, streamlined information handling does not guarantee more effective decisions. Even if data is readily available, there is no assurance it will be used appropriately; and since computerized information systems are indifferent to the kinds of data collected, officials may or may not be better informed as a consequence of availing themselves of such systems. Adequate and timely information is clearly essential in urban management, but decision-making is also subject to political and organizational influences. The introduction of new technology in the absence of comprehensive reforms aimed at rationalizing the decision-making process is likely to be an expensive tour de force. Moreover, the need to justify substantial investment of resources underwrites the bureaucratic tendency to focus on problems whose information requirements can be handled conveniently with the tools at hand.

The power payoffs of urban information systems are manifest in organizational changes. Intermediate steps in data utilization tend to be eliminated, and those officials who are conversant with the new techniques are favored with "better" information. Lower and intermediate level officials lose power to higher levels; high level staff officials, in particular, gain power since politicians and top level executives must either expand their staffs or overwork existing ones. Administrators and operating officials gain power at the expense of lawmakers. Government bureaucracy, as a whole, gains power at the expense of the general electorate and non-government people. Well-organized and sophisticated groups gain at the expense of those who are less organized. Within the city government, there is an increase in the power of those who control automated data systems, and also an increase in the power of technically educated officials at the expense of old style political advisors.

4.   Planning in a Democracy

In recent years, the term "crisis" has forced its way into our social lexicon. We have witnessed an energy crisis, a food crisis, and countless political crises which have threatened the stability of world order. One of the defining features of a crisis is its unexpected character. It is largely our inability to respond appropriately to a given set of conditions that precipitates a crisis. The succession of these untoward events points to the need for social planning, and the inadequacy of traditional methods. Through our failure to anticipate the consequences of excessive dependence on automobile traffic, we are now faced with a transportation crisis in urban areas. The failure to manage resources on a rational basis has led to overuse and scarcities. Despite the evolution of economic, fiscal, and monetary controls, our society suffers from chronic over- and under-production, inflation, and unemployment. The ability to plan is in itself insufficient to deal with these problems— the will to implement policies which may be politically unpopular is equally important. But without such an ability, the will is ineffectual.

Planning requires information to identify problems, formulate and implement solutions, and evaluate results.[9] Unfortunately, the companion requirement for careful selection and analysis of data is in practice often a luxury.

> The typical difficulty faced by policy makers in defining problems is that a problem usually exists only in a political context. The political system is convulsive; it acts when the electorate perceives that a crisis exists, whether the crisis is one of inflation, unemployment, pollution, the failure of the educational system, or crime in the streets. But the public perception of a crisis often antedates the presentation of statistical evidence that there is indeed a crisis. Hence, when the legislature or the executive is

faced with an aroused public, time is not available to design a
survey or experiment, gather the requisite data, and perform a
careful analysis pointing toward an optimal policy recommenda-
tion. In addition, when the public perceives a crisis there may be
no general agreement on the nature of the problem, the important
variables to be measured, or the way to relate the variables in a
study. (Wallis,1971,p. 83)

Clearly, it is not possible to devise an information system which can
anticipate the data needs of all contingencies, especially when
decision-making is conducted under strong pressures for immediate
results.

The influence of broad policy studies on administration has not
been as effective as it might be. Radical departures from traditional
practices are rarely undertaken, and budgets usually reflect
short-term goals. The recurrent crises which plague contemporary
society testify to the inadequacy of this *ad hoc* approach to changing
social conditions. Long-range planning is seen by some observers as
a necessity. Michael(1968b) believes it to be inevitable.

The convergence of certain social and technological trends will
lead to much more extensive use of long-range planning even
though we are ill prepared institutionally, methodologically, and
personally to do it well; and ... the type of education needed to
realize the opportunities and avoid the threats in this situation is
not at all likely to be available as soon as we will need it or on the
required scale. (Michael,1968b,p. 3)[4]

Perhaps the most significant consequence of increased reliance
on long-range planning is the corresponding growth in the importance of information and expert knowledge. The complex problems
to be resolved depend on extensive data and specialized methods of
analysis. Fundamental to long-range planning is the formulation of
important social objectives, and thus the exclusive character of this
dependence poses a serious challenge to the democratic process.
Herein lie the opportunities and the threat. Computer-based
systems could make the requisite information accessible to the
general public, thus facilitating participation in policy formation. If,
on the other hand, access is restricted either by design or through
lack of knowledge, goals will eventually come to be set by an elite
body of planners.

Like many other issues, planning is not an either-or proposition
which we are free to accept or reject. Nor is it an alien concept in the
democratic capitalist state. Corporations and other private organizations, as well as governments, make long-range plans which impinge
on society. The central question is, in whose interests is the

planning carried out? Private corporations are subject to community control to a very limited extent, and the profit motive is not a reflection of the community's interests. Planning in a governmental framework also carries no guarantee that the public good will be the guiding principle, since politicians are influenced by special interest lobbying. In the end, there appears to be no substitute for an informed public, actively participating in the policy making process.

Fromm(1968) views the challenge of planning as a choice between the present "alienated bureaucratic procedure" and "humanistic management." The modern hierarchical organization is a one-way system, with control exercised from the top. It is inherently irresponsible in its pursuit of efficiency and indifference to human needs and expectations. The organizational structure of bureaucracy militates against the use of information technology to promote interaction and communication across levels in the hierarchy. Two complementary guarantees are necessary to achieve an open decision process: generalized access to information and the power to use it. The latter is obviously more difficult to satisfy. Although it is ambiguous because we have little experience with genuine power sharing in large organizations, one critical feature is a mechanism for establishing a continuing dialogue between managers and workers or ordinary citizens. This is not likely to emerge spontaneously, since it presupposes a fundamental shift in values from productivity and efficiency to human well-being.

Large-scale social planning is a response to increasing complexity, and there does not appear to be any ready alternative within the compass of our political experience. Thus apart from utopian anarchistic schemes, we are faced with the problem of making government planning receptive to diverse views, and responsive to human needs. The threat to democratic institutions posed by centralized planning suggests the desirability of achieving a balance between free and managed social change taken as the bounds of a spectrum of alternatives. One of the shortcomings of large-scale social planning derives from imperfect understanding of social phenomena. Naturally, as knowledge increases, so does our ability to act appropriately; but if sweeping programs were formulated by government planners, based as they must be on the best available imperfect models, the consequences of errors could be of disastrous proportions. The results of reliance on fiscal and monetary policies to manage the economy indicate the effects of such inadequacies. Centralized planning may promote efficiency in operations, but it also creates vulnerability. At the other extreme, redundancy sometimes leads to duplication and waste, but small-scale errors are less obtrusive.

Historically, extensive social planning is the legacy of socialist ideology. Concern over the trend toward central economic management in Great Britain led Hayek(1944) to remark

> [F]ascism and communism are merely variants of the same totalitarianism which central control of all economic activity tends to produce ... It is now even widely recognized that democratic socialism is a very precarious and unstable affair, ridden with internal contradictions and everywhere producing results most distasteful to many of its advocates. (p. viii)[11]

The basic danger of planning is the autonomy required by the planner. In order to have a free hand to deal with unforseen events, central governments require the power to make decisions on issues which cannot be specified in advance.

> To say that in a planned society the Rule of Law cannot hold is ... not to say that the actions of the government will not be legal ... It means only that the use of the government's coercive powers will no longer be limited and determined by pre-established rules. The law can, and to make a central direction of economic activity must, legalize what to all intents and purposes remains arbitrary action. (Hayek,1944,p. 82)

5. Computers and Political Power

Our discussion of surveillance (Chapter 9) focused on the problem of balancing the individual's right to privacy against society's need for information. In the context of the broader issue of the effects of databanks on democratic institutions, the central problem can again be posed in terms of achieving a balance: between the individual's "right to participate" and government's "need for autonomy" in decision-making. Shifts in power along the lines indicated for urban governments lead to greater centralization of decision-making and a consequent decline in participation by the average citizen in the political process.

Michael(1968a) points to the increasing dependence of those with political power on esoteric knowledge, and the decreasing ability of the concerned citizen to get the knowledge he needs to participate. Weizenbaum(1971) confirms this development in his analysis of the "two cultures" surrounding the use of computers. Exclusive social groupings based on privileged information have a long history in our culture. The underlying rationale for the

Pythagorean mystery cult may be different from that of the Communist party of the U.S.S.R., but both organizations share the tendency to promote a power elite based to some extent on access to secrets or priviledged information. The comparison may appear ludicrous, but perhaps the only real difference lies in the nature of the secrets. Just imagine the change in the course of history if the alchemists had succeeded in their efforts to transmute base metals into gold.

The association of power with esoteric knowledge has many facets. Power has a built-in tendency to preserve itself, so that control of information may very well provide a basis for "adjusting" the external world to suit a particular government agency. This sort of thing is already a common occurrence as governments struggle to survive under conditions of economic instability. Although not unique to the contemporary world of computer-based information systems, the problems are made more acute, since access to databanks is restricted and information is often unavailable for challenge. Another aspect of the same underlying issue, is the possibility of partisan use of incomplete or selectively emphasized technological knowledge.

For the concerned citizen, decision-making based on information in restricted databanks, poses some very difficult problems. How is the ordinary citizen to judge whether he knows enough about a policy? How will he know what data were used in arriving at a particular policy choice? Michael's solution to this problem is similar to Fano's. Allow maximum access to procedures of social planning and evaluation. The citizen ought to be able to look over the shoulder of the planner and decision-maker. A computer utility could provide the technical means for this capability.

Perhaps the most interesting claim for this approach is that it might lead to more openness on the part of government and greater citizen involvement in decision-making. Moreover, it is claimed that unfettered development of information systems with relatively open databanks will allow for the possibility of social experimentation.

The theme of social experimentation is explored in depth by Sackman(1968). Out of the mists of computer-based military command and control systems comes the real-time information system which monitors events in a specified environment, and controls the outcome of such events in a desired direction. Such systems give rise to the possibility of a new class of social institutions— one which is able to meet and deal with problems at the time they occur and in time to modify their outcome. Real-time systems involve a fusion of information and action and thus raise critical questions concerning the social control of "information power."

According to Sackman, social change via real-time information systems is self-change, since information power in a democracy resides in the public; that is to say, the public ideally authorizes and warrants social change. A new level of participant democracy is required. Here Sackman recommends the usual package of educational changes and *ad hoc* legal and regulatory devices to prevent concentration of information power. But the central part of his new philosophy is social experimentation— the possibility of which he attributes to computers and the development of real-time information systems.

Social experimentation is linked to the philosophical tradition of American pragmatism as exemplified in the works of Charles Peirce, William James and John Dewey. Dewey's work is particularly important in this regard.[12] He proposed operational measures of effectiveness for human organizational and social performance, a position which places a high value on freedom of social inquiry. As noted before, Sackman conjectures that the public information utility may be the instrumentality through which Dewey's dream could be realized. A public information utility could in principle provide for citizen participation in social experimentation through the agency of real-time information systems.

The possibilities of incorporating information technology into the political life of our society seem unlimited. If every home were equipped with a communications terminal connected to a nation-wide computer network, and if the network's (presumably rich) information resources were accessible to all users, the ordinary citizen would have the means for making intelligent decisions and communicating opinions to others. This vision of the future underlies speculation on citizen participation in politics and government administration. There are, of course, many different forms of participation. The range of alternatives runs from opinion polling and electronic voting to direct participatory democracy.[13] Opinion polling by means of an information utility would be a reasonably straightforward extension of existing practices designed to provide legislators and government officials with information on public attitudes. Extending a partial legislative authority to the whole citizenry would require considerably more adjustment.

The most far reaching alternative is direct participatory democracy. What this might mean is not entirely clear, but it would entail the evolution of political structures to facilitate public discussion and decision-making. It is not likely that society would be willing to dispense with executives or managers, so that the emphasis would be on policy formation, planning, and legislation. Developments in this direction are made possible by the accesibility of information and expert knowledge, and the ability to share experience among the members of the community. Whether or not people would take advantage of the opportunities is another matter.

Umpleby(1972) examines the various arguments against the use of a mass information utility as the vehicle for direct democracy. The "establishment social scientist" views increased citizen participation as a threat to civil liberties and democratic procedures. Liberal traditions are believed to be more secure in a political system dominated by a wealthy, educated minority than in one ruled by the capricious and highly impressionable masses. Technologically oriented observers fear that there would be a decline in the information and technical knowledge brought to bear on public decision-making, which would ultimately result in the dissolution of effective government. Although the "technologists" and "pluralists" differ in the value accorded to different forms of knowledge and the motives for using such knowledge in decision-making, they both accept the principle of elitist rule. Radical elements are also opposed to citizen participation, but for entirely different reasons. They argue that the new media will inevitably come to be owned and operated by powerful vested interests who will exploit it for their own partisan objectives. Instead of contributing to genuine power sharing, the technology would then serve as a vehicle for preserving existing privilege by enabling elite groups to exercise inordinate influence on public discussion.

Predicting the consequences of unknown forms of citizen participation in public decision-making is hazardous at best. Perhaps the greatest source of uncertainty derives from possible changes in public attitudes. Conceivably, political scientists will be astounded to discover that people actually become more involved when given the opportunity for genuine participation. On the other hand, we may witness the emergence of powerful forms of political control disguised as interactive systems; there is the distinct possibility of continued citizen acquiescence in "rule by experts." The destruction of democratic institutions need not result from conscious acts, nor from the sinister designs of power hungry men. Coercion can become institutionalized without anyone being particularly aware of it.

1 For example, Westin and Baker(1972) and Ware(1973); see also the Wallis(1971) report on the federal statistical program in the U.S.

2 As noted in Chapter 2, the United States Federal Government is the largest single user of computers.

3 Lenk(1973) attributes this state of affairs to the wide discrepancies between promise and reality, and suggests using the term "integrated data base" to "characterize the main element of advanced automation."

4 The following account is based on Hansen(1973).

5 We have already encountered some of Kaysen's recommendations in Chapter 9.

6 This parallels the decision-making paradigm discussed in Chapter 4.

7 Copyright 1972, Association for Computing Machinery, Inc., reprinted by permission.

8 See the discussion of management information systems in Chapter 4.

9 In Chapter 11 we will examine the application of systems analysis methods to social planning.

10 From THE UNPREPARED SOCIETY: Planning for a Precarious Future, by Donald N. Michael, Basic Books, Inc., Publishers, New York.

11 Copyright 1944 by the University of Chicago, reprinted by permission.

12 See Chapter 8.

13 See Umpleby(1972) for a discussion of some recent proposals.

Chapter 11.
Systems Analysis and Political Decision-Making

Growing social complexity has occasioned efforts to rationalize public decision-making. The problems of government administration and policy-planning no longer yield to traditional methods. There are too many people involved and too much at stake in the governing of cities and countries to permit informal administration by elected officials and political appointees. Regulating the economy of a nation, for example, requires a knowledge of technical matters associated with monetary and fiscal policies, their effects on trade balance, capital investment, productivity of labor, and levels of employment. It would be unthinkable for national governments to operate without extensive technical staffs. The same observation holds for urban governments. The coordination and planning of urban transportation systems, and various municipal services such as garbage collection, fire protection, and law enforcement require considerable technical sophistication.

Since communities have limited resources, the problem of optimizing functions is quite important. In the past, under simpler living conditions, the intuition of an experienced program director was sufficient in most cases to guarantee near optimal solutions. An astute postmaster in a small city could probably assign routes to postmen so as to minimize the cost of delivering mail, without having to formalize the problem. Similarly, the experienced fire chief could probably determine the best operational strategy for his fire companies. In the modern urban environment, however, intuition is not enough. This is the age of the expert with his bag of specialized tools and knowledge.

As indicated before in our discussion of databanks (Chapter 10), it is useful to distinguish between the two principal areas of decision-making in government: administration (including both line and staff functions) and policy-planning. The rise of scientific techniques in the execution of ongoing administrative tasks is not particularly controversial. Problems arise with planning because policy choices depend on priorities and values as well as technical questions. Computer simulation, for example, is a powerful tool for exploring alternative courses of action; but great care must be exercised in its use, to avoid biased outcomes.

The systems approach is perhaps the most promising analytical framework yet devised for the study of complex social phenomena. Its principal contribution to scientific method lies in its insistence on conceptualizing interacting events as a totality or unified whole. Systems analysis seeks to identify relations among the parameters which influence behavior and to construct models in which that influence can be ascertained. The applicability of this conceptual approach to problems of public policy can best be understood by looking at an example. Planning for the transportation needs of a large city requires anticipating the effects of a number of interacting factors. Transportation facilities influence land development, which in turn has an effect on the distribution of population. The construction of highways linking inner city areas with outlying regions may stimulate the growth of suburbs, and thus lead to increased demand for transportation facilities. In order to incorporate these interactions in a planning strategy, it is necessary to formulate a model of the urban system in which the mutual effects of the factors influencing transportation needs can be investigated.

Several allied techniques for analyzing complex systems have been developed. The term "operations research" was first used to describe the analytic methods applied to military problems during World War II by Great Britain and the United States. Since the war, these techniques have been elaborated and refined in both military and industrial applications. The computer has, of course, played a central role in this development, providing the computational power needed to transform conceptual schemes into practical instruments.

Our aim here is to assess the impact of the systems approach, and the methods usually associated with it, on the formation of public policy. After describing the methods and comparing them with traditional practices in government, we will examine some of the problems peculiar to the modeling of social systems. Since computer simulation is one of the principal techniques for investigating such systems, we will present a detailed example in order to clarify the issues. Opposition to the use of simulation and other techniques is not entirely a matter of institutional resistance to change. As observed in the preceding chapter, dependence on specialized knowledge tends naturally to limit participation in decision-making. The discussion will conclude with an exploration of the effects of systems methods on the exercise of authority in the public interest.

1. Methods of the Information Age

The problem-solving methodology associated with information-processing systems constitutes an analytical perspective, an attempt to apply rational, analytical principles to decision-making. This rational or scientific approach to decision-making provides a general framework for analyzing a problem and a host of techniques for resolving specific questions. The framework appears in many guises but is most often called systems analysis.[1] In a recent survey of business systems analysis techniques, Couger(1973, p. 167) explains:

> Systems analysis consists of collecting, organizing, and evaluating facts about a system and the environment in which it operates. ... The objective of systems analysis is to examine all aspects of the system— equipment, personnel, operating conditions, and its internal and external demands— to establish a basis for designing and implementing a better system.[2]

Our intention in the present brief review is to identify some of the methods which have evolved within the framework of systems analysis and to indicate their function in public administration. We will first discuss the systems approach to planning and budgeting and then consider the specialized techniques of simulation and optimization.

In government circles, the systems analysis approach spawned the method of program budgeting, with its Planning, Programming, and Budgeting Systems (PPBS).[3] Program budgeting is a marriage of program planning and budgeting. The basic idea is to make budgeting more responsive to program requirements so that priorities will be reflected more accurately in resource allocation. The first step in translating plans or projected programs into action is obtaining the necessary funding. Program planning and budgeting systems furnish categories of expenditures based on the program itself rather than the needs of the accounting department. Ideally, this forces the planner to make priorities explicit and to document the need for funds for particular activities.

Program planning and budgeting seek to substitute formal procedures for much of the intuitive decision-making of the experienced manager. To the extent that formal procedures are in fact explicit representations of managers' rational decision processes, this approach may be deemed "automated common sense."(Ramo,1968) However, as Churchman(1969, p. 215) observes, "The manager in most cases cannot make explicit what steps he has taken and he feels no need to do so." Systems analysis emphasizes the problem as a whole and the need to achieve a clear definition of its characteristics. Program goals must be identified, strategies for achieving them explored, and criteria for evaluating alternative courses of action established. The aim is an optimal organization of resources designed to secure the desired system performance.

Although the underlying systems approach of program budgeting is more important than the particular forms of PPBS, there are some distinguishing features which such systems have in common. The main feature is a conceptual framework which in effect constitutes a functional model of the real system. This framework typically identifies 1) program inputs and their costs, 2) outputs in the form of end products or services, 3) effects (benefits and harmful consequences), and 4) alternatives. Relationships among inputs, outputs, and effects are handled by specialized analytical tools which, of course, depend upon the gathering of appropriate data.

According to Gross(1969), most PPB systems consist of two parts: an analytic capability, and what he terms a "specialized information cycle." The former involves a technical staff, possibly supplemented by private consultants, which reports directly to a high-ranking agency official. The responsibility of this staff is to carry out studies of system characteristics. These studies may involve anything from cost-benefit analysis to applications of optimization techniques. The specialized information cycle of a PPB system is the apparatus for providing information essential to the making of major decisions by top officials. The form in which information is presented is quite critical for effective decision-making. Policy planners require material outlining program objectives and broad strategy for achieving them, as well as the principal options available and tentative recommendations. They also require the results of special studies which form the analytical basis for the broader program issues. Ideally the information provided by PPB systems to decision-makers helps to bring into the open many previously hidden and tacit considerations, and thus promotes constructive debate on policy issues.

No less important than the general perspective of systems analysis is the collection of specialized techniques for resolving specific problems. Perhaps the most important of these techniques are the ones developed for the simulation of large-scale systems and various methods of optimizing system performance. It is here that the computer plays a major role. The idea of simulating a system antedates the computer, but the development of the technique would have been severely limited without it. Simulation is best understood in terms of models; a computer simulation is a dynamic model of a system, or to use Oettinger's terminology (see Chapter 6), it is the dynamic expression of a theory. The particular intellectual contribution of simulation is the ability to deal with highly complex systems as a whole.

Starting with a model which identifies system parameters, it is possible to study the influence of these parameters and their mutual interactions on performance. The behavior of many systems of practical interest, which are too complex to be handled by classical mathematical methods, can often be investigated by means of computer simulations. Under certain simplifying assumptions, the growth of population can be predicted on the basis of mathematical theories of branching processes. However, realistic models of regional demographic trends are beyond the reach of these analytical methods. In addition to birth and death rates, it is necessary to account for migration patterns, which in turn depend on a variety of economic, political, and social conditions. These factors can be incorporated into a simulation model by defining variable quantities whose values can be manipulated to reflect different assumptions. The effects of locating a business or factory at a particular site might be represented by increasing the weight of some "economic activity indicator" which is used to evaluate the "growth pressure" in a given region. Similarly, the influence of highway construction or the development of public facilities such as parks can be taken into account.

Simulation makes it possible to test different hypotheses, and to explore alternatives; it provides the planner with a means for investigating the implications of policies in a laboratory setting. Determining optimal conditions for urban traffic flow can be accomplished by simulating the effects of various arrangements of directed streets (one-way or two-way), and traffic control patterns. The impact of proposed public expenditures on welfare programs might be studied as part of an economic activity simulation, which incorporates mechanisms for indicating the effects of increased consumer spending on such factors as industrial output and employment. Many more examples could be cited. Suffice it to say that simulation is becoming an important tool in public policy formation.

Optimization techniques constitute another class of methods for the study of complex systems. This class includes linear and dynamic programming, the techniques of combinatorial optimization, and other mathematical methods. All of them share the objective of determining a system configuration which optimizes some function which can often be interpreted as minimizing loss or maximizing gain. As an illustration, consider the problem of collecting the mail from deposit boxes distributed throughout a city. For simplicity, suppose there is one truck which starts from a central post office, visits each box, and then returns to the starting point. Economy demands that a sequence of visits be arranged so as to minimize the total distance travelled. This is an instance of a celebrated problem in combinatorial optimization, known as the "travelling salesman problem." It is particularly noteworthy because it occurs in many different forms, and methods for solving it efficiently have yet to be devised.

The foregoing discussion merely touches on some salient aspects of management science, which are of interest in public administration.[4] A variety of methods have been developed for handling scheduling, resource allocation, and other problems which are beyond the scope of the present survey. It is worth pointing out here that the techniques of simulation and optimization were developed in an engineering context. Their use has become a subject of controversy largely because of efforts to apply them to social systems in a context of public policy formation.

2. Traditional Methods and the Systems Approach

The application of systems analysis methods to problems of public administration constitutes more of an evolutionary trend than a break with tradition. As suggested before, the principal innovation of the new approach lies in the attitude toward administrative tasks which naturally flows from it. The ancillary techniques designed to solve particular problems are of secondary importance. Systems analysis is in keeping with the growth of bureaucratic organization. The attitude which it encourages is characterized by the use of formalized procedures and explicit analysis applied according to established rules. Emphasis on a system as a whole provides a rationale for identifying goals, and analyzing behavior relative to those goals. Traditional approaches to decision-making differ in being less formalized, and more dependent on intuition, personal talent, and charisma; the analysis of problems relies less on explicit procedures. But it is important to note that the difference is one of degree rather than kind.

The systems approach tends to shift the boundary between structured and unstructured decision-making, toward the latter.[5] This type of shift is quite predictable on the basis of Weber's theory of bureaucratic organization, since it enhances the technical advantages of bureaucracy.

> Bureaucratization offers above all the optimum possibility for carrying through the principle of specializing administrative functions according to purely objective considerations. Individual performances are allocated to functionaries who have specialized training and who by constant practice learn more and more. The "objective" discharge of business primarily means a discharge of business according to *calculable rules* and "without regard for persons." (Weber; in Gerth and Mills, 1946, p. 215)

The new analytic methods extend the "principle of specializing functions according to purely objective considerations." By making goals and procedures in decision-making explicit, they reduce the scope of subjective personal judgments.

The advantages of the systems approach over conventional methods of administration and planning are clearly evident in some applications of program budgeting. When properly used, the systematic method for establishing priorities and allocating resources serves to inform discussion, and to promote greater efficiency and improved services. As a case in point, let us examine the problems connected with drawing up a budget for a municipal government agency. The conventional approach to budgeting does not indicate what is done with funds; categories of expenditures are distinguished mainly for accounting purposes. Yale Law Journal(1967, p. 823) reports on a revealing study of police department budgeting in a major American city.

> In ... hearings ... each division captain gave a brief speech describing the pressures on his division and stating that even barely adequate service in the coming year would require more men. The budget officer has special knowledge of police operations, which enabled him to ask intelligent questions about police policy and efficiency. But the police officials parried questions about policy with assertions that their present practices were clearly "the most efficient." The police rarely offered factual support for these claims, but on most questions the budget official had no facts with which to refute them.[6]

Clearly this approach is poorly designed to reveal any policy decisions to the city government. The basis of claims for funding needs is obscured, and no intelligent method for appropriate channeling of funds is provided.

> The form of the traditional budget document is one important reason why time spent scrutinizing the police budget does not contribute to review and control of police policy. The traditional accounting-style budget is designed to keep track, in minute detail, of the expenditure of public funds.

> It is an excellent device for assuring that public funds are not lost or stolen, but tells almost nothing about what is done with them. It does not show how police resources are being allocated, either by neighborhood or by function. (Yale Law Journal, 1967, p. 824)

The use of accounting categories as opposed to program functions leaves planners, as well as the public, singularly uninformed on a department's activities. Discussion of funding focuses on wages, office supplies and capital investment. Economy measures sought by the city council reduce to questions of whether or not to "put radios in patrol cars." Setting priorities for services defaults to the department. The result is that the needs of the public become a secondary issue, and resources are not allocated on a rational basis, as evidenced by fewer patrol cars in areas with a high crime-rate than in those with a low one. Resistance to program budgeting in this case stems from the police department's desire to preserve its autonomy and maintain control over its policies— a position which is clearly not in the public interest.

In principle, a program budget would allow the public to observe and modify existing practices. Such an approach indicates the spending on each of the tasks to be performed, thus revealing priorities and objectives. This feature is often a source of resistance because of fear of disclosure. In many cases, policies have no real foundation or are based on concealed prejudices. If a department were placed in the position of having to defend its policies, and document its claims to the city council, there would be less opportunity for concealment.

In addition to providing a basis for informed discussion of substantive policy issues, program budgeting is useful for the agency itself in implementing its programs. The task-oriented nature of program budgeting lends itself to the application of cost-benefit analysis as a guide to efficient resource allocation. Although not a panacea for misguided policies, it would allow for more rational use of public funds, wider participation in decision-making, and perhaps improved services.

The question of rational management figures prominently in all phases of public administration and planning. As noted earlier, the systems approach does not signal a radical departure from conventional practices. It constitutes a further elaboration of scientific methods which can be applied to practical problems. Churchman's(1968) defense of systems methods may be somewhat exaggerated. Several levels of opposition must be distinguished. In government and other large organizations, the principle of rational bureaucratic procedures is well-established. Opposition to the new methods stems from political motives rather than rejection of scientific methods. It is not surprising that managers who are untrained in the new techniques would be unreceptive to changes which challenge their prestige and authority. The discussion of police department budgeting reveals a more serious form of this resistance, namely, the unwillingness to relinquish political power. Criticism of the systems approach by social scientists and those not directly engaged in management activities raises issues which we will treat later.

The contrast between the relatively informal, intuitive, decision-making framework of conventional management, and the systems approach is striking and important; but it should not be interpreted as reflecting a struggle between anti-rationalists and rationalists. Churchman's(1968) emphasis on the differences between conventional and scientific management is somewhat misleading. The exemplary, traditional ("anti-planning") manager is described as a gifted individual with a great deal of experience and insight. Such a manager typically analyzes various aspects of a problem, obtains information from the staff and ultimately decides on a course of action. However, this description is not entirely inappropriate for the administrator who avails himself of the fruits of systems analysis. The main difference between the "anti-planning" manager and his scientific counterpart lies in a further development of the objective character of bureaucratic functions. The new approach simply reduces the opportunities for the exercise of personal will in the management of organizations.

3. Simulation as a Tool of the Planner

Prophets, diviners, and oracles have always occupied a special place in human affairs. The ability to foretell the future forms the basis of many myths and legends in which knowledge of what is to come is ardently sought by some and sedulously avoided by others.

The world has not lacked for its prophets of doom and prophets of opportunity. With the exception of occasional cranks and latterday soothsayers, the function of prophesy has been institutionalized in modern times. Rational methods of prediction have been codified in historical and scientific research, and the need for systematic future gazing is universally recognized. Stability and orderly growth demand knowledge of the consequences of actions. The highly interdependent character of contemporary life intensifies this need, and the emergence of the planner bears witness to our efforts to secure the benefits of foreknowledge.

Predicting the future may or may not be associated with a deterministic view of the universe. For the planner, Omar Khayyam's "moving finger" is irrelevant. The unfolding of human history is seen as one particular realization of a stochastic process, and the task of anticipating desirable courses of action reduces to making judicious choices among feasible alternatives. Computers afford the planner a vehicle for performing *Gedanken* experiments capable of guiding the selection process. Such is the role of simulation in the formation of public policy. Decision-making is characteristically a multistage process carried out under conditions of uncertainty. The value of simulation lies in its ability to reduce some of the uncertainty by providing timely answers to hypothetical questions of the form: if such and such action is taken at time t, what will be the likely effects at time t+h? Of course, the reliability of the answers depends on the soundness of the underlying model.

The use of simulation as a practical aid to decision-makers has a history similar to that of the management information system and the databank concept: too much promised too soon. Social phenomena turn out to be more intractable than the engineering problems for which simulation along with other systems methods were developed. Nevertheless, these techniques have achieved a substantial measure of respectability and widespread support in the public sector.[7] Simulation efforts have been undertaken at all levels of government, and encompass everything from urban transportation systems to global climate and ecology.[8] The tool has been applied to ecological, transportation, and socioeconomic systems. One of the most ambitious and controversial projects is the world model of the Club of Rome which is based on the work of Forrester(1971). In the interests of clarity and concreteness, we will examine one particular simulation in some detail. The choice of a land-use model is somewhat arbitrary, but the simulation to be discussed is a good illustration of a complex program designed as an aid to urban planners; moreover, it has actually been put to some use.

The San Francisco land-use simulation was developed for the City and County of San Francisco during the early 1960's as part of the Community Renewal Program which was established by Congress in 1959.[9] It was designed to predict the consequences of public policies for the development of residential property; commercial and industrial land-use was excluded from consideration on the grounds that San Francisco is a relatively compact residential and commercial city as opposed to an industrial center. The geographic unit was defined by the political boundaries of the city proper. Wolfe and Ernst(1967, pp. 57-58) list four general purposes that the simulation was intended to achieve:

1. To develop alternative, long-range strategies and programs for renewal and development of the city, and to indicate the costs and benefits of each strategy and program.
2. To serve as an ongoing tool of the city government, to permit the city officials to have available on a continuing basis a method for testing the consequences of various renewal actions before they have actually taken place.
3. To identify key statistical symptomatic indicators which should be maintained on a continuing basis so that the city can be aware of the rate and direction of changes affecting it and take appropriate responsive action.
4. To improve the flow of information and utilize more effectively and in greater detail the available information.

The model's environment is the inventory of residential housing at a given time. It operates by adjusting the existing inventory so as to equilibrate demand for housing with private investment opportunities. The adjustments are made for two-year periods, and a complete simulation run involves nine iterations, thus providing an eighteen year forecast. At the beginning of an iteration, the model is furnished with information concerning public-action programs and policies, population, investment climate, and "location decisions of households," as well as the stock of housing. The program uses this information to determine a new equilibrium for housing usage.

The housing inventory is based on "neighborhoods" defined to correspond roughly to census tracts. Each neighborhood is assigned a "location category" reflecting its physical and economic characteristics. The smallest "dwelling unit" in the inventory is a two-acre parcel characterized by one of several different "housing types" and "conditions." Public actions are incorporated into the model in the form of zoning regulations, assessment changes, construction of amenities such as parks, and other changes which affect property values. However, the principal determinant of land-use in the simulation is private action. This is represented by the decisions of private developers which are based on calculations of expected investment returns. The model takes into account changes in rentals, depreciation and demolition of property, and a variety of other factors in balancing demand with development activity.

Certain strategic decisions made at the outset limit the model's applicability. The restriction to the City of San Francisco was dictated by political considerations, in view of the fact that surrounding municipalities were not integrated into a metropolitan authority. As a result, the movement of population within the region, and the influence of area-wide transportation systems could be treated only in an indirect fashion. Another serious limitation is the exclusion of industrial and commercial property. Since there is competition for land and resources between residential and commercial development interests, the latter exerts an influence on the housing inventory.

The accuracy of predictions based on the simulation depends also on the testing and validation of the model. If the requisite data is available, one can in principle observe a model's predictive ability for a period whose characteristics are known. In the present case, the model used 1960 census data as input. Since the data from the 1950 census was not in a strictly comparable form, it could not be used for testing purposes. Instead, the model was "calibrated to the construction activity in San Francisco during the period 1960-1964 by an extensive series of tuning runs." Other factors conspire to limit accuracy. Investment climate is influenced by general economic conditions and social attitudes. Willingness to invest in residential housing depends to some extent on competing alternatives, and it is affected by community response to proposed construction of major new building units.

The various qualifications and caveats which must be observed in interpreting the results of simulation runs place a heavy burden on planners, politicians, and the general public. Results must be taken as suggestions of possible outcomes rather than firm predictions. Accounting for simulation results in terms of the underlying model requires ingenuity, and in some cases the explanations do not afford acceptable interpretations of the real world. In such cases, the results are not too useful. Thus interpretation of the simulation's "suggestions" demands familiarity with the specifications of the model, as well as a knowledge of the housing characteristics and construction activities in the city of San Francisco. The excessively detailed character of the database on which the simulation operates is a further obstacle to its effective use. Wolfe and Ernst attribute this overabundance of detail to the city planners' "insistence on a level of detail which bordered on impracticality." Commenting on the San Francisco land-use model and two other projects of comparable magnitude, Wolfe and Ernst(1967, p. 57) are careful to indicate shortcomings.

1. Each has cost far more to produce than was originally planned!
2. Each badly overran the original planned completion date!
3. Not one has yet received effective use for the purpose which inspired their original design.

Moreover, Brewer(1973, p. 114) observes: "the model is still nowhere near completion and has been set aside by responsible civic officials."

Despite unfulfilled expectations, the simulation project is seen as an important contribution to city planning. In the hands of skilled and knowledgeable practitioners, it can be used to gain insight into the dynamics of land-use. Unexpected results sometimes suggest new ways of looking at problems, and the model-building exercise is a valuable educational experience for the planners involved. Nevertheless, intrinsic limitations and inadequate validation make the simulation an unreliable instrument for hypothesis testing. The feasibility of suggestions for improvements has not been demonstrated, and it is not at all clear that the benefits justify the considerable investment of public resources required.

4. Modeling Social Systems

It is difficult to take issue with an approach which contributes to informed policy making and also improves the efficiency of government operations. However, it should be noted that despite all the verbiage about program budgeting systems, they amount to no more nor less than an attitude toward problem-solving; the specialized technical methods of management science are not essential. So, one may accept the positive contributions of the systems approach to policy-planning, and yet find fault with the use of particular techniques for the analysis of social systems. In what follows, we will focus principally on computer simulation.

As one of the leading contributors to their development, Jay W. Forrester is a staunch advocate of the use of computer models for investigating the behavior of social systems.[10]

A computer model embodies a theory of system structure. It states assumptions about the system. The model is only as good as the theory which lies behind it. A good computer model is distinguished from a poor one because it captures more of the essence of the social system that it presumes to represent. Making a computer model requires that we be explicit about the assumptions on which our mental models are based. When assumptions are clearly stated, they encourage deeper discussion and lead to better selections from the vast numbers of fragments which are contained in our mental models. Making a computer model enforces a rigor and discipline that is missing in discussion and writing. (Forrester, 1971, p. 15)[11]

Since all decisions are based on models, the only question, according to Forrester, is which models to choose; the choice must be guided exclusively by consideration of our current best efforts at model construction. What is more, computer-based models are seen to be better than intuitive ones. Restricted to the physical world these observations would not generate very much controversy. What is so different about social systems?

A fundamental criticism leveled against simulation of social systems derives from the belief that social science theory is not sufficiently advanced to support realistic models. An extreme version of this sceptical view avers that our knowledge of social phenomena has not advanced beyond the stage of description and taxonomy, and it is thus premature to attempt constructing computer-based models designed to predict behavior. Forrester(1971, p. 26) counters this argument by observing

[W]hat justification can there be for the apparent assumption that we do not know enough to construct models but believe we do know enough to directly design new social systems by passing laws and starting new social programs? I am suggesting that we do indeed know enough to make useful models of social systems. Conversely, we do not know enough to design the most effective social systems directly without first going through a model-building experimental phase.

Which is to say that this is the best we can do, so why insist on using inferior methods simply because our best efforts are not perfect.

Assuming that systems models represent our best efforts, then, of course, Forrester is right. However, even without challenging the assumption, there remain some thorny issues. The technical methods used in decision-making are *not*, unfortunately, without influence in the political process. As Hoos(1969) points out, the new methods come replete with the enormous prestige of the scientific enterprise, so that there is a built-in tendency for policy-makers to accept the results of simulations as gospel truth, in spite of the fact that the underlying societal models are highly imperfect. If decision-makers were sufficiently sensitive to the pitfalls of uncritical acceptance of projections based on simulation models, no doubt the requisite caution would be exercised in interpreting them. But such scholarly caution cannot readily be expected from the typical politician or decision maker. The crucial question is whether or not the risk of error is offset by the apparent gain in precision.

Models of social systems in the context of policy-planning are usually designed for the purpose of resolving questions about government services. The systems approach to welfare-operations in California described by Hoos(1967) is an instructive example. One of the key questions investigated in the study was the social benefit of proposed services. This is not, however, a purely technical problem. Evaluating the benefits of social services involves value judgments which do not yield to quantitative analysis. For example, it may be possible to compare the cost of welfare payments with increased consumer buying power, and derive some measure of the effect of welfare expenditures on unemployment rates. Assessing the costs of welfare relative to possible improvements in recipients' attitudes toward authority is quite another matter. The phenomenon of urban riots suggests that potential benefits of this nature are not mere frills.

Perhaps the most significant criticism of simulations of social systems is the self-reflexive character of such efforts. One of the unsettling discoveries of modern physics was the realization that under certain conditions the observer has an indeterminate effect on what he observes. In the sphere of social phenomena, the effect of observer on observed is everywhere inescapable. The attitudes and values of the investigator are reflected in the assumptions made and in the so-called facts selected for consideration. The results and conclusions of the investigator have, in turn, an effect on the object of study.

> [I]n the social sciences we have to deal with short statistical runs, nor can we be sure that a considerable part of what we observe is not an artifact of our own creation. An investigation of the stock market is likely to upset the stock market. We are too much in tune with the objects of our investigations to be good probes. In short, whether our investigations in the social sciences be statistical or dynamic - and they should participate in the nature of both - they can never be good to more than a very few decimal places, and, in short, can never furnish us with a quantity of

verifiable, significant information which begins to compare with that which we have learned to expect in the natural sciences. We cannot afford to neglect them; neither should we build exaggerated expectations of their possibilities. There is much which we must leave, whether we like it or not, to the un-"scientific," narrative method of the professional historian. (Wiener, 1961, p. 164)

Defining the objectives and philosophies of social systems is a value-laden enterprise, constrained by the observer's point of view and ideological orientation. Suppose one were to investigate the penal system from the systems point of view. A basic philosophical question concerning its objectives would have to be decided at the outset. Should the model embody a rehabilitative or retributive principle of justice? The answer is not to be found in any "stubborn irreducible facts"; either choice would reflect the views of the observer as much as any objective social reality. In addition to the subjective nature of problem definition, there is an inherent ambiguity in the concept of solution. What constitutes a "solution" to a social problem? Can it be specified with the precision claimed for the systems approach? The impossibility of definitive answers makes the promises of systems analysis inappropriate and misleading. For example, the suggestion of a particular reform in the penal system cannot be seen as the solution to a problem in the strict sense. Rational criteria alone are insufficient to characterize compelling social action. The assignment of costs and benefits to different courses of action is not a factual exercise.

Beyond the question of intractability and value dependent choices, the very foundation of the systems approach to social phenomena may be faulty. Invoking Sorokin's critique of the system concept as applied to society, Hoos(1972, p. 28) argues that the mere fact of analogy between two entities does not guarantee structural equivalence.

> Just because human society may be considered a kind of unity in which the members are interdependent, and an organism is a unity of interrelated parts, it does not follow, [Sorokin] argued, that society is an organism. By the same token, the solar system, an automobile, a plant, an animal, a river, or a man represent a kind of unity with interdependent parts, but this does not mean that they are identical. Nor does establishment of their truismatic relationship imply that their intrinsic substance, or the rules governing their behavior or performance, or the methods best applicable to an understanding of the dynamics of one are proper with respect to another.[12]

It should be pointed out here that this argument does not contradict Forrester's claim that one should use the best available models in decision-making. It is necessary first to determine just what the best models are. As the example of the land-use model shows, simulation has yet to demonstrate its superiority over the "narrative method of the professional historian." At the very least, one must guarantee that the results of simulations are used with extreme care; and that every effort is made to highlight, rather than obscure, the biases built into the model. The reliability of the management science approach to social systems is further compromised by the tendency to "substitute ignorance for objectivity," as Hoos(1967) expressed it. This occurs when systems analysts untrained in the given subject area attempt to build a model without consulting the specialists. In such cases, the collection of data is apt to substitute for serious thought.

5.   Systems Analysis and the Public Interest

Let us return once again to Forrester's remarks about models. We have already touched on some of the reasons for handling our "best" models with care, all of which have to do with problems of hidden bias. Another class of reasons derives from the politics of resource utilization. Once produced, a large-scale simulation represents a considerable investment of resources. This fact alone argues strongly for the use of the product, regardless of quality and constraints.

A simulation of an urban area intended as an aid to city planners may suffer from all manner of weaknesses, yet if it is used to determine policy, the weaknesses are likely to be ignored. If there were a natural corrective mechanism at work, there would be some chance of checking inappropriate applications. However, even assuming that such a model would be accessible in some form to the general public, it is clear that only those groups with technical training or the resources to hire consultants would be in a position to challenge its assumptions and organization. Instead of encouraging debate by making priorities explicit and tracing the consequences of different courses of action, large-scale simulations may provide a compelling framework for decision-making. Under such conditions, influence would naturally shift toward those capable of making use of the model.

Forrester's position is thus seen to be misleading on two counts. First, simulations are prey to hidden bias stemming from the inescapable value judgments present in the analysis of social phenomena. This poses an internal problem which affects the "objectivity" of results and our confidence in them. Second, there is a kind of political bias which militates against using the results of simulations with the proper restraint. Substantial development costs for simulations of social systems promote their use, and the cost of making modifications acts as an effective deterrent to discussion of the model itself.

Thus far in our examination of the systems approach to public planning and policy formation, we have not questioned the societal configuration which occasions its invocation. If this configuration is regarded as sacred and immutable, there is no alternative but to debate the merits of different strategies for dealing with social complexity. But is this view well founded? Is the interest of the community best served by centralized management of mass social systems? The notion of optimality is as relevant here as it is in the systems approach to specific social problems. Since analogies require qualification, we will simply mention the dinosaur's fate without comment. Part of the difficulty encountered in the use of systems methods derives from the diffuse character of society. Objectives elude definition because the public interest is not a unitary thing, and the point of view of the analyst will almost certainly be at variance with that of some group or other. This does not challenge the propriety of rational methods in decision-making, but rather the scale of public programs and social organization.

Whether or not society can be modeled as a system homologous to an organism or a machine, there is probably a threshold function which defines the optimal size of social units. Economy of scale may turn to diseconomy beyond a critical value for the scale of an enterprise. Thus it is reasonable to suggest that our emphasis on the forging of management techniques for larger and larger organizations may be misplaced. Perhaps we ought to experiment with different forms of control to ascertain the optimal sizes of communities. The most disturbing feature of the methods we have been discussing is not their shortcomings as techniques but the harm that can come from their application in large communities. This problem is, of course, common to all decision methods, from which one might conclude that redundancy is as much an optimizing principle as is economy of scale.

The systems approach to problem-solving could in principle be applied to the size question. However, in addition to the limitations connected with value-laden choices and ideological biases, there is yet another difficulty. A "principle of least effort" or a "Procrustes syndrome" (tailoring problem definitions to fit into a particular conceptual framework) conditions the methodology's application and is manifest in its peculiar definition of rationality. This effect has been observed in the context of a game known as the Prisoner's Dilemma. The game derives from an anecdote concerning two captured criminals, say A and B, held by a public prosecutor on suspicion of the same capital offense. If A informs on B, B will be sentenced to life imprisonment while A receives a light sentence. The analogous outcome occurs if B informs on A. In the case where neither informs on the other, both receive medium sentences; whereas if both of them inform on the other each one goes to jail for life. Thus, each suspect has two strategies: inform on the other (D) or remain silent (C).

The essential ingredients of the situation are captured in a game represented by the following list of strategy choices and associated payoffs to the players, where the first symbol corresponds to A's choice.

CC: both receive 5 cents
CD: A loses 10 cents, B gains 10 cents
DC: A wins 10 cents, B loses 10 cents
DD: both lose 5 cents

Rapoport(1964, p. 49) observes:

> [T]he principal feature of this game is the fact that strategy D dominates strategy C for both players. On the face of it, therefore, we seem to be confronted with the simplest type of two-person game, namely, one in which each player has a clearly dominating strategy, one that is sure to be better than the other no matter what the other player does.

However, it is intuitively clear that both players would be better off if each chose strategy C. Rapoport(1964, p. 50) explains the apparent paradox as follows.

> The dilemma results from a bifurcation of the idea of rationality. If one asks, "With which strategy am I better off?" The answer is unequivocally, "With strategy D." The choice of strategy C is dictated by collective interest. If one asks, "Where are we both better off?" The answer is, "With strategy C." Thus, strategy D is dictated by self-interest while strategy C is dictated by collective interest.

The analysis of real world decisions is, of course, far more complicated, but the bifurcation of rationality is evident in the application of systems methods in the public domain. It is both more expedient and more rewarding for the systems analyst to assign utilities to outcomes on the basis of vested interests rather than community interests.

One should be wary of systems analysts bearing promises of simple, straightforward solutions. The prestige of science makes it easy for a speaker of the systems language to dupe the unsophisticated politician and the public with meaningless jargon. The systems analyst is at least part salesman, and the profit motive leads to interesting results. Highly sensitive political questions are transformed magically into problems of technique or administration. This is evident from the imaginative euphemisms and circumlocutions used to characterize social issues. Riot control translates into "constabulary capabilities for low level conflict." Psychological warfare becomes "cross-cultural studies" or "communication, by word or action, intended to influence or persuade." The intellectual distortion resulting from the Procrustes syndrome does little to promote the collective interests of the community.

---

[1] For a comprehensive study of its philosophy and practice, see Churchman(1968).

[2] Copyright 1973, Association for Computing Machinery, Inc., reprinted by permission.

[3] See Gross(1969) for a discussion of the origins of PPBS.

[4] Couger's(1973) survey of management science methods is a good entry point into the literature.

[5] See the discussion of Simon's characterization of decision-making in Chapter 4.

[6] Reprinted by permission of The Yale Law Journal Company and Fred B. Rothman and Company from *The Yale Law Journal*, Vol. 76, pp. 822-838.

[7] Hoos(1972, p. 5) presents some estimates of public expenditures for systems analysis in the United States in 1966, the total for the year among cities and states being $22.5 million.

[8] See, for example, Bekey(1971).

[9] This discussion is based largely on Wolfe and Ernst(1967) and Benton(1971). See Brewer(1973) for a comprehensive assessment of the San Francisco and Pittsburgh simulation projects conducted under the Community Renewal Program.

[10] Forrester's work in simulation of social systems provided the foundation for the world model of the Club of Rome (see Chapter 1).

[11] Reprinted with permission from *World Dynamics* Second Edition, by Jay W. Forrester. Copyright © 1973 Wright-Allen Press, Inc., Cambridge, Mass., 02142, USA.

[12] Copyright © 1972 by The Regents of the University of California; reprinted by permission of the University of California Press.

Chapter 12.
Information, Power and Complexity

The role of technology in our society has become the subject of intense controversy during the past few years. Erstwhile champions of the era of industrial and technological expansion have metamorphosed into villains of a mounting ecological crisis. The blind faith of our Victorian forebears in the virtues of unending progress has been laid to rest with the dead of two global and countless local wars. Where there was once faith and optimism, we now find cynicism and despair. Yet the change in attitude toward technology does not signal a fundamental departure from its constitutive role in our society. With sociologically insignificant exceptions, the change in attitude has been from one of expectation of reward to acceptance of the inevitable. Virtually all participants in the current debate over technology share the assumption that continued development is inevitable, barring some catastrophe.

In its simplest form this assumption of inevitability is a response to the seeming futility of challenging established authority. The characteristic feature of the position which springs from this assumption is that society is evolving into ever more complex forms which necessitate the continued elaboration of technology. Our contention is that this reasoning entails an implicit ideological commitment to the maintenance of centralized power. The desirability of promoting the self-interest of a few is confused with the inevitability of social evolution. As a result, advocates urge accelerated implementation of the latest technical innovation, while opponents are content to impose formal restrictions on machine-based power.

It is certainly no accident that information technology appeared on the scene in earnest at mid-century. The computer and the large-scale information-processing systems spawned by it emerged at a time when pyramidal social organization seemed to require ever increasing direction from the apex. What could be more natural than the birth of a technique for processing massive amounts of information, just when our highly complex and differentiated society required such a capability for its continued functioning. It appears to be a case of necessity mothering invention. No doubt there is some truth in this observation, especially within the framework of a localized view of history. However, to see in this particular response to particular social conditions a sign of the inevitable and the necessary is to indulge in a form of egocentric projection, no different in principle from the anthropomorphic animism observed among primitive peoples.

The appeal to social complexity as an evolutionary principle which necessitates the growth of central power is a modern equivalent of the theory of the divine right of kings. History makes it abundantly clear that power cannot be exercised for long without a cogent claim to legitimacy. Whether authority be sanctioned by divine providence or as an expression of a collective will, it seeks justification in moral agency. Through the replacement of the active hand of God by natural law, scientific rationalism has contributed to a shift in the basis of legitimacy from divine to natural or social necessity. Contemporary views owe much to social Darwinism, wherein society is likened to a hierarchically structured organism with its differentiated components integrated according to subordinate-superordinate relationships. The analogy with biological organisms is buttressed by examples taken from the physical world and is expressed more generally by means of the notion of complexity as applied to arbitrary systems. In all of these analogies, the legitimacy of social authority is embedded in natural law or evolutionary principles. The unfolding of providential designs is thus transmuted into a species of social necessity.

In what follows, we will explore the intellectual and moral significance of social complexity in legitimizing the centralization of power in our society. The first issue to be considered is the notion of complexity itself. Close examination reveals a multiplicity of different concepts, some of which are closely related to certain ideas of information. This connection leads us to examine the function of information both in systems which operate under uncertainty and in organizational structure. Proceeding from this analysis, we will attempt to characterize social complexity, and identify its principal manifestations. The main purpose of this inquiry is, of course, to illuminate the dependence of contemporary beliefs in the necessity of continued elaboration of information technology on the acceptance of increasing complexity as an inevitable consequence of social evolution. To this end, we will investigate the role of computers as instruments of social authority designed to cope with complexity by promoting the centralization of power.

1. An Anatomy of Complexity

The notion of complexity seems far removed from moral and political issues, but in fact it is ever present both as background and in the form of a common species of argumentation. Complexity is generally taken to be a meaningful feature of the real world, exhibited by intricate patterns, complicated interactions, differentiated structures, abundance of choice, things with many parts, etc. These instances serve to elucidate the concept in ordinary usage, and exemplify its intellectual content as background to analysis and decision-making. Somewhat closer to our present concern is the influence of the notion of complexity on attitudes toward problem-solving. Problems perceived as complex are usually thought to be beyond the scope of the ordinary person. Complication typically signifies something of a technical nature and calls for the special competence of an expert in a given subject area. In some cases, such as solving a system of differential equations, the division of labor is sensible and unambiguous - mathematicians are trained to solve mathematical problems. Moreover, to set up a production process for a certain chemical, one calls on the services of a chemist or chemical engineer; designing a bridge requires the specialized knowledge of a civil engineer. But some kinds of problems are not so clearcut. To whom does one turn to decide whether or not a bridge *should* be built? Various experts can contribute to particular aspects of this question, such as determining the number of vehicles that might use the bridge, or estimating construction costs, etc. Still there are issues which do not fall within the competence of any particular specialist. What if limited resources force a choice among a new school, a bridge, and a hospital? Assuming a need for all three, how is the choice to be made?

There is no specialized branch of knowledge for resolving questions of priority. Thus belief that all complex problems must be handled by experts leads to moral and political difficulties. Clearly, the "argument from complexity" entails a fallacious transference. Since the intellectual division of labor is so pervasive, one is inclined to assume that every issue has its appointed discipline. This misguided assumption contributes to the erosion of individual responsibility for decisions affecting the community. The transformation of political questions into technical problems obscures the values and priorities upon which policy objectives are based. In the context of social development, the argument from complexity is used to support the contention that consolidation of power in centralized bureaucracies is both natural and essential to the preservation of society. This justification for the concentration of authority feeds on the widespread acceptance of the expert as the arbiter of complex problems. In order to demonstrate the misguided character of this argument, it is necessary to take a closer look at the concept of complexity itself.

Perhaps the most important observation about complexity is that it does not appear to be an intrinsic property of things or processes. Its dependence on our knowledge and methodology is evidenced by the multiplicity of different meanings attached to the term and the absence of a unifying framework for its analysis. A broad distinction is often drawn between disorganized and organized complexity (Weaver,1948). The disorganized variety refers to situations with no *apparent* structure, an example of which is a collection of particles randomly distributed in some medium, whose motions do not exhibit patterned behavior. The main criterion for this distinction is methodological. Disorganized complexity is characteristic of problems whose analysis requires statistical methods. Such a problem is one with a large number of variables which behave erratically or in an unknown manner, but whose aggregate behavior exhibits statistical regularities.

According to Weaver(1948), organized complexity is characteristic of "problems which involve dealing simultaneously with a sizeable number of factors which are interrelated into an organic whole." As the name suggests, organization is the critical feature of such problems. A system with a large number of interacting components whose behavior is structured or patterned reveals organized complexity. Biological functions, chemical interactions, genetic mechanisms, economic systems, etc., provide examples of this type of complexity. Despite the diversity of problems included in this category, the idea of "organic whole" leaves little doubt as to the principal frame of reference. The underlying model is based on an analogy with biological organisms, and the criteria for structure or pattern is embedded in some form of purposive or goal-seeking behavior.

As indicated above, the taxonomy of problems according to different types of complexity is motivated by methodological considerations. Statistical methods are inappropriate for problems of organized complexity since one is not interested in average behavior; moreover, the techniques developed in the nineteenth Century to deal with a small number of variables are inadequate.

> These new problems, and the future of the world depends on many of them, require science to make a third great advance, an advance that must be even greater than the nineteenth-century

conquest of problems of simplicity or the twentieth-century victory over problems of disorganized complexity. Science must, over the next 50 years, learn to deal with these problems of organized complexity. (Weaver,1948,p.540).[1]

Naturally, the entire discussion would be somewhat incomplete if it did not suggest future directions. The computer coupled with the methods of operations research and their progeny are seen to be likely candidates for handling organized complexity. These developments, then, come to be linked with the world's salvation in the future.

The organismic model of complexity is carried further by Simon(1962), although he is careful to eschew any hint of metaphysical presuppositions which may cling to the relationship between the whole and its parts. Hierarchical organization is the distinguishing feature of this formulation. "[O]ne path to the construction of a non-trivial theory of complex systems is by way of a theory of hierarchy. Empirically, a large proportion of the complex systems we observe in nature exhibit hierarchic structures."(Simon,1962).[2] The concept of hierarchy allows for defining organization in terms of a decomposition of the parts of a system into interacting subassemblies. This constitutes a generalization of the structure of an organism in the sense that it encompasses relations between components which in principle need not reflect dominance patterns. However, as observed in Chapter 4, Simon's hierarchical model of complex organization is based on a certain type of goal-seeking behavior. The evolution of systems organized for efficient production replaces the simpler notion of command hierarchies as the expected form of "natural" growth processes, thus providing a more abstract foundation for theories of social Darwinism.

Since the concept of complexity is relevant to virtually all phenomena, there is a strong tendency to view it as a property of existence. Part of the reason for this is purely linguistic. When someone uses the word "complexity" to describe an event or an object, it does convey some meaning, but the content is too diffuse to be of much use analytically. On the other hand, when the meaning is made precise, it ceases to have the generality of a universal property. The tantalizing character of this elusive notion is illustrated by an observation of Von Neumann concerning the ability of a system to reproduce itself.

There is thus this completely decisive property of complexity, that there exists a critical size below which the process of synthesis is degenerative, but above which the phenomenon of synthesis, if properly arranged, can become explosive, in other words, where synthesis of automata can proceed in such a manner that each automaton will produce other automata which are more complex and of higher potentialities than itself.(Von Neumann,1966,p.80)

Of course, as Von Neumann points out, "none of this can get out of the realm of vague statement until one has defined the concept of complication correctly." But the correct definition depends on the nature of the problem, and also on what we know about it as well as the methods used for analyzing it.

That complexity is not a unitary concept, but a host of essentially different attributes of sytems and objects is clearly evident from mathematical studies. Measures of complexity have been investigated for computations, algorithms, graphs, and various algebraic systems. Consider the question for an algorithm. The reason algorithmic complexity is important is that it is associated with the cost of executing computer programs. Typically, complexity in this context measures the number of basic operations which must be performed, and thus gives some indication of the execution time and relative cost. But this is by no means the only feature of an algorithm which determines its "complexity." Storage requirements and structural features are also of interest, and these lead to very different formulations. Complexity based on execution time gives no information about internal organization, so that algorithms of widely divergent character which perform a computation in a comparable number of steps would not be distinguished. This is not to say that computation time is an inappropriate index of complexity, but that others are needed for different purposes.

Studies of the complexity of mathematical structures such as graphs confirm this conclusion. The characterization of an object's complexity is relative to a particular structural feature, and different measures need not correlate with one another at all. For example, a graph which is highly complex on the basis of one measure, may turn out to be exceedingly simple when analyzed from a different point of view.[3] The dependence of complexity on our knowledge and objectives is captured by Stafford Beer's remarks on the nature of systems.

A pattern is a pattern because some *one* declares a concatenation of items to be meaningful or cohesive. The onus for detecting systems, and for deciding how to describe them, is very much on ourselves. I do not think we can adequately regard a system as a fact of nature, truths about which can be gradually revealed by patient analytical research. A viable system is something we detect and understand when mapped into our brains, and I suppose the inevitable result is that our brains themselves actually impose a structure on reality. (Beer,1960,p.12)[4]

2. Information, Choice and Structure

Complexity and information are closely related. In the disorganized case, it is intuitively clear that as complexity increases, so does the amount of information required to specify any particular outcome or configuration. Consider the problem of guessing the winner in a lottery. Assuming that the winning ticket is drawn at random from all the entries, the "complexity" of the task is proportional to the number of entries. One way to make this precise is to define the information associated with any outcome of the draw, as the number of yes-no type questions required to determine that outcome uniquely.[5] Thus if there are eight entries, exactly three questions suffice: the first can be chosen to eliminate half of the possibilities; the second, to eliminate half of the remaining entries; and the third, to specify a unique outcome. Information as used here is equivalent to uncertainty, in that the specification of an outcome involves the removal of uncertainty about the state of affairs. The amount of information (or uncertainty) depends on the statistical properties of the selection to be made.

Organized complexity can also be analyzed in terms of information, but, in this case, information signifies something else. Instead of determining outcomes subject to statistical considerations, one is interested in specifying structures. Suppose we would like to characterize the complexity of an organic molecule. An important structural feature has to do with the different ways in which a molecule can enter into combinations with other molecules. This property is partly a function of topological structure and may be expressed in terms of a molecule's symmetry: the more symmetric, the fewer the modes of combination. The "amount of information" needed to specify symmetry properties can thus be taken as a measure of structural complexity.[6]

The preceding examples illustrate the main technical uses of the concept of information, and indicate their respective relationships to the study of complexity. Our main objective is to probe the different forms of social complexity, but the present preliminaries are needed to clarify some important distinctions which apply in the context of social phenomena. Although the theme of this book is information-processing, we have not attempted to present a formal definition of information. For most practical purposes, our intuitive notions are sufficient, and context can usually be counted upon to provide the appropriate interpretations. The management of large data files, for example, is normally conducted independently of the semantic meaning of information items contained therein. On the other hand, the semantic component is clearly relevant to the design of systems which require facilities for extracting "information" from a database in order to answer questions posed by users, such as might be needed in computer-assisted instruction applications. The need for a formal treatment arises when one starts to theorize about the role of information generally. Then it becomes apparent that the different senses of the word must be respected.

As suggested above, information comes in two models. The first, illustrated by our lottery example, is known as selective information, and forms the basis of the theory of information elaborated by Shannon(1959) and others.[7] This theory was formulated in the context of communication systems and is concerned with the problem of transmitting messages over channels whose behavior is characterized probabilistically. In other words, interference (noise) in the transmission medium may introduce errors in the messages transmitted, so that it is necessary to operate within certain restrictions imposed by the channel, and design codes to insure reliability. For present purposes, the point to be made is that the definition of information is based on statistical considerations. A message may be characterized as the outcome of an experiment, or as an element of an ensemble which occurs with a given relative frequency.[8] The possible outcomes of a lottery provide a concrete example of such an ensemble.

The second type of information actually includes a variety of subspecies which are commonly referred to by the terms structural and semantic information. We have already discussed an instance of the structural type. In cases where one is concerned with structure or meaning, the selective notion of information does not apply, at least not in any obvious way. The meaning of a word or a message has nothing to do with our expectation of its occurrence in a communication medium; uncertainty is not at issue, choice is not the fundamental consideration. The problem here involves capturing the relationship between a sign or symbol and its referents.

Similarly, structure is a relational property which depends upon the interaction of the different parts of a system. There is no general theory of structural or semantic information comparable to that developed for the statistical variety, although various special cases have been considered. Part of the difficulty stems from the ambiguities described earlier in connection with studies of organized complexity. The requisite unifying concepts are not forthcoming.

The connection between information and organized complexity is especially transparent in the problem of providing a description of a system. In fact, the "information" contained in a description could be taken as an index of complexity. For purposes of measuring complexity, one might wish to identify descriptions with the objects they describe, but this would require looking at all possible descriptions, which is not a feasible procedure. To avoid this difficulty, the object and its description must be distinguished, and a "grammar" of allowable descriptions established. Such a strategy would facilitate a measure of complexity (relative to a grammar) which could be used to determine the "goodness" of any particular description. This approach is in accord with our earlier observation, to the effect that complexity is a function of knowledge and methodology. The information in a description is a direct reflection of what we know about a system, rather than any intrinsic system property.

The importance of choosing an appropriate description may be seen from a simple example given by Simon(1960). Consider a two-dimensional array of letters. If certain subarrays are repeated, one can take advantage of this redundancy to simplify the description. In such cases, the number of symbols required to specify the array can be reduced. Generally, by a judicious choice of basic elements or building blocks, it is possible to obtain greater economy of description. Since many systems are composed of a relatively small number of subsystems and some interactions among components may safely be neglected, such choices are feasible.

Having considered some of the characteristics of the different types of information, we turn finally to their special roles in organization. To say that information is the life blood of organization is probably not too great an exaggeration. Our primary interest lies in social organization, but suitable examples of organized activity are also provided by biological organisms, artificial control systems, computers, etc. Consider the ways in which information is processed by the human organism. Signals from the environment impinge on sensory receptors such as the eye and the ear; they are encoded into neural impulses and in this form are transmitted to the brain. The process of transmission may be modeled by means of a noisy communication channel, thus introducing the selective theory of information. However, when messages are interpreted and translated into action, the semantic component of information comes into play. Information is essential to the integration and coordination of the various functions and activities of an organism. Both internal homeostatic controls and mechanisms mediating responses to external stimuli are driven by information. Most of these uses have parallels in social systems.

3. Social Complexity

That society is becoming ever more complex, no one seems to doubt. One source of this belief lies in the observation that social organization is more differentiated now than in the past. Division of labor and specialization of function are all-pervasive features of a society which appears to us as an exceedingly intricate web of interdependent elements. Industrialization and its concomitant urbanization are the principal formative influences in the emergence of this intricate web. According to Faunce(1968)

> One of the best-documented effects of the emergence of manufacturing industries in the early stages of the Industrial Revolution was an increase in the degree of division of labor. This pattern of effects could clearly be seen in England during the period we have been describing and was repeated in Continental European countries and the United States as they became industrialized during the next century. Agricultural societies are relatively undifferentiated ... India, with its highly elaborated caste structure, however, is a clear exception to this generalization. Althoggh industrialization is obviously not the only process capable of producing an extensive division of labor, it may still be said that all industrial societies are characterized by a high level of occupational specialization, while agricultural societies, with few exceptions, are not.[9]

In addition to structural differentiation, complexity is manifest in social choice. Mobility characterizes all spheres of social existence. The individual is free to choose an occupation, a place to live, a mate, a life style, etc.; and none of these choices are exclusive forever. It is largely this diversity of options which generates the enormous volume of transactions typically cited to justify computer applications. The itinerant character of modern life necessitates extensive record-keeping in order to provide social services. Physical transfer of cash is too clumsy to meet the needs of a fluid business community and a public in perpetual motion, so that mountains of checks must be handled and credit card transactions processed. Educational institutions offer training programs in much the same way as department stores market the seasons' fashions. The ubiquitous media feature entertainment to satisfy our craving for novelty. Even our maladies, such as the once fashionable "information-input overload," reflect a super abundance of possibilities. In short, prodigal choice is the hallmark of contemporary life, from the garage to the bedroom.

The apparently anomalous example of India as a non-industrialized but highly differentiated society provides some insight into the divergent sources of social complexity. Freedom of choice is not a necessary consequence of structural differentiation. In the elaborate caste structure of India, behavior is rigidly prescribed; yet social scientists regard Indian society as complex. The specialization of function which is common to the predominantly agrarian society of India and the industrialized West warrants the ascription of complexity to both. But the relative absence of individual choice in the former, testifies to a significant difference. Both societies exhibit organized complexity, whereas only the latter reveals a high degree of disorganized complexity. This distinction helps to clarify the import of the argument from complexity as it applies to the question of the centralization of authority.

A highly structured social system in which patterns of behavior are mediated endogenously requires a minimum of coercion to insure satisfactory performance. In such a case, admittedly an ideal situation, deviance is truly aberrant behavior. By contrast, where internal weakness supports exaggerated choice, exogenous controls become necessary. The disorganized complexity characteristic of our own society raises the specter of chaos. And it is this aspect of complexity to which the modern Hobbesian responds with visions of a computer-based future. Social experimentation does not require the technological apparatus so dear to the advocates of real-time information systems. In any event, it is superfluous when the community is ill-disposed and ill-equipped to discover its own interests and identity. One may object to free information flow on grounds analogous to Marx's objections to the unconscionable practices of free trade in the early nineteenth century. Development of the instruments for controlling potential chaos is not likely to underwrite the emergence of Dewey's ideal public.

Contemporary society may be compared to a rambling edifice which has grown by accretion. Unlike the great cathedrals which inspire our admiration for the virtues of a simpler age, it is singularly deficient in architectural integrity. For lack of a compelling aesthetic, we describe its form in terms of complexity. But even so, we fail to distinguish between structure and mere diversity. The edifice has become problematic because its internal flaws and contradictions are beginning to surface. Now and then, part of the structure collapses, and we are forced into taking remedial action. Many programs have been proposed for coping more systematically with these problems. Two divergent approaches deserve comment. According to conventional wisdom, the defects of the building can be checked by installing sensors in the various components and monitoring them at a central location. In this way, it is believed that deterioration can be reversed and new development undertaken by an enlightened team of planners making effective use of the information available from the sensors. The rationale here is based on transmuting selective information into structural gold.

Perhaps the modern alchemists will be more successful than their ignorant ancestors. But there is another alternative: reduce the disorganized complexity. It is possible in principle to alter the structure by creating a constellation of smaller buildings, each with its own autonomous organization.[10] In such an arrangement, genuine experimentation might prevail, without the risks attendant upon large-scale enterprise. Local integrity is a more manageable goal. The sacrifice of choice for its own sake seems like a small price to pay for stability and coherence. These ends are certainly not alien to the conventional program, but under it they are likely to obtain as side effects of oppressive control; and, in the long-run, stability cannot be maintained by police and armed guards.

The politics of complexity lead to many distortions. A historical trend demanding a particular course of social action is more powerful than the will of any individual and creates the conditions of its own rationality. Since decision-makers are in the business of eliminating alternatives, complexity for a corporate manager or government official is likely to signify a situation with many choices. This primary understanding, based as it is on concrete experience, produces a distorted picture of reality when coupled with what everyone knows about the division of labor and specialization of function. Identification of the two types of complexity sustains one's faith in the rectitude of the technological approach to the control of chaos. From such a position, it is difficult to see that the technology itself may contribute to increasing disorganized complexity.

The possibility of complexity with limited individual choice points up the critical importance of values in preserving social stability. Social complexity need not generate the problems of control that we face. It is the absence of a coherent system of values rather than any intrinsic structural complexity which accounts for the disorder threatening our society. Vulnerability is a more appropriate concept. The massive concentration of capital resources in industries which depend on one another for production and distribution of commodities demand protection against social disorder caused by the lack of coherence in contemporary life. Our society is extremely vulnerable not simply because of the functional and structural interdependence of people and institutions, but as a consequence of stretched or broken threads in the social fabric. This is a feature of modernity better described by poets than social scientists.

> Turning and turning in the widening gyre
> The falcon cannot hear the falconer;
> Things fall apart; the centre cannot hold;
> Mere anarchy is loosed upon the world,
> The blood-dimmed tide is loosed, and everywhere
> The ceremony of innocence is drowned;
> The best lack all conviction, while the worst
> Are full of passionate intensity.
> (W.B. Yeats, 1924)[11]

4. Centralization of Power

The rapid increase in the range of social choice has been and continues to be met by increasing centralization of power. Expanding computer application in decision-making is viewed by proponents as a natural response to the need for centralization of function in complex organizations. Government, for example, is charged with the responsibility for making decisions which affect many different sectors of society: industry, labor, education, health services, etc. In order for government decision-makers to plan intelligently, it is essential for them to have access to reliable information regarding all aspects of proposed policy. Since data collection and record-keeping functions are spread among many government agencies, and the volume of information required by government decision-makers is so great, it is argued that some form of centralized information processing is required.

This argument is historically familiar and resembles the litany of reasons periodically intoned before the public to justify defense expenditures. The connection between improved administrative controls and military activities is not a fortuitous one, as Max Weber explains.

> [T]he bureaucratic tendency has chiefly been influenced by needs arising from the creation of standing armies as determined by power politics and by the development of public finance connected with the military establishment. In the modern state, the increasing demands for administration rest on the increasing complexity of civilization and push towards bureaucratization. (Weber; in: Gerth and Mills,1946,p. 212)

Computer technology forms part of the technical apparatus appropriated by the modern state to consolidate its regulatory powers. Centralized management is facilitated by the achievements of technology in transportation, communication, and now information-processing. "The bureaucratic structure goes hand in hand with the concentration of the material means of management in the hands of the master."(Weber)

The creation of information-processing systems with databanks for use by administrators and policy planners seems at first glance to have much to recommend it. There is some evidence to suggest that there would be considerable reductions in operating costs of many government agencies. What is more, one might anticipate more informed policy decisions and improved social services simply on the basis of the availability of more extensive and reliable information. The proponents of databanks are also aware of the dangers of possible abuse: access by unauthorized persons, either in business or criminal organizations, and manipulation by corrupt government officials for private ends. However, it is felt that the possible abuses constitute a tolerable risk which can be minimized by taking security measures to control and monitor access.

As we have indicated repeatedly, the persuasive character of information systems in government and industry derives from their ability to mitigate the effects of disorganized complexity. The modern state exists on the edge of chaos; disorder is endemic to the mass society. This is the anarchy of which Wiener(1961,p. 148) spoke.

> There [are] those who see nothing good in the anarchy of modern society, and in whom an optimistic feeling that there must be some way out has led to overvaluation of the possible homeostatic elements in the community. Much as we may sympathize with these individuals and appreciate the emotional dilemma in which they find themselves, we cannot attribute too much value to this type of wishful thinking. It is the mode of thought of the mice when faced with the problem of belling the cat. Undoubtedly it would be very pleasant for us mice if the predatory cats of this world were to be belled, but— who is going to do it? Who is to

assure us that ruthless power will not find its way back into the hands of those most avid for it?

For the most part, the debate over databanks and computer utilities has centered about tactical considerations of the sort summarized above. The strategic impact has largely been ignored. Since the issue has such broad implications this response is not surprising. However, one is entitled to question the seductive character of the framework for tactical analysis. Does the problem in fact reduce to weighing on one hand the benefits of improved bureaucratic organization and consequent improvements in decision-making and social services, against, on the other hand, the dangers of invasion of privacy and abuse of public trust? Can we be so certain that the goals we want to achieve as a society will best be served by accomplishing these limited objectives? There is really no way to answer this question honestly by anticipating the future. The present state of futurist projection is little better than the prophesying by diviners and oracles of old. The more prudent course calls for understanding the historical forces which have shaped our present values and attitudes, so that we may gain deeper insight into the biases underlying desired futures and perhaps influence the emergence of a desirable future.

Weizenbaum(1969) discusses some of the consequences of population growth as evidenced by what he terms the "homogenization of life styles." It is a paradox of disorganized complexity that great diversity should amount to so much sameness. For all the different models of automobiles, gadgets of every description, and liberated mores, our "life styles" are as standardized and interchangeable as the parts produced in our factories. The computer is seen as a necessary but not sufficient instrument for dealing with this condition. Although not explicitly stated, the process of homogenization is seen to be encouraged by the increasing centralization of control made possible through the use of computers. Weizenbaum's concern over the emergence of two separate cultures distinguished according to their ability to utilize computing facilities supports this view. However, it appears from the discussion that the danger of power concentration derives quite simply from inappropriate applications of computer technology. No account is taken of historical trends. Although we may ignore history, history is unlikely to ignore us.

There is a pronounced trend in the history of the modern period toward the centralization of power. Coping with the current problem requires an understanding of the underlying historical trend.

Bertrand de Jouvenel(1962) describes the transformation of power in Western history.

> The history of the West, from the time of Europe's fragmentation into sovereign states, shows us an almost uninterrupted advance in the growth of governmental Power. The only way of failing to see it is to fix exclusive attention on the forms which Power takes: a picture of pure fantasy is then formed, in which monarchs appear as masters to whose exactions there are no bounds, to be succeeded by representative governments whose resources are proportionate to their authority, until in the end democracy succeeds and receives from a consenting people only what it chooses to give to a Power which is its servant.
>
> These are imponderables. But there are also ponderables— the dimensions of armies, the weight of taxation, the number of officials. The measurable scale of these implements provides an exact index of the growth of Power. Begin at the reign of Philip Augustus [king of France from 1180 to 1223]. Without taxation to maintain him, the king lives, like other landlords, off his own estate. Without an army at his command, he keeps a meager bodyguard who feed at his own table. Without officials, he depends for the discharge of public business on ecclesiastics whom he employs and on servants whom he appoints. Even his public treasury, as well as his private fortune, has an ecclesiastical home and is left in the hands of the monks who act as his bankers. Though I am his subject, my path never crosses that of this head squire; he demands no tax from me, claims from me no military service, and passes no law which can possibly affect my life.
>
> By the end of the reign of Louis XIV, what a change is here for my countrymen! After a struggle lasting for centuries, the people have been brought to fill the royal coffers at regular intervals. The monarch maintains out of his revenues a standing army of two hundred thousand men. His intendants make him obeyed in every province, and his police harry the malcontents. He gives out laws and sets his dragoons at those who do not worship God in what he considers the right way; an enormous army of officials animates and directs the nation. Power has imposed its will. It is now no longer one small dot in society but a great stain at the center of it, a network of lines which run right through it.
>
> An infliction, you say? Is not the revolution which overthrows the king going to pull down his structure, attack his apparatus of command, which it will partly at any rate destroy, and reduce the taxation paid by the people? By no means; instead it will introduce the conscription which the monarchy long desired but never had the strength to realize. True it is that

Calonne's budgets will never be seen again; but the reason simply is that they will be doubled under Napoleon and trebled under the Restoration. The intendant will have gone, but the prefect will have taken his place. And so the distension grows. From one regime to another, always more soldiers, more taxes, more laws, more officials. (Jouvenel, 1962, pp. 127-128)[12]

McDermott(1969) confirms the trend toward centralization of power in the contemporary world; but his discussion of the rise and spread of the democratic ethos in Europe and North America appears at first glance to contradict it. However, all the contributing factors (printing press, development of transportation and communication, growth in organized means of popular social expression, etc.) which McDermott views as having narrowed the gap between ruler and ruled, served also to create a mass society in which the sovereign power of a king was replaced by the far more commanding sovereignty of the peoples' representatives. According to de Jouvenel, it is in the nature of power to expand.

> [I]t is through the interplay of [an egoistical urge combined with the will to serve society] that the tendency of Power is towards occupying an ever larger place in society; the various conjunctures of events beckon it on at the same time that its appetite is driving it to fresh pastures. Thus there ensues a growth of Power to which there is no limit, a growth which is fostered by more and more altruistic externals, though the motive-spring is still as always the wish to dominate. (Jouvenel, 1962, p. 119)

We have already examined several instances of this tendency. The introduction of computers in large corporations has led to the centralization of decision-making (see Chapter 4). Whisler(1967) discovered in his study of effects of computers on management, that the middle ranks in the corporate hierarchy are either eliminated or have their scope of action severely reduced. The gap between top and bottom widens. Similar developments are observed in the area of governmental decision-making. There is considerable evidence to support McDermott's contention that there is a growing rift between the ruling class and the lower orders of society.

5. The Myth of Complexity

The claim of social necessity for technological development obscures the motive of those in power to consolidate and enlarge their power. Jouvenel explains how the public interest is used to justify and accomplish extensions of power.

To raise contributions, Power must invoke the public interest. It was in this way that the Hundred Years' War, by multiplying the occasions on which the monarchy was forced to request the cooperation of the people, accustomed them in the end, after a long succession of occasional levies, to a permanent tax, an outcome which outlived the reason for it.

It was in this way, too, that the Revolutionary Wars provided the justification for conscription, even though the files of 1789 disclosed a unanimous hostility to its feeble beginnings under the monarchy. Conscription achieved fixation. And so it is that times of danger, when Power takes action for the general safety, are worth much to it in accretions to its armoury; and these, when the crisis has passed, it keeps. (Jouvenel, 1962, p. 129)

The argument for further development of computer technology in administration and policy-planning may be paraphrased as follows. Society is becoming ever more complex, and thus it is necessary to make use of the computer in order to deal with the potential chaos of this complexity. Armer(1966) paints a glowing picture of the opportunities in both industry and government for effectively utilizing the speed and accuracy of the computer. Of course there are problems, but they are not insurmountable. These problems are the negative consequences of technological development, which must be faced, according to Mesthene(1968), by encouraging institutional innovation. Westin(1967a) regards the development of information systems as inevitable and desirable. This new technology is not without certain negative features (invasion of privacy, abuse of public trust, etc.), but new legislation and regulatory mechanisms can be designed to handle them. Michael(1968) focuses on the use of computers in social planning. He has some of the same fears as Weizenbaum regarding participation in decision-making, and offers up continual education as a partial solution. Fano(1972) goes much further in suggesting that a "procognitive system" such as envisioned by Licklider(1965) is essential for the preservation of our society (see Chapter 6). That is to say, unless information is made universally accessible, we will not be able to deal with the challenge of complexity.

There is a missing component in all of these arguments, namely the fact that increasing complexity is a concomitant of the centralization of power and not a "natural" feature of social evolution. A vicious cycle is created by the technocratic response to conditions of increased complexity. Each extension of power leads to ever greater social complexity by undermining the integrity and cohesiveness of local communities. We are paying a heavy price for our mobility. As the constraining influences of family and community weaken, there appears to be greater lawlessness and thus the "need" for centralized bureaucratic control in the form of administrators, policy planners, and police becomes evident. The claim that this is a necessary or inevitable development rests on an elitist view of social organization; it is an argument in support of special priviledge. The myth of complexity consists in the conviction that we must abandon any hope of altering the conditions on which the apparent need for further consolidation of power is based.

As indicated earlier on, the notion of complexity is not an intrinsic system property. It can only be defined for a particular aspect of a system. From an individual standpoint, the breakdown of the extended family which resulted from industrialization exemplifies the often tragic over-simplification of human relations brought about by technology. The rich kinship structures of the past have either been drastically weakened or completely destroyed. In some parts of the world, even the nuclear family is virtually extinct. Do the myriad superficial associations normally formed in the contemporary world which substitute for the deep bonds of a vanishing family life constitute a net increase in complexity? This is certainly a moot point.

There can be little doubt that centralized decision-making undermines the integrity and cohesiveness of local communities. Social institutions cannot exercise effective moral suasion unless they play a vital role in community affairs. Like most other abilities, the exercise of responsibility atrophies from disuse. If we are unwilling to take responsibility for making decisions which affect us, eventually we will lose the option altogether. Since the industrial revolution, we have moved from standardized interchangeable parts in manufacturing to standardized, interchangeable people in society. But life is not lived in the aggregate. It has taken thousands of millennia for life to emerge from the primeval ooze, for individuals to become differentiated from the aggregate. Modern civilization seems determined to crawl back into that primeval state, Asimov's(1973) direct mail advertising to the contrary, notwithstanding. The computer is just another tool in the long history of the democratization of violence. The French revolution made conscription a permanent feature of our collective experience, thus democratizing the physical violence of warfare. Now, we are engaged in the more subtle process of democratizing psychic violence through the use of computers by centralized bureaucracies.

The temptation to use a tool because it is available and there is something at hand which calls for its use is a formidable one to resist. But when the stakes are high enough, resistance to temptation becomes a virtue. One may agree that centralized policy-planning and social services require centralized databanks and information systems, and that information technology is adequate to the task of guaranteeing against the obvious abuses; and yet one may take issue with the creation of such systems. The obvious forms of abuse are not the most worrisome ones. The frightening prospect here is the abrogation of community responsibility and its consequences, namely, the exercise of overwhelming power by legitimately constituted governments. We have already compromised our responsibility for making informed judgments on many matters of local and national policy by deferring to so-called "experts." The next step if taken, would constitute a dangerous extension of Hobbesian social contract. The stability afforded by a paternalistic Leviathan may be desirable so long as potentially destructive acts are rectifiable through community action. It is certainly not clear, however, that it is possible to extend the powers of Leviathan indefinitely without sacrificing the principle of rectifiability.

> Surely some revelation is at hand;
> Surely the Second Coming is at hand.
> The Second Coming! Hardly are these words out
> When a vast image out of *Spiritus Mundi*
> Troubles my sight: somewhere in the sands of the desert
> A shape with lion body and the head of a man,
> A gaze blank and pitiless as the sun,
> Is moving its slow thighs, while all about it
> Reel shadows of the indignant desert birds.
> The darkness drops again; but now I know
> That twenty centuries of stony sleep
> Were vexed to nightmare by a rocking cradle,
> And what rough beast, its hour come round at last,
> Slouches towards Bethlehem to be born?
> (W.B. Yeats, 1924)

[1] Reprinted by permission, *American Scientist*, journal of Sigma Xi, The Scientific Research Society of North America.

[2] In Chapter 4, we discussed Simon's conception of hierarchy in connection with social organizations, particularly corporations.

3 See Mowshowitz(1968b).
4 Reprinted by permission of the Society for General Systems Research.
5 This approach is similar to the procedure followed by the parlor game "Twenty Questions," where one must identify an object by a series of questions.
6 The technical details are beyond the scope of the present discussion; see Mowshowitz(1968a).
7 For a comprehensive treatment of the subject, see Ash(1965) or Gallager(1968).
8 More precisely, an ensemble is a set of messages with an associated probability distribution.
9 From *Problems of an Industrial Society* by W.A. Faunce. Copyright 1968 by McGraw-Hill Book Company. Used with permission of McGraw-Hill Book Company.
10 This is essential to the growth of "convivial tools." See Illich(1973).
11 Reprinted with permission of Macmillan Publishing Co., Inc. From *The Collected Poems of W.B. Yeats* by W.B. Yeats. Copyright 1924 by Macmillan Publishing Co., Inc., renewed 1952 by Bertha Georgie Yeats.
12 From *On Power* by Bertrand de Jouvenel, translated by J.F. Huntington. Copyright 1949 by The Viking Press, Inc. Reprinted by permission of The Viking Press, Inc.

Part IV.
Identity and
Uncertainty: The Machine
as Mirror Image

Thus far we have examined the impact of computer technology on social organizations and social structure. The focus has been on issues surrounding the behavior of groups rather than individuals. We surveyed the accomplishments of computer applications in industry and social services. Although consideration of the individual was not absent, the principal concern was with effects on organization. We also treated the use of information-processing systems in controlling disorder from the same point of view. In the remaining chapters the emphasis shifts from social organization to the individual. We will attempt to deal more systematically with the effects or information technology on individual attitudes, values and expectations.

The transformation of society brought about by the industrial revolution and expanding technological development has placed severe strains on traditional modes of human interaction. Since the late nineteenth century, observers have pointed to a growing uncertainty reflected in individual behavior and a concomitant preoccupation with the problem of personal identity. David Riesman(1956) captured the essence of this uncertainty in his discussion of the other-directed person of the modern era. Lacking strong internalized guidelines for behavior, the modern individual typically takes his cues from his peer group and the mass media.

> The other-directed person must be able to receive signals from far and near; the sources are many, the changes rapid. What can be internalized, then, is not a code of behavior but the elaborate equipment needed to attend to such messages and occasionally to participate in their circulation. As against guilt-and-shame controls, though of course these survive, one

prime psychological lever of the other-directed person is a diffuse anxiety. This control equipment, instead of being like a gyroscope, is like a radar. (Riesman, *et al.*, 1956, p. 42)

The so-called problem of personal identity has become so pervasive as to make its way into commercial advertising. Products are touted for their personalizing virtues rather than how well they function. The rapid changes in literary and artistic fashions also bear witness to our preoccupation with a crisis of identity. This search for definition and direction is attributed by many observers to the fluidity of mass society.

> Difficulty in affirming a positive image of self is pervasive in industrial societies. Industrial man frequently participates in activities in which he has invested little of his self and in which he is consequently self-estranged in the classic sense of this term as developed by Marx and Fromm. Freed from the bonds of small-group pre-industrial society, the individual is confronted with the problem of maintaining self-esteem in an unstable, fragmented, and poorly integrated social order. The result is a sense of powerlessness, meaninglessness, and normlessness. (Faunce, 1968, pp. 131-132)[1]

In order to frame subsequent discussion, let us consider some of the factors which have contributed to this state of affairs. The process of industrialization which began in earnest in the eighteenth century is clearly one of the underlying causes. Before the factory became the dominant form of social production, most manufacturing was carried out on a very small scale, and, what is more, the bulk of humanity was engaged in agriculture. Survival, for both the peasant and the artisan was largely a family affair, in which all members contributed in their own peculiar way. The emergence of large-scale industrial enterprises changed all of this. One of the fundamental requirements of early capitalism was a cheap supply of labor. This need, embodied in the social forces which created an impoverished class of former peasants and artisans, turned the human being into an instrument of labor, a commodity to be bought and sold in the market place. This reduction of individual worth to an economic value in a free market, and the wretched squalor of life in the new industrial centers, effectively destroyed the cohesion of family life among the proletariat. Individual goals were no longer embedded in family life, and the stark conditions of subsistence living made family discipline impossible.

The undermining of the authority of the family was not confined to the oppressed proletariat. The middle classes were ultimately affected both by the brutalization of the proletariat, and their own belief in the ethic of economic reductionism. The first casualty of the industrial revolution was the extended family. But the forces set in motion have not yet been fully spent. When the worst abuses of industrialization were curbed, another feature of the new order became more noticeable. The reduction of the individual's social worth to his productive capacity in a competitive labor market had the effect of making people more or less interchangeable, a clear parallel to the interchangeability of parts in manufacturing. This economic indifference to human attributes, which were once so important in the family, provided the basis for the social mobility which characterizes the contemporary world. Although mobility opens new horizons and creates opportunities, it also undermines stability and gives rise to uncertainty. Perhaps the last act in the unfolding drama initiated by the industrial revolution will be the complete dissolution of the family.

A more subtle influence of industrialization derives from the relationship between human beings and technological artifacts. In a period when an individual's worth came to be defined in terms of productive capacity or the accumulation of capital, machines were being developed to replace or augment human skills in the factory. Setting the stage in this way, clearly puts the human being at a disadvantage. In economic terms, worth can be measured precisely, and people are often slower, less accurate, and less reliable than machines. Since no one is likely to admit being inferior to a machine, the search for an alternative source of identity or purpose becomes imperative.

It is one of the ironies of modern life that the source of this identity crisis should become an instrument of symptomatic relief. Our society has substituted status for meaning, and in the quest for personal definition through status-roles, machines and gadgets play an important part. For example, among certain groups, owning a particular type of automobile is not only a mark of wealth, but serves to articulate the owner's personality. Commercial advertising panders to these uncertainties and confusion; the pathetic character of dependence on artifacts such as cars to achieve personal definition is underscored by the cynical manipulation of the consuming public by large corporations.

The difficulty of achieving a coherent sense of self has been increased by the development of computers. No doubt Isaac Asimov (see Chapter 6) would take issue with this remark, in view of the potentialities of direct mail advertising aided by sophisticated information retrieval systems. However, no matter how accurate the interest profiles, there is no escaping the fact of manipulation by corporate interests; and there is really little difference between this type of manipulation and the more crass variety associated with the promotion of technological artifacts as adjuncts to personality. In the long-run, the principal effect of computers on the individual is likely to be their encroachment on human identity. The last enclave of human skills is now under siege. Once thought beyond the reach of non-human agency, it has now become clear that tasks requiring intelligence can be performed by machines.

In what follows we will examine the impact of the computer on individual behavior. Our cultural and intellectual life may be viewed in terms of the changing conception of man's place in the universe. Various intellectual achievements have eliminated seeming discontinuities between man and the cosmos, the biosphere, and the unconscious. What remains is the apparent discontinuity between men and machines. We will consider the implications of this view in our discussion of man-machine interaction in the contemporary world. The question of machine encroachments on human identity and uniqueness is brought into sharp focus by developments in artificial intelligence. Our treatment of these developments will stress the problematic character of man-machine coexistence. Finally, we will turn to the literary record of men and machines as a vehicle for probing the human significance of modern technology, and to recapitulate the major themes of the book.

[1] From *Problems of an Industrial Society* by W.A. Faunce. Copyright 1968 by McGraw-Hill Book Company.

Chapter 13.
Man-Machine Interaction

The emergence of machines which challenge man's pride of place among rational creatures serves to aggravate an already profound anxiety manifest in contemporary affairs. It is not enough that our purpose in life be reduced to waiting for Godot; we must now accept conditions on the nature of this Godot. Nietzsche's overman may very well turn out to be a machine. That the Theatre of the Absurd should be followed by a computer act may be dramatically defensible, but in human terms it reveals moral weakness and decay. It means, according to Weizenbaum(1972) "that we have permitted technological metaphors ... and technique itself to so thoroughly pervade our thought processes that we have finally abdicated to technology the very duty to formulate questions." (p. 611) Different observers use different terms to characterize this tendency. Some speak of cultural lag, the inability of institutions and values to keep pace with the rapid changes in technology; others bemoan the destruction of the old order or the collapse of traditional values.

One thing is quite clear. In the process of reshaping the world according to the objective vision of science, we have destroyed the foundations of the old myths. Philosophers have been aware of this for some time. Nietzsche proclaimed the death of God a hundred years ago.

> Whither is God [cried the madman]. I shall tell you. *We have killed him*— you and I. All of us are his murderers. But how have we done this? How were we able to drink up the sea? Who gave us the sponge to wipe away the entire horizon? What did we do when we unchained this earth from its sun? Whither is it moving now? Whither are we moving now? ... This tremendous event is still on its way, still wandering— it has not yet reached the ears of man. (Nietzsche, 1882, pp. 95-96)[1]

The full implications of the death of God are little clearer for us than they were for Nietzsche. The one major lesson of the intervening period has been the problematic nature of any second coming; we are justifiably more suspicious of millennial pretensions. Although science and technology have contributed most to our current predicament, there is no indication that they can furnish the myths and moral structures with which to extricate ourselves.

What is the significance of this observation concerning cultural and moral decay? Is it an accidental feature of certain dislocations on the road to perpetual material progress? Or does it signal the decline of our civilization as claimed by Oswald Spengler? Although we cannot hope to resolve this question, we can gauge its importance by examining some of the central issues. Barrett(1958, p. 25), in his examination of contemporary philosophical issues, points to the decline of religion as the critical element in modern Western history. "In losing religion, man lost the concrete connection with a transcendent realm of being; he was set free to deal with this world in all its brute objectivity." What has replaced religion as a "psychic container," a framework in which to define one's life? The closest we can come to a new spiritual home are the twin principles of production and consumption. Van den Haag(1957, p. 174) writes: "If one lives and dies discontinuously and promiscuously in anonymous surroundings, it becomes hard to identify with anything, even the self, and uneconomic to be attached to anything, even one's own individuality."

Perhaps the most revealing aspect of the new order built by science and technology is the debased role of the arts. Art, literature, and music function decoratively in our society. That universities certify as educated, students who are virtually illiterate, testifies to this fact. According to Read(1955, p. 35): "We must wait, wait perhaps for a very long time, before any vital connection can be re-established between art and society." The decorative function of art is apparent from the lack of any real appreciation on the part of the ordinary person. "Do not let us deceive ourselves: the common man, such as we produce in our civilization, is aesthetically a dead man." (p. 60). By the same token, literature is treated largely as a form of amusement or as a means of escape. The dance, too, has suffered a similar fate. Writing on the decline of the choral dance, Halmos(1952, p. 31) states that: "The dance today is a degenerated survival of an ancient group language, a language which was meant to be a medium of solidarity, of self-expression and release. In our times it is an empty form at best, when it does not serve other ulterior ends."

Of course, one might protest that this gloomy prognosis is too one-sided. Have we not evolved a dynamically experimental culture with new forms of expression? After all, culture is the symbolic expression of the values and goals of society, and our society is often characterized by its institutionalization of change. The difficulty here stems from the concepts we use to analyze culture.

Perhaps future historians will find it possible to reconcile the emergence of a new culture and a new morality with the absence of religion, and with art forms which play no significant role in human social behavior. Be that as it may, for us caught between a culture which is at least familiar and an unknown future which may or may not materialize, it is difficult to be optimistic. In terms of what we have, our greatest hope is our science and technology, and this recognition gives us little solace.

In what follows, we will examine various aspects of man-machine interaction. First, we will look at the impact of mechanization on the modern world, especially the effects of coexistence with machines on the individual's view of nature and himself. Models of the human being are strongly influenced by machines. This influence leads us to consider the role of the human-machine dichotomy in the formation of our self-image. Computers serve as a tool for extending human intelligence, and it is held in some quarters that current man-computer systems may evolve into symbiotic relationships. We will investigate the nature of such projected symbiosis and trace its consequences. To round out the picture of the individual's interaction with machines, we will report on contemporary attitudes toward computers. Finally, we will discuss ethical problems which arise in the practice of science and technology, and consider some of the broader issues associated with professional conduct in computer science.

1.   The Human Meaning of Mechanization

Technological artifacts are an integral part of the human landscape. The instruments, machines and gadgets we use routinely affect our bodily functions, our movements, and our interactions with other people. It is easy enough to produce an *ad hoc* catalogue of effects but rather difficult to ascertain the extent of our dependence on the products of technology. This is so because patterns of behavior often crystallize in response to an invention. Mumford's(1934) discussion of glass making provides an example. The use of glass in architecture changed the character of indoor living. It made possible a lengthened working day— particularly in cold or inclement weather— and also facilitated the development of various optical instruments which have had a profound effect on our view of the world. Spectacles in particular may have contributed to the revival of learning experienced during the Renaissance. In any case, the use of corrective lenses certainly altered, quite literally, people's vision of reality. The introduction of mirrors too must be credited with modifying our self-image.

Giedion(1949) documents the progress of mechanization, its effects on human employments and living circumstances. Agriculture, the principal occupation of most of the earth's inhabitants since the dawn of civilization, has in the West been transformed by machines and modern production methods into large-scale capital enterprises involving a small fraction of the population. The highly skilled craftsman has largely disappeared, having been mechanized into oblivion; and many ancient crafts have atrophied from lack of practitioners. Our daily bread is baked by machine; our living-space and the objects that fill it have also been transformed by technology. Mass production has introduced a remarkable uniformity in home furnishings, and "labor-saving" devices have completely changed the character of domestic activities.

One of the most critical changes in the role of technology in the modern period is the shift in our relationship to instruments of production. From the Medieval period to the present, the artisan has given way to the machine. The growth of specialization, and the organization of production into larger and larger social units, culminating in the mechanized, automated factory of today has created a tremendous gap between producer and consumer. This gap is manifest in many ways. The expendable character of consumer goods and the consequent waste of productive capacity and resources reveal a careless attitude toward the productive process.[2] Even if an individual participates in production, his role is likely to be so specialized as to make it quite impossible for him to relate to the article being produced.[3] The psychological result is the alienated condition of modern man.

> Alienation as we find it in modern society is almost total; it pervades the relationship of man to his work, to the things he consumes, to the state, to his fellow man, and to himself. Man has created a world of man-made things as it never existed before. He has constructed a complicated social machine to administer the technical machine he built. Yet the whole creation of his stands over and above him. He does not feel himself as a creator and center, but as the servant of a Golem, which his hands have built. (Fromm, 1955, pp. 124-125)[4]

The transformation of the human environment brought about by modern science and technology is unprecedented in scope and intensity. Events of comparable significance must be sought in the transition from the nomadic existence of prehistoric man to the settled agriculture which formed the basis of civilization. Whereas the latter took place over a period of tens of thousands of years, the development of the modern world is reckoned in centuries, and the industrial revolution erupted a mere two hundred years ago. In this brief time span, man's relationship to nature and the conditions governing communal life have undergone radical changes. The seemingly endless procession of inventions, experiments, and new forms of social organization has prompted contemporary observers to speak of change itself as a dimension of modern life. It would appear that cultural evolution has accelerated to the point where major modifications are registered within an individual's lifetime. Perhaps the most striking feature of this new dispensation is the challenge it poses to the plasticity of human behavior. The individual's ability to adapt to rapidly changing conditions is one of the most popular issues of our time. Transience, novelty, choice, and diversity are frequently used to characterize the contemporary scene.[5] Impermanence is as much a feature of human relationships as it is of architecture and consumer goods. Technology has so altered the relative costs of goods and services, that it is often less expensive to replace an article than it is to repair it. The same attitude prevails in family life.

The mere existence of machines and mechanized procedures cannot account for these modified ground rules; but, as we have stressed repeatedly, neither can science and technology be comprehended as pure instrumentalities. Human values are not disembodied principles which are to be accepted or rejected according to individual likes and dislikes; they represent the codification of established practices embedded in social institutions. Technology affects behavior by altering the form and content of these practices, and ultimately reshapes the structure of communities. The thrust of technological development in modern history suggests directed activity rather than random applications. Productive efficiency and large-scale organization are too pervasive to be accidental, but not sufficiently universal or eternal to be regarded as intrinsic to social evolution. It is more in keeping with historical trends and our knowledge of human societies to interpret the progress of mechanization as one particular response to the environment. For example, after the fact, we can build theories to explain the peculiar evolution of the factory system, and modern methods of transportation and communication. But it must be remembered that such theories account for what has happened, not what could have happened. To assert that technology has become an autonomous agent of change is not to attribute an occult quality to the growth of modern society which transcends human choice. It simply means that mechanization has affected social organization and individual behavior in such a way as to create a foundation for further development along certain lines. We have cultivated a special relationship to technology wherein needs and conflicts are almost invariably formulated as technical problems requiring technical solutions.

This special relationship is evident from the ways we use and interact with machines. Mechanization is so much a part of the modern experience that we have found it necessary to create a specialized discipline to act as matchmaker between machines and human beings. "Human factors engineering, or human engineering, is concerned with ways of designing machines, operations, and work environments so that they match human capacities and limitations." (Chapanis, 1965, p. 8). The practical utility of this branch of engineering and applied psychology is obvious. For example, designing instrument panels and controls for an aircraft so as to minimize the chance of pilot error is unquestionably a desirable objective. However, one looks in vain for a discipline dedicated to raising questions about the desirability of technical development. Such questions are pursued haphazardly, not because they are unimportant, but because our society is by and large committed to the extension of technology. Whether in agriculture, industry, government administration, or recreation, technical innovation is assumed beneficial unless proven otherwise; and there are no established procedures for constructing or presenting proofs.

The mechanization of agriculture and allied occupations is a particularly important illustration of the working of our peculiar commitment to technology. Here it would seem, the improvements brought about through the use of machines, chemical fertilizers and pesticides, scientific methods of stock breeding and seed selection, etc. are entirely unproblematic. The world's food supply has been increased dramatically, and production is more stable and reliable than ever before. These remarkable achievements overwhelm criticism; yet not all the effects are desirable. Mechanization led to specialization, large-scale operations, and uniformity in agricultural products. "The consumer is educated to remain content with little variety." (Giedion, 1948, p. 133). This may be a small price to pay for increased yields, but it is not clear that the factory model is the most appropriate one for agriculture. Giedion(1948) speaks of the encounter between mechanization and the organic. The disappearance of the self-sufficient farmer signals a break in the continuity of man with nature whose long-term consequences defy analysis.

Moreover, there are basic uncertainties concerning the possible effects of large-scale mechanized farming on the soil and the environment.

> Mechanization comes to a halt before the living substance. A new outlook must prevail if nature is to be mastered rather than degraded. The utmost caution is imperative. This calls for an attitude turning radically away from the idolatry of production. (Giedion, 1948, p. 256)

The extension of mechanized methods to human interaction also warrants extreme care. Press's(1974) call for a moratoriam on the construction of community information utilities is a modest but eminently sound proposal. If we are to come to terms with technology, we must deal with the content of applications as well as their form. The idea of "humanizing" computer systems, for example, amounts to little more than a calculated use of cosmetics to alter visible form.[6] Like human engineering it does not raise questions about the desirability of any particular application, and may serve to obscure substantive criticism in the same way that workers' attitudes are manipulated by industrial and personnel psychologists. Human resilience and adaptability have limits, and the effects of changes in modes of interaction are unpredictable.

> Is what we are witnessing today the convulsions of a transition period, different from earlier periods, yet penetrated like them with the need for continuity? Or does it represent a remolding of life into ways for which a form is as yet lacking, and of which the structural alteration of farming, man's basic calling, stands as the first symptom? (Giedion, 1948, p. 168)

2.   The Man-Machine Dichotomy

Against this background of uncertainty, the problem of personal identity comes into sharp focus. Weizenbaum(1972) attributes greater significance to the unseen "side effects" of computer technology than to its visible impact on society. Side effects here refer to influences on attitudes and values, as opposed to more immediate effects on social organizations or institutions. The subtle influence of technology on man's self-image is in effect the distilled essence of its impact on society, what remains after accidental features have disappeared. Weizenbaum believes that the computer will induce profound changes in man's image of himself. He points to an apparent paradox involving the juxtaposition of autonomous machines and non-autonomous people, and claims that "[t]o understand it, we must realize that man's commitment to science has always had a masochistic component." (p. 610) Mazlish(1967), on the other hand, attributes the paradox to "man's pride, and his refusal to acknowledge" the continuity between men and machines. What is more, this refusal is seen as "the substratum upon which the distrust of technology and an industrialized society has been reared." Ultimately, Mazlish continues, "this last rests on man's refusal to understand and accept his own nature— as a being continuous with the tools and machines he constructs." (p. 278)

Both Weizenbaum and Mazlish appeal to the conventional view of science in intellectual history, as elaborated by Freud and others. Science is credited with having broken down various seeming discontinuities between man and the universe. First, Copernicus removed the earth from the center of the cosmos, and Galileo established a material connection between the earth and the heavenly bodies. Then, Darwin firmly rooted the human species in the animal world. Finally, Freud pointed to the continuity in psychic life between conscious and unconscious phenomena. To complete the picture, Mazlish urges the continuity of men and machines.

A simple question occurs to one at this point. Is the scientific framework the only legitimate one in which to consider discontinuities between human existence and cosmic reality? Perhaps Freud set up a straw man in order to make a point. Consider each of the supposed discontinuities more carefully. Can it be said that myths of creation entail a discontinuity between man and the cosmos? In a world system based on a creative principle in which everything is organized according to a divine scheme, there is no discontinuity. The discontinuity bridged by Copernicus and Galileo was a gap in Christian theology, a gap created by the acceptance of the freedom of natural phenomena from divine intervention.

The tremendous impact of Darwin's theory of evolution testifies more to the changes in Western society brought about by the industrial revolution than it does to any basic discontinuity between man and the animal kingdom. What does the removal of the schizm ultimately accomplish? Was not the rift itself a product of the age? The triumph of technology in the industrial revolution meant the triumph of the principle of conquest and mastery of nature. The degradation of the natural world was an inevitable consequence of this attitude. It is small wonder that the nineteenth century choked on the suggestion of consanguinity with something it regarded as inferior, fit only for conquest and manipulation.

What of Freud's accomplishment? The claim here is that the continuity between mental health and mental illness was established. Again, one cannot take issue with the claim, only with its significance regarding fundamental discontinuities in our worldview. Was it always the case that madmen were regarded as a separate species, and that madness itself was something entirely different from normal behavior? Not at all. Foucault(1967) traces the history of madness in Western civilization. He shows that the dichotomy between reason and unreason emerged in the classical period.

> Confinement was an institutional creation peculiar to the seventeenth century. ... [I]n the history of unreason, it marked a decisive event: the moment when madness was perceived on the social horizon of poverty, of incapacity for work, of inability to integrate with the group. ... The concrete space of classical society reserved a neutral region ... Here reason reigned in the pure state, in a triumph arranged for it in advance over a frenzied unreason. (p. 61)

The position taken by Mazlish reminds one of the commercial baking of bread. The product is said to be enriched because something of what was removed in the process of manufacturing is reintroduced as an additive. The exhortation to accept the continuity of men and machines because the same concepts apply to both is tantamount to advocating acceptance of a condition simply because it is distasteful. After all, is there any compelling intellectual justification for accepting the industrialized world on its own terms? Weizenbaum's remark about the masochistic component in science is seen to have some real foundations.

Since the dawn of consciousness, man has seen something of himself in his surroundings. The spirits and demigods on which his fate once depended constituted a curious amalgam of essentially human characteristics. The universe was ordered and purposeful, however unresponsive and unfathomable. The myths of primitive peoples bear witness to the importance of projection of human needs and expectations on the natural world. All the principal functions of tribal existence were seen to be controlled by benign or malevolent spirits. From the primal act of creation through the recurrent cycle of generation and decay in nature, primitive man imbued the structure of the universe with his own longings and limitations. The operation of projection in cultural evolution is well-known, but there is a companion principle of equal importance which is virtually ignored. This is what one might call mirror vision, mistaking the image of a model for reality itself.

Once a myth becomes well-established, it is impossibly difficult to disentangle it from the "truth" it serves to articulate. So it is not surprising to discover that our attempts to grapple with reality often reflect a struggle with our own creative imagination. The myth of Narcissus provides illuminating insight. Narcissus presents an object lesson in the perils of hybris. There is a powerful tendency in man to deify his own image. This coupled with projection of himself into his surroundings leads to a circular view. First, we paint the world with our own image, and then we use that painting to build a model of ourselves which clearly must reflect a construction of the human environment that already embodies human characteristics. The pattern of projection and mirror vision is by no means limited to primitive peoples. The sustaining myths of our own civilization reveal a similar organization. Classical Greek and Roman culture indulged a host of deities with human traits, and curiously enough both men and gods were subject to cosmic forces which suggest more of human affairs than the structure of the universe. Although the consolidation of the monotheistic principle constituted a major spiritual shift in Western cultural evolution, it did not significantly alter the projective aspect of the earlier demi-gods and deities.

Science is not entirely immune from this subtle form of anthropomorphism. The scientific enterprise lays claim to objectivity in its relentless pursuit of truth. But what is meant by objectivity? Can one ignore the world-view which underlies the model-building of the scientist, and consider only the extent to which he intrudes upon his observations? The edifice of science is built on empirical observation coupled with inductive generalization and deductive reasoning. The building blocks are the observations; rational thought provides the mortar. What of the design of the edifice: does it shape itself, or is the plan hidden in the recesses of the human mind and will? The metaphor is of course simplistic insofar as it ignores the dynamic aspects of evolving scientific theory; but it does serve to illuminate a flaw in the universalistic pretensions of scientific method. It is the values and expectations of the scientist as an exemplar of a cultural tradition and social order which dictates the choice of subject matter to be scrutinized, the particular observations to be entertained, and the tentative hypotheses to be submitted to the rigors of testing.

Western man, like Narcissus, has become intoxicated with his own image in nature and his creations. Every artifact of human culture presents itself to man as a mirror in which his reflection threatens the uniqueness of his identity. In modern times, the emphasis has shifted from nature to machines. The Medieval period refined the principle of godhead in nature with consummate skill and artistry. The legacy of the Renaissance, and more characteristically the Enlightenment, is the relative isolation of the natural world from spiritual principles. Science waged a winning struggle against teleology in the operation of natural forces; but it never succeeded in expunging the face of man from its own ontology. One of the peculiar intellectual achievements of science is the displacement of man's image from nature to cultural artifacts.

The discontinuity between men and machines is a pseudo issue. We see ourselves in machines precisely because of the operation of projection and mirror vision. We are humbled by our artifacts only because our identity is bound up with them. In effecting a schism between the spritual and natural world, we have essentially abandoned the former, consoling ourselves with the thought that somehow the epistemological nature of the one would illuminate the other. The rigid distinction we draw between the physical and the spiritual lends credence to the model of man as a machine. If we are nothing but a spiritual nature superimposed on a physical body, we can separate the physical part and study its properties in isolation. Then the terms applicable to our artifacts become appropriate to ourselves. Current difficulties stem from the disappearance of a discernible spiritual nature. We are no longer animated by a soul. We have become pure mechanism controlled or purposefully guided by more or less arbitrary moral principles.

At first, the projective impulse was narcissistic; but, ultimately, this seemingly innocent indulgence hardened into a fixed view of the world, supported by myriad rationalizations which disguise its origins. Moreover, what were originally ambiguous and complex human qualities, subjectively perceived, became simplified for *genus machina*. Now, unwittingly we borrow back these attributes to construct an impoverished model of ourselves.

3. *Symbiosis or Parasitism*

Our attitudes toward machines are obviously influenced by the way we use them. Until recently there was little question about the respective roles of men and machines in combination. Man has always been the intelligent partner, providing direction and control. Current developments cast some shadows on this arrangement. Licklider(1960), for example, envisions a man-computer symbiosis growing out of current man-machine systems. Existing systems are of two main types. In one, human capabilities are extended through the use of machines controlled by human operators. Examples range from the construction worker operating a crane or a steam shovel, to the scientist using a computer to find an approximate solution to a system of differential equations. The other type is exemplified by numerically controlled machines such as automatic milling devices which are merely "tended" by human operators. True symbiotic relationships between men and machines have yet to emerge, although the development of interactive computing systems has brought us closer to realizing Licklider's criteria for such relationships.

Symbiosis is a biological term meaning "an association of two different organisms (usually two plants, or an animal and a plant) which live attached to each other, or one as a tenant of the other, and contribute to each other's support."[7] It is also used in an extended sense to signify "mutually beneficial association without bodily attachment." Applied to the human organism and the computer, the term is somewhat misleading in that it implies some measure of independence for the latter. Nonetheless, the idea is suggestive in a figurative sense, as it relates to cognitive behavior. Man-computer symbiosis refers mainly to systems designed to handle problem-solving and decision-making. The advance over simple mechanical extensions and fully automated processes described above lies in the possibility of bringing the computer into the formulative stages of problem-solving and utilizing its analytical potential in real-time to facilitate decision-making.[8] Licklider envisions interactive systems which allow for genuine dialogue between the problem solver or decision-maker and the computer.[9] Often the most difficult part of solving a problem involves identifying what it is or finding an appropriate representation. A dialogue system could provide a means for testing different formulations and hypotheses. For the decision-maker, such a system holds out the possibility of exploring alternative strategies before the conditions requiring action have changed.

The need for man-computer symbiosis derives, according to Licklider, from the enormous amount of preparatory effort associated with "technical thinking." A great many tasks which are essentially clerical in nature must be performed in order to get into a position to think. One searches for information, makes preliminary calculations, transforms data into usable forms, etc. All of these tasks could in principle be expedited by the use of an interactive computing system, and thus free the thinker to devote more of his time to intellectual problems. This would entail a more appropriate division of labor in the cognitive domain than ordinarily obtains, namely, using the computer's speed and accuracy, and the human's flexibility to better advantage. The respective roles of the parties to the partnership would of course evolve over time, but initially they could be expected to conform to a straightforward allocation of functions. Direction and control are seen to rest with the human being. The problem-solver establishes goals and supplies the motivation for particular questions, formulates hypotheses and proposes models and procedures. In addition, the discovery of references to relevant ideas and the responsibility for exceptional cases and untoward situations remain in human hands. The machine's part consists primarily of answering questions posed by the problem-solver. This includes testing models and hypotheses against data, performing simulations, carrying out procedures and displaying results.

This type of man-computer symbiosis has been attempted in the design of management information systems, with the disappointing results discussed in Chapter 4. However the technical obstacles are gradually being overcome, and it is reasonable to suppose that sophisticated interactive systems approximating Licklider's proposed symbiotic relationship will emerge in the not too distant future. The implications of this development embrace many of the issues associated with computer applications in industry, education, and government. From an individual standpoint, the central question concerns the locus of control. The projects we undertake are determined to a great extent by the instruments we have available. For example, a rank amateur can build a cabinet with the aid of power tools, whereas it takes a skilled craftsman to achieve the same result with hammer, saw, and chisel. This certainly does not argue against the use of sophisticated tools, but it does reveal a source of dependence, since eventually the skilled craftsman will disappear when there is no longer any discernible need for his services. The net effect of such a loss is a reduction in flexibility and redundancy. It may not be apparent at once, but in the long-run there is likely to be a degradation in the quality and variety of cabinets. What this observation suggests about problem-solving and decision-making has to do with the constraints imposed by the information-processing system on the kinds of questions that can be formulated and the data available for testing. Considerable skill is needed to make intelligent use of such a system.

In recent years, the sedentary habits of citizens in affluent countries have become a matter of public concern. The use of machinery has reduced the physical requirements of most jobs, and as a result people have fewer opportunities to exercise their muscles. Whether or not "fitness programs" can compensate for the lack of physical activity in primary pursuits remains to be seen. The obvious analogy with intellectual functions is instructive. Caution must be exercised in the elaboration of the potential man-computer symbiosis. Loss of vitality may occur in subtle ways. The tendency to accept, uncritically, results displayed by a sophisticated interactive system cannot be ignored, nor is it likely to be eliminated by the ritual incantation of words to the contrary. Moreover, the problem is not confined to the highly trained scientist or professional manager. Assuming the eventual deployment of community information utilities, the dangers of dependence on machines for the framing of questions and selection of evidence become generalized.

Speculation on the future use of computers as intellectual aids raises some important general issues. The question of social need may be spurious, but the tendency toward greater and greater interdependence of men and machines is quite real. Scientists, managers, and government decision-makers already make considerable use of computing systems to assist in the solution of problems. The probable consequences of forging closer ties between men and machines are unclear. Is the outcome likely to be a symbiosis involving the intimate cooperation of two dissimilar entities; or will it end in parasitism, with the host's identity a contentious matter? Samuel Butler raised the possibility of the latter in his novel *Erewhon*. The narrator quotes from a treatise by an earlier Erewhonian philosopher who presents a counter argument to the conventional view that machines are necessarily instruments subject to man's will. "Man's very soul is due to the machines; it is a machine-made thing: he thinks as he thinks, and feels as he feels, through the work that machines have wrought upon him, and their existence is quite as much a *sine quo non* for his, as his for theirs." (Butler, 1872, p. 180)

The struggle between master and servant need not take the form of overt conflict. As Butler suggests the "servant glides by imperceptible approaches into the master." It is not necessary to attribute anything like a determinate will to machines in order for this to take place. The only necessary precondition is that the servant become indispensable to the master. This theme is developed by Harry Kressing(1965) in a novel about a rather unusual cook. The cook insinuates himself into the household of a wealthy family and masterfully manipulates the appetites of his employers. Eventually the family comes to depend on his services to such an extent that the cook becomes the *de facto* head of the household and then proceeds to destroy the family and dissipate its wealth. It is doubtful that this book was intended as an allegory of technological development, but it serves the purpose nicely.

We run the risk of being manipulated by the instruments we have created for the purpose of satisfying our insatiable appetites. Even Licklider's technical thinker may be in for some real surprises. The direction of research, the questions raised, and the facts deemed relevant may all be resolved by the machine servant.

4.   Popular Attitudes Toward Computers

Thus far in our examination of the impact of computers, no account has been given of the general public's response to the new technology. Figures on the number and value of computing installations, together with details of the distribution of applications gives some indication of the computer's social importance; but these indices do not reveal its effect on the lives of ordinary citizens. Since its first commercial uses in the early 1950's, the computer has become a highly visible instrument. This is due partly to coverage in the popular media and partly to contacts with computers on the job. Although comprehensive surveys have been compiled only recently and information on secular trends is virtually non-existent, the various "snapshots" of current attitudes are useful for correcting possible misapprehensions. The following discussion is based on two major surveys, one conducted jointly by the American Federation of Information Processing Societies (AFIPS) and TIME Magazine in 1971 and the other by Canada's Department of Communications (DOC) in the same year. Both samples were of approximately the same size (1001 for the AFIPS-TIME study, and 1030 for the DOC survey); and representative cross sections of the respective populations of the United States and Canada were chosen.[10]

The surveys reveal widespread acquaintance in some form with computers or computer applications. Almost half of the American respondents report some contact with computers in their work experience; and 72% of the Canadian sample indicate "having contact in their homes with something printed out by computer." That only 13% of the Canadians interviewed report direct contact with computers may reflect differing subjective interpretations of the question, but it is also consistent with the fact that there are fewer computers per capita in Canada than in the United States.

This might also account for relative differences in enthusiasm for applications, since favorable attitudes appear to increase with familiarity. Computers are seen to enjoy the prestige generally accorded to technology. 85% of the Americans surveyed believe that life is better because of inventions and technology, and 71% affirm that computers in particular have had a beneficial over-all effect on life. It is also interesting to note that the average person's perception of the computer's capabilities is not quite so misguided as one might have suspected. The AFIPS-TIME study presented several statements purportedly describing the nature and function of computers. Of the sample, 72% strongly agree with the description of a computer as an electronic device for storing information; 69% believe the computer to be an automatic electronic machine for performing calculations; and 61%, a super fast adding machine. However, a substantial percentage (39%) still holds with the view of a computer as an electronic brain or "thinking machine." The Canadian survey found that 60% of the respondents perceive the computer as a very efficient mathematical machine, whereas only 16% believe it to be an intelligent machine.

An overwhelming majority (91%) of the American sample believes that "computers are affecting the lives of all of us"; 87% feel that computers allow us to do many things that would otherwise be impossible; 60% vs. 33% recognize the importance of computers to American business; and 95% indicate awareness of the existence of information files on individual citizens. Some of the effects are regarded as beneficial, others ambiguous, and a few harmful. We will look first at effects viewed as beneficial. A majority (68% vs. 22%) believes that computers have contributed to improving the quality of consumer goods and services; 65% vs. 26% see computers as a factor in raising the standard of living; and 86% vs. 12% think computers will create more leisure time in the future. The use of computer-based information files is believed (63% vs. 29%) to help make government more effective; and 53% vs. 28% feel that the government uses safeguards to insure accuracy. When queried as to whether certain computer uses should be increased or decreased, 78% vs. 6% indicated that surveillance of criminals should be increased; 70% vs. 6% concurred in extending the gathering and analysis of census data; and 56% vs. 17% agreed that surveillance of activist or radical groups should be increased. In the Canadian survey, only 47% vs. 35% were found to believe that computers will improve the standard of living, although 73% vs. 18% think computers will give us more leisure time. By a margin of 53% to 31% Canadians feel that computers will facilitate better decisions in business and government, and 58% vs. 28% see improvements in the quality of education. Benefits are also thought to obtain from computer applications in scientific research (86% vs. 6%), as well as from applications which make information more readily available (85% vs. 7%).

On the negative side, Americans show concern about unemployment, depersonalization, loss of individual freedom, and computer errors. More than half (51% vs. 36%) disagree with the assertion that computers create more jobs than they eliminate. A majority (55% vs. 38%) of the sample is of the opinion that "people are becoming too dependent on computers," and 54% vs. 40% believe that "computers are dehumanizing people and turning them into numbers." In addition, 58% vs. 33% feel that there is too much information about individuals in circulation, and 53% vs. 40% fear a loss of individual freedom as a result of the use of computerized information files. Respondents affirmed by a small margin (47% vs. 44%) that computer processing of bills often leads to mistakes; but 77% vs. 20% believe that computers do not always give accurate information. Responses to questions concerning human as opposed to computer reliability are mixed. The Canadian survey reveals similar concerns over possible negative effects. A large majority (71% vs. 21%) believes computers "cause unemployment"; 52% vs. 29% think computers are "reducing people to 'just numbers'"; and 69% vs. 19% see computers as prone to errors because they are unable to "take human factors into account."

Since the impact of computers on privacy has provoked considerable controversy in both official circles and the media, it is somewhat surprising to discover that 54% vs. 38% of the American sample believe computers do not represent a real threat to people's privacy. Moreover, 52% vs. 13% are favorably disposed to increased use of credit card billing systems, and as noted above, a majority thinks surveillance of radical or activist groups should be increased. Canadians reveal a slightly more skeptical attitude in their concern (52% vs. 36%) over the possibility of breaches of confidence resulting from computer applications. There is evidently some confusion about the implications of data surveillance in the United States, since the views just noted conflict with negative attitudes concerning personal information in circulation, and the loss of individual freedom. In addition, 62% vs. 36% claim to be concerned about information being kept by organizations. This inconsistency may be partially explained by distinguishing between what people perceive to be in their own personal interest and more abstract questions about society as a whole. Individuals who feel threatened by "crime in the streets" may be inclined to support the maintenance of computerized police records, and 83% of the sample are in favour of such record-keeping. Other types of computerized files associated with public services such as health-care and education are also looked upon with favor. Where self-interest is concerned, there seems to be relatively little anxiety about invasion of privacy. The convenience of using credit cards outweighs the fear of too much information being kept.

On the other hand, when the issues are less immediate, certain misgivings come to the fore. In the abstract, too much information on file is seen to reduce individual freedom. This interpretation is reinforced by the apparent correlation between favorable attitudes toward computer applications and benefits derived from them. Generally speaking, people with higher incomes and more education, who do in fact receive a disproportionate share of the benefits of computers, tend to express more favorable attitudes than other groups. Of course, one expects self-interest to have a strong influence on opinion, but failure to draw connections between short-term gains and long-term losses may ultimately lead to ruin.

Survey statistics tell only part of the story of popular attitudes. It is difficult to gauge the social significance of relatively isolated phenomenona, but the appearance of "grass roots" activity in the computer field is of some interest. Several groups have been formed in American and Canadian cities for the purpose of "bringing computer technology to the people."[11] This is not, strictly speaking, a populist movement since many of the principals are highly trained in computer technology. Nevertheless, it does constitute a response to popular disenchantment with the use of technology by powerful government and private interests.[12] Much of the effort of these groups seems to be devoted to providing information on services available in the community, but there are also projects underway designed to facilitate the exchange of information among people with similar interests. The possible consequences of these community-based enterprises are a matter of pure speculation. They may serve as valuable educational experiences and even provide a genuine public service whose control is firmly planted in the community. On the other hand, they could equally well serve the interests of big government once respectability is achieved. Given the public confusion over the impact of information technology on concentration of power and social control, the latter is not entirely unlikely.

5. The Moral Imperative

Computer technology shares in the ethical dilemma of science and technology as a whole. Dilemma suggests problematic choices, and in the present instance these arise from a peculiar attitude toward the pursuit of knowledge. According to the now orthodox view, science is morally indifferent to its subject matter. A fundamental distinction is drawn between epistemological and normative issues. There is no necessary connection between the search for knowledge and how that knowledge is used. In a modified form, the same position is taken by technologists: participation in design and construction is separated from the use made of the product. It is a matter of indifference to the scientist (*qua* scientist) that the results of his work may be used for harmful purposes. Armed with this rationale the physicist, mathematician, biologist, etc., labor with conscience undisturbed by visions of bombs and man-made epidemics. The dichotomy between truth and value does not absolve the individual from making moral judgments, it simply rules them out of the pursuit of knowledge itself; the individual scientist may take a stand on ethical matters, but in so doing acts as an ordinary citizen or human being. Thus, in one role, a scientist may contribute to the development of nuclear energy, laser technology, etc., and in another protest against their use for destructive purposes.

Modern history suggests that the ethical neutrality of science and technology is not entirely satisfactory. Science has become a social enterprise; it has long ceased to be an individualistic undertaking, practiced primarily by aristocratic dilletantes. Like all enterprises which enjoy substantial public support and have a systematic impact on society, science has social responsibilities. In fact, these responsibilities are exercised by default. By refusing to make judgments on the propriety of his professional activities, the scientist gives tacit approval to the goals of the institution which employs him. The technologist who works on weapons systems by day and protests against war by night exhibits a dangerously irresponsible attitude. In this case, the freedom to protest functions as a safety valve in the political system. The condemnation of war is a meaningless expression of intention, clearly subverted by contrary action. So long as the scientist refuses to examine the consequences of his own contribution to the enterprise of which it is a part, that enterprise derives the benefit of his unspoken approval.

Science and technology are more than mere instrumentalities which can be neatly disentangled from the social matrix in which they function. Neither the praise for social benefits nor the blame for harmful effects can be attributed to science as a purely intellectual activity. Discoveries and inventions are elaborated in institutional settings: universities, government laboratories, industrial research centers, none of which operates in a vacuum. These are social organizations having special interests and objectives, and constitute an integral part of a social, economic, and political system. Industrial research and development are supported primarily for the purpose of generating products and services which may ultimately lead to profitable exploitation. Governments devote public resources to scientific research in order to make use of new results in what is conceived to be the public interest. Weapons systems as well as cures for cancer must be seen in this light. Universities too are no longer isolated from the community at large; research objectives parallel those in the private and public sectors. The practice of science and technology is no more entitled to sidestep responsibility for its results on the grounds of disinterested knowledge than any other human endeavor which affects the course of social evolution.

Susskind(1973) explores the issue of dividing "responsibility between the technologist and the society that uses him." He chooses two revealing examples to illustrate the interaction between technical activities and social goals. On the one hand, there is the case of technology in the service of the Nazi program of mass extermination; at the other extreme, we see technology serving the agricultural policy launched by the United States government in the nineteenth century.

> Our two cautionary tales, taken from opposite ends of the moral spectrum, thus show the futility of trying to apportion credit or blame for the effects of technological operations between society and those it employs to carry them out. But has not the technical expert, because of his special knowledge, a duty to do more than to make an objective presentation of the various solutions to a problem and to draw up balance sheets of the technical advantages and disadvantages of each? Should he sometimes set aside his scientific objectivity and make a special plea for one solution or another on the basis of nontechnical considerations? Will society be better or worse served if its decision makers cannot rely on the objectivity of the technical information on which they must base their decisions?

What is evidently wanted is a set of balance sheets in which the relative merits of each solution to a technical problem are analyzed both on technical grounds such as safety, ease of operation, cost, reliability, maintainability, complexity, and esthetics, and on ethical grounds such as moral considerations, effects on the quality of human life, liberty, dignity, and other human values. (Susskind, 1973, pp. 115-116)[13]

The social necessity of morally responsible action by scientists and technologists in the work they perform goes beyond the need for professional codes in the conventional sense. Such codes are typically restricted to questions of competence and based on the values of the market place. Consideration of the propriety of undertaking a particular project requires, as Susskind suggests, broad ethical guidelines which touch on all aspects of human conduct.[14] The ethical neutrality of the scientist has been questioned on other grounds than social necessity. Rapoport(1957) argues that the pursuit of science itself involves an ethical position which is closely linked to the strategic principles of inquiry.

Scientific inquiry is based on a belief in the existence of objective truth together with rules of evidence for discovering it. The possibility of universal agreement, achieved not through coercion but by independent discovery, suggests guidelines for conduct. Scientific practice contains, if not the germ of a complete ethical system, at least the foundations of a broad code of conduct for scientists. The achievement of desirable social goals requires the same commitment to truth as the pursuit of objective knowledge, and there is no satisfactory way of separating the ends of knowledge from the means of discovery.

What then are the implications for the computer professional? Does he have any greater responsibility than the ordinary person for guiding the use and development of computer technology? Both Weizenbaum(1972) and Berkeley(1962) believe that he does. Weizenbaum is concerned with the effect of computers on man's self-image and thus urges a greater responsibility on the part of computer scientists for pronouncements on computer capabilities. He also points out the importance of precise statements concerning the fallibility and limitations of systems. Decision-making can be strongly influenced by management information systems, and it can happen that assumptions and design features are imperfectly understood by the user. There is a danger of introducing a disastrous rigidity into decision-making as a result of ritual insistence on the perfection of machines.

Berkeley argues that technology has become midwife to the birth of all sorts of monstrosities, and asks what is the horror point beyond which one will not go. The scientist-technician is compared to a locksmith confronted with a dubious proposition. The locksmith reasons thus with himself: "it is hard to make a living, and anyway if I don't do the job someone else will." This self-serving rationalization is clearly reprehensible; but often the details of real situations obscure this judgment.

Berkeley focuses on the development of nuclear weapons systems. The role of computer scientists in fashioning guidance systems is likened to that of the locksmith in his parable. Although direct participation in military research and development is a dramatic example, it is not the only one. We have witnessed the problematic role of the computer throughout our society. Automation may increase productivity, but it also puts people out of work and tends to centralize decision-making. Management information systems entail serious problems of appropriate use, and also contribute to further concentration of power. Computer-assisted instruction is a mixed blessing even under ideal conditions. Government use of computers for statistical purposes and for monitoring individual behavior may improve some public services, but there is the very real possibility of extensions of legitimate power which limit individual freedom. The computer scientist functions as locksmith in all these cases. The difficulty lies in making fine discriminations, and principled decisions. It is all too easy to fall prey to what Berkeley calls "the argument of the beard"— rationalizing an action on the grounds that one's own contribution will not lead immediately to disastrous consequences. Unfortunately, the price of such ostrich-like indifference to ends may be very high indeed.

---

[1] From *The Portable Nietzsche* edited and translated by Walter Kaufman. Copyright 1954 by the Viking Press, Inc. Reprinted by permission of The Viking Press, Inc.

[2] Packard(1960) documents this waste in a popular account of the subject.

[3] Recall the discussion in Chapter 5.

[4] From THE SANE SOCIETY by Erich Fromm. Copyright © 1955 by Erich Fromm. Reprinted by permission of Holt, Rinehart and Winston, Publishers.

[5] Toffler's(1970) popular study stresses these elements as facts of life which must be incorporated into strategies for survival in a future-oriented society.

[6] See the guidelines proposed by Sterling(1974).

[7] *The Oxford English Dictionary*, 1971.

[8] This is basically the aim of management information systems; see Chapter 4.

[9] The characteristics of such systems were discussed in Chapter 6 in connection with computer-assisted instruction.

[10] For further details on methodology and results, see AFIPS-TIME(1972), and Communications Canada(1973). Although the issues probed in the two studies are somewhat different, a few direct comparisons are possible.

[11] For example, Colstad and Lipkin(1975) report on the development of a public information system in the San Francisco Area.

[12] Further evidence for this response may be seen in Nelson's(1974) effort to explain computers to the layman.

[13] From *Understanding Technology* by Charles Susskind. Copyright 1973 by Johns Hopkins University Press. Reprinted by permission.

[14] Susskind(1973, p. 117) argues that it is not as difficult as often claimed to formulate such guidelines, and presents a set of principles which are consonant with humanistic values.

Chapter 14.
Machine Intelligence and Human Identity

The computer has made it possible to realize intelligent behavior in an artificial medium. In the past two decades programs have been developed which perceive configurations, draw inferences, solve problems, and even exhibit a rudimentary understanding of natural language. It must be noted, of course, that intelligent machines are in their infancy and do not begin to match human capabilities except perhaps in certain highly restricted domains. Nevertheless, judging strictly on the basis of performance, it must be conceded that machines which play championship level checkers and solve elementary calculus problems do exhibit intelligence. One may argue about the locus of intelligence, whether it resides in the machine or in its designer; and one may be skeptical of the possibilities for further extensions. But there is little doubt that machines can perform tasks which are normally thought to require intelligence on the part of human beings.

The emergence of intelligent machines is a tribute to the reductionist spirit of scientific inquiry. From the scientific point of view, intelligent behavior poses no more of a mystery than any other exceedingly complex natural phenomenon. Our understanding of it has been hampered in the past by the lack of appropriate concepts and methods. Just as the secrets of the cosmos have been probed successfully with the aid of telescopes, and the microscope exposed the hitherto invisible world of microorganisms, the computer is now being used to explore the inner workings of perceptual and cognitive processes. The automation of arithmetic and logical operations made possible the mechanization of computational processes. This in turn contributed to the development of the computer (see Chapter 2) and laid the foundation for employing the computer to investigate intelligence. The latter is defined operationally in terms of the various forms of behavior in which it is embedded, and these forms of behavior are modeled by means of computational processes.

A new intellectual discipline known as artificial intelligence (AI) has crystallized around computer-based investigations of intelligent behavior, and it has come to occupy a prominent position within the field of computer science. Although there is no universally accepted definition of research in AI, there is some agreement among workers in the field as to the principal areas of concern. Most of the research in AI seems to be directed toward one of two different but complementary objectives. First, there are the various efforts to further the development of intelligent skills in machines. Examples include game playing programs and the construction of robots. The particular interest of investigations of this type ranges from building practical devices or systems (such as industrial robots or systems for medical diagnosis) to the elaboration of a general theory of intelligent behavior. The other main objective of AI research involves the study of human cognitive or problem-solving behavior. Pursuit of this objective exemplifies the use of the computer as actor in scientific research (see Chapter 6); computer programs serve as dynamic expressions of theories of cognition.

Few definitions of human uniqueness have been as persuasive as that founded on man's ability to reason. It is therefore not surprising that the birth of machines which challenge a central pillar of human identity should be a source of intense controversy. In a less direct fashion, the positivist tradition in psychology and scientific thought generally poses the same challenge. The analytic reduction of human behavior to mechanistic principles denies the human being any claim to a special position in the universe fundamentally different from that of other organized systems. This point of view made it possible to envisage the construction of intelligent machines long before computers appeared on the scene.[1] But the actual construction of such mechanical entities has transformed speculation into palpable reality, and, one might argue, it has delivered the *coup de grace* to vitalism in psychology. Abstract theories may be ignored outside of the annals of learned societies, but this is not so for their concrete issue. Eventually we must recognize the existence of intelligent machines. To call them by another name or to redefine the notion of intelligence are temporary expedients at best, and merely serve to obscure the intensely problematic character of man-machine interaction.

The threat to human identity posed by intelligent machines may be traced to a colonialist attitude fostered in modern man by the cultural imperialism of science. This peculiar development is largely a product of the success of science and technology in manipulating the material world, a success built on two closely related dualistic principles. The first divides reality into spiritual and material spheres; the second distinguishes between subjective and objective knowledge. Through its unyielding fidelity to rules of evidence based on objective methods, the scientific enterprise constructed a formidable system of knowledge about the material world. However, like the successful entrepreneur who faults the poor for lack of enterprise, science now chides humanity for its feeble response to the conditions of modern life. What has happened is that we have come to identify the scientific conception of valid experience with the whole of experience and the material side of existence with the whole of existence. Robbed of our spiritual nature and denied access to all but one modality of experience, we prostrate ourselves before our own artifacts. Such is the hold of the colonialist mentality, that we cannot imagine how it would be possible to build an autonomous culture.

The controversy surrounding artificial intelligence is a microcosm of the contending intellectual forces which have shaped contemporary views of the human being. Thus, at the risk of exaggerating its importance, we propose to explore the accomplishments of AI in light of the search for identity. In order to provide some perspective, we will briefly survey the field of AI as well as the social uses of intelligent machines. After discussing the role of science and technology in the formation of models of behavior, we will examine the influence of the reductionist principle on our attitudes toward intelligent machines. In conclusion, we will consider the ethical implications of the apparent removal of the discontinuity between men and machines.

1. Computers and Intelligence

The use of computers to study intelligence dates from various research efforts initiated in the mid 1950's. Since intelligence is linked to mind and thought processes, the early work generated a great deal of controversy, and research in the area continues to provoke heated debate. This is to be expected for a new science which challenges established ideas, especially when the ideas have the status of sacred cows. AI research has adopted a characteristically scientific attitude toward its subject matter. Intelligence is viewed as a property of behavior, and as such it can be analyzed in terms of methods for constructing systems whose performance exhibits certain desired features. In a widely referenced paper, Minsky(1961, p. 27) expresses this operational interpretation of intelligence.

> My own view [of the question "what is intelligence"] is that this
> is more of an aesthetic question, or one of sense of dignity, than a

technical matter! To me "intelligence" seems to denote little more than the complex of performances which we happen to respect, but do not understand. So it is, usually, with the question of "depth" in mathematics. Once the proof of a theorem is really understood its content seems to become trivial. (Still there may remain a sense of wonder about how the proof was discovered.)[2]

Although philosophical problems concerning mind are not entirely ignored, workers in AI have attempted to defuse the issue by defining their goals in technical terms.[3] In what follows, we will review major developments in AI and discuss some of the difficulties encountered in the design of intelligent machines.

The construction of computer programs which perform intellectual tasks has a twofold aim. Such programs furnish a vehicle for investigating the fundamental mechanisms of intelligence, and also allow for applying and testing current observations and knowledge. Nilsson(1974) refers to research efforts embodying these goals as "first-level applications" of AI.[4] Projects aimed at producing programs capable of proving non-trivial mathematical theorems, playing master-level chess, and understanding natural language fall into this category. These projects are distinguished from the "second-level applications" whose principal objective is the solution of specialized problems such as designing industrial robots to handle dangerous materials.[5] Nilsson identifies eight topic areas among the first-level applications which have contributed substantially "to our basic understanding of intelligence." We will give a brief summary of each one.

Considerable effort has been devoted in recent years to the construction of game playing programs. Chess, in particular, because of its complexity has attracted a great deal of attention, and several programs have been devised. In fact, computer chess tournaments are held periodically for rival programs. Although first rate performance has been achieved in checkers, the best chess playing program still falls short of master level play. An area of some interest outside of AI involves systems designed to aid human professionals in solving technical problems. Examples include programs which can solve certain types of problems in integral calculus, and produce symbolic solutions to various kinds of mathematical equations. In addition to symbolic manipulation of mathematical expressions, a program has been developed which uses mass spectrogram and nuclear magnetic resonance data to infer the structure of chemical compounds. In some cases this program performs better than highly trained chemists. Automatic theorem proving is another active area of artificial intelligence research.

Early work focused largely on restricted problem domains such as propositional logic and elementary plane geometry, but techniques have been developed for dealing with more complex mathematical systems. Some new theorems have actually been discovered by interactive theorem provers, but automated mathematics is a rather distant prospect. AI research has also been directed toward automatic programming. This entails the automatic generation or verification of computer programs, where verification means proving that a program acts in a particular way. Automatic program generation has been accomplished in restricted problem areas, such as formulating plans for robots operating in a simple environment.

The building of robots is perhaps the most widely known activity in AI, since it is most often associated with machine intelligence in the popular mind. Robot projects have been conducted at several different centers in the United States and elsewhere. The main purpose of these projects is to build a device capable of responding appropriately to commands and inputs (usually visual stimuli impinging on a television camera "eye") from its environment. Typical responses include building structures from simple blocks, assembling pieces of equipment, and moving from one location to another over a terrain strewn with various obstacles. To accomplish tasks of this nature, a robot might be expected to have some general reasoning capability and language processing skills, be able to perceive visual stimuli, and have manipulative and locomotive abilities. These requirements cut across several areas of artificial intelligence, and the robot projects have provided testing grounds for problem-solving strategies. One of the problems faced by the robot designer concerns the interpretation of visual images of the world, and machine vision is an active research area in its own right. Some of the earliest work in AI was directed toward automatic pattern recognition, mainly of two-dimensional configurations such as alphanumeric characters. This type of work has followed an independent course and now forms part of the second-level applications of AI. More germane to machine vision in artificial intelligence is the description and interpretation of complex three-dimensional scenes, such as arise in a "blocks world" inhabited by a robot faced with the problem of perceiving the components of a structure consisting of blocks.

The design of systems for processing natural language, both written and spoken, occupies a central position in artificial intelligence. Problems of language processing surface in a variety of contexts involving man-computer interaction. A long-range goal of computer-assisted instruction is the achievement of genuine dialogue between student and computer; truly effective management information systems would permit a decision-maker to communicate with a computer program capable of drawing inferences and answering questions on a database consisting of statements in natural language; and the sophisticated information retrieval system envisioned by Licklider (see Chapter 6) requires a similar facility. Some progress toward machine understanding of natural language has been made, but workers in the field are not inclined to underestimate the difficulties.[6] The last area in Nilsson's taxonomy, the interface between artificial intelligence and psychology, will be discussed in Section 3.

Permeating these first-level applications of AI are certain fundamental principles, ideas and structures associated with the use and representation of knowledge, which Nilsson calls "core topics." Four such topics are singled out for comment.[7] Artificial intelligence takes reasoning to mean the use of knowledge to draw inferences, make predictions, formulate plans, answer questions, and obtain further knowledge. The various applications areas are conceived partly to illuminate these different aspects of using knowledge or reasoning. Modeling and representation of knowledge are also of fundamental importance to artificial intelligence. In order to make use of knowledge, it is necessary to choose appropriate representations. This is one area where the computer has helped to clarify certain epistemological problems. Processing visual images, for example, calls for making strategic decisions on how to represent a scene. Such decisions are critical both for efficient processing and for determining what knowledge can be extracted from the description.

Many problems in artificial intelligence require searching through a "space" of alternatives to find one which is optimal according to some given criterion. Although this is a straightforward procedure in principle, the number of alternatives in any but the simplest tasks is so great that even the speed of the computer is beggared by comparison. A game, for example, can be represented by a tree-like structure in which the nodes correspond to positions, and the edges joining them signify legal moves from one position to another. In this representation, the problem of finding an optimal strategy reduces to searching the game tree for acceptable paths between the nodes corresponding to initial and final positions. An exhaustive search of the game tree for checkers would require examining 10^{40} alternatives, while for chess the number is estimated to be 10^{120}. Exhaustive search under such conditions is entirely infeasible, so that methods for reducing the number of choices explored must be sought. This has led to the development of "heuristic search" techniques for making use of special knowledge from the problem domain to aid in finding a solution. The fourth core area embraces computer systems and languages designed especially for use in AI applications. Since the implementation of complex computer programs is an indispensable part of AI research, these systems and languages are essential to its methodology.

2.   The Uses of Intelligent Machines

Intelligent machines as conceived by AI practitioners have yet to leave their imprint on society. Systems currently in use which exhibit intelligent behavior are relatively crude and not sufficiently widespread to be credited with a significant social impact. Moreover, it is difficult to differentiate between the effects of ordinary computer applications and those which depend in an essential way upon mechanical intelligence. The introduction of robot assemblers in manufacturing, for example, is part of a larger trend toward automated production processes which currently bears little relation to artificial intelligence. Tomorrow's computer applications, however, are very likely to draw more heavily on the skills being developed in today's AI laboratories. A large variety of industrial, commercial and service oriented applications await further advances in machine intelligence. Thus, it is with a view toward the future that we focus on intelligent machines as a distinctive component of computer utilization. Our intention here is to explore the potential influence of succeeding generations of intelligent artifacts on succeeding generations of human beings. To this end, we will look at some present day commercial products as the first step in the social evolution of intelligent machines.

Firschein, et al.(1973) identify three characteristics which set AI products apart from more conventional computer-based systems: an ability to communicate in natural language, problem-solving skills, and a capability for interacting directly with the real world through sensors and effector mechanisms. Commercially available products exhibit these properties in varying degrees. The more advanced robots designed for industrial use come equipped with television "eyes," and are capable of performing assembly tasks and manipulating objects on a conveyor belt. Such devices are beginning to appear on automobile assembly lines. Another industrial application involving problem-solving and motor skills is the "automated warehouse" in which computer-controlled loading devices are directed to particular storage bins. Sensory capabilities are evident in medical monitoring systems which are designed to detect various forms of biological activity and transmit information to a central facility for analysis. An important area in which pattern recognition techniques are being used is personal identification. This is accomplished in one device by comparing hand measurements with coded information on an ID card.

A number of products making use of technology associated with artificial intelligence incorporate some form of natural language processing. Voice communications plays a particularly important role. Credit transactions may soon be expedited by a voice verification system currently in the development stage. This system operates by matching a set utterance spoken by an individual with a pre-recorded version. Voice activated systems for supermarket checkout and airline baggage routing are now commercially available. Prices dictated by clerks are automatically recorded, and baggage is routed to its destination by orally giving flight numbers or other information. A voice response system with a 16,000 word vocabulary and a sentence forming capability is also being marketed. Automatic production of recorded telephone messages is likely to become commonplace in the not too distant future.

Perhaps the largest potential market for AI related products is the military. Automatic sensing devices linked to remote computing installations have already been employed on a large-scale by the United States Armed Forces in Southeast Asia.[8] Dickson(1974) describes the military's vision of future warfare.

> War will be much less dependent on men because dogface ground troops, and even trained air pilots, will become less and less necessary. In their place will emerge controllers and technicians housed in remote centers where they will direct robot planes and fire power in response to computer read-outs and blips on screens. The new American military dream depends on a highly lethal, portable array of integrated, plug-in gadgets which, once installed, sets up a zone out of which, presumably, no living thing can escape.[9]

The sensors used in Vietnam to trigger anti-personnel weapons and transmit information to commanders to assist in directing firepower were crude devices. Further advances in pattern recognition and automated diagnosis are required to produce more discriminating weapons systems. Simple acoustic, seismic, and chemical detectors do not distinguish between troops and civilians, friend and foe, nor do the explosive charges they detonate. Moreover, they are easily foiled as in the case of the "ammonia sniffers" which were neutralized by hanging buckets of urine in the trees. More subtle and powerful instruments for monitoring troop movements from afar await the application of sophisticated problem-solving techniques to data gathered by devices with improved perceptual capabilities.

Artificial intelligence promises to play an increasingly prominent role in computer applications of the future. Firschein, *et al.*(1973) conducted a Delphi study among AI experts to assess probable future developments and their likely social consequences.[10] The participants were presented with a list of hypothetical AI products grouped according to their potential social effects, and responses were solicited on the following issues: composition of the list, appropriateness of suggested applications and implications of the products, potential significance of the products, time estimates for prototypes and commercial development, likelihood and desirability of the suggested applications and implications. Products judged to be of high potential significance and likely to be developed commercially by 1985 include automatic identification systems based on recognizing voice, face, fingerprints, etc.; automatic medical diagnosis; autonomous industrial robots; and automated inquiry systems with the ability to engage in genuine dialogue. Other potentially significant products were thought to require more time to emerge. According to the experts, by the beginning of the next century we will have computer-controlled artificial organs which can substitute for natural ones; robot tutors whose performance is on a par with good human teachers; reliable models for predicting the effects of economic policies; automated intelligence systems for augmenting human intellectual abilities; and robot servants capable of operating in a household environment. Products considered to be of medium potential significance include mobile police or military robots; systems capable of creative work in music, art, literature and mathematics; computer psychiatrists; automatic language translators and talking typewriters. These are expected to appear in commercial form by the turn of the century.

The predicted arrival times may be overly optimistic, but what is more interesting is the fact that almost all of the products received overall "desirable" ratings.[11] Individual responses did, however, take cognizance of some potentially dangerous effects. Concern focused on the possible use of various systems for political censorship, indoctrination, monitoring of citizens, and control of behavior. It was also recognized that robot soldiers and other intelligent weapons systems might contribute to "aggressive actions by some nations." As suggested earlier, the consequences of second-level applications of AI must be seen in the broader context of computer technology. Most of the conclusions reached by Firschein, *et al.*(1973) concerning "societal implications" apply to the general use of computers. In particular, long-range trends toward decreased human interaction, displacement of human workers, and centralization of political decision-making are all enhanced by increased dependence on computers. Intelligent machines, however, do increase the poignancy of certain issues. The challenge to human identity and uniqueness posed by the existence of intelligent machines accentuates the alienation of modern man; and the ethical problems created by our ability to act through mechanical devices, such as dropping bombs on remote targets, acquire a new concreteness in the form of autonomous robots. We will discuss these issues in the last two sections.

3.   Models of Human Behavior

Technology influences human behavior not only through its impact on the physical and social environment, but also by the way it affects our view of the world. A central component of world-view is the conception one has of oneself. In the modern period, science and technology have played prominent roles in shaping man's self-conception. The lines of influence are not entirely clear, but it is possible to trace the evolution of certain dominant metaphors associated with technology which have suggested areas of inquiry concerning human behavior. From the mechanical devices of the seventeenth century to the general-purpose digital computer of the present day, technology has furnished concepts which thinkers have adapted for use in fashioning models of the human being. Information-processing technology may be unique in that it serves as a tool for the study of behavior as well as providing a rich source of metaphors. The investigation of intelligence, perception, and other behavioral attributes in machines has suggested new ways of looking at human behavior. Our aim in the present discussion is to indicate the ways in which notions drawn from information-processing have influenced contemporary conceptions of the human being.

The current adaptation of technological metaphors to the human condition is but the latest chapter in modern intellectual history. Rapoport(1955) traces the influence of successive "technological phyla" on intellectual development. The first phylum to exhibit properties suggesting attributes of living things was that of clockwork mechanisms. Clockworks are activated by stored mechanical energy and give the appearance of autonomous behavior. Although Descartes evidently found the comparison between clockworks and animals compelling, his observation did not lead to any significant line of inquiry, since energy storage in living things is not in the form of mechanical stress. Efforts to investigate biological transformations of energy were not undertaken until the emergence of the next phylum, the heat engines. "The comparison between heat engines and organisms passed beyond the metaphorical stage and bore real scientific fruits." (Rapoport, 1955). In particular, the analogy between food and fuel led to the principle of energy conservation in living things, one consequence of which was the demise of vitalism in physiology.

The essential contribution of technology to our understanding of physiological phenomena lies in the model of energy storage, transformation and utilization suggested by thermodynamical systems. This model gave rise to questions with empirically testable consequences about organic processes. The emergence of a new phylum of machines, whose principal function is the processing of information, signals the start of an intellectual revolution in psychology analogous to earlier developments in physiology. Information-processing is the active principle in organization, and as such it lends itself to analysis of the organizing behavior which is characteristic of perception, memory, and intelligence. The modes of information storage, transmission, and transformation in computers suggest hypotheses about human behavior which can be investigated systematically. Exploration of plausible behavioral mechanisms by means of computer simulation facilitates theoretical analysis. In designing a program to solve problems, for example, one is forced to examine different ways of representing knowledge, and strategies for using knowledge. These issues are suggested by the information-processing model of problem-solving tasks, and attempts to implement particular solution methods in computer programs serve to sharpen our understanding and contribute to the development of a theory of behavior. It remains to be seen whether or not this approach will lead to significant psychological experiments capable of testing the validity of the proposed mechanisms.

Simon and Newell(1964) state the basic assumptions of the information-processing model of man.

> 1.   A science of information-processing can be constructed that is substantially independent of the specific properties of particular information-processing mechanisms.

2. Human thinking can be explained in information-processing terms without waiting for a theory of the underlying neurological mechanisms.

3. Information-processing theories of human thinking can be formulated in computer programming languages and can be tested by simulating the predicted behavior with computers.[12]

The focus of this approach, according to Newell(1973), is "on tasks that are highly symbolic." Behavior requiring "continuous motor skills or an intimate dependence on sensory systems" is of peripheral concern. Thus, the central problems of information-processing psychology lie in such areas as cognition, and memory. Although these theories deal "with phenomena of substantial complexity," they do not cover "the full complexity of human affairs."[13]

The pervasive influence of the information-processing model can be seen from its impact on various areas of psychological research. We will look briefly at some examples. Simon and Newell(1964) discuss the components of a theory of problem-solving in the context of chess playing. The actual theory is a computer program formulated in a particular programming language. Its underlying structure reflects the distinction between the representation and use of information. The chess player's behavior is analyzed in terms of two types of information-processing capabilities: one for representing and storing information, the other for extracting and using the information available. The former includes processes for internal storage of encoded representations of stimuli, and means for representing in memory the various moves under consideration. Extraction and use of information are accomplished by processes which facilitate the discovery of new relations in a position, permit the generation of moves with specified properties, and organize searches for winning combinations. The object of the theory is to predict the behavior of a chess player, and the basic processes are designed to model what goes on in the mind of a player as he scrutinizes a given board position. The critical feature of information-processing models is that they posit operationally defined processes in place of the ambiguous notions of intuition, imagination, inspiration, etc. to account for behavior. This has the dual advantage of providing a well-defined, testable model, and allowing for the use of computer programs as dynamic expressions of theory.

The study of memory is an area where information-processing concepts have proved especially fruitful. Analogies with machine-based processes yielded models which have led to important discoveries. The notions of immediate and long-term memory, rehearsal, and decay, and their functions in recalling and forgetting, become precisely defined with reference to information-processing systems. Questions which might not otherwise be raised at all become natural in this setting. The mechanisms of information storage in a computer, for example, suggest modeling rehearsal as a feature of immediate memory, with transfer of items to long-term memory occurring as a function of the length of time they have been in immediate memory. Other areas of psychology have also been enriched by information-processing concepts. Our understanding of perceptual processes, verbal learning, and psycholinguistic phenomena has been advanced through the use of computer simulation and process models.

Artificial intelligence occupies a central position in the development of information-processing models of behavior. Although its particular results may not be applicable directly to all psychological studies, it serves as a source of intellectual tools and constructs. It is in this sense that Newell(1973) forwards the view of AI as "theoretical psychology." The core topics (in Nilsson's sense) of artificial intelligence contribute to the development of "the science of information-processing systems so that other specific systems more relevant to psychological questions can be better constructed and analysed."

4. Some Consequences of Reductionism

The impulse to place limits on experience springs from diverse human needs. Common sense tells us that to cope effectively with reality, we must discipline our expectations and make judicious choices. An inescapable consequence of choice is the exclusion of possibilities. "Life consists in giving up the state of availability."[14] By focusing on one particular thing, we inevitably exclude others from consideration. Our society has made a virtue of necessity by placing a high value on specialization. This is reflected in cultural as well as economic affairs. Our concern here is with one aspect of specialization, namely, the reduction of experience accomplished by science and technology. The intellectual achievements of the scientific enterprise are due in large measure to restrictions placed on the subjects of inquiry and the types of experience admissible as evidence. Moreover, the growth of scientific knowledge is characterized by the search for unifying principles which reduce apparent complexity to simple order. Modern technology reveals the same evolutionary pattern. The resolution of complex skills into simple component tasks made it possible to use machinery in large-scale production. We have examined this reductionist tendency in a number of contexts.[15] Common to all of them is a compression of the range of human experience. The emergence of intelligent machines threatens to advance this movement one step further. From an intellectual standpoint, the model of man as an information processor is simply a means for gaining insight into human behavior. But the consequences of the model transcend its intellectual function. Like the defeat of vitalism which owes so much to an earlier technological metaphor, the reduction of thought to computational processes casts a shadow over the whole spectrum of human activity. In this section and the next, we will explore the implications of this intellectual development.

The reductionist position of artificial intelligence with regard to thought processes exemplifies the application of scientific analysis to ill-formed problems. One of the earliest and perhaps most comprehensive statements of this position is presented in a now classic paper of Turing(1950). What emerges from Turing's discussion is that traditional notions of thought are essentially useless as scientific hypotheses. In particular, the question "Can machines think?" is meaningless apart from an operational definition of hhinking. Thus Turing reformulates the question in terms of a procedure which he calls the "imitation game." In this game, a human interrogator converses (by means of a teletypewriter) with two unidentified respondents, one of whom is a machine and the other a human being. The object for the interrogator is to determine which of the two is the machine and which is the human being. The imitation game has come to be known as "Turing's Test," and serves as a criterion for machine intelligence. If in repeated trials with different human subjects, the interrogator is unable to distinguish between the person and the machine with substantially better than 50% accuracy, the machine may be said to simulate human intelligence. Turing's reformulation is unquestionably a legitimate intellectual exercise, but it is not clear that all the relevant features of our intuitive notions of thinking are captured in the operational definition.[16]

Turing's Test eliminates the ambiguity in the question "Can machines think?" by reducing its content. The reduction is necessary in order to isolate a process which may be realized in structurally inequivalent entities. This means that differences in the constituent parts and organization of machines and human beings are irrelevant to the question of whether or not they exhibit intelligent behavior. As Armer(1960, p. 392) puts it, "Intelligent behavior on the part of a machine no more implies complete functional equivalence between machine and brain than flying by an airplane implies complete functional equivalence between plane and bird." Minsky(1961, p. 27) carries the reductionist argument somewhat further.

> [W]e should not let our inability to discern a locus of intelligence lead us to conclude that programmed computers therefore cannot think. For it may be so with *man*, as with *machine*, that, when we understand finally the structure and program, the feeling of mystery (and self-approbation) will weaken.[17]

As power corrupts, success blinds. Scientific reductionism has provided us with useful models of different forms of behavior. We have come to understand the role of energy in organisms, and we are beginning to learn about the organizing functions of information. However, there appears to be a tendency to make unwarranted extensions of these models. This does not involve any simple identification of men and machines; we are too sophisticated to commit such an egregious error. The problem arises from a kind of part-whole confusion. Faced with an ambiguous question, the scientist attempts to recast it in a form that gives it determinate meaning and also makes it tractable. There is, of course, no guarantee that the particular resolution arrived at is the only one possible. This is especially true for "meaningless questions." For example, the fact that the question "Can machines think?" is deemed meaningless does not deter anyone from believing that it makes sense in terms of Turing's Test. Thus to suppose a question meaningless does not imply that it has no content whatsoever. If that were the case, nothing at all could be extracted from it. What is being suggested here is that a particular formulation of a meaningless question may leave behind a residue of unresolved issues. This may or may not be the case for the operational definition of intelligent behavior, but there is no justification for assuming that all of human experience can be interpreted in the framework of the information-processing model.

Participation in a successful enterprise sustains the illusion of infallibility. We are reminded of this every day as impregnable fortresses collapse, wonder drugs produce dangerous side-effects, nuclear reactors leak radiation, and economic policies lead to ruin. The presumption of intellectual infallibility leads to inflated claims, but this is not the real issue. Reductionism is a social as well as intellectual phenomenon. To search for causes is futile, but it is painfully clear that each particular manifestation reinforces the rest. Excessive specialization of function and fragmentation of knowledge complement each other in degrading human experience. The one by inhibiting growth, the other by limiting horizons. There is more pride in the effort to reduce human behavior to mechanistic principles than in the refusal to accept the consequences of reductionism. What is more, the former is a vindictive pride akin to the predator's disdain for its victim. Humanity is victimized by insensitivity to the experiential limitations of scientific knowledge.

It may be true that intelligence is a behavioral attribute of information-processing systems and that both human and machine intelligence can be unified in a general theory. But this does not imply the spiritual interchangeability of men and machines. Reductionism urges us to accept a view of ourselves in which all experience is resolved into what can be represented in a discrete symbol processor. The information-processing model of man presupposes the intertranslatability of all modalities of experience, their distinctive formative principles being submerged in universal computational processes. So we will have computer music, computer art, computer poetry, and what have you. Yet one must ask what function these expressions will serve in human culture. Apart from a purely formalist aesthetics, what meaning, can mechanical creativity have? The reductionist principle creates a factory of the spirit, a unity which comprehends only sameness.

> It is in the basic symbolic function and its various directions that the spiritual consciousness and the sensory consciousness are first truly differentiated. It is here that we pass beyond passive receptivity to an indeterminate outward material, and begin to place upon it our independent imprint which articulates it for us into diverse spheres and forms of reality. Myth and art, language and science, are in this sense configurations *towards* being: they are not simple copies of an existing reality but represent the main directions of the spiritual movement, of the ideal process by which reality is constituted for us as one and many— as a diversity of forms which are ultimately held together by a unity of meaning. (Cassirer, 1953, p. 107)

5.   Identity and Conduct

The threat to human identity posed by intelligent machines is the latest in a series of cultural shocks linked to the advance of science and technology. As we observed in the previous chapter, man has lost his special place in the cosmos, become rooted in a biological continuum, been deprived of an autonomous inner self, and is now confronted with the continuity of human and machine behavior. Our primary concern here is with the most recent challenge. The existence of intelligent machines is likely to have far-reaching effects on human activity. Although the issues may seem abstract, changes in world-view have a direct impact on institutions and behavior. The overwhelming importance attributed to intelligence or rational thought in defining human worth and dignity makes us especially vulnerable. It would appear that technology is assaulting the last stronghold of human uniqueness. In what follows, we will analyze this assault, and consider the question of the social desirability of developing intelligent machines.

It is futile to reject truth on the grounds that it is too disconcerting to contemplate.[18] However, the disconcerting consequences of an insight may arise from inappropriate interpretation. Let us suppose for the sake of discussion that there is no more to the question "Can machines think?" than Turing's Test. What implications does this have for human conduct? Clearly, the main effect is on our notions of virtue. As a distinguishing feature of the human being, rational thought is bound up with the moral order of things. It confirms our superiority and supports our claim to moral ascendancy over the rest of creation. Thus acceptance of the principle of machine thought undercuts our uniqueness and casts further doubts on our resemblance to the image of God. A corollary to the loss of unique virtue is the erosion of responsibility. Moral ascendancy confers obligation as well as privilege, and after losing the former we are not likely to exercise the latter. If Skinner's(1971) technology of behavior were available, perhaps this would not be a problem. However, while waiting for the new dispensation to emerge, we have no choice but to go on thinking in terms of freedom and dignity.

The key element in this interpretation of the consequences of machine intelligence is the part played by rational thought in human affairs. Basing human identity on a presumably unique attribute of behavior is a risky enterprise, whether that attribute is strength, intelligence, or anything else. However, this requires some qualification. Human identity has no meaning apart from a given culture, so we must examine the context in which rational thought plays its fateful role. Modern society is in a state of flux, and our institutions are in disarray. Communities have been transformed into mobile populations so there are few anchor points at which to fix individual definition. Religious practice exerts little influence, and moral sanctions are largely vestigial forms inherited from inoperative traditions. These conditions tend to underscore the utility of rational behavior but rarely as part of community activity. This is a detached and individualistic rationality. As such it is particularly vulnerable to attack, and lacking community foundations it capitulates without a struggle.

Our dependence on reason as a defining characteristic of human identity is reinforced by science and technology. The scientific enterprise offers itself as a universal system of knowledge in which rational principles reign supreme. Unfortunately, it does not constitute a complete and autonomous culture, and is not sufficient to deal with all the problems of human existence. Technology too cultivates a detached rationality; it has become an active agent in modern society, rather than a passive instrument of community action. The point to be made is not that rationality is a completely misguided choice for a definition of man, but in a disembodied state it is too brittle. Indeed, this would be the case for any other abstract principle which has lost its connection with the concrete human practices of group life. The question "Can machines think?," especially as formulated by Turing, should have little effect on human attitudes. That it does signals something amiss in the society which poses it. From the standpoint of human conduct, a more important question is "can machines share human culture?" Certainly, one must admit the possibility of an affirmative answer.

Assuming the reductionist attitude toward experience, there is nothing to preclude such an eventuality. As Block and Ginsburg(1968) point out "[n]ow that we have the electric shaver, electric toothbrush, electric scalp massager and electric buttocks vibrator, can man-machine sexual relationships be far behind?" Contemporary society already shows a marked advance toward a machine culture. At work, in school and at play, we have become standardized, interchangeable parts in a mechanized parade. Considering the longevity of most human relationships, it would undoubtedly be more economical and maybe just as rewarding for individuals to choose general-purpose robot companions with modifiable attributes. Perhaps the most telling sign of what we can anticipate is the centralization of decision-making in bureaucratic organizations. Substitution of exogenous for endogenous social control testifies to the collapse of community authority, so that it is a matter of indifference whether one interacts with humans or machines.

The extent to which modern culture has progressed toward the reductionist ideal can be summed up in what may be termed the "argument from machines": human behavior cannot possess properties not realizable in machines. Minsky(1965), for example, uses this argument to dispense with free will. The concept of volition is seen to arise from imperfect understanding of human behavior since we would not attribute such a notion to a thoroughly understood machine or program. Minsky argues further that the idea of free will "has its genesis in a strong primitive defense mechanism" that mediates an ingrained dislike of compulsion. Thus, determinism is transformed into a species of behavioral control, and our "logically futile" resistance to compulsion accounts for our unwillingness to extend the analysis of machines to human beings. In this view determinism is a coercive principle whose rectitude derives largely from its unpalatability.

The question of the desirability of producing intelligent machines cannot be separated from the larger issue of cultivating excessive dependence on technology. However, some problems are more salient in the special case. Wiener(1960) expresses concern that machines constitute a threat to human beings. "It is my thesis that machines can and do transcend some of the limitations of their designers, and that in doing so they may be both effective and dangerous." That we may lose control to machines is not idle speculation. The characteristics we expect of our so-called machine slaves are contradictory. Subservience and intelligence are not compatible in a slave. In a response to Wiener's argument, Samuel(1960) counters with the observation that slaves do not possess human needs or will. However, he fails to take account of the fact that the nature of the slave is invisible to the slaveholder, and the latter is profoundly influenced by the institution of slavery itself. The intelligent machine slave is no more likely to be a pure instrument of the master's will than its human counterpart.

Intelligent machines are a symbol of modern technology. The possibility of some form of machine autonomy suggests the operation of technology as an independent force in social development. Moreover, the dominant responses to the idea of machine intelligence reveal characteristic attitudes toward technology. Both the arrogance and outrage which surface in discussions of the implications of artificial intelligence stem from the same underlying insecurity. Our more pressing cultural need is to come to terms with the instruments we have created, but this will not be possible until we forge an authentic identity for ourselves.

1   See Cohen(1966).

2   Copyright 1961 by the Institute of Radio Engineers, Inc. Reprinted with permission, from the *Proceedings of the IRE*, January 1961, pp. 8-30.

3   For example, Hayes(1973) suggests defining AI as "the study of intelligence as computation," and indicates that this is consistent with the views of several of the principal workers in the field.

4   The present discussion of AI research is based largely on Nilsson's(1974) review paper. For a comprehensive textbook treatment of the subject with an extensive bibliography, see Jackson(1974).

5   We will discuss these applications in Section 2.

6   For a relatively non-technical account of the subject by a leading figure, see Winograd(1974).

7   As Nilsson indicates, these core topics are too closely intertwined to be regarded as strictly separate issues.

8   The significance of this effort may be gauged from the expenditures devoted to the "automated battlefield" concept. Dickson(1974) estimates spending at five to six billion dollars annually.

9   Reprinted by permission from *The Progressive*, 408 West Gorham Street, Madison, Wisconsin 53703. Copyright © 1975[4], The Progressive, Inc.

10 The Delphi method is an iterative approach to opinion polling which makes use of respondent feedback to reach a consensus; for a general discussion, see Gotlieb and Borodin(1973, pp. 104-105). See also Kling's(1973) critique of the Firschein study.

11 As Kling(1973) points out, technical competence in AI does not necessarily imply expertise on social issues. Beyond that one must reckon with a natural personal bias on the part of anyone judging the effects of his own work.

12 Reprinted by permission, *American Scientist*, journal of Sigma Xi, The Scientific Research Society of North America.

13 Simon(1969, p. 25) takes a more extreme position in supposing that the "apparent complexity" of man's behavior is "largely a reflection of the complexity of the environment in which he finds himself."

14 Ortega y Gasset(1956, p. 156)

15 Recall the discussion in Chapters 1, 2, 5 and 13.

16 It is not our intention to become drawn into the debate over the nature of minds and machines. There is a large literature on the subject which the interested reader may access through Anderson(1964), Dreyfus(1972) and Papert(1968). Minsky's descriptor-indexed bibliography in Feigenbaum and Feldman(1963) is a useful guide to material on this and other topics in AI.

17 Copyright 1961 by The Institute of Radio Engineers, Inc. Reprinted, with permission, from the *Proceedings of the IRE*, January 1961, pp. 8-30.

18 Turing(1950) terms this line of argument against the possibility of machine intelligence the "Heads in the Sand Objection."

Chapter 15.
Literary Perspectives on the Machine

The pervasive effects of technology on modern life acquire human dimensions in literature; the imaginative works of poets and storytellers transform abstract issues into the concrete longings, fears, and expectations of individual human beings. Unconstrained by the "objective" procedures of scientific and historical methods, the creative imagination moves freely between the actual and the potential. The historical record serves mainly as a point of departure for what might be, so that analysis and exploration may transcend the purely factual and embrace moral judgments as well as representation. Concerns and purposes are as varied as the human condition itself. Expressions of awe and wonder mingle with prophesy and catharsis. The experience reflected in the many works dealing with men and machines is a valuable source of insight. Our aim in discussing the literary response to technology is twofold. In addition to pursuing the historian's interest in documenting the cultural impact of economic and political change, we propose to examine the intellectual content of certain recurrent themes, which reveal universal human problems.

Our study of the role of computers in contemporary society has emphasized the continuity of present developments with traditional practices and beliefs. We have tried to show that computer technology is problematic largely because it is conditioned by modes of thought and action inherited from the past. The literary record of the machine is particularly instructive on this point. Poetic license allows for the elaboration of visions of reality uncluttered by scholarly preoccupations. And through these visions we may glimpse a kernel of truth which transcends the particularity of contemporary events. Utopian writers of the nineteenth century, for example, built imaginary worlds based on the factory system and the harnessing of unlimited sources of energy. The value of these often fanciful projections resides less in their verisimilitude to the world of the future, than in what they teach us about the potentialities of historical, social trends. These imaginary worlds hold up a mirror to reality, in which potential developments are reflected as accomplished facts; so, if we look carefully, we may discern something of our own world-view and the consequences which follow from it.

The amount of material dealing with technology in human affairs is truly formidable, but the present discussion is not intended as a comprehensive study of the major works representing the different genre. Nor do we propose to survey fictional accounts of the computer. Our aim is to examine some literary pieces which illuminate the issues surrounding the development and use of computers, such as we have explored more formally in the preceding chapters. This end is best served by focusing on themes and problems rather than literary forms. However, we are inclined to favor utopian writings because of their comprehensive scope and the central position accorded to technology and social organization.

To set the stage for subsequent discussion, we will survey the range of attitudes toward machines reflected in several different types of literature. The themes we have chosen to explore parallel the main divisions of this book. First, is the promise of computer technology which springs from its expected contribution to the goal of progress. This expectation has a long history and is articulated in projections of an ordered society based on rational principles of organization. We will consider contrasting utopian works which embody this idea and provide some perspective on current concerns. The second major theme deals with the negative side of technology's promise. As industrialization succeeded in changing the shape of society, and promoted the growth of powerful nation states, enthusiasm turned to skepticism and disillusionment. The part played by technology in facilitating political and social control is a salient feature of twentieth-century fiction dealing with men and machines. Once again, we will concentrate primarily on one particular idiom, the anti-utopian novel.

Perhaps the most problematic aspect of technology is the creative human ability it represents. The tension between creator and artifact increases as the latter acquires (or seems to acquire) some measure of autonomy. Modern technology has suggested many epithets to describe society: "the age of steam," "the age of electricity," "the atomic age," "the computer age," etc. But none is more appropriate than "the age of anxiety." The third main theme deals with this tension and anxiety generated by man's challenge to the gods. This issue has a special significance for computer technology, since the myth of mechanical intelligence has become a disturbing reality. Our final theme is one which has permeated the entire work: the conquest of will. We will appeal to the literary record to illuminate the discussion of Part IV concerning the mechanistic reduction of human experience, and the spirit of conquest which has marked its progress.

1. The Problematic Machine

The literary record is filled with man's ambivalence toward machines. Dreams of an age of plenty and ease find expression in the imagery of technological cornucopia; but these dreams often turn into nightmares when the unrestrained application of power threatens to subjugate the human being. Machines have been depicted as benefactors and oppressors, slaves and masters. We have been captivated by their beauty and appalled by their ugliness. If there is anything constant in our relationship to them, it is an abiding fascination with their capabilities and limitations. The instruments fashioned by *homo faber* have exercised the imagination throughout history, but our concern here is principally with the modern period, from the beginning of the industrial revolution onwards. During this period technology became indissolubly linked with fundamental social change, and its potentialities for good and evil intruded upon the consciousness of thinkers, poets, writers, and artists alike. In what follows, we will sample the troubled responses to technology revealed in poetry and fiction.

For purposes of discussion, it is useful to distinguish several major categories of fiction which bear on technology. First, there is what might loosely be termed social commentary.[1] This category includes realistic pieces dealing with the impact of technology on individuals or social structure. Charles Dickens' novel *Hard Times*, Emile Zola's *Germinal*, and John Steinbeck's *The Grapes of Wrath* fall within this class. The journalistic writings of the so-called "muckrakers" such as Upton Sinclair's *The Jungle* and Frank Norris' *The Octopus* might also be included. Utopian novels constitute a second category.[2] Works of this type are characterized by their construction of a complete social order, which may be cast as a positive or negative "ideal." Edward Bellamy's *Looking Backward* and William Morris' *News from Nowhere* exemplify the positive variety; Aldous Huxley's *Brave New World* and George Orwell's *1984* are well-known examples of negative utopias. Berneri(1950,p.2) points to another important division in this class.

> Two main trends manifest themselves in utopian thought throughout the ages. One seeks the happiness of mankind through material well-being, the sinking of man's individuality into the group, and the greatness of the State. The other, while demanding a certain degree of material comfort, considers that happiness is the result of the free expression of man's personality and must not be sacrificed to an arbitrary moral code or to the interests of the State.

The third category is science fiction, which is defined by the thematic centrality of scientific and technological possibilities. Examples which touch on computer technology include Arthur C. Clarke's *2001*, Olof Johannesson's *The Tale of the Big Computer*, and Robert Heinlein's *The Moon is a Harsh Mistress*. There is, of course, considerable overlap among these three classes of fiction, but the labels are useful for referring to general properties peculiar to each one.

The advantages of new sources of energy coupled with new modes of production led inexorably to the destruction of the old order. Industrialization altered the foundations of society. To be sure, this passage did not go unmarked. William Blake was an early critic of the emerging industrial society, and the well-known phrase "dark satanic mills" from the preface to his poem "Milton" has become a symbol of the depredations of industrial technology. It was not simply the fact of change that created a sense of malaise. The requirements of mechanical efficiency were gradually extended to all aspects of life. In *Hard Times*, Dickens paints a dismal picture of material and spiritual impoverishment. Factory discipline prevails not only at work and in school, but it serves to define the terms of human interaction.

> *Hard Times* criticizes not a person, but an emotional atmosphere, a state of mind symbolized by the machine. ... Within the novel, plot and symbol are organized to indicate the major theme of nineteenth- and twentieth- century literature, the suppression of emotional impulse by the false application of the machine metaphor. (Sussman, 1968, p. 62).

The fate of Steinbeck's Okies in *The Grapes of Wrath* is a consequence of the same mechanical logic. Families were driven from their land because they had ceased to be productive units. What is more, the tractors used to plow over their holdings were operated by their own neighbors. The operator was simply the tool of impersonal organizations, but his self conscious rationalization is characteristic of advancing mechanistic consciousness.

For those who saw in technology a means of improving the lot of mankind, the harsh realities of nineteenth century development were accidental features born of inappropriate or iniquitous social structure. The utopian projection furnished a vehicle for exploring the beneficent potentialities of technology under ideal social conditions. Berneri(1950, p.207) explains the connection between utopian schemes and the nineteenth century social reform movement.

> The history of utopias in the nineteenth century is closely linked with the creation of the socialist movement, and it is sometimes difficult to distinguish between schemes which belong to the realm of utopian thought and those which come within the province of practical social reform.

In the utopian writings of this period, technology is rarely problematic in itself. The underlying economic organization of society, the ownership of property and the means of production, the distribution of wealth, etc. are seen to determine how machines are used. Cultural disposition is a secondary issue, and the scientific world-view is a neutral component of society, subordinate to organizational goals. We will examine several representative utopian works in subsequent sections.

As the industrial revolution consolidated its advance, the machine penetrated the aesthetic landscape. Casual perusal of anthologies of modern poetry, for example, yields dozens of "odes" to machines and technological artifacts. This signifies growing familiarity but not necessarily acceptance. Although the occasions for reform are not likely to disappear, the problems have changed. Blake's "dark satanic mills" are not as dark and satanic as they once were; and the impoverished conditions of life observed by Dickens and Zola have been ameliorated. The trade union movement succeeded in bringing the forces of capital under the rule of a more just law. With some notable exceptions, as in the negative utopias, machines have come to be represented as natural components of modern life. The tractor in *The Grapes of Wrath* is an instrument of oppression, but it is not an alien thing; the automobile becomes a means of salvation with its driver fully integrated into the mechanism.

> Al, at the wheel, his face purposeful, his whole body listening to the car, his restless eyes jumping from the road to the instrument panel. Al was one with his engine, every nerve listening for weakness, for the thumps or squeals, hums, and chattering that indicate a change that may cause a breakdown. He had become the soul of the car. (Steinbeck, 1940, p. 167)[3]

This growing familiarity with machines facilitated a narrowing of focus to more limited issues than comprehensive social reform. Isaac Asimov's story of the robot "Robbie" illustrates the new dispensation for our mechanical artifacts. Here the machine appears firmly under man's control and exists only to serve human ends. To make the point perfectly clear, Asimov postulates "the three laws of robotics":

1- A robot may not injure a human being, or through inaction, allow a human being to come to harm.

2- A robot must obey the orders given it by human beings except where such orders would conflict with the First Law.

3- A robot must protect its own existence as long as such protection does not conflict with the First or Second Law. (Asimov, 1950, p. 6)

The master-slave relationship is a compelling theme in science fiction. In a short story "With Folded Hands" by Jack Williamson, Asimov's Second Law leads to a resolution radically different from that envisioned in "Robbie." The unyielding solicitude of humanoid robots programmed to obey their "Prime Directive: to serve and obey, and guard man from harm," reduces the human being to a parasite.

Ascher(1963) explores a variety of issues treated by science fiction writers which concern computers in particular.[4] These issues range from the sinister possibility of "conscious" malevolence to quirks associated with the computer's literal character. Current preoccupations with control of decision-making, depersonalized computer applications, and the challenge to human skill and creativity are common themes in contemporary science fiction. The twentieth century's concrete experience with machines has certainly not allayed the fear and outrage expressed during the industrial revolution. New developments, particularly the computer, have reinforced the problematic in technology. This is especially evident in the negative utopias which envision a dehumanized world dominated by mechanistic principles. Contemporary literature has little patience for the naive view of the nineteenth century. Science and technology are no longer seen as neutral instruments at the disposal of free human masters.

2.   Abundance and Freedom from Toil

The industrial revolution promised to increase the availability of goods and ease the burdens of work. Despite, or perhaps because of the great human sacrifice which this promise entailed, dreams of industrial development in the future focused on the material foundations of existence. The harsh realities of life coupled with the seemingly boundless potentialities of technology provided motive and basis for utopian visions of ideal societies. Solutions to the age old problems of poverty and inequality were seen to be at hand; material progress held the key to man's salvation. Improving the material conditions of life would raise the living standard of the poor and miraculously eliminate the inequalities perpetuated by social institutions.

The materialistic preoccupations of nineteenth century Utopias are in sharp contrast to the concerns of earlier works. "While utopias in the past had stressed the need for detachment from material goods, those of the nineteenth century sought happiness in the satisfaction of an ever increasing number of material needs." (Berneri,1950,p. 210) For example, in Thomas More's *Utopia* the austere quality of life was calculated to avoid the corrupting influence of luxury; it was not dictated by necessity.[5] The ideal commonwealths of the Renaissance were (with some exceptions) concerned with the perfection of the human being through the improvement of physical, mental, and moral faculties. Sweeping changes in economic and social organization are doubtless responsible for the differences in utopian objectives. In particular, the process of industrialization accelerated a shift in the focal point of moral doctrine from the spiritual to the mundane. Elaboration of power and the development of new forms of social organization were central to the experience of the nineteenth century, and this experience is reflected in the literature of the period.

As Berneri points out, nineteenth century utopian writers were strongly influenced by socialist thought. Thus, technology often plays a subsidiary role in the ideal commonwealth; the main emphasis was on the organization of society. *The Coming Race* of Bulwer-Lytton is a notable exception. The shape of the imaginary civilization of this tale was determined by the discovery of an extraordinary form of energy known as "vril." Possession of vril became universal among all the people of the "civilized" nations of this underground world, and consequently it was believed to be impossible for any one group to gain an advantage through its use. In particular, conventional types of government became unnecessary. Bulwer-Lytton's conception of the consequences of vril is reminiscent of the contemporary doctrine of nuclear deterrence. Unfortunately for us, he did not elaborate on the social mechanisms needed to sustain the desired equilibrium. *The Coming Race* anticipated modern utopias in the role it assigned to machinery, since much of the work was handled by machines and robot-like devices.

The dominant model of social structure in nineteenth century utopias derives from industrial and military organization. Etienne Cabet in *Voyage en Icarie* envisioned a kind of democratic state socialism; Edward Bellamy's *Looking Backward* portrays a society patterned after an "industrial army." The essential features of these utopias are remarkably similar. Individual behavior is minutely controlled by the state. Much of the daily routine is prescribed by law, and the tasks set for individuals are singularly uninteresting. Distribution of goods and services is accomplished through centralized agencies. Spontaneous formation of groups based on shared experience and common interests is replaced by the establishment of artificial associations. One of the few departures from the industrial-military model is William Morris' *News From Nowhere*. We will take a closer look at the works of Bellamy and Morris inasmuch as they represent opposing viewpoints in nineteenth century utopian thought.

Edward Bellamy's *Looking Backward* exemplifies the nineteenth century creed of material progress. The novel's widespread popularity shortly after it first appeared in 1888 gives some indication of the representative character of Bellamy's vision of the ideal society. The story itself is a romance about the future, which unfolds through the experience of the hero. The narrator-hero is an insomniac who often has recourse to a mesmerist to put him to sleep. On one of these occasions the trance proves sufficiently deep to preserve him in a state of suspended animation in his underground vault for 113 years, from 1887 until 2000.[6] The hero of Bellamy's tale is introduced to American society in the year 2000 by the person who rouses him from his hypnotic trance. It is through the latter that we learn of the nature of society. The new order emerged through a peaceful social revolution which occurred at the beginning of the twentieth century. In broad outline, this new order is part of the actual experience of the twentieth century. Bellamy turns out to have been more of a prophet than a utopian visionary.

Economic life is controlled by a centralized state monopoly. Production and distribution of goods and services are accomplished through the organization of an industrial army, which consists of a very well-defined and disciplined hierarchy with managers at the top and workers at the bottom. Service in the industrial army is compulsory for men and women between the ages of twenty-one and forty-five. Despite the military discipline, replete with service ranks comparable to those of a conventional army, perfect social equality prevails. Each individual is given a credit card with a fixed amount of credits (the same for everyone) for commodities and services. Although goods are not over-abundant, there is an ample supply.

The society envisioned by Bellamy is an amalgam of nineteenth century developments in large-scale social production, and various reform programs aimed at curbing the abuses of an uncontrolled market economy. The operation of these tendencies are clearly evident in Bellamy's treatment of human relationships. There is equality between men and women with recognition of the peculiar needs of both, but the conventional family structure of the nineteenth century is preserved. *Looking Backward* is very much a part of the nineteenth century tradition of utopian visions, which Berneri(1951, p. 216) characterizes as "depressingly uninspiring."

> They aim at setting up a vast machinery which will ensure a perfect running of society and bring material well being to everyone. But in these intricate mechanisms man's individuality is completely lost. The State becomes an all-wise, all-providing God which can never make any mistakes— and if it did no one would have the power to correct them.

William Morris's *News from Nowhere* published in 1890 is an anomaly in this dreary tradition. Although the narrative is set in the twenty-first century, the novel is more a portrait of the potentialities of human development than a projection of a future society. In contrast to the standard nineteenth century utopian fare, the individual is not reduced to a machine to be cared for by the apparatus of the state. Morris does not fall prey to the usual conceits of nineteenth century utopian writers. He does not imagine that he has the ultimate program for reshaping the social order. The vision of *News from Nowhere* is antithetical to that of *Looking Backward*. government has become unnecessary, and production of goods is accomplished through a federation of autonomous communities whose economic life is a mixture of agriculture and industry. Morris did not subscribe to the belief in material progress as the salvation of man. Happiness is not equated with abundance or consumption. The role of work or craft is seen as an essential component of life. In this respect, Morris anticipated the contemporary search for a more authentic individuality rooted in an intimate relationship between producer and consumer.

> The wares which we make are made because they are needed: men make for their neighbours' use as if they were making for themselves, not for a vague market of which they know nothing, and over which they have no control: as there is no buying and selling, it would be mere insanity to make goods on the chance of their being wanted; for there is no longer any one

who can be compelled to buy them. So that whatever is made is good, and thoroughly fit for its purpose. Nothing can be made except for genuine use; therefore no inferior goods are made. Moreover, as aforesaid, we have now found out what we want, so we make no more than we want; and as we are not driven to make a vast quantity of useless things, we have time and resources enough to consider our pleasure in making them. All work which would be irksome to do by hand is done by immensely improved machinery; and in all work which it is a pleasure to do by hand machinery is done without. There is no difficulty in finding work which suits the special turn of mind of everybody; so that no man is sacrificed to the wants of another. From time to time, when we have found out that some piece of work was too disagreeable or troublesome, we have given it up and done altogether without the thing produced by it. Now, surely you can see that under these circumstances all the work that we do is an exercise of the mind and body more or less pleasant to be done: so that instead of avoiding work everybody seeks it: and, since people have got defter in doing the work generation after generation, it has become so easy to do, that it seems as if there were less done, though probably more is produced. (Morris, 1891, pp. 112-113)

3. Control of Behavior

The focus of nineteenth century utopian writers was on the organization of production and distribution of goods. With some notable exceptions such as William Morris, their characteristic response to the industrial and technological development of the period was to envision a well regulated society controlled by a central government. The individual is conditioned and seduced into his appointed role, but, if necessary, he may be coerced. The overriding concern with producing enough goods to satisfy needs obscured the authoritarian character of the centralized state. The experience of the twentieth century has led to a radically different view of man's relationship to technology.[7]

The main trend of literature between the two wars has been one of extreme scepticism regarding the power of the State to transform society. The rise of new regimes, frankly communistic or vaguely socialist, but always totalitarian and ready to sacrifice the individual to the interests of the State, forced intellectuals to adopt either an attitude of complete subservience to the State and become little more than paid propagandists, or to claim defiantly the rights of the individual.

There has also been a turning-away from the faith in the inevitability of progress. For most writers of the nineteenth century, scientific discoveries and industrial development were going to increase automatically the happiness of mankind, but modern generations see the dangers as well as the advantages which "progress" can bring. (Berneri,1951,p. 310)

One of the earliest of the anti- or negative utopias of the twentieth century was Eugene Zamiatin's *We* published in 1924.[8] The story takes place one thousand years after the consolidation of the United State as ruler of the entire world. The United State is about to extend its power into the universe with the launching of the Integral, a machine designed for space travel. Zamiatin pictures a world in which every aspect of life has been reduced to mechanical precision. The agents of the State know every movement and every thought of each citizen. The roles of spy and confessor or psychological counsellor have been fused into one, and there is no such thing as a private life for the individual. People live in apartments with glass walls so that nothing can be concealed from the agents of the state (except during the personal hour when curtains may be drawn). Activities are determined by a table of hours and the condition of man is one of near perfect unfreedom.

> Naturally, having conquered hunger (that is, algebraically speaking, having achieved the total of bodily welfare), the United State directed its attack against the second ruler of the world, against love. At last this element also was conquered, that is, organized and put into a mathematical formula. It is already three hundred years since our great historic Lex Sexualis was promulgated: "A Number may obtain a license to use any other Number as a sexual product."
>
> The rest is only a matter of technique. You are carefully examined in the laboratory of the Sexual Department where they find the content of the sexual hormones in your blood, and they accordingly make out for you a Table of sexual days. Then you file an application to enjoy the services of Number so and so, or Numbers so and so. You get for that purpose a checkbook (pink). That is all. (Zamiatin,1924,p. 22)[9]

Aldous Huxley's *Brave New World* appeared in 1932. This satire on American society was strongly influenced by Zamiatin's We. The main focus is on the control of disorder, achieving a stable society. Huxley goes much further than Zamiatin in imagining complete genetic and social control through the production of "bottle babies," and their subsequent conditioning. In a foreword to the novel, written in 1946, Huxley explains his view of the new totalitarianism.

> There is, of course, no reason why the new totalitarianism should resemble the old. Government by clubs and firing squads,

by artificial famine, mass imprisonment and mass deportation, is not merely inhumane (nobody cares much about that nowadays); it is demonstrably inefficient and in an age of advanced technology, inefficiency is the sin against the Holy Ghost. A really efficient totalitarian state would be one in which the all-powerful executive of political bosses and their army of managers control a population of slaves who do not have to be coerced, because they love their servitude. (p. xii)

This reveals a difference between Huxley and Zamiatin. In *We*, the State had to resort to primitive corrective measures in the form of torture and exemplary murder.

Fifteen years after he wrote *Brave New World*, Huxley remarked that his initial projection of the anti-utopia 600 years into the future could probably be shortened to a century. Although the technical means for producing bottle babies may be in the distant future, the other characteristic features of *Brave New World* are very close indeed. The use of drugs and other techniques for modifying behavior has become a political as well as a medical fact. The psychiatric hospital has become a tool for the control of dissident elements in the Soviet Union; and the realm of personal accountability for citizens of the Western democracies is steadily shrinking with the widespread adoption of tests of mental competence in judging anti-social behavior. Moreover, the sexual promiscuity of *Brave New World* is a fact of contemporary life. In some American cities the number of divorces exceeds the number of marriages. "As political and economic freedom diminishes, sexual freedom tends compensatingly to increase. ... In conjunction with the freedom to daydream under the influence of dope and movies and the radio, it will help to reconcile [the dictator's] subjects to the servitude which is their fate." (Huxley, p. xiii)

George Orwell's *1984* (published in 1949) is closer to Zamiatin's *We* than to Huxley's *Brave New World*. The nightmarish futures depicted by Zamiatin and Orwell bear a close resemblance to the Nazi and Stalinist dictatorships. Huxley's new order is largely a projection of existing trends in the industrialized Western democracies. All three of these negative utopias are concerned with the future of the individual in societies which are evolving ever more powerful means of control. Without computers, the actual means of surveillance used by Zamiatin's guardians, and Orwell's Big Brother are necessarily vague. However, the principle remains unchanged with the advent of the computer. Kurt Vonnegut's novel *Player Piano*, published in 1952, has computers managing production and distribution. The ordinary citizen is reduced to accepting make-work type jobs in the Army or the Reconstruction and Reclamation Corps. In a very amusing episode, Vonnegut examines the distinction between citizen and slave. The urbane Dr. Ewing J. Halyard of the United States Department of State fails to convince the visiting Shah of Bratpuhr that a group of idling workers from the Reconstruction and Reclamation Corps are free citizens.

A recent book by Ira Levin, *This Perfect Day* (1970) leans heavily on Zamiatin, Huxley, and Orwell. What is new is that society is managed by a central computer called Unicomp. Following Huxley, Levin incorporates behavior modification through chemotherapy as a form of control. The essence of the plot is similar to those of *We* and *1984* in that the hero is a deviant person who ultimately discovers the existence of islands not yet integrated into the "Family," and thus stumbles on the possibility of "coming alive" as a thinking, feeling human being, free of the dulling effects of chemotherapy.

In a world in which the human being is reduced to a machine-like existence, it makes little difference to the ordinary person whether social decisions are made by a human or a machine. However, actual control by computers adds a new dimension to the negative utopia. In Olof Johannesson's *Tale of the Big Computer*, the preservation of the human race hangs in the balance. The computer narrator speculates on the "human problem."

> We may take it that economic considerations, both industrial and national, must play a very large part. Our society is incomparably the richest of any that have existed before, none of which can claim the epithets "welfare state" or "affluent society" with more justice than our own. But wealth must never be an excuse for wastefulness; on the contrary, the great moral obligations entailed by wealth must ever be borne in mind. Only by strict application of economic laws and the avoidance, by more rational organization, of unnecessary expenditure can we make ourselves worthy of the blessings of prosperity, and so win the right to possess and to increase our riches. This applies not only to individuals but also to communities, our own included. So for purely economic reasons also we must question whether our society can afford mankind. (Johannesson,1969,p. 127)

4.   Challenge to the Gods

Together with developments in the life sciences, computer technology has sparked considerable literary exploration of the implications of creating new beings. Of course, this speculation on the awesome power of creation antedates the computer. The human imagination has reveled in fantasies of power since time immemorial. However, modern science and technology conspire to translate fantasy into reality. Mary Shelley's *Frankenstein* published in 1818 is one of the more well-known modern treatments of this theme. As Mazlish(1967) points out, Frankenstein's creation runs amok not because of an intrinsically evil disposition, but because it is spurned by Frankenstein. This illustrates one way in which the challenge to the gods sets uncontrollable events in motion. The novel's subtitle *The Modern Prometheus* emphasizes the idea of challenge. The critical aspect of Dr. Frankenstein's creature is the fact that it possesses a will independent of its creator. The consequences are far more dangerous than those suggested by the parable of the sorcerer's apprentice. In the latter case, there is also a problem of control, but the solution is more straightforward. The forces set in motion by the apprentice are uncontrolled but not uncontrollable, since they do not issue from a sovereign will.

The conflict between people and robots in Karel Capek's *R.U.R.* points to the problematic relationship between creator and artifact. Initially the robots are seen to be completely subservient; whatever problems result from their manufacture and deployment appear to derive from errors in human judgment regarding their proper use. Eventually, however, the robots develop consciousness, and turn on their creators. The slave becomes the master. There is poetic justice in this reversal— man usurps the power of the gods, and in the end is destroyed by the presumption of that power. The so-called "human problem" which emerges at the end of Johannesson's *Tale of the Big Computer* suggests the same conclusion.

Man's relationship to his mechanical creations constitutes a curious love affair. As we see our own creativity and skill mirrored in our artifacts, we cannot despise them without despising ourselves. We are overcome with pride and transfixed by the measure of our own greatness. Yet these creatures mock our strength, blaspheme our sacred rites, destroy our institutions, scorn our intelligence, impugn our integrity, and challenge our creativity. For all of this we are not always grateful, but our tolerance knows no bounds. Perhaps we have no alternative. In any case, it is hard to imagine an appropriate form of retribution. The obvious parallels are not too helpful on this account, although the idea of a mechanical heaven and hell might serve a useful purpose. Here as elsewhere the greatest imponderable is free will. Two-thousand years of philosophical and theological speculation have yet to produce a definitive answer for man in relation to God, but we may suppose that the problem for machines and man is not quite so complex. In its most dramatic form, the possibility that machines may exhibit free will has been represented by writers from Samuel Butler to Arthur C. Clarke in terms of consciousness. This is not the only form it may take.

The question of whether or not machines can or will become autonomous creatures has greater significance in terms of the unfolding of historical forces. To what extent is man able to modify the development of technology? Have our mechanical creations become so much a part of our aspirations and the social means for their realization that we are powerless to move in other directions? These are some of the vital questions raised by twentieth century literary accounts of the machine. The widespread appeal of *Brave New World* and *1984* show that these concerns are quite real. There is a pervasive fear that we have indeed compromised our ability to control technology, that the evolution of our machine-based civilization has become an autonomous process; and this is a source of acute anxiety. Tales of malevolent robots and recalcitrant computers are poignant allegories of modern history which we ignore at our peril.

In many cases the consequences of man's challenge as a creator are more subtle than the overt destruction of the human race which occurs in *R.U.R.* The existence of creatures which rival or surpass man's capabilities poses a grave threat to human identity. An inverted form of this threat is implicit in the negative utopias discussed earlier. The elaboration of mechanisms for controlling and monitoring individual behavior turns the human being into an inferior creature. The threat to identity is an internal one, posed by society itself. As the human being is transformed into a machine, the latter threatens to obliterate all traces of the former. In Zamiatin's *We* the State ultimately has recourse to an operation designed to destroy human imagination.

> The enemies of happiness are awake! Hold to your happiness with both hands. Tomorrow all work will stop and all numbers are to come to be operated upon. Those who fail to come will be submitted to the machine of the well-doer. (Zamiatin, 1924, p. 180)

The twentieth century has yielded refinements of Zamiatin's crushing vision. Beyond the making of robots, and the transformation of human beings into robots, the diabolical logic of technique must master the inner workings of the soul. David Karp's novel *One* explores the possibility of completely remaking the individual ego.

This is not a simple matter of coercion or control. The state is not content with the outward forms of loyalty and obedience; it insists on absolute mastery of thought, behavior, and the unconscious will. Contemporary developments in the use of drugs, psychosurgery, and psychotherapy to modify behavior provide a real basis for this projection. Our creations are seen to turn on us with a vengeance.

In the end the State triumphs over the individual human soul. After his operation, the narrator in *We* reports

> Next day, I, D-503, appeared before the Well-Doer and told him everything known to me about the enemies of happiness. Why, before, it had seemed hard for me to go, I cannot understand. The only explanation seems to be my illness— my soul. (Zamiatin, 1924, p. 217)

1984 concludes on a similar, chilling note.

> He gazed up at the enormous face. Forty years it had taken him to learn what kind of smile was hidden beneath the dark mustache. O cruel, needless misunderstanding! O stubborn self-willed exile from the loving breast! Two gin-scented tears trickled down the sides of his nose. But it was all right, everything was all right, the struggle was finished. He had won the victory over himself. He loved Big Brother. (Orwell, 1949, p. 245)

However, the very possibility of the struggle of the protagonists of *We* and *1984* is enough to establish a new myth of regeneration. In virtually all the negative utopias, the authoritarian State either tolerates or is powerless to eliminate all traces of behavioral deviance. In *We* there are human colonies living between the cities with their green walled enclosures; *Brave New World* preserved remnants of the old civilization in the interests of science; the thought control in *1984* is imperfect; and the society of *This Perfect Day* has yet to incorporate all regions of the world into its system of control. Even though rebellion turns out in most cases to be futile, one is left with the hope that the human spirit will not be obliterated for ever.

In spite of the destruction of humanity by the robots in *R.U.R.*, the play ends on a hopeful note. Some of the robots acquire human characteristics, and the possibility of a new race of human beings presents itself. Of course, there is another side to the myth of regeneration. Perhaps history will repeat itself, for as Moliere observed "the only thing immortal in man is his stupidity." This theme is developed by Walter Miller in his novel *A Canticle for Leibowitz* which appeared in 1959. The story begins after a nuclear war destroyed most of the civilized world.[10] What happens is essentially a recapitulation of the history of Western civilization from the dark ages to the present. In the denouement, another nuclear war threatens the new civilization.

5. The Conquest of Will

The fate of civilization as depicted in *A Canticle for Leibowitz* is not entirely accidental. It is linked to the peculiar world-view fostered by science and technology. The conquering spirit of this world-view is irrepressible and has taken root everywhere. Karl Shapiro traces its tortuous development in his poem "The Progress of Faust," whose last stanza leaves off where Miller's grim prophecy begins.

> Backwardly tolerant, Faustus was expelled From the Third Reich in Nineteen Thirty-nine. His exit caused the breaching of the Rhine, Except for which the frontier might have held. Five years unknown to enemy and friend He hid, appearing on the sixth to pose In an American desert at war's end Where, at his back, a dome of atoms rose. (Karl Shapiro; in Untermeyer,1955,p. 372)

Man's capacity for self-deception in the face of imminent disaster is perhaps a necessary component of the will to power. Even the Abbot Zerchi, who knew better, appealed to the rationality of the world built by science to forestall the inevitable at the conclusion of Miller's novel.

> Now— *now* the princes, the presidents, now they know— with dead certainty. They can know it by the children they beget and send to asylums for the deformed. They know it, and they've kept the peace. Not Christ's peace, certainly, but peace, until lately— with only two warlike incidents in as many centuries. Now they have the bitter certainty. My sons, they cannot do it again. Only a race of madmen could do it again. (Miller, 1961, p. 227)[11]

The compelling character of the destructive potentialities of technique is attributed by some writers to man's dependence on technology as a mediator of experience. It is not simply the use of machines and gadgets that defines this dependence. Our reliance on them is merely the outward manifestation of a pervasive attitude toward experience. "Multiplication of forms and improvements of technology inevitably make all experience a commodity." (Boorstin,1964,p. 179). The ability to grasp what is real is attenuated by the interposition of interpretive media, by excessive filtering, blocking, and laundering of experience. To the extent that we inhibit the capacity to interact with the world on a direct basis, we risk a one-sided and faulty view of reality and ultimately become maladaptive. Surely the resort to nuclear confrontation is maladaptive. The anti-hero in Max Frisch's novel *Homo Faber* exemplifies the under-dimensioned personality, mass produced for modern society by the technological ethos. Mr. Faber is an engineer, who possesses a kind of lethal Midas Touch. His attitude is exploitative and opportunistic; he flows, essentially unmoved, from one disastrous encounter to another. The attitude and the behavior are revealed in a self-conscious revery.

> Discussion with Hanna— about technology (according to Hanna) as the knack of so arranging the world that we don't have to experience it. The technologist's mania for putting the Creation to a use, because he can't tolerate it as a partner, can't do anything with it; technology as the knack of eliminating the world as resistance, for example, of diluting it by speed, so that we don't have to experience it. (I don't know what Hanna means by this.) The technologist's worldlessness. (I don't know what Hanna means by this.) (Frisch, 1959, p. 178).

The mechanistic reduction of experience takes many forms. It appears in the realm of knowledge as the positivistic rejection of anything other than measurable quantities and operational procedures. The atomization of human task performance is a basic ingredient in the progress of industry. Administration by impersonal bureaucracies is based on the formalization of human roles. There is no disputing the contribution of reductionism to the achievement of a systematic understanding of natural phenomena, unparalleled productive capacity, and effective political organization. But like the fabled helper of the sorcerer's apprentice, the principle of reductionism has no internal limit, and our civilization appears to have lost the ability to control its operation. In *The Machine Stops*, E. M. Forster creates a world in which direct contact with nature is entirely eliminated. People live in complete physical isolation from one another in hermetically sealed, air conditioned cubicles— underground, and all forms of interaction are mediated through the machine. The only remaining modality of experience is the intellectual, and even that is reduced to the exchange of topical "ideas" received n-th hand; the very thought of direct experience inspires terror. Ultimately, the decay of human vitality leads to the collapse of civilization. The breakdown is gradual and imperceptible, and the habits of total passivity render people incapable of taking effective action.

> No one confessed the Machine was out of hand. Year by year it was served with increased efficiency and decreased intelligence. The better a man knew his own duties upon it, the less he

understood the duties of his neighbor, and in the world there was not one who understood the monster as a whole. Those master brains had perished. They had left full directions, it is true, and their successors had each of them mastered a portion of those directions. But Humanity, in its desire for comfort had over-reached itself. It had exploited the riches of nature too far. Quietly and complacently, it was sinking into decadence, and progress had come to mean the progress of the Machine. (Forster, 1928, p. 285)[12]

Most of the stories we have cited, bear witness, implicitly or explicitly, to an inherent contradiction in the conquering spirit of science and technology. The conquest of nature, space, and time is seen as a paradoxical victory over the human ego. As man extended his dominion over the natural world, he became alienated from the sources of his vitality. Through obsessive exercise of the will to power in the elaboration of technique, the will itself became enfeebled and subject to control by autonomous forces linked to mechanical progress. The process by which this came about is exceedingly complex, but science and technology are dominant factors. Success in one area invites emulation in others. The scientific outlook laid the foundation for systematic investigation of natural phenomena. But in order to probe the secrets of nature, it was necessary to cultivate a peculiar kind of restraint. The intellect had to be disciplined to reject all but objectively verifiable observations, and this required the resolution of human experience into easily manipulatable units. This procedure has its counterpart in the evolution of industrial technology and social organization.[13] In both cases, it is reflected in the imperative to divide and conquer.

A social order built on this imperative ultimately domesticates the heroic impulse which fashions it. Herein lies the paradox. As the division of labor grows in the pursuit of knowledge, in economic and political affairs, and all other areas of social conduct, human behavior becomes more rigidly defined and circumscribed. Appearances to the contrary are mere illusions. Control, too, becomes a specialized function distinguished from the activity it regulates. The advance of the Jacquard Loom over the music box marks the progress of the modern conception of social control. Once the separation is established, the demands of efficiency, or, in contemporary parlance, "economy of scale," lead inexorably to the centralization of control. In human terms, specialization of function and centralization of control entail a compression of the ego and a reduction in individual autonomy. These complementary developments are explored in science fiction as well as the negative utopias.

The specialization of social roles is facilitated by mechanized grading schemes (Zamiatin, Orwell, Forster, Bennett, Levin) or by genetic programming (Huxley), and serves as an effective instrument for the control of behavior. With or without the aid of computers, the effect is the same. Human consciousness gives way to mechanical consciousness embodied in the Perfect State. Life is so arranged that no untoward challenge can disturb the machine-made equilibrium.

The objective is the elimination of personal struggle. Human happiness is identified with contentment, and the latter is seen to obtain when the exigencies of life are substantially less demanding than the individual's capabilities for coping with them. The resemblance to sound industrial practice is not fortuitous, and neither is the underlying motive. Redundancy is made to serve technological ends, rather than human ones. And just as muscles and skills atrophy from disuse, so does the exercise of judgment and responsibility. Christopher Hodder-Williams comes to grips with these issues in *Fistful of Digits* , where a world-wide computer network and advanced behavioral engineering techniques serve the sinister designs of a clandestine organization.

> Eventually the mechanical interlock of technology must conquer all individual will. You might conceivably postpone it, but it could only be postponement; because for as long as man could not stand by himself and rely on himself in preference to the easy way out, then inevitably he would wind up handing over the mastery of his own wits... (Hodder-Williams, 1972, p. 273).

Questioning the beneficence of scientific rationality and technological progress is almost as heretical as denigrating patriotism. Poets are held of little account in our society, so their license is free for the asking. Operating without poetic license, however, opens one to a variety of charges, ranging from lack of objectivity to muddled mysticism. In weighing such charges, it is essential to bear in mind that rationality is not the exclusive preserve of science and technology. Other modalities of experience have their own peculiar rationality. The belief in the social necessity and inevitability of computer utilities, databanks, management information systems, and sundry computer applications is not based on reason alone. It is the reflection of a political faith built into the scheme of modern history, with an internal logic akin to that portrayed in the Theatre of the Absurd. If the past is any guide to the future, we cannot afford to acquiesce in moral bankruptcy. There are always other choices so long as the paralysis of will is not complete.

1   The works of Victorian writers discussed by Sussman(1968) include some in this category, but his study encompasses essays, poetry and other genre.

2   For a survey of utopian writing from Plato to the twentieth century, see Berneri(1950) and Mumford(1922).

3   From *The Grapes of Wrath* by John Steinbeck. Copyright 1939, Copyright © renewed 1967 by John Steinbeck. Reprinted by permission of The Viking Press, Inc.

4   See also Baer's(1972) discussion of selected works dealing with computers.

5   More's *Utopia* first appeared in 1516.

6   H.G. Wells used a similar literary device to enter the world of the future in *When the Sleeper Wakes.*

7   The early utopian writings of H.G. Wells (*A Modern Utopia* and *Men Like Gods*) would appear to be transitional works.

8   Written in Russian, it was first published in English translation— it was never published in Russia because of official censorship.

9   From *We* by Eugene Zamiatin, translated by Gregory Zilboorg. Copyright 1924 by E.P. Dutton and Co.; renewed, 1952, by Gregory Zilboorg. This and the following passages are reprinted by permission of the publishers, E.P. Dutton and Co., Inc. Non-exclusive worldwide rights granted by permission of the Estate's agents: Agence Hoffman, Paris.

10 The plot in Margot Bennett's novel *The Long Way Back* is based on a similar projection.

11 Copyright 1959 by Walter M. Miller, Jr., reprinted by permission of Harold Matson Company, Inc.

12 Reprinted by permission of the publisher, Harcourt Brace Jovanovich, Inc., and The Society of Authors as the literary representative of the Estate of E.M. Forster.

13 Recall the discussion in Chapter 2 of the parallels between the growth of the scientific outlook, the resolution of industrial processes (such as occurred in silk weaving), and the reduction of computational processes into primitive operations.

Bibliography

Abrams, M.E., ed. (1972). *Spectrum 71: A Conference on Medical Computing*. London: Butterworths.

Adams, S. (1970). MEDLARS - medical information retrieval, in: Sanders(1970), pp. 287-295.

AFIPS-TIME (1972). A National Survey of the Public's Attitudes Toward Computers. Montvale, N.J.: AFIPS Press.

Alford, Robert R. (1962). The political economy of health care: dynamics without change. *Politics and Society* 2, pp. 127-164.

Allery, G.D. (1974). Data communication and public networks, in: *Information Processing* 74. Amsterdam: North-Holland, pp. 117-122.

Anderson, Alan Ross, ed. (1964). *Minds and Machines*. Englewood Cliffs, N.J.: Prentice-Hall.

Anderson, Allan, H.; *et al.* (1966). *An Electronic Cash and Credit System* . New York: American Management Association.

Anderson, J. (1970a). The development of medical recording, in: Anderson and Forsythe(1970), pp. 3-13.

Anderson, J. (1970b). Aims of medical information, in: Anderson and Forsythe(1970), pp. 22-27.

Anderson, J.; Forsythe, J.M., eds. (1970). *Information Processing of Medical Records* . Amsterdam: North-Holland Publishing Co.

Anderson Ronald E.; Fagerlund, E. (1972). Privacy and the computer: an annotated bibliography, *Computing Reviews* 13, pp. 551-559.

Arendt, Hannah (1958). *The Origins of Totalitarianism*. Cleveland, Ohio: World Publishing Co.

Armer, Paul (1960). Attitudes toward intelligent machines, *Symposium on Bionics*, Wadd Technical Report 60 600, pp. 13-19. Reprinted in Feigenbaum and Feldman(1963), pp. 389-405.

Armer, Paul (1966). Computer aspects of technological change, automation, and economic progress, in: *The Outlook for Technological Change and Employment*, Appendix Volume I to *Technology and the American Economy*. Report of the National Commission on Technology, Automation and Economic Progress. Washington, D.C.: Government Printing Office, pp. 205-232. Extract in Taviss(1970), pp. 123-129.

Ascher, Marcia (1963). Computers in science fiction, *Harvard Business Review* **41** , pp. 40-45.

Ash, Robert (1965). *Information Theory*. New York: Wiley.

Asimov, Isaac (1950). *I, Robot*. New York: Doubleday and Company.

Asimov, Isaac (1973). The individualism to come, *New York Times*. Special Advertising Supplement, January 7, 1973.

Babbage, Charles (1864). *Passages from the Life of a Philosopher*. Reprinted in 1969, Augustus M. Kelley, New York. Excerpts are also reprinted in Morrison and Morrison(1961).

Bacon, Francis (1627). *New Atlantis*. Reprinted in: Hugh G. Dick, ed. *Selected Writings of Francis Bacon*. New York: The Modern Library, 1955.

Baer, Robert M. (1972). *The Digital Villain*. Reading, Mass.: Addison-Wesley.

Ball, Marion J., ed. (1973a). *How to Select a Computerized Hospital Information System* . Basel: S. Karger.

Ball, Marion J. (1973b). Fifteen hospital information systems available, in: Ball(1973a), pp. 10-27.

Bangs, F.K.; Hillestad, M.C. (1970). *Automated Data Processing for Education: Curricular Implications*. Detroit, Michigan: Management Information Services.

Baran, Paul (1967). The future computer utility, *The Public Interest* **8**, pp. 75-87.

Barquin, Ramon C. (1974). Computing in Latin America, *Datamation* **20** (March 1974), pp. 73-78.

Barrett, William (1958). *Irrational Man: A Study in Existential Philosophy*. New york: Doubleday and Company.

Barth, John (1966). *Giles Goat-Boy*. Greenwich, Conn.: Fawcett Publications.

Bartol, Robert A.; Bartol, Kathryn M. (1973). Soviet information-handling problems: the possibilities in computer usage, *Computers and Automation* **22** (June 1973), pp. 16-18.

Bauer, Walter F. (1968). Computer/communication systems: patterns and prospects, in: Gruenberger(1968), pp. 13-37.

Beckett, Samuel (1955). *Molloy*. New York: Grove Press.

Beer, Stafford (1960). Below the twilight arch: a mythology of systems, *General Systems* **5**, pp. 9-20.

Beer, Stafford (1971). The liberty machine, *Futures* **3**, pp. 338-348.

Bekey, George A., ed. (1971). *Simulation Councils Proceedings—* Mathematical Models of Public Systems, Vol. 1, No. 1. La Jolla, Calif.: Simulation Councils, Inc.

Bell, Daniel, ed. (1969). *Toward the Year 2000: Work in Progress*. Boston: Beacon Press.

Bellamy, Edward (1888). *Looking Backward*. Reprinted in 1960, New American Library, New York.

Beman, Lewis (1973). I.B.M.'s travails in Lilliput, *Fortune*, November 1973.

Bemer, R.W., ed. (1971). *Computers and Crisis: How Computers Are Shaping Our Future* . New York: Association for Computing Machinery.

Bennett, Margot (1954). *The Long Way Back*. London: The Bodley Head.

Bentham, Jeremy (1823). *An Introduction to the Principles of Morals and Legislation* . Reprinted in 1948, Hafner, New York.

Benton, William K. (1971). *The Use of the Computer in Planning*. Reading, Mass.: Addison-Wesley.

Berg, Ivar (1974). "They won't work:" the end of the Protestant ethic and all that, in: O'Toole(1974), pp. 27-39.

Berkeley, Edmund C. (1962). *The Computer Revolution*. New York: Doubleday and Company.

Berkeley Scientific Laboratories, Inc. (1971). A Study of Automated Clinical Laboratory Systems, U.S. Department of Health, Education, and Welfare, Springfield, Va.: NTIS.

Bernal, J.D. (1965). *Science in History*. New York: Hawthorn Books.

Berneri, Marie Louise (1951). *Journey Through Utopia*. London: Routledge and Kegan Paul.

Bisco, Ralph, L., ed. (1970). *Data Bases, Computers, and the Social Sciences*. New York: John Wiley.

Bitzer, Donald L.; Easley, J.A. (1965). Plato: a computer-controlled teaching system, in: Sass and Wilkinson(1965), pp. 89-103.

Bitzer, Donald L.; Easley, J.A. (1969). Plato III - a computer-based system for instruction, in: *Proceedings of the XVIth International Congress of Applied Psychology* (Amsterdam, 18-22 August 1968). Amsterdam: Swets and Zeitlinger, 1969.

Bitzer, Donald L.; Hicks, Bruce L.; Johnson, Roger L.; Lyman, Elizabeth R. (1967). The Plato System: current research and developments, *IEEE Trans. On Human Factors in Electronics HFE-8*, pp. 64-70.

Bitzer, Donald L.; Skaperdas, D. (1970). The economics of a large-scale computer-based education system: Plato IV, in: Holtzman(1970), pp. 17-29.

Black, Harold; Shaw Edward (1967). Detroit's data banks, *Datamation* 13 (March 1967), pp. 25-27. Reprinted in Westin(1971), pp. 30-34.

Blau, Peter M. (1956). *Bureaucracy in Modern Society*. New York: Random House.

Blauner, Robert (1964). *Alienation and Freedom: The Factory Worker and His Industry* . Chicago: University of Chicago Press.

Block, Henry; Ginsburg, Herbert (1968). The psychology of robots, *Psychology Today* , April 1968. Reprinted in Pylyshyn(1970), pp. 246-255.

Blum, Albert A. (1968). Computers and Clerical Workers, Document D 1-68 of the Third International Conference on Rationalization, Automation and Technological Change, sponsored by the Metalworkers' Industrial Union of the Federal Republic of Germany. Oberhausen, Germany. Reprinted in Taviss(1970), pp. 69-80.

Boguslaw, Robert (1965). *The New Utopians: A Study of System Design and Social Change* . Englewood Cliffs, N.J.: Prentice-Hall.

Boorstin, Daniel J. (1964). *The Image: A Guide to Pseudo-Events in America*. New York: Harper and Row.

Borodin, A.; Gotlieb, C.C. (1972). Computers and employment, *Communications of the ACM* 15, pp. 695-702.

Bowden, B.V., ed. (1953). *Faster than Thought*. London: Sir Isaac Pitman and Sons.

Bowen, Howard R.; Magnum, Garth L., eds. (1966). *Automation and Economic Progress*. Englewood Cliffs, N.J.: Prentice-Hall.

Boyle, James A. (1969). Automated diagnosis, *Computers and Automation* 18 (June 1969), pp. 20-22.

Brewer, Garry D. (1973). *Politicians, Bureaucrats, and the Consultant: A Critique of Urban Problem Solving*. New York: Basic Books.

Bright, J.R. (1958). The impact of automation on the work force, in: *Automation and Management*. Cambridge, Mass.: Harvard University, 1958, pp. 170-188.

British Medical Association (1969). *Computers in Medicine*. London: B.M.A. House.

Britten, Geoffrey M.; Wener, Mario, eds. (1970). *Automation and Data Processing in the Clinical Laboratory*. Springfield, Ill.: Charles C. Thomas.

Bronstein, Sanford K. (1973a). The impact of automated medicine on improved service to patients, in: Bronstein(1973b), pp. 3-5.

Bronstein, Sanford K., ed. (1973b). *Automation in Medicine*. Mount Kisco, N.Y.: Futura Publishing.

Bulwer-Lytton, Edward George (1870). *The Coming Race.* Reprinted in *The Novels and Romances of Edward Bulwer-Lytton* (Vols. XXII-XXIII). Boston: Little, Brown and Co., 1896-1898.

Burtt, Edwin Arthur (1954). *The Metaphysical Foundations of Modern Physical Science* . Garden City, N.Y.: Doubleday.

Bury, J.B. (1920). *The Idea of Progress, an Inquiry into its Origin and Growth.* Reprinted in 1955, Dover, New York.

Bush, Vannevar (1945). As we may think, *Atlantic Monthly* **176** (July 1945), pp. 101-108.

Butler, Samuel (1863). Darwin among the machines. Reprinted in Lewis(1963), pp. 183-187.

Butler, Samuel (1872). *Erewhon.* Reprinted in *Erewhon and Erewhon Revisited* . New York: Random House, 1927.

Cabet, Etienne (1842). *Voyage en Icarie.* Paris: J. Mallet et Cie.

Capek, Karel (1923). *R.U.R.* Reprinted in Lewis(1963), pp. 3-58.

Carbonell, J.R. (1970). A.I. in C.A.I.: an artificial intelligence approach to computer-assisted instruction, *IEEE Trans. on Man-Machine Systems* **MMS-11** (December 1970), pp. 190-202.

Cassirer, Ernst (1953). *The Philosophy of Symbolic Forms.* Volume One: *Language.* New Haven, Conn.: Yale University Press.

Chapanis, Alphonse (1965). *Man-Machine Engineering.* Belmont, Calif.: Wadsworth.

Chartrand, Robert L., ed. (1972). *Computers in the Service of Society.* New York: Pergamon Press.

Cheatham, Thomas E. (1972). Chinese computer science: a visit and a report. *Computers and Automation* **21** (November 1972), pp. 16-17.

Churchman, C. West (1968a). Real time systems and public information, in: *Proc. 1968 Fall Joint Computer Conference.* Montvale, N.J.: AFIPS Press, pp. 1467-1468.

Churchman, C. West (1968b). *The Systems Approach.* New York: Dell Publishing Company.

Clarke, Arthur C. (1968). *2001: A Space Odyssey.* London: Hutchinson.

Cohen, John (1966). *Human Robots in Myth and Science.* London: George Allen and Unwin.

Collen, M.F. (1970). Problems with presentation of computer data, in: Anderson and Forsythe(1970), pp. 407-411.

Collen, Morris J. (1973). How automated health testing aids the physician in doing a better job for a greater number of patients, in: Bronstein(1973b), pp. 19-31.

Colstad, Ken; Lipkin, Efrem (1975). Community memory: a public information system. Preprint of paper presented at the Computer Science section of the IEEE meeting in San Francisco, February 1975.

Communications Canada (1972a). *Branching Out.* Vols. I and II. Report of the Canadian Computer/Communications Task Force. Ottawa: Information Canada.

Communictions Canada (1972b). *Privacy and Computers.* Ottawa: Information Canada.

Communications Canada (1973). Survey of Public Attitudes Towards the Computer. Ottawa: Information Canada.

Couger, J. Daniel (1973). Evolution of business system analysis techniques, *Computing Surveys* 5, pp. 167-198.

Crossman, E.R.F.W.; Laner, S. (1969). The impact of technological change on manpower and skill demand: case-study and policy implications. Department of Industrial Engineering and Operations Research, University of California, Berkeley.

Darby, Charles A., Jr.; Korotkin, Arthur L.; Romashko, Tania. (1972). *The Computer in Secondary Schools.* New York: Praeger.

Davies, Donald W. (1974). Packet switching, message switching and future data communication networks, in: *Information Processing* 74. Amsterdam: North-Holland, 1974, pp. 147-150.

DeCarlo, Charles R. (1967). Changes in management environment and their effect on human values, in: Myers(1967), pp. 244-274.

De Grazia, Sebastian (1962). *Of Time, Work, and Leisure.* New York: Doubleday and Company.

Deighton, Len (1966). *The Billion Dollar Brain.* New York: G. P. Putnam's Sons.

Denenberg, Herbert S. (1975). The medical malpractice mess, *The Progressive*, May 1975.

Derry, T.K.; Williams, Trevor I. (1960). *A Short History of Technology.* London: Oxford University Press.

De Sola Pool, Ithiel (1967). Computer simulations of total societies, in: Klausner(1967).

Dewey, John (1927). *The Public and Its Problems.* New York: Holt, Rinehart and Winston.

Dial, Oliver E. (1968). Urban information systems: a bibliographic essay, Report of the Urban Systems Laboratory, Massachusetts Institute of Technology. Reprinted in Westin(1971), pp. 322-327.

Dickson, Paul (1974). Tomorrow's automated battlefield, *The Progressive*, August 1974.

Diebold, John (1962). Testimony submitted to the sub-committee on automation and energy resources, 86th Congress, Second Session, in: Philipson(1962), pp. 12-76.

Dorn, Philip H. (1972). Systems and stumbling blocks: yesterday and tomorrrow, in: Gruenberger(1972), pp. 13-21.

Dostoyevsky, Fyodor (1864). *Notes from Underground*, (translated by Constance Garnett). Reprinted in 1960, Dell Publishing Co., New York.

Downs, Anthony (1967). A realistic look at the final payoffs from urban data systems, *Public Administration Review* **27**, pp. 204-209. Reprinted in Westin(1971), pp. 311-321.

Dreyfus, Hubert L. (1972). *What Computers Can't Do: A Critique of Artificial Reason* . New York: Harper and Row.

Duggan, Michael A.; McCartan, Edward F.; Irwin, Manley, eds. (1970). *The Computer Utility: Implications for Higher Education*. Lexington, Mass.: Heath Lexington Books.

Dunlop, Robert A. (1970). The emerging technology of information utilities, in: Sackman and Nie(1970), pp. 25-49.

Dunn, Edgar S., Jr. (1965). Review of Proposal for a National Data Center (Statistical Evaluation Report No. 6) U.S. Executive Office of the President, Bureau of the Budget, Office of Statistical Standards, December, 1965. Reprinted in: U.S. Congress(1966).

Dunn, Michael D. (1973). Hospital information systems: what they are, in: Ball(1973), pp. 6-9.

Durkheim, Emile (1897). *Suicide*, (translated by J.A. Spaulding and G. Simpson). Reprinted in 1951, The Free Press, Glencoe, Illinois.

Durkheim, Emile (1902). *The Division of Labor*, (translated by George Simpson). Reprinted in 1947, The Free Press, Glencoe, Illinois.

EDUCOM (1972). *Computing in Higher Education 1971*. Princeton, N.J.: The Interuniversity Communications Council.

Ellis, Allan B. (1974). *The Use and Misuse of Computers in Education*. New York: McGraw-Hill.

Ellul, Jacques (1964). *The Technological Society*, (translated by John Wilkinson). New York: Vintage Books.

Enslow, Philip H. Jr. (1973). Non technical issues in network design— economic, legal, social, and other considerations, Computer **6** (August 1973), pp. 21-30.

Eulau, Heinz (1970). Some political effects of the information utility on potential decision-makers and the role of the representative, in: Sackman and Nie(1970), pp. 187-199.

Evans, C.R. (1972). Psychological assessment of history taking by computer, in: Abrams(1972), pp. 9-31.

Fano, Robert M. (1968). The computer utility and the community, in: Gruenberger(1968), pp. 39-51.

Fano, Robert M. (1972). On the social role of computer communications, *Proc. IEEE* **60**, pp. 1249-1253.

Farber, David J. (1972). Networks: an introduction, *Datamation* **18** (April 1972), pp. 36-39.

Farber, Seymour M.; Wilson, Roger H.L., eds. (1961). *Control of the Mind*. New York: McGraw-Hill.

Faunce, William A. (1968). *Problems of an Industrial Society*. New York: McGraw-Hill.

Feigenbaum, Edward A.; Feldman, Julian, eds. (1963). *Computers and Thought*. New York: McGraw-Hill.

Feurzeig, W.; Papert, S.; Bloom, M.; Grant, R.; Solomon, C. (1971). Programming-Languages as a Conceptual Framework for Teaching Mathematics, Bolt, Beranek and Newman, Cambridge, Mass., Report No. 2165, Vols. 1,2,3, June 1971.

Firschein, Oscar; Fischler, Martin A.; Coles, L. Stephen; Tenenbaum, Jay M. (1973). Forecasting and assessing the impact of artificial intelligence on society, in: *Advance Papers of the Conference, Third International Joint Conference on Artificial Intelligence*, Stanford University, Stanford, Calif., 20-23 August 1973.

Fiske, Edward B. (1975). Education feeling no-growth pains, *New York Times*, Annual Education Section, January 15, 1975.

Forbes, R.J. (1968). *The Conquest of Nature*. New York: New American Library.

Forbes, R.J.; Dijksterhuis, E.J. (1963). *A History of Science and Technology*. Vols. 1 and 2. Middlesex: Penguin Books.

Forrester, Jay W. (1961). *Industrial Dynamics*. Cambridge, Mass.: MIT Press.

Forrester, Jay W. (1967). Comments on the conference discussion, in: Myers(1967), pp. 275-281.

Forrester, Jay W. (1971). *World Dynamics*. Cambridge, Mass.: Wright-Allen Press.

Forster, E.M. (1928). The Machine Stops, in E.M. Forster. *The Eternal Moment and Other Stories*. New York: Harcourt Brace Jovanovich, 1928.

Foucault, Michel (1965). *Madness and Civilization*, (translated by Richard Howard). New York: Pantheon Books, a division of Random House Inc.

BIBLIOGRAPHY

Franklin, Bruce (1972). Chic bleak in fantasy fiction, *Saturday Review*, July 15, 1972.

Frayn, Michael (1965). *The Tin Men*. New York: Ace Publishing.

Friedricks, G. (1972). Computer and worker, in: Marois(1972), pp. 367-380.

Frisch, Max (1959). *Homo Faber*, (translated by Michael Bullock). New York: Harcourt Brace Jovanovich.

Fromm, Erich (1955). *The Sane Society*. New York: Holt, Rinehart and Winston.

Fromm, Erich (1968). *The Revolution of Hope: Toward a Humanized Technology*. New York: Harper and Row.

Galbraith, John Kenneth (1967). *The New Industrial State*. Boston: Houghton Mifflin.

Gallager, Robert G. (1968). *Information Theory and Reliable Communication*. New York: Wiley.

Gallati, Robert R.J. (1971). The New York State Identification and Intelligence System, in: Westin(1971), pp. 40-46.

Garfield, Sidney R. (1973). A clear look at the economics of medical care, *IEEE Transactions on Biomedical Engineering*. **BME-20** (May 1973), pp. 175-179.

Gassmann, H.P. (1973). Computer usage in Western Europe, in: *Proc. 1973 National Computer Conference*. Montvale, N.J.: AFIPS Press, 1973.

Gerth, H.H.; Mills, C. Wright, eds. (1946). *From Max Weber: Essays in Sociology* . New York: Oxford University Press.

Giedion, Siegfried (1948). *Mechanization Takes Command: A Contribution to Anonymous History*. New York: Oxford University Press.

Gilchrist, Bruce; Weber, Richard E., eds. (1973). The State of the Computer Industry in the United States, a Report of the AFIPS Statistical Research Program. Montvale, N.J.: AFIPS Press.

Glinski, G.S. (1969). Computing in Canada, *Datamation* **15** (September 1969), pp. 66-72.

Goldstine, H.H. (1972). *The Computer from Pascal to von Neumann*. Princeton, N.J.: Princeton University Press.

Goodlad, John I.; O'Toole, John F., Jr.; Tyler, Louise L. (1966). *Computers and Information Systems in Education*. New York: Harcourt Brace Jovanovich.

Gotlieb, C.C.; Borodin, A. (1973). *Social Issues in Computing*. New York: Academic Press.

Greist, John H.; Van Cura, Lawrence J.; Kneppreth, Norwood P. (1973). A computer interview for emergency room patients, *Computers and Biomed. Research* **6**, pp. 257-265.

Gross, Bertram (1969). The new systems budgeting, *Public Administration Review* **29** , pp. 113-133. Reprinted in Westin(1971), pp. 357-374.

Gruenberger, Fred, ed. (1968). *Computers and Communications—Toward a Computer Utility* . Englewood Cliffs, N.J.: Prentice-Hall.

Gruenberger, Fred, ed. (1971). *Expanding Use of Computers in the 70's*. Englewood Cliffs, N.J.: Prentice-Hall.

Gruenberger, Fred, ed. (1972). *Information Systems for Management*. Englewood Cliffs, N.J.: Prentice-Hall.

Guzy, James (1973). The domination of the computer industry by IBM. *Computers and Automation* **22** (February 1973), pp. 8-10.

Haessler, Herbert A. (1969). Recent developments in automating the medical history, *Computers and Automation* **18** (June 1969), pp. 24-27.

Hall, P. (1970). Information science, the patient and the medical record, in: Anderson and Forsythe(1970), pp. 31-40.

Hall, P. (1972). Information processing and patient care, in: Marois(1972), pp. 381-392.

Halmos, Paul (1952). *Solitude and Privacy*. London: Routledge and Kegan Paul.

Hamilton, Peter (1972). *Computer Security*. Princeton: Auerbach Press.

Handlin, Oscar (1965). Science and technology in popular culture, *Daedalus* **94** (Winter 1965), pp. 156-170.

Hansen, Morris H. (1971). The role and feasibility of a national data bank, based on matched records, and alternatives, in: Wallis(1971), Vol. II, pp. 1-61.

Harman, Alvin J. (1971). *The International Computer Industry*. Cambridge, Mass.: Harvard University Press.

Harrington, Michael (1965). *The Accidental Century*. New York: Macmillan.

Hayek, Friedrich A. (1944). *The Road to Serfdom*. Chicago: The University of Chicago Press.

Hayes, P.J. (1973). Some comments on Sir James Lighthill's report on artificial intelligence, AISB European Newsletter, July 1973, pp. 36-54.

Heinlein, Robert A. (1966). *The Moon is a Harsh Mistress*. New York: G. P. Putnam's Sons.

Hicks, B.L.; Hunka, S. (1972). *The Teacher and the Computer*. Philadelphia: W.B. Saunders.

Hobbes, Thomas (1651). *Leviathan*. Reprinted in 1950, E. P. Dutton, New York.

Hodder-Williams, Christopher (1972). *Fistful of Digits*. London: Hodder Paperbacks Ltd.

Hodges, Henry (1970). *Technology in the Ancient World*. New York: Alfred A. Knopf.

Hoffman, Lance J. (1969). Computers and privacy: a survey. *Computing Surveys* **1** , pp. 85-103.

Holland, Wade B. (1969). Soviet computing, 1969: a leap into the third generation, *Datamation* **15** (September 1969), pp. 55-60.

Holtzman, Wayne H., ed. (1970). *Computer-Assisted Instruction, Testing and Guidance* . New York: Harper and Row.

Hook, Sidney, ed. (1960). *Dimensions of Mind*. New York: Macmillan.

Hoos, Ida R. (1967). Systems analysis, information handling, and the research functions: implications of the California experience, Working Paper, Space Sciences Project, University of California, Berkeley, 1967. Reprinted in Westin(1971), pp. 409-418.

Hoos, Ida R. (1969). A realistic look at the systems approach to social problems, *Datamation* **15** (February 1969), pp. 223-228. Reprinted in Westin(1971), pp. 444-450.

Hoos, Ida R. (1971). Information systems and public planning, *Management Science* **17**, Series 2, pp. 658-671.

Hoos, Ida R. (1972). *Systems Analysis in Public Policy, A Critique*. Berkeley: University of California Press.

Hootman, Joseph T. (1972). The computer network as a marketplace, *Datamation* **18** (April 1972), pp. 43-46.

Huizinga, Johan (1955). *Homo Ludens*. Boston: Beacon Press.

Huse, Edgar F. (1967). The impact of computerized programs on managers and organizations: a case study in an integrated manufacturing company, in: Myers(1967), pp. 282-302.

Huxley, Aldous (1932). *Brave New World*. Reprinted in 1946, Harper and Row, New York.

Huxley, Aldous (1958). *Brave New World Revisited*. New York: Harper and Row.

Illich, Ivan (1973). *Tools for Conviviality*. New York: Harper and Row.

Inglis, Brian (1972). *Poverty and the Industrial Revolution*. London: Panther Books.

Irwin, Manley R. (1972). The possibility of the computer utility as a regulated utility, in: Chartrand(1972), pp. 111-119.

Iverath, Axel (1973). Report on the Swedish Data Act, The Federation of Swedish Industries, Stockholm, December 1973.

Jackson, Philip C. (1974). *Introduction to Artificial Intelligence.* New York: Petrocelli.

Jaeckel, Martin T. (1972). Forrester's *Urban Dynamics*: a sociologist's inductive critique. *IEEE Transactions on Systems, Man, and Cybernetics* SMC-2 (April 1972), pp. 200-216.

Jaffe, A.J.; Froomkin, Joseph (1968). *Technology and Jobs.* New York: Praeger.

Jaki, Stanley L. (1969). *Brain, Mind and Computers.* New York: Herder and Herder.

Johannesson, Olof (1968). *The End of Man?* (Originally published as *The Tale of the Big Computer*). *New York: G.P. Putnam's.*

Josephson, Eric; Josephson, Mary, eds. (1962). *Man Alone: Alienation in Modern Society.* New York: Dell Publishing Co.

Jouvenel, Bertrand de (1962). *On Power* (translated by J.F. Huntington). New York: The Viking Press.

Jungk, Robert (1960). *Brighter than 1000 Suns.* Harmondsworth: Penguin Books.

Kahn, Herman; Wiener, Anthony J. (1967). *The Year 2000: A Framework for Speculation on the Next Thirty-Three Years.* New York: Macmillan.

Kanner, Irving F. (1973). Automated medical records for the general practitioner, in: Bronstein(1973), pp. 49-68.

Karp, David (1953). *One.* New York: Grosset and Dunlap.

Kaysen, Carl (1966). Report of the Task Force on the Storage of and Access to Government Statistics. Executive Office of the President. Bureau of the Budget, Washington, D.C., October 1966. Reprinted in U.S. Congress, Senate(1967).

Kaysen, Carl (1967). Data banks and dossiers, *The Public Interest* 7, pp. 52-60.

Kestenbaum, Lionel (1971). The regulatory context of information utilities: varieties in law and public policy, in: Sackman and Nie(1970), pp. 73-101.

Klausner, Samuel Z., ed. (1967). *The Study of Total Societies.* New York: Praeger.

Kling, Rob (1973). Notes on the social impacts of artificial intelligence. *SIGART Newsletter*, No. 42, October 1973, pp. 26-31.

Knox, William T. (1973). Systems for technological information transfer, *Science* 181 (August 1973), pp. 415-419.

Kochen, Manfred, ed. (1967). *The Growth of Knowledge.* New York: Wiley.

Korzybski, Alfred (1921). *Manhood of Humanity: the Science and Art of Human Engineering* . New York: E.P. Dutton.

Kranzberg, Melvin; Pursell, Carroll W., Jr., eds. (1967). *Technology in Western Civilization*, Vols. I and II. New York: Oxford University Press.

Kressing, Harry (1965). *The Cook.* New York: Random House.

Kriebel, Charles H. (1972). MIS technology - a view of the future, in: *Proc. of the 1972 Spring Joint Computer Conference.* Montvale, N.J.: AFIPS Press, 1972, pp. 1173-1180.

Kriebel, Charles H.; Van Horn, Richard L. (1971a). Management information systems, in: Kriebel, *et al.*(1971b), pp. 13-39.

Kriebel, Charles H.; Van Horn, Richard L.; Heames, J. Timothy, eds. (1971b). *Management Information Systems: Progress and Perspectives.* Pittsburgh, Pa.: Carnegie Press.

Kuhn, Thomas S. (1970). *The Structure of Scientific Revolutions.* Chicago: University of Chicago Press.

Kuo, F.F.; Mills, W.H. (1972). The European Computer Scene 1972: Part I, the United Kingdom, Office of Naval Research London Report ONRL-R-6-72, March 21, 1972.

Kurita, Shohei (1973). Computer use in Japan, in: *Proc. 1973 National Computer Conference.* Montvale, N.J.: AFIPS Press.

Laslett, Peter (1970). The sovereignty of the family. *The Listener,* April 7, 1970. Reprinted in Josephson(1962), pp. 86-93.

Lasswell, Harold D. (1965). Policy problems of a data-rich civilization, in *International Federation for Documentation, 31st Meeting and Congress, Proceedings of the 1965 Congress.* Washington, D.C.: Spartan Books, 1965.

Lenk, Klaus (1973). *Automated Information Management in Public Administration.* Paris: Organization for Economic Cooperation and Development.

Levin, Ira (1970). *This Perfect Day.* Greenwich, Conn.: Fawcett World Library.

Lewis, Arthur O. Jr., ed. (1963). *Of Men and Machines.* New York: E.P. Dutton.

Licklider, J.C.R. (1960). Man-computer symbiosis, *IRE Transaction on Human Factors in Electronics* **HFE 1**, pp. 4-10. Reprinted in Pylyshyn(1970), pp. 306-318.

Licklider, J.C.R. (1965). *Libraries of the Future.* Cambridge, Mass.: MIT Press.

Licklider, J.C.R. (1970). Social prospects of information utilities, in: Sackman and Nie(1970), pp. 3-24.

Lilley, S. (1945). Machinery in mathematics: an historical survey of calculating machines, *Discovery* **6**, Nos. 5 and 6, pp. 150-156, pp. 182-185.

Lilley, Samuel (1957). *Automation and Social Progress*. London: Lawrence and Wishart.

Lilley, Samuel (1965). *Men Machines and History*. New York: International Publishers.

Lincoln, Thomas L. (1973). Medical Computing: Pros and Cons. Technical Report, Rand Corporation, Santa Monica, California, February 1973.

Lipinski, Andrew J. (1970). Communications, computers and the enhancement of social intelligence, in *Information Systems: Current Development and Future Expansion*. Montvale, N.J.: AFIPS Press, 1970, pp. 61-74.

Lipner, Steven B. (1969). Requirements for the development of computer-based urban information systems, in *Proc. of the 1969 Spring Joint Computer Conference*. Montvale, N.J.: AFIPS Press, 1969, pp. 523-528.

Locke, John (1690). *Treatise of Civil Government*. Reprinted in 1937, Appleton-Century-Crofts, New York.

Lundell, E. Drake, Jr. (1971). U.S. Computers 'aid' S. African Apartheid, *Computerworld*, December 8, 1971.

Lusted, Lee (1968). *An Introduction to Medical Decision Making*. Springfield, Ill.: Childs Thomas.

Mann, Floyd C.; Hoffman, Richard L. (1960). *Automation and the Worker*. New York: Holt, Rinehart and Winston.

Mansfield, Edwin (1968). *The Economics of Technological Change*. New York: W.W. Norton and Co.

March, James G.; Simon, Herbert A. (1958). *Organizations*. New York: John Wiley.

Marcuse, Herbert (1964). *One-Dimensional Man*. Boston: Beacon Press.

Margolin, Joseph B.; Misch, Marion R., eds. (1970). *Computers in the Classroom*. New York: Spartan Books.

Marois, M., ed. (1972). *Man and Computer: Proceedings of the First International Conference on Man and Computer*, Bordeaux, June 22-26, 1970. Basel: S. Karger.

Martel, C.C.; Cunningham, I.M.; Grushcow, M.S. (1974). The BNR network: a Canadian experience with packet switching technology, in *Information Processing 74*. Amsterdam: North-Holland, 1974, pp. 160-164.

Matson, Floyd W. (1964). *The Broken Image: Man, Science and Society*. New York: George Braziller.

Mauser, Ferdinand F.; Schwartz, David J., Jr. (1966). *American Business: An Introduction*. New York: Harcourt Brace Jovanovich.

Mayne, J.G. (1970). Clinical data acquisition, in: Anderson and
Forsythe(1970), pp. 100-104.

Mazlish, Bruce (1967). The fourth discontinuity. *Technology and
Culture* 8, pp. 1-15. Reprinted in Pylyshyn(1970), pp. 195-207.

McCarthy, J. (1972). The home information terminal, in:
Marois(1972), pp. 48-57.

McCracken, Daniel D. (1974). A report of the ACM Committee on
Computers and Public Policy: a problem-list of issues
concerning computers and public policy. *Comm. ACM* 17,
pp. 495-503.

McDermott, John (1969). Technology: the opiate of the intellectuals.
New York Review of Books 13, July 31, 1969.

McLachlan, G.; Shegog, R.A., eds. (1968). *Computers in the Service
of Medicine*. Vols. I and II. London: Oxford University Press.

McNeill, W.H. (1969). *History of Western Civilization, a Handbook*.
Chicago: University of Chicago Press.

Meadows, Donella H.; Meadows, Dennis L.; Randers, Jorgen;
Behrens, William W. III. (1972). *The Limits to Growth. A
Report for the Club of Rome's Project on the Predicament of
Mankind*. New York: New American Library.

Merriam, W.R. (1903). The evolution of American census-taking.
Century Magazine 65, pp. 831-842.

Mesthene, Emmanuel G. (1968). How technology will shape the
future. *Science* 161 (July 12, 1968), pp. 135-143.

Mesthene, Emmanuel G. (1970a). Computers and the purposes of
education, in: Holtzman(1970), pp. 384-392.

Mesthene, Emmanuel G. (1970b). *Technological Change*. New
York: New American Library.

Michael, Donald N. (1962). Cybernation: the silent conquest, A
Report to the Center for the Study of Democratic Institutions,
Santa Barbara, California. Reprinted in Philipson(1962),
pp. 78-128.

Michael, D.N. (1964). Speculations on the relation of the computer to
individual freedom and the right to privacy, *The George
Washington Law Review* 33, pp. 270-286.

Michael, Donald N. (1968a). On coping with complexity: planning
and politics, *Daedalus* 97 (Fall 1968), pp. 1179-1193. Reprinted
in Westin(1971), pp. 291-300.

Michael, Donald N. (1968b). *The Unprepared Society: Planning for
a Precarious Future* . New York: Basic Books.

Mill, John Stuart (1859,1879). *On Liberty* and *Utilitarianism*.
Reprinted in: Edwin A. Burtt, ed. *The English Philosophers
from Bacon to Mill*. New York: Random House, 1939.

Miller, Arthur R. (1971). *The Assault on Privacy*. Ann Arbor, Michigan: University of Michigan Press.

Miller, Samuel (1803). *A Brief Retrospect of the Eighteenth Century*. Extract reprinted in Lewis(1963), pp. 114-125.

Miller, Walter M. (1961). *A Canticle for Leibowitz*. New York: Bantam Books.

Mills, C. Wright (1956). *The Power Elite*. London: Oxford University Press.

Minsky, Marvin (1961). Steps toward artificial intelligence, in: *Proceedings of the IRE* **49**, pp. 8-30. Reprinted in Feigenbaum and Feldman(1963), pp. 406-456.

Minsky, Marvin (1968). Matter, mind, and models, in *Proceedings 1965 IFIPS Congress* , pp. 45-49. Reprinted in Marvin L. Minsky, ed. *Semantic Information Processing*. Cambridge, Mass.: MIT Press, 1968, pp. 425-432.

Mishan, E.J. (1969). *The Costs of Economic Growth*. Harmondsworth: Penguin Books.

Moore, Omar Khayyam (1964). Autotelic responsive environments and exceptional children, in: Jerome Hellmuth, ed. *The Special Child in Century* **21**. Seattle, Wash.: Special Child Publications, 1964, pp. 87-138.

Morris, William (1891). *News from Nowhere*. Reprinted in 1912, Longmans Green and Co., London.

Morrison, Philip; Morrison, Emily, eds. (1961). *Charles Babbage and his Calculating Engines*. New York: Dover.

Morse, Philip M., ed. (1967). *Operations Research for Public Systems*. Cambridge, Mass.: MIT Press.

Mowshowitz, Abbe (1968a). Entropy and the complexity of graphs: I. An index of the relative complexity of a graph, *Bull. of Math. Biophysics* **30**, pp. 175-204.

Mowshowitz, Abbe (1968b). Entropy and the complexity of graphs: IV. Entropy measures and graphical structure, *Bull. of Math. Biophysics* **30**, pp. 533-546.

Mumford, Lewis (1922). *The Story of Utopias*. Reprinted in 1962, Viking Press, New York.

Mumford, Lewis (1934). *Technics and Civilization*. New York: Harcourt Brace Jovanovich.

Mumford, Lewis (1967). *The Myth of the Machine: I. Technics and Human Development*. New York: Harcourt Brace Jovanovich.

Mumford, Lewis (1970). *The Myth of the Machine: II. The Pentagon of Power*. New York: Harcourt Brace Jovanovich.

Murray, F.J. (1961). *Mathematical Machines*, Vol. 1. New York: Columbia University Press.

Myers, Charles A., ed. (1967). *The Impact of Computers on Management.* Cambridge, Mass.: MIT Press.

Nanus, Burt; Wooton, Leland M.; Borko, Harold (1973). The Social Implications of the Use of Computers across National Boundaries. Montvale, N.J.: AFIPS Press.

Nelson, Theodor H. (1974). *Computer Lib.* Chicago: Hugo's Book Service.

Newell, Allen (1973). Artificial intelligence and the concept of mind, in: Schank and Colby(1973), pp. 1-60.

Nietzsche, Friedrich (1882). *The Gay Science,* in: Walter Kaufmann *The Portable Nietzsche.* New York: The Viking Press, 1954.

Nietzsche, Friedrich (1892). *Thus Spoke Zarathustra,* in: Walter Kaufmann. *The Portable Nietzsche.* New York: The Viking Press, 1954.

Nievergelt, J.; Farrar, J.C. (1972). What machines can and cannot do, *Computing Surveys* 4, pp. 81-96.

Nilsson, Nils J. (1974). Artificial intelligence, in: Information Processing 74. Amsterdam: North-Holland Publishing, 1974, pp. 778-801.

Novick, D.; Levin, M.A. (1971). Financial industry's need for computer technology in the 70's, in: Gruenberger(1971), pp. 103-106.

OECD (1969). Gaps in Technology: Electronic Computers, A Report of the Organization for Economic Cooperation and Development, Paris.

Oettinger, Anthony G. (1966). The uses of computers in science, *Scientific American* 215 (September 1966), pp. 161-180.

Oettinger, Anthony G. (1968). The myths of educational technology, *Saturday Review* 51 (May 18, 1968), pp. 76-91.

Oettinger, Anthony G. (1969). *Run, Computer Run: the Mythology of Educational Innovation .* Cambridge, Mass: Harvard University Press.

Ortega y Gasset, Jose (1956). *The Dehumanization of Art.* New York: Doubleday and Company.

Orwell, George (1949). *1984.* New York: Harcourt Brace Jovanovich.

O'Toole, James, ed. (1974). *Work and the Quality of Life.* Cambridge, Mass.: MIT Press.

Packard, Vance (1960). *The Waste Makers.* New York: David McKay Co.

Packard, Vance (1964). *The Naked Society.* New York: David McKay Co.

Papert, S. (1968). The Artificial Intelligence of Hubert L. Dreyfus: A Budget of Fallacies. AI Memo 154. Cambridge, Mass.: MIT Project MAC.

Papert, Seymour (1971a). Teaching children to be mathematicians vs. teaching about mathematics. MIT AI Laboratory Memo No. 249, July 1971.

Papert, Seymour (1971b). Teaching children thinking. MIT AI Laboratory Memo No. 247, October 1971.

Parker, Donn B.; Nycum, Susan; Oura, S. Stephen (1973). Computer Abuse, Technical Report, Stanford Research Institute, Menlo Park, California, November 1973.

Parker, Edwin R. (1970). Information utilities and mass communication, in: Sackman and Nie(1970), pp. 51-70.

Parker, J.B.; Scott, W.A. (1953). Navigation, in: Martin Davidson, ed. *Astronomy for Everyman*. London: J.M. Dent and Sons, 1953, pp. 447-473.

Parkhill, D.F. (1966). *The Challenge of the Computer Utility*. Reading, Mass.: Addison-Wesley.

Patterson, R. (1957). Spinning and weaving, in: Singer, *et al.*(1957), Vol. III, pp. 151-180.

Philipson, Morris, ed. (1962). *Automation: Implications for the Future*. New York: Random House.

Piel, Gerard (1962). *Science in the Cause of Man*. New York: Alfred A. Knopf.

Poage, James. (1975). Federal law protecting your right to privacy, *Computers and Society* 6 (Summer 1975), pp. 3-8.

Pouzin, Louis (1974). CIGALE, the packet switching machine of the CYCLDES computer network, in *Information Processing 74*. Amsterdam: North-Holland, 1974.

Press, Laurence I. (1974). Arguments for a moratorium on the construction of a community information utility. *Comm. ACM* 17, pp. 674-678

Pyke, T.N. Jr.; Blanc, R.P. (1973). Computer networking technology - a state of the art review, *Computer* 6 (August 1973), pp. 13-19.

Pylyshyn, Zenon W., ed. (1970). *Perspectives on the Computer Revolution*. Englewood Cliffs, N.J.: Prentice-Hall.

Ramo, Simon(1968). The systems approach: automated common sense, *Nation's Cities* 6 (March 1968), pp. 14-19. Reprinted in Westin(1971), pp. 93-98.

Randell, Brian (1972). On Alan Turing and the origins of digital computers, in: B. Meltzer and D. Michie, eds. *Machine*

Intelligence, Vol. 7. Edinburgh: Edinburgh University Press, 1972, pp. 3-20.

Randell, Brian, ed. (1973). *The Origins of Digital Computers: Selected Papers*. Berlin: Springer-Verlag.

Rapoport, Anatol (1955). Technological models of the nervous system, *Methodos* 7 , pp. 131-146. Reprinted in Sayre and Crosson(1963), pp. 25-38.

Rapoport, Anatol (1957). The scientific approach to ethics and its consequences, *Science* **125**, pp. 796-799.

Rapoport, Anatol (1964). *Strategy and Conscience*. New York: Harper and Row.

Rawles, J.M. (1972). Computer-assisted monitoring, in: Rose(1972), pp. 92-105.

Read, Herbert (1955). *The Philosophy of Modern Art*. New York: Meridian Books.

Reich, Charles A. (1970). *The Greening of America*. New York: Random House.

Reichenbach, Hans (1962). *The Rise of Scientific Philosophy*. Berkeley, Calif.: University of Calfornia Press.

Reynolds, James (1802). (Alleged Author). *Equality: A History of Lithconia*. Extract reprinted in Lewis(1963), p. 125.

Rezler, Julius (1969). *Automation and Industrial Labor*. New York: Random House.

Rhee, H.A. (1968). *Office Automation in Social Perspective*. Oxford: Basil Blackwell.

Riesman, David (1964). *Abundance for What?* New York: Doubleday and Company.

Robinson, Herbert W.; Knight, Douglas E., eds. (1972). *Cybernetics, Artificial Intelligence, and Ecology*. New York: Spartan Books.

Roethlesberger, F.J.; Dickson, W.J. (1939). *Management and the Worker*. New York: Wiley.

Rose, J., ed. (1972). *Computers in Medicine*. London: John Wright and Sons.

Rosen, Saul (1969). Electronic computers: a historical survey, *Computing Surveys* **1**, pp. 7-36.

Roszak, Theodore (1969). *The Making of a Counter Culture*. New York: Doubleday and Company.

Rousseau, Jean Jacques (1762). *The Social Contract*. Reprinted in 1947, Hafner Publishing Co., New York.

Rowe, B.C., ed. (1972). *Privacy, Computers and You*. Manchester, England: The National Computing Centre Limited.

Ruggles, Richard (1965). Report of the Committee on the Preservation and Use of Economic Data to the Social Science Research Council, Washington, D.C. Reprinted in: U.S. Congress(1966).

Ryan, G.A.; Monroe, K.E. (1971). *Computer Assisted Medical Practice*— The AMA's Role . Chicago: American Medical Association.

Sackman, Harold (1967). *Computers, System Science, and Evolving Society*. New York: John Wiley.

Sackman, Harold (1968). A public philosophy for real time information systems, in *Proc. of the 1968 Fall Joint Computer Conference*. Montvale, N.J.: AFIPS Press, 1968, pp. 1491-1498. Reprinted in Westin(1971), pp. 222-236.

Sackman, Harold (1970). The information utility, science, and society, in: Sackman and Nie(1970), pp. 143-166.

Sackman, Harold; Nie, Norman, eds. (1970). *The Information Utility and Social Choice* . Montvale, N.J.: AFIPS Press.

Samuel, Arthur L. (1960). Some moral and technical consequences of automation -- a refutation. *Science* **132** (September 16, 1960), pp. 741-742. Reprinted in Philipson(1962), pp. 174-179.

Sanders, Norman, ed. (1970). *Computer Applications in the Field of Medicine*. Rome: UNIVAC International Executive Center.

Sandler, Harold; Fryer, Thomas B.; Rositano, Salvador A.; Lee, Robert D. (1973). The application of aerospace technology to patient monitoring. *IEEE Transactions on Biomed. Engin.* BME-20, pp. 189-194.

Sass, Margo A.; Wilkinson, William D., eds. (1965). *Computer Augmentation of Human Reasoning*. Washington, D.C.: Spartan Books.

Sayre, Kenneth M.; Crosson, Frederick J., eds. (1963). *The Modeling of Mind: Computers and Intelligence*. New York: Simon and Schuster.

Schank, Roger C.; Colby, Kenneth Mark, eds. (1973). *Computer Models of Thought and Language*. San Francisco: W.H. Freeman.

Schmitz, Homer H. (1973). Cost effectiveness of Deconess Hospital information system, in: Ball(1973), pp. 51-55.

Shannon, Claude E.; Weaver, Warren (1959). *The Mathematical Theory of Communication* . Urbana, Ill.: University of Illinois Press.

Sharpe, William F. (1969). *The Economics of Computers*. New York: Columbia University Press.

Shelley, Mary (1818). *Frankenstein; or, The Modern Prometheus*. Reprinted in 1967, Bantam Books, New York.

Shepard, Jon M. (1971). *Automation and Alienation: A Study of Office and Factory Workers* . Cambridge, Mass.: MIT Press.

Sherman, H.; Reiffen, B.; Komaroff, A.L. (1973). Aids to the delivery of ambulatory medical care, *IEEE Transactions on Biomed. Engin.* **BME-20**, pp. 165-174.

Silberman, Charles E. and the Editors of *Fortune*. (1966). *The Myths of Automation*. New York: Harper and Row.

Silverberg, Robert, ed. (1968). *Men and Machines*. New York: Universal Publishing and Distributing Corp.

Simon, Herbert A. (1962). The architecture of complexity, *Proc. Amer. Philosophical Society* **106**, pp. 467-482.

Simon, Herbert A. (1965). *The Shape of Automation for Men and Management*. New York: Harper and Row.

Simon, Herbert A. (1969). *The Sciences of the Artificial*. Cambridge, Mass.: MIT Press.

Simon, Herbert A.; Newell, Allen (1964). Information processing in computer and man, *American Scientist* **52**, pp. 281-300. Reprinted in Pylyshyn(1970), pp. 256-273.

Singer, Charles; Holmyard, E.J.; Hall, A.R.; Williams, Trevor I. (1954-58). *A History of Technology* , *Vols. I-V*. Oxford: Oxford University Press.

Singer, J. Peter. (1969). Computer-based hospital information systems. *Datamation* **15** (May 1969), pp. 38-45.

Skinner, B.F. (1971). *Beyond Freedom and Dignity*. New York: Alfred A. Knopf.

Smigel, Erwin O. (1965). The problem of leisure time in an industrial society, in: Industrial Relations Monograph No. 25, *Computer Technology—* Concepts for Management. New York: Industrial Relations Counselors, Inc., pp. 103-120.

Smith, Adam (1776). *The Wealth of Nations*. Reprinted in 1963, R.D. Irwin, Homewood, Illinois.

Smith, David Eugene (1958). *History of Mathematics*, Vols. I and II. New York: Dover.

Smith, David Eugene (1959). *A Sourcebook in Mathematics*, Vols. 1 and 2. New York: Dover.

Smith, Thomas M. (1967). Origins of the computer, in: Kranzberg and Pursell(1967), Vol. 2, pp. 309-323.

Smith, Thomas M. (1970). Some perspectives on the early history of computers, in: Pylyshyn(1970), pp. 7-15.

Snaith, A.H. (1972). The future of computing in community medicine, in: Abrams(1972), pp. 186-194.

Spangle, C.W. (1972). The present role of governments in the world computer industry, *Computers and Automation* **21** (December 1972), pp. 16-19.

Spengler, Oswald (1926-28). *The Decline of the West*, 2 Vols. New York: Alfred A. Knopf.

Steinbeck, John (1940). *The Grapes of Wrath*. New York: Viking Press.

Sterling, Theodore D. (1974). Guidelines for humanizing computerized information systems: report from Stanley House, *Comm. ACM* **17**, pp. 609-613.

Stevens, Chandler H. (1971). Citizen Feedback: the need and the response, *Technology Review* **73**, pp. 39-45.

Streatfeild, Guy, ed. (1973). *Futures* **5**, No. 1.

Sturman, Gerald M. (1972). Computers and urban society, *Comm. ACM* **15**, pp. 652-657.

Suppes, Patrick (1966). The uses of computers in education, *Scientific American* **215** (September 1966), pp. 206-220.

Suppes, Patrick (1968). Computer technology and the future of education, *Phi Delta Kappa* **49**, pp. 420-423. Reprinted in Taviss(1970), pp. 203-209.

Suppes, Patrick; Morningstar, Mona (1970). Four programs in computer-assisted instruction, in: Holtzman(1970), pp. 233-265.

Susskind, Charles (1973). *Understanding Technology*. Baltimore, Md.: Johns Hopkins University Press.

Sussman, Herbert L. (1968). *Victorians and the Machine: The Literary Response to Technology*. Cambridge, Mass.: Harvard University Press.

Sypher, Wylie (1971). *Literature and Technology*. New York: Vintage Books.

Taviss, Irene, ed. (1970). *The Computer Impact*. Englewood Cliffs, N.J.: Prentice-Hall.

Taylor, E.G.R. (1957). Cartography, survey, and navigation 1400-1750, in: Singer, *et al.* (1957), Vol. III, pp. 530-557.

Taylor, Thomas (1970). Computers in medicine, *Science Journal* **6**, pp. 81-86.

Testerman, Jack D.; Jackson, Juanice (1973). A comprehensive annotated bibliography on computer assisted instruction, Parts I and II, *Computing Reviews* **10**, pp. 483-499 and pp. 543-553.

Toffler, Alvin (1970). *Future Shock*. New York: Random House.

Turing, A.M. (1950). Computing machinery and intelligence, *Mind* **59**, pp. 433-460. Reprinted in Anderson(1964), Feigenbaum and Feldman(1962), and Pylyshyn(1970).

Umpleby, Stuart A. (1970). Citizen sampling simulations: a method for involving the public in social planning, *Policy Sciences* **1**, pp. 361-375.

Umpleby, Stuart A. (1972). Is greater citizen participation in planning possible and desirable? *Technological Forecasting and Social Change* **4**, pp. 61-76.

United Nations (1971). The Application of Computer Technology for Development. United Nations Publication E/4800 ST/ECA/136, New York.

United States Congress, House (1966). Committee on Government Operations Special Subcommittee on Invasion of Privacy. *The Computer and the Invasion of Privacy, Hearings before the Special Subcommittee*. 89th Cong., 2nd. sess., July 1966. Washington, D.C.: U.S. Government Printing Office.

United States Congress, Senate (1967). Committee on the Judiciary, Subcommittee on Adminstrative Practice and Procedure. *Computer Privacy, Hearings Before the Subcommittee*. 90th Congress, 1st Session, March 1967. Washington, D.C.: U.S. Government Printing Office.

Untermeyer, Louis, ed. (1955). *Modern American and Modern British Poetry*. New York: Harcourt Brace Jovanovich.

Vallbona, Carlos (1970). Computer usage in future health care systems, in: Anderson and Forsythe(1970), pp. 374-386.

Vallbona, Carlos; Tobias, Paul R.; Moffet, Charles; Baker, Robert L.; Beggs, Susan (1973). Computer support for a neighborhood health clinic: design and implementation. *IEEE Transactions on Biomed. Engin.* **BME-20**, pp. 189-194.

Van den Haag, Ernest; Ross, Ralph (1957). *The Fabric of Society*. New York: Harcourt Brace Jovanovich.

Van Tassel, Dennis (1972). *Computer Security Management*. Englewood Cliffs, N.J.: Prentice-Hall.

Von Neumann, John (1966). *Theory of Self-Reproducing Automata* (Edited and completed by Arthur W. Burks). Urbana, Ill.: University of Illinois Press.

Vonnegut, Kurt Jr. (1967). *Player Piano*. New York: Avon Books.

Walker, Charles R., ed. (1968). *Technology, Industry and Man: The Age of Acceleration*. New York: McGraw-Hill.

Wallis, W. Allen (1971). *Federal Statistics*, Vols. I and II. Washington, D.C.: U.S. Government Printing Office.

Ware, Willis H. (1973). *Records, Computers and the Rights of Citizens*. Washington, D.C.: U.S. Government Printing Office.

Wasserman, Anthony I. (1975). A problem-list of public policy issues concerning computers and health care, *Comm. ACM* **18**, pp. 279-280.

Weaver, Warren (1948). Science and complexity, *American Scientist* *36*, pp. 536-544.

Weber, Max (1904-5). *The Protestant Ethic and the Spirit of Capitalism*. Reprinted in 1958, Charles Scribner's Sons, New York.

Weiss, Harold (1974). Computer security: an overview, *Datamation 20* (January 1974), pp. 42-47.

Weizenbaum, Joseph (1969). The two cultures of the computer age, *Technology Review* **71**, pp. 54-57.

Weizenbaum, Joseph (1972). On the impact of the computer on society, *Science* **176** , pp. 609-614.

Wells, H.G. (1899). *When the Sleeper Wakes*. New York: Harper and Bros.

Wells, H.G. (1904). *A Modern Utopia*. New York: Charles Scribners' Sons.

Wells, H.G. (1923). *Men Like Gods*. New York: Macmillan.

Westin, Alan F. (1967a). Legal safeguards to insure privacy in a computer society, *Comm. ACM* **10**, pp. 533-537.

Westin, Alan F. (1967b). *Privacy and Freedom*. New York: Atheneum.

Westin, Alan F., ed. (1971). *Information Technology in a Democracy*. Cambridge, Mass.: Harvard University Press.

Westin, Alan F. (1973). Databanks in a free society: a summary of the project on computer databanks, *Computers and Automation* **22** (January 1973), pp. 18-22.

Westin, Alan F., Project Director; Baker, Michael A., Assistant Project Director (1972). *Databanks in a Free Society*. New York: Quadrangle Books.

Whisler, Thomas L. (1967). The impact of information technology on organizational control, in: Myers(1967), pp. 16-60.

Whisler, Thomas L. (1970). *The Impact of Computers on Organizations*. New York: Praeger.

White, D. (1970). Information processing of medical records, in: Anderson and Forsythe(1970), pp. 387-400.

Whitehead, Alfred North (1925). *Science and the Modern World*. New York: Macmillan.

Whitehead, Alfred North (1929). *The Aims of Education*. New York: Macmillan.

Wiener, Norbert (1954). *The Human Use of Human Beings: Cybernetics and Society*. New York: Doubleday and Company.

Wiener, Norbert (1960). Some moral and technical consequences of automation, *Science* **131** (May 6, 1960), pp. 1355-1358.

Wiener, Norbert (1961). *Cybernetics*. Cambridge, Mass.: MIT Press.

Wiener, Norbert (1964). *God and Golem, Inc*. Cambridge, Mass.: MIT Press.

Wilkes, M.V. (1968). *Time-Sharing Computer Systems*. New York: American Elsevier.

Willis, Donald S. (1973). Who knows you: a look at commercial data banks, *Computers and Automation* **22** (March 1973), pp. 18-21.

Winograd, Terry (1974). Artificial intelligence: when will computers understand people, *Psychology Today*, May 1974.

Withington, Frederic G. (1966). *The Use of Computers in Business Organizations*. Reading, Mass.: Addison-Wesley.

Wolf, A. (1935). *A History of Science, Technology, and Philosophy in the 16th and 17th Centuries*, Vols. 1 and 2. London: George Allen and Unwin.

Wolf, A. (1939). *A History of Science, Technology, and Philosophy in the 18th Century* , Vols. I and II. New York: Macmillan.

Wolfe, Harry B.; Ernst, Martin L. (1967). Simulation models and urban planning, in: Morse(1967), pp. 49-81.

Yale Law Journal (1967). Program budgeting for police forces, *The Yale Law Journal* **76**, pp. 822-838. Reprinted in Westin(1971), pp. 375-382.

Yeats, William Butler (1924). *The Collected Poems of W.B. Yeats*. New York: Macmillan.

Zamiatin, Eugene (1924). *We*, (translated by Gregory Zilboorg). New York: E.P. Dutton.

Selected References by Chapter

Chapter 1

Bacon (1627)
Bell (1969)
Bernal (1965)
Berneri (1951)
Burtt (1954)
Bury (1920)
Butler (1863)
Butler (1872)
Derry (1960)
Dostoyevsky (1864)
Durkheim (1897)
Durkheim (1902)
Ellul (1964)
Forbes (1968)
Forbes *et al.* (1963)
Giedion (1948)
Harrington (1966)
Hodges (1970)
Illich (1973)
Inglis (1972)
Jungk (1960)
Kahn (1967)
Kranzberg (1967)
Kuhn (1970)
Lewis (1963)
Lilley (1965)
Matson (1964)
McCracken (1974)
Meadows (1972)
Mesthene (1970b)
Miller (1803)
Mumford (1934)
Press (1974)
Reich (1970)

Reichenbach (1962)
Reynolds (1802)
Roszak (1969)
Smith (1776)
Weber (1904-5)
Whitehead (1925)
Wiener (1954)

Chapter 2

Babbage (1864)
Bernal (1965)
Bowden (1953)
Cohen (1966)
Goldstine (1973)
Huizinga (1955)
Kranzberg (1967)
Lilly (1945)
McNeil (1969)
Merriam (1903)
Morrison (1961)
Murray (1961)
Parker (1953)
Patterson (1957)
Randell (1972)
Randell (1973)
Rosen (1969)
Rousseau (1762)
Singer (1954-58)
Smith (1958)
Smith (1959)
Smith (1967)
Smith (1970)
Taylor (1957)
Wolf (1935)
Wolf (1939)

Chapter 3

Barquin (1974)
Bartol (1973)
Beman (1973)
Cheatham (1972)
Gassmann (1973)
Gilchrist (1973)
Glinski (1969)
Gotlieb (1973)
Gruenberger (1968)
Guzy (1973)
Harman (1971)
Holland (1969)
Kuo (1972)
Kurita (1973)
Mansfield (1968)
Mishan (1969)
Nanus (1973)
OECD (1969)
Sharpe (1969)
Spangle (1972)
U.N. (1971)

Chapter 4

Bemer (1971)
Blau (1956)
Chartrand (1972)
Couger (1973)
DeCarlo (1967)
Dorn (1972)
Forrester (1967)
Galbraith (1969)
Gruenberger (1972)
Hobbes (1651)
Huse (1967)
Kriebel (1972)
Kriebel *et al.* (1971a)
Kriebel *et al.* (1971b)
March (1958)
Mauser (1966)

Mills (1956)
Myers (1967)
Simon (1965)
Whisler (1967)
Whisler (1970)
Withington (1966)

Chapter 5

Berg (1974)
Blauner (1964)
Blum (1970)
Borodin (1972)
Bowen (1966)
Bright (1958)
Butler (1872)
Crossman (1969)
De Grazia (1962)
Diebold (1962)
Durkheim (1897)
Friedricks (1972)
Jaffe (1968)
Laslett (1970)
Lilley (1957)
Lilley (1965)
Mann (1960)
Mansfield (1968)
Marcuse (1964)
Marois (1972)
Michael (1962)
Mumford (1934)
Philipson (1962)
Rezler (1969)
Rhee (1968)
Riesman (1964)
Roethlesberger (1939)
Shepard (1971)
Silberman (1966)
Smigel (1965)
Taviss (1970)
Walker (1968)
Weber (1904-5)

Chapter 6

Asimov (1973)
Bangs (1970)
Bitzer (1965)
Bitzer (1967)
Bitzer (1969)
Bitzer (1970)
Bush (1945)
Carbonell (1970)
Darby (1972)
De Sola Pool (1967)
EDUCOM (1972)
Ellis (1974)
Feurzeig (1971)
Fiske (1975)
Goldstine (1972)
Goodlad (1966)
Hicks (1972)
Holtzman (1970)
Kochen (1967)
Korzybski (1921)
Licklider (1965)
Margolin (1970)
Marois (1972)
Mesthene (1970a)
Moore (1964)
Nietzsche (1892)
Oettinger (1966)
Oettinger (1968)
Oettinger (1969)
Papert (1971a)
Papert (1971b)
Piel (1962)
Sass (1965)
Suppes (1966)
Suppes (1968)
Suppes (1970)
Testerman (1973)
Whitehead (1929)

Chapter 7

Abrams (1972)
Adams (1970)
Alford (1962)
Anderson (1970a)
Anderson (1970b)
Anderson *et al.* (1970)
Ball (1973a)
Ball (1973b)
Bemer (1971)
Berkeley Labs (1971)
Boyle (1969)
British M.A. (1969)
Britten (1970)
Bronstein (1973a)
Bronstein (1973b)
Collen (1970)
Collen (1973)
Dennenberg (1975)
Dunn (1973)
Evans (1972)
Garfield (1973)
Greist (1973)
Haessler (1969)
Hall (1970)
Hall (1972)
Kanner (1973)
Lincoln (1973)
Lusted (1968)
Marois (1972)
Mayne (1970)
McLachlan (1968)
Rawles (1972)
Rose (1972)
Ryan (1971)
Sanders (1970)
Sandler (1973)
Schmitz (1973)
Sherman (1973)
Singer (1969)
Snaith (1972)

Taylor (1970)
Vallbona (1970)
Vallbona (1973)
White (1970)

Chapter 8

Allery (1974)
Anderson (1966)
Armer (1966)
Baran (1967)
Bauer (1968)
Bemer (1971)
Chartrand (1972)
Comm. Canada (1972a)
Davies (1974)
Dewey (1927)
Duggan (1970)
Dunlop (1970)
Enslow (1973)
Fano (1968)
Fano (1972)
Farber (1972)
Gruenberger (1968)
Gruenberger (1971)
Hootman (1972)
Irwin (1972)
Kestenbaum (1971)
Licklider (1970)
Marois (1972)
Martel (1974)
McCarthy (1972)
Novick (1971)
Parker (1970)
Parkhill (1966)
Pouzin (1974)
Press (1974)
Pyke (1973)
Sackman (1968)
Sackman (1970)
Sackman *et al.* (1970)
Weizenbaum (1972)
Wilkes (1968)

Chapter 9

Anderson (1972)
Bentham (1823)
Comm. Canada (1972b)
Dewey (1927)
Hamilton (1972)
Hobbes (1651)
Hoffman (1969)
Iverath (1973)
Kaysen (1967)
Lasswell (1965)
Locke (1690)
Lundell (1971)
Michael (1964)
Mill (1859,1879)
Miller (1971)
Packard (1964)
Parker (1973)
Poage (1975)
Rousseau (1762)
Rowe (1972)
van Tassel (1972)
Ware (1973)
Weiss (1974)
Westin (1967a)
Westin (1967b)
Westin (1971)
Westin (1973)
Westin *et al.* (1972)

Chapter 10

Armer (1966)
Beer (1971)
Bemer (1971)
Benton (1971)
Bisco (1970)
Black (1967)
Chartrand (1972)
Dial (1968)
Downs (1967)

Dunn (1966)
Eulau (1970)
Fromm (1968)
Gallati (1971)
Hansen (1971)
Hayek (1944)
Kaysen (1966)
Knox (1973)
Lenk (1973)
Lipner (1969)
Marois (1972)
Michael (1968a)
Michael (1968b)
Ruggles (1966)
Sackman (1967)
Sackman (1968)
Sackman *et al.* (1970)
Stevens (1971)
Sturman (1972)
Taviss (1970)
Umpleby (1970)
Umpleby (1972)
U.S. Congress (1966)
U.S. Congress (1967)
Wallis (1971)
Ware (1973)
Weizenbaum (1969)
Westin (1971)
Westin (1973)
Westin *et al.* (1972)
Willis (1973)

Chapter 11

Bekey (1971)
Benton (1971)
Bisco (1970)
Boguslaw (1965)
Brewer (1973)
Chartrand (1972)
Churchman (1968a)
Churchman (1968b)
Couger (1973)

Forrester (1961)
Forrester (1971)
Gerth (1946)
Gross (1969)
Hoos (1967)
Hoos (1969)
Hoos (1971)
Hoos (1972)
Jaeckel (1972)
Klausner (1967)
Knox (1973)
Lenk (1973)
Morse (1967)
Rapoport (1964)
Sackman (1967)
Streatfeild (1973)
Taviss (1970)
Westin (1971)
Wiener (1961)
Wolfe (1967)
Yale Law J. (1967)

Chapter 12

Armer (1966)
Ash (1965)
Asimov (1973)
Beer (1960)
Boguslaw (1965)
Fano (1972)
Faunce (1968)
Gallager (1968)
Gerth (1946)
Huxley (1958)
Illich (1973)
Jouvenel (1962)
Licklider (1965)
McDermott (1969)
Mesthene (1968)
Michael (1968b)
Mowshowitz (1968a)
Mowshowitz (1968b)
Mumford (1967)

Mumford (1970)
Shannon (1959)
Simon (1962)
von Neumann (1966)
Weaver (1948)
Weizenbaum (1969)
Weizenbaum (1972)
Westin (1967a)
Whisler (1967)
Wiener (1961)
Wiener (1964)
Yeats (1924)

Chapter 13

AFIPS-TIME (1972)
Arendt (1958)
Barrett (1958)
Berkeley (1962)
Butler (1872)
Chapanis (1965)
Colstad (1975)
Comm. Canada (1973)
Foucault (1965)
Fromm (1955)
Giedion (1948)
Halmos (1952)
Josephson (1962)
Kressing (1965)
Laslett (1970)
Licklider (1960)
Lipinski (1970)
Mazlish (1967)
Mumford (1934)
Nelson (1974)
Nietzsche (1882)
Packard (1960)
Pylyshyn (1970)
Rapoport (1957)
Read (1955)
Skinner (1971)
Spengler (1926-28)
Sterling (1974)

Susskind (1973)
Toffler (1970)
van den Haag (1957)
Weizenbaum (1972)

Chapter 14

Anderson (1964)
Armer (1960)
Block (1968)
Cassirer (1953)
Dickson (1974)
Dreyfus (1972)
Feigenbaum (1963)
Firschein (1973)
Hayes (1973)
Hook (1960)
Jackson (1974)
Jaki (1969)
Kling (1973)
Minsky (1961)
Minsky (1968)
Newell (1973)
Nievergelt (1972)
Nilsson (1974)
Ortega y Gasset (1956)
Papert (1968)
Philipson (1962)
Pylyshyn (1970)
Rapoport (1955)
Robinson (1972)
Samuel (1960)
Sayre (1963)
Schank (1973)
Simon (1969)
Simon *et al.* (1964)
Skinner (1971)
Turing (1950)
Wiener (1960)
Winograd (1974)

Chapter 15

Ascher (1963)
Asimov (1950)
Baer (1972)
Barth (1966)
Beckett (1955)
Bellamy (1888)
Bennett (1954)
Berneri (1951)
Boorstin (1964)
Bulwer-Lytton (1870)
Butler (1872)
Cabet (1842)
Capek (1923)
Clarke (1968)
Deighton (1966)
Ellul (1964)
Forster (1928)
Franklin (1972)
Frayn (1965)
Frisch (1959)
Handlin (1965)
Heinlein (1966)
Hodder-Williams (1972)
Huxley (1932)
Johannesson (1968)
Karp (1953)
Levin (1970)
Lewis (1963)
Mazlish (1967)
Miller (1961)
Morris (1891)
Mumford (1922)
Orwell (1949)
Shelley (1818)
Silverberg (1968)
Steinbeck (1940)
Sussman (1968)
Sypher (1971)
Untermeyer (1955)
Vonnegut (1967)

Wells (1899)
Wells (1904)
Wells (1923)
Zamiatin (1924)

Index